UNIVERSITY CASEBOOK SERIES®

2023 SUPPLEMENT TO

HART AND WECHSLER'S

THE FEDERAL COURTS AND THE FEDERAL SYSTEM

SEVENTH EDITION

WILLIAM BAUDE
Harry Kalven, Jr. Professor of Law
University of Chicago Law School

JACK L. GOLDSMITH
Learned Hand Professor of Law
Harvard Law School

JOHN F. MANNING
Morgan and Helen Chu Dean and Professor of Law
Harvard Law School

JAMES E. PFANDER
Owen L. Coon Professor of Law
Northwestern University Pritzker School of Law

AMANDA L. TYLER
Shannon Cecil Turner Professor of Law
University of California, Berkeley School of Law

FOUNDATION
PRESS

© 2016–2022 LEG, Inc. d/b/a West Academic
© 2023 LEG, Inc. d/b/a West Academic
      860 Blue Gentian Road, Suite 350
      Eagan, MN 55121
      1-877-888-1330

Printed in the United States of America

ISBN: 979-8-88786-028-2

PREFACE

This supplement brings the Seventh Edition up to date by discussing judicial decisions that have come down, statutes that have been enacted, and secondary literature that has been published since the Seventh Edition went to the publisher in January 2015. The most important changes from the 2022 Supplement involve decisions from the Supreme Court's 2022 Term. This year's supplement has deferred consideration of recent contributions to the Federal Courts literature in contemplation of the appearance of a new Eighth Edition in 2024.

As in the past, material in footnotes is intended primarily for scholars and researchers. We announce to our own classes that they need not read the footnotes in the editorial Notes unless we specifically assign them. (Students should of course read footnotes that we have included in principal cases.)

We are grateful to a large number of outstanding research assistants running back to 2015. Special thanks for help during this past year go to Sofia Debbiche, Tom Koenig, Sierra Polston, Georgios Sarris, and Owen Smitherman.

WPB
JLG
JFM
JEP
ALT

July 2023

SUMMARY OF CONTENTS

TABLE OF CONTENTS

TABLE OF CASES

The principal cases are in bold type.

TABLE OF AUTHORITIES

UNIVERSITY CASEBOOK SERIES®

2023 SUPPLEMENT TO

HART AND WECHSLER'S

THE FEDERAL COURTS AND THE FEDERAL SYSTEM

SEVENTH EDITION

CHAPTER I

THE DEVELOPMENT AND STRUCTURE OF THE FEDERAL JUDICIAL SYSTEM

INTRODUCTORY NOTE: THE JUDICIARY ARTICLE IN THE CONSTITUTIONAL CONVENTION AND THE RATIFICATION DEBATES

Page 1. Add at the end of the second paragraph of footnote 1:

See also Gienapp, The Second Creation: Fixing the American Constitution in the Founding Era (2018).

Page 1. Add at the end of footnote 1:

One of the most important sources for the Convention debates is James Madison's Notes on the 1787 Constitutional Convention. Bilder, Madison's Hand: Revising the Constitutional Convention (2015), reveals that Madison's revisions to his notes over the course of the decades that followed the Convention were far more extensive than scholars have previously recognized. By comparing the version of Madison's notes first published in 1840 to earlier sources, including a copy made of Madison's then-existing notes in 1790 for Thomas Jefferson, and using technology to date Madison's many revisions, Bilder shows the evolution of Madison's thinking on many important issues debated at the Convention while calling into question the reliability of his description of the debates regarding certain topics. For discussion emphasizing the significance of Bilder's findings and probing the conclusions she draws, consult Rakove, *A Biography of Madison's Notes of Debates*, 30 Const.Comment. 317 (2016).

Page 3. Add at the beginning of footnote 14:

For an overview of the various schools of thought concerning the continuing influence of the Articles on constitutional meaning and a detailed comparison of the provisions of the Articles and the Constitution, consult Maggs, *A Concise Guide to the Articles of Confederation as a Source for Determining the Original Meaning of the Constitution*, 85 Geo.Wash.L.Rev. 397 (2017). For analysis of the way state constitutions at the time of the Constitutional Convention may have influenced the drafting of the federal Constitution, see Maggs, *A Guide and Index for Finding Evidence of the Original Meaning of the U.S. Constitution in Early State Constitutions and Declarations of Rights*, 98 N.C.L.Rev. 779 (2020).

Page 3. Add at the end of footnote 14:

A recent addition to the literature on the Convention, and on the decision to move beyond amending the Articles, Klarman, The Framers' Coup: The Making of the United States Constitution (2017), describes the relevant events as effectively an undemocratic coup. For probing analysis, consult Fried, *The Cunning of Reason: Michael Klarman's* The Framers' Coup, 116 Mich.L.Rev. 981 (2018); Finkelman, *The Nefarious Intentions of the Framers?*, 84 U.Chi.L.Rev. 2139 (2017). Ellis, The Quartet: Orchestrating the Second American Revolution, 1783–1789 (2015), details the roles that Washington, Hamilton, Madison, and Jay played in the transition from the Articles of Confederation to the Constitution, giving special attention to Washington's influence as chair of the Constitutional Convention.

Page 3. Add at the end of footnote 18:

Recent scholarship stresses the importance of studying the constitutional vision advanced by Federalists in the period between 1787 and 1800—the Constitution's "formative years"—during which time the Federalist constitutional ideology predominated before fading thereafter. For an overview of how such studies may alter modern assessments of the Founding period and discussion of how many aspects of constitutional meaning remained contested during this period, see *Symposium: The Federalist Constitution*, 89 Fordham L.Rev. 1669 (2021).

Page 6. Add at the end of footnote 31:

For an explication of the significant changes made by the Committee on Style, as well as Gouverneur Morris's role as drafter, consult Treanor, *The Case of the Dishonest Scrivener: Gouverneur Morris and the Creation of the Federalist Constitution*, 120 Mich.L.Rev. 1 (2021). Treanor argues that in altering the vesting language of Article III, Morris sought to provide a textual basis for his view that favored mandating the creation of inferior federal courts while downplaying the Madisonian Compromise. Treanor further posits that Morris altered the wording of the Supremacy Clause in order to provide a textual anchor for the practice of judicial review. For a skeptical analysis of both contentions, consult Schwartz, *Framing the Framer: A Commentary on Treanor's Gouverneur Morris as "Dishonest Scrivener"*, 120 Mich.L.Rev. Online 51 (2023) (arguing that the relevant changes made by the Committee of Style were not as significant as Treanor suggests and that language supporting Morris's vision of the federal courts had already been embraced by the delegates).

Page 17. Add at the end of footnote 105:

Mask & MacMahon, *The Revolutionary War Prize Cases and the Origins of Diversity Jurisdiction*, 63 Buff.L.Rev. 477 (2015), argues that the experience of the Continental Congress in entertaining appeals from state tribunals in prize cases, as discussed on p. 6, footnote 36 of the Seventh Edition, persuaded influential Framers of the importance of national courts free of geographic bias. According to the authors, their findings "rehabilitate[ ] the view that geographic bias was a driving force behind the grant of diversity jurisdiction."

NOTE ON THE ORGANIZATION AND DEVELOPMENT OF THE FEDERAL JUDICIAL SYSTEM

Page 22. Add after the second sentence of footnote 8:

See also Lee, *Article IX, Article III, and the First Congress: The Original Constitutional Plan for the Federal Courts, 1787–1792*, 89 Fordham L.Rev. 1895, 1895 (2021) (observing that "the federal courts were originally established, in significant part, to reduce tensions with foreign governments by subordinating states' conflicting interests and protecting foreigners and providing them favorable forums for resolving maritime and commercial disputes with Americans"); Moore, *Trimming the Least Dangerous Branch: The Anti-Federalists and the Implementation of Article III*, 56 Tulsa L.Rev. 1 (2020) (arguing that the Judiciary Act's failure to grant sweeping federal question jurisdiction to the district courts resulted from the influence of Anti-Federalists).

Page 24. Add a new footnote 27a at the end of the third sentence of Section A, Paragraph (3)(b):

[27a] Once the potential existed for ties on the circuit courts, see Seventh Edition p. 27 & note 38, the Supreme Court reviewed a number of federal criminal cases over which it would not otherwise have enjoyed appellate jurisdiction. See Nash & Collins, *The Certificate of Division and the Early Supreme Court*, 94 S.Cal.L.Rev. 733 (2021) (documenting that the Court reviewed 44 such cases during the Chief Justiceships of Marshall and Taney).

Page 32. Add at the end of the first paragraph:

(Congress did adopt legislation in 1937 that, among other things, called for three-judge panels in cases seeking injunctive relief against the execution of federal laws, which remained in place until 1976.[86a])

[86a] See Act of Aug. 24, 1937, ch. 754, 50 Stat. 751; Act of Aug. 12, 1976, Pub.L.No. 94–381, 90 Stat. 1119. For background on the 1937 legislative changes, see Cushman, *The Judicial Reforms of 1937*, 61 Wm. & Mary L.Rev. 995 (2020).

Page 35. Insert the following in place of the final sentence of the second paragraph of Section G, Paragraph (3):

Appeals of such applications are reviewable by the Foreign Intelligence Surveillance Court of Review, made up of three Article III judges also selected by the Chief Justice.

Page 36. Add at the end of the carryover paragraph at the top of the page:

Congress adopted some of these proposals in the USA FREEDOM Act of 2015, which established procedures for the appointment of amici to appear before the FISC in cases involving "a novel or significant interpretation of the law" or where otherwise appropriate. The Act also provides for the certification of questions of law to higher courts and calls for the declassification of significant FISC decisions, orders, and opinions.[110a]

[110a] See Uniting and Strengthening America by Fulfilling Rights and Ensuring Effective Discipline over Monitoring (USA FREEDOM) Act of 2015, Pub.L.No. 114–23, 129 Stat. 268 (2015), codified at 50 U.S.C. § 1861.

Page 38. Add at the end of footnote 126:

In response to the decision in Kuretski v. Commissioner, 755 F.3d 929, 932 (D.C.Cir.2014), declaring that "[t]he Tax Court exercises Executive authority as part of the Executive Branch," Congress amended various provisions governing the Tax Court and added the following language to the court's chartering provision: "The Tax Court is not an agency of, and shall be independent of, the executive branch of the government." See Protecting Americans from Tax Hikes Act of 2015, Pub.L.No. 114–113, 129 Stat. 2242, codified at 26 U.S.C. § 7441.

Page 39. Add a new footnote 137a at the end of the first paragraph of Section H, Paragraph (2):

[137a] For a discussion of important differences between administrative law judges ("ALJs") and administrative judges ("AJs"), including the procedures by which they are appointed, the protections that they enjoy from removal, and their roles within agencies, along with the view that ALJs are superior to AJs because of their higher likelihood of impartiality and greater insulation from agency pressures, see Barnett, *Against Administrative Judges*, 49 U.C. Davis L.Rev. 1643 (2016) (arguing that AJs are "the real hidden judiciary"). In Lucia v. SEC, 138 S.Ct. 2044 (2018), the Supreme Court held that ALJs presiding over enforcement actions in the Securities and Exchange Commission (SEC) are not merely employees, but "Officers of the United States", a class of government officials subject to the Appointments Clause. See Art. II, § 2, cl. 2. Accordingly, the Court held the appointment of SEC ALJs by SEC staff, rather than the by the Commissioners themselves, ran afoul of that Clause. Relying on Freytag v. Commissioner, 501 U.S. 868 (1991), which reached the same conclusion with respect to special trial judges of the United States Tax Court, the Court emphasized the extensive powers that the SEC ALJs exercise and the potential for their decisions to become final where the Commission declines to review them. See also Buckley v. Valeo, 424 U.S. 1 (1976) (per curiam) (defining officers for Appointments Clause purposes as exercising "significant authority"). The holding in Lucia raises important questions, including how many other ALJs and possibly AJs may fall under its purview depending on how they are appointed. It may also have ramifications with respect to how ALJs and AJs may be removed by agency heads where the Appointments Clause applies, a matter that the Court declined to take up in Lucia despite the government's invitation to do so. In Lucia's wake, the President issued an executive order declaring that under the decision, "at least some—and perhaps all—ALJs are 'Officers of the United States' and thus subject to the Constitution's Appointments Clause." Accordingly, the order directs that going forward, ALJs shall be exempt from "competitive examination and competitive service selection procedures" through which they had previously been appointed and be appointed at the discretion of agency heads. Exec. Order No. 13,843, § 1, 83 Fed. Reg. 32,755 (July 13, 2018). The Solicitor General followed the order with separate guidance expanding the order's application to non-ALJs who act as adjudicators and explaining that the Department of Justice will defend existing statutory limitations on the removal of ALJs only insofar as those limitations are construed to be "suitably deferential" to the Department head at issue. Memorandum from the Solicitor General, U.S. Dep't of Justice, to Agency Gen. Counsels, Guidance on Administrative

Law Judges After Lucia v. SEC (S. Ct.) (July 2018). More recently, in United States v. Arthrex, Inc., 141 S.Ct. 1970 (2021), the Supreme Court concluded that Administrative Patent Judges ("APJs") are inferior officers for purposes of the Appointments Clause and held that as such, their decisions must be subject to direct review by a principal officer, in this case the Director of the Patent and Trademark Office. In so doing, the Court substituted expanded review by the Director for the lower court's invalidation of the tenure protections afforded APJs. These developments together have the potential to introduce extensive changes to the status of, and appointment and removal processes governing, both ALJs and AJs.

Page 40. Add a new footnote 146a at the end of the last paragraph of Section H, Paragraph (3)(a):

[146a] For broad discussion of the role of magistrates in the Article III framework, consult *Symposium: Magistrate Judges and the Transformation of the Federal Judiciary*, 16 Nev.L.J. 775 (2016).

Page 41. Add a new paragraph at the beginning of Section I and before Paragraph (I)(1):

The Federal Judicial Branch today, "while tiny in comparison to the Executive Branch, is nevertheless a large and complex institution, with an annual budget exceeding $7 billion and more than 32,000 employees." Ayestas v. Davis, 138 S.Ct. 1080 (2018) (citing Administrative Office of the U.S. Courts, The Judiciary FY 2018 Congressional Budget Office Summary Revised 9–10 (June 2017)).

Page 42. Add at the end of footnote 159:

Updated 2022 figures from the Administrative Office of the U.S. Courts revealed that civil filings in the district courts have risen from the level reported in 2013 to 309,102 in the 2021–2022 period. This follows a huge spike in civil filings related to a single defendant in multidistrict litigation cases in the 2019–2020 period, highlighting how such cases can make up a substantial portion of total district court civil filings. After a substantial decline since 2015, diversity filings in the district courts rose 17% in 2017–2018, to 88,547, rose further in 2018–2019 to 104,803, and rose dramatically in 2019–2020 to 284,603 (again, due in part to multidistrict litigation cases). But in 2020–2021, diversity cases fell 41%; they fell further in 2021–2022 to 141, 125. Bankruptcy petitions continued their declining trend during the same period, numbering 395,373 in the 2021–2022 period. Meanwhile, 2020 figures revealed that criminal filings have fallen considerably from the 2013 fiscal year. Specifically, the number of such filings between 2021–2022 was 71,111. See Administrative Office of the U.S. Courts, 2022 Judicial Business, Analysis & Tables C, C-2, D, D-2, F; Administrative Office of the U.S. Courts, 2021 Judicial Business, Analysis & Tables C, C-2, D, D-2, F; Administrative Office of the U.S. Courts, 2020 Judicial Business, Analysis & Tables C, C-2, D, D-2, F; Administrative Office of the U.S. Courts, 2019 Judicial Business, Analysis & Tables C, C-2, D, D-2, F; Administrative Office of the U.S. Courts, 2018 Judicial Business, Analysis & Tables C, C-2, D, D-2, F.

Page 43. Add at the end of footnote 163:

For an elaboration of these points and a broader discussion of how the federal courts constitute American lawyers' " 'common intellectual heritage,' " consult Resnik, *Revising Our "Common Intellectual Heritage": Federal and State Courts in Our Federal System*, 91 Notre Dame L.Rev. 1831 (2016) (from a Symposium honoring Daniel Meltzer) (quoting Meltzer, *The Judiciary's Bicentennial*, 56 U.Chi.L.Rev. 423, 427 (1989)).

Page 45. Add at the end of footnote 172:

Updated 2022 figures from the Administrative Office of the U.S. Courts revealed a decline in filed appeals from the 2013 figure to 44,546 in 2021 and 42,900 in 2022. Filings by *pro se* litigants accounted for just shy of half of new filings in 2020–2021. See Administrative Office of the U.S. Courts, 2022 Judicial Business, Analysis & Tables B, B-9; Administrative Office of the U.S. Courts, 2021 Judicial Business, Analysis & Tables B, B-9.

Page 47. Insert the following in place of the second paragraph of Section I, Paragraph (3):

The number of cases filed annually in the Court has risen over time, though it has fallen in recent years. During the 2020 Term, the Court docketed 6,239 cases[185] (in comparison with 1,957 in the 1960, 3,419 in the 1970, 4,174 in the 1980, 5,502 in the 1990, 7,924 in the 2001, and 8,580 in the 2013 Terms). Of the total in the 2020 Term, 10 came within the Court's original jurisdiction.[186]

[185] *The Supreme Court, 2020 Term—The Statistics*, 135 Harv.L.Rev. 491, 498 (2021).

[186] See *id.*

Page 47. Insert the following in place of the second sentence of the third paragraph of Section I, Paragraph (3):

The Court rendered opinions in just 62 cases in the 2020 Term and 60 cases in the 2021 Term,[187] in comparison with 132 in the 1960, 141 in the 1970, 159 in the 1980, 129 in the 1990, 95 in the 1994, and 88 in the 2001 Terms.

[187] *The Supreme Court. 2021 Term—The Statistics*, 136 Harv.L.Rev. 505 (2022); *The Supreme Court, 2020 Term—The Statistics*, 135 Harv.L.Rev. 491 (2021). By comparison, the Court rendered 72 opinions in the 2018 Term, and 59 in the 2019 Term. See *The Supreme Court, 2018 Term—The Statistics*, 133 Harv.L.Rev. 412 (2019); *The Supreme Court, 2019 Term—The Statistics*, 134 Harv.L.Rev. 610 (2020). The lower number of opinions issued in the 2019 Term resulted at least in part from the fact that the COVID-19 global pandemic began during this period and curtailed the number of oral arguments held at the end of the Term.

Page 47. Add at the end of footnote 187:

An empirical study of 93,000 certiorari petitions filed between the 2001 Supreme Court Term and the start of the 2015 Term found that factors influencing the probability of a petition being granted include whether the federal government supports a grant, the attorneys involved, and the lower court that rendered the decision. See Feldman & Kappner, *Finding Certainty in Cert: An Empirical Analysis of the Factors Involved in Supreme Court Certiorari Decisions from 2001–2015*, 61 Vill.L.Rev. 795 (2017).

CHAPTER II

THE NATURE OF THE FEDERAL JUDICIAL FUNCTION: CASES AND CONTROVERSIES

1. INTRODUCTION AND HISTORICAL CONTEXT

NOTE ON ADVISORY OPINIONS

Page 54. Add a new footnote 2a at the end of Paragraph (1):

[2a] Recent historical scholarship argues that the prohibition against advisory opinions in American Founding-Era practice was in fact part of a global phenomenon throughout the anglophone world in the late eighteenth century, including in England and British India. Burset, *Advisory Opinions and the Problem of Legal Authority*, 74 Vand.L.Rev. 621 (2021). According to Burset, the refusal to issue advisory opinions was a judicial response to a contemporary global dispute about the nature of common law authority, and had little to do with the specifics of the American Constitution. If this is so, does it imply that the prohibition on advisory opinions may be less deeply rooted than the conventional wisdom has it? Or the opposite?

NOTE ON MARBURY V. MADISON

Page 69. Add at the end of footnote 4:

For a defense of Marbury on nearly every point, including a rejection of the claim that the opinion was "disingenuously manipulative * * * in order to create an occasion for the exercise of judicial review," see Treanor, *The Story of Marbury v. Madison: Judicial Authority and Political Struggle*, in Federal Courts Stories (Jackson & Resnik eds. 2010), at 29.

NOTE ON MARBURY V. MADISON AND THE FUNCTION OF ADJUDICATION

Page 79. Add at the end of Paragraph (7)(b):

See also Sessions v. Morales-Santana, 582 U.S. 47 (2017), also discussed pp. 32, 34, *infra*, in which the Court ruled a provision of the immigration laws invalid on equal protection grounds even though applicable remedial law precluded an award of citizenship to the complaining party, who therefore remained subject to removal from the United States. To remedy the equal protection violation, the Court concluded that the Government, in the absence of other corrective action by Congress, should eliminate the disparity of which the respondent complained by ceasing to confer citizenship on others on a gender-discriminatory basis. To a protest from Justice

Thomas, joined by Justice Alito, that the equal protection ruling was "unnecessary" in light of the Court's remedial determination, Justice Ginsburg's majority opinion rejoined: "[D]iscrimination itself … perpetuat[es] 'archaic and stereotypic notions' incompatible with the equal treatment guaranteed by the Constitution." Does the Justices' disagreement turn on what it means for constitutional rulings to be unnecessary? If so, in what way?

Page 81. Add at the end of Paragraph (7)(c):

Divisions among the Justices about whether a construction is sufficiently plausible to trigger the avoidance canon are not infrequent. See, e.g., Jennings v. Rodriguez, 138 S.Ct. 830 (2018) (involving a division, by 5–3, about whether three immigration provisions could plausibly be read to require periodic bond hearings for long-term detainees). See also Katyal & Schmidt, *Active Avoidance: The Modern Supreme Court and Legal Change*, 128 Harv.L.Rev. 2109 (2015) (arguing that recent decisions invoking the avoidance doctrine have engaged in "constitutional adventurism of a uniquely pernicious sort" by announcing new rules of constitutional law and relying on them as a predicate for substantially rewriting statutes).[13]

[13] Fish, *Constitutional Avoidance as Interpretation and as Remedy*, 114 Mich.L.Rev. 1275 (2016), argues for re-conceptualizing avoidance doctrine as including not only an interpretive component, but also a remedial one, through which courts seek to save statutes from facial invalidity. Courts have traditionally dealt with judicial responses to identified statutory overbreadth or vagueness via separability doctrine. For discussion, see Seventh Edition pp. 170–174.

---

2. ISSUES OF PARTIES, THE REQUIREMENT OF FINALITY, AND THE PROHIBITION AGAINST FEIGNED AND COLLUSIVE SUITS

NOTE ON HAYBURN'S CASE

Page 86. Add at the end of Paragraph (4):

Pfander & Birk, *Article III Judicial Power, the Adverse-Party Requirement, and Non-Contentious Jurisdiction*, 124 Yale L.J. 1346 (2015), seek comprehensively to revise long-settled assumptions that Article III jurisdiction requires adverse parties in all cases. The authors trace a history of "non-contentious" jurisdiction from Roman times through the English Court of Chancery sitting in Westminster to colonial and early American courts that had sundry powers to rule on ex parte or otherwise uncontested petitions to establish or register legal rights or interests. According to the authors, historical or modern residues of that tradition can be seen not only in naturalization proceedings (as in Tutun), but also, inter alia, in uncontested prize and salvage cases in admiralty, appointments of bankruptcy trustees, issuances of warrants, entries of default judgments, class action settlements, and consent decrees. In the authors' view, Article III requires adverse parties in "controversies", but not necessarily in all "cases", some of which can be non-contentious. "The lesson of Hayburn's

Case", they write, "is not that the federal courts lack power to hear ex parte proceedings, but that they can act only where their decision will have a binding, legally determinative effect." Seeking to distill normative lessons from historical practice, Pfander & Birk conclude: "[W]hile no adverse party need appear in non-contentious proceedings, federal courts should exercise jurisdiction only if the party invoking federal power has a concrete interest in the recognition of a legal claim. * * * The courts also should exercise non-contentious jurisdiction only where they have been called upon to employ judicial judgment in the application of law to the facts and only where their decisions will enjoy the finality long viewed as essential to the federal judicial role. The courts must be especially mindful of the potential for cases heard on the non-contentious side of their dockets to affect the rights of absent parties, and due process will continue to require that third parties receive notice of, and an opportunity to participate in, matters that concern them."

Pfander & Birk are unquestionably correct that federal courts routinely act on ex parte motions and render uncontested rulings in a number of contexts. As the authors acknowledge, many of these rulings come in proceedings that are potentially contested (as in Tutun) or are ancillary to the resolution of live disputes (as, for example, in the appointment of bankruptcy trustees). That said, their study generates an important question: Is there a large enough residual category to warrant the development of forward-looking principles—such as those that they propose—to identify, limit, and structure exercises of "non-contentious jurisdiction" under Article III.

Woolhandler, *Adverse Interests and Article III*, 111 Nw.U.L.Rev. 1025 (2017), answers in the negative. According to Professor Woolhandler, the examples adduced by Pfander and Birk show at most that Article III does not require adverse arguments in every case; the authors fail to refute the more fundamental proposition that Article III jurisdiction always requires parties with adverse interests. Pfander & Birk, *Adverse Interests and Article III: A Reply*, 111 Nw.U.L.Rev. 1067 (2017), retort that Woolhandler adopts a conceptualization of Article III's requirements that emerged only in the late nineteenth century and that she offers no theory adequate to explain earlier discussion of and practice involving non-contentious jurisdiction. Pfander has expanded further on these and other arguments in a recent book, Pfander, Cases Without Controversies: Uncontested Adjudication in Article III Courts (2021).

————

3. SOME PROBLEMS OF STANDING TO SUE

A. PLAINTIFFS' STANDING

NOTE ON STANDING TO SUE

Page 117. Add at the end of footnote 11:

In Students for Fair Admissions v. Harvard, 143 S.Ct. 2141 (2023), the Court found organizational standing under Hunt's three-part test, and went on to hold that (unlike in Hunt) where "an organization has identified members and represents them in good faith, our cases do not require further scrutiny into how the organization operates."

Page 119. Add at the end of Paragraph (3)(b):

The Court relied on Justice Powell's concurring opinion in United States v. Richardson in Carney v. Adams, 141 S.Ct. 493 (2020), which held that the plaintiff, a lawyer and political independent, lacked standing to challenge a provision of the Delaware Constitution that imposed party-membership criteria for appointment to the state's major courts. Despite general averments that he wished to apply to become a judge, the plaintiff had not established that he was "able and ready" to seek appointment to any particular court, and he therefore had not shown the requisite "personal," "concrete," and "imminent" injury.

Page 119. Add at the end of Paragraph (3)(c):

(d) Trump v. Hawaii, 138 S.Ct. 2392 (2018), upheld the standing of three U.S. citizens or permanent residents to challenge a presidential proclamation that restricted entry into the United States by nationals of six predominantly Muslim countries. In doing so, the Court declined to decide whether injury to a "claimed dignitary interest" in being free from religious establishments and the designation of a "disfavored faith" sufficed for standing. The individual plaintiffs had alleged adequate injury in the "real-world effect that the Proclamation has had in keeping them separated from certain relatives who seek to enter the country."

(e) Uzuegbunam v. Preczewski, 141 S.Ct. 792 (2021), found that a plaintiff satisfied the requirements for standing by seeking nominal damages for a past deprivation of free speech rights (to engage in religious proselytization on the campus of a public college) even in the absence of allegations of quantifiable economic harm. In an opinion by Justice Thomas, the Court held, by 8–1, that the plaintiff had alleged an injury in fact, caused by the defendants, and that nominal damages would redress his injury. Justice Thomas's opinion relied heavily on English and American common law, which he said allowed suits seeking nominal damages based on the premise that "*every* legal injury necessarily causes damage," even when "there was no apparent continuing or threatened injury for nominal damages to redress." "By permitting plaintiffs to pursue nominal damages whenever they suffered a personal legal injury, the common law avoided the oddity of privileging small-dollar economic rights over important, but not easily quantifiable, nonpecuniary rights", he wrote.

Chief Justice Roberts dissented. He maintained that the Court's reliance on English common law was inapt, since English courts were not subject to the constraints of Article III. He further argued that the American common law cases clearly established only that plaintiffs could sue for nominal damages as a form of relief against ongoing or threatened future harms. Viewing the issue through a more contemporary lens, the Chief Justice also thought allowance of nominal damages for purely past injuries irreconcilable with "modern justiciability principles" that do not permit standing to challenge every invasion of a statutorily conferred right and that authorize suit only when judicial relief will "compensat[e] the plaintiff for a past loss" or prevent "an ongoing or future harm."

For discussion of the impact of Uzuegbunam v. Preczewski on mootness doctrine, see p. 44 *infra*.

Page 119. Add at the end of footnote 15:

In cases under the Establishment Clause challenging governmental displays of crèches, crosses, and the Ten Commandments, the Supreme Court has often ruled on the merits, typically without discussion of standing. In American Legion v. American Humanist Ass'n, 139 S.Ct. 2067 (2019), which rejected a challenge to the display of a cross as a war memorial, the majority took no notice of any standing issue. But Justice Gorsuch, in an opinion concurring in the judgment that Justice Thomas joined, would have dismissed on standing grounds. More broadly, he would have rejected "the plaintiffs' 'offended observer' theory of standing" and, further, would have held the implied recognition of standing in a number of prior religious display cases to be error. According to Justice Gorsuch, the plausibility of the "offended observer" theory depends on a mistaken test of substantive constitutional validity, under which displays of religious symbols are unconstitutional if a "reasonable observer" would perceive them as "endorsing" religion. See, *e.g.*, County of Allegheny v. American Civil Liberties Union, Greater Pittsburgh Chapter, 492 U.S. 573, 620–21 (1989) (opinion of Blackmun, J.); *id.* 631 (O'Connor, J., concurring in part and concurring in the judgment). In Justice Gorsuch's view, the Article III standing requirement of injury-in-fact renders the "offended observer" theory untenable, and he would have rejected that theory along with the "endorsement" test (and the test of Lemon v. Kurtzman, 403 U.S. 602 (1971), on which it sometimes functioned as a gloss). Justice Ginsburg's dissenting opinion, which Justice Sotomayor joined, described "Justice Gorsuch's 'no standing' opinion [as] startling in view of the many religious-display cases this Court has resolved on the merits." She also suggested that it would have intolerable consequences. Without further elaboration, Justice Ginsburg approvingly cited an amicus brief that she described in a parenthetical as "explaining why offended observer standing is necessary and proper."

In demanding that the Court reject "offended observer" standing, Justice Gorsuch traced the mismatch between the Court's Establishment Clause jurisprudence and the Article III demand for injury-in-fact to the Court's "misadventure" in seeking "a 'grand unified theory' of the Establishment Clause [that] left us only a mess." Would it be just as fair to direct the same criticism at the Court's effort to develop a "grand unified theory" of Article III standing built on a demand for injury-in-fact? Cf. Fallon, *The Fragmentation of Standing*, 93 Tex.L.Rev. 1061, 1062 (2015) ("Since the Court began in the 1970s to characterize standing as turning almost entirely on a single, transubstantive, tripartite test * * * commentators have complained about inconsistencies and anomalies in application.").

Page 123. Add at the end of Paragraph (4)(c):

In Trump v. New York, 141 S.Ct. 530 (2020), also discussed p. 47 *infra*, the Court found that the plaintiffs lacked standing to challenge a memorandum directing the Secretary of Commerce to provide information that would facilitate the President's exclusion of unlawful immigrants from the population base used in apportioning the states' representation in Congress and disbursing certain federal funds. Emphasizing uncertainty concerning the number of unlawful immigrants that the Secretary would be able to identify and that the President would be able to exclude from his tally, the Court held that the plaintiffs had not established a "substantial risk" of either reduced representation or diminished funding. Justice Breyer, joined by Justices Sotomayor and Kagan, dissented. He argued that despite uncertainties as to precise numbers, "the memorandum presents the 'substantial risk' that our precedents require." (The Commerce Department subsequently announced a delay in its reporting of even preliminary census data until after the end of the Trump administration, and the Biden administration revoked the challenged memorandum.)

Most recently, in Whole Woman's Health v. Jackson, 142 S.Ct. 522 (2021) the Court concluded that plaintiffs lacked standing to sue a private individual, Mark Lee Dickson, who might have filed state lawsuits against them under the Texas abortion statute S. B. 8. The Court relied on sworn statements by Dickson that he did not intend to sue the plaintiffs under S. B. 8, and concluded that the plaintiffs had not established an injury traceable to his conduct. It apparently rejected (without explanation) the plaintiffs' arguments that those disavowals were too limited and conditional to eliminate their risk of injury. This portion of the decision was not contested by the dissenting justices. For additional discussion of Whole Woman's Health, see *infra* pp. 126–137.

Page 124. Add at the end of footnote 19:

See also Boddie, *The Sins of Innocence*, 68 Vand.L.Rev. 297 (2015) (arguing that presumed injuries to white plaintiffs seeking to enjoin affirmative action programs rely on racialized conceptions of innocence and make standing both a product and an instrument of racial inequality).

Page 125. Add at the end of footnote 20:

Town of Chester v. Laroe Estates, Inc., 581 U.S. 433 (2017), applied the principle that plaintiffs must separately demonstrate standing for all forms of relief that they seek to intervenors as of right under Fed.R.Civ.P. 24(a)(2) who seek relief not requested by the plaintiffs.

Hessick, *The Separation-of-Powers Theory of Standing*, 95 N.C.L.Rev. 673 (2017), argues from the premise that standing doctrine exists solely to protect the separation of powers to the conclusion that there should be no Article III standing barrier to suits that do not present separation-of-powers concerns, including actions to enforce either "private" or "public" rights against state officials. Notwithstanding supporting dicta in a few Supreme Court decisions, is the premise of Professor Hessick's argument sounder than a number of the decisions with which his conclusion would conflict?

Page 125. Add at the end of Paragraph (5)(c):

In Department of Commerce v. New York, 139 S.Ct. 2551 (2019), the Court ruled that some plaintiff states and possibly other parties had standing to challenge the citizenship question in the 2020 census questionnaire. In an opinion by Chief Justice Roberts, the Court upheld standing based on the prediction that the "citizenship question would result in noncitizen households responding to the census at lower rates than other groups, which in turn would cause them to be undercounted and lead to" such harms to the states as "los[ing] out on federal funds that are distributed on the basis of state population." For a Court that was unanimous on this point, the Chief Justice reasoned: "The Government invokes our steady refusal to 'endorse standing theories that rest on speculation about the decisions of independent actors,' Clapper v. Amnesty Int'l USA, 568 U.S. 398, 414 (2013), particularly speculation about future unlawful conduct, Los Angeles v. Lyons, 461 U.S. 95, 105 (1983). But * * * evidence at trial established that noncitizen households have historically responded to the census at lower rates than other groups, and the District Court did not clearly err in crediting the Census Bureau's theory that the discrepancy is likely attributable at least in part to noncitizens' reluctance to answer a citizenship question. Respondents' theory of standing thus does not rest on mere speculation about the decisions of third parties; it relies instead on the predictable effect of Government action on the decisions of third parties." Compare Allen v.

Wright, Seventh Edition p. 103, and Simon v. Eastern Ky. Welfare Rights Org., Seventh Edition p. 124, both denying standing on the ground that anticipated harm resulting from actions by third parties was too speculative to support standing.

Page 125. Add Paragraphs (5)(d), (5)(e), 5(f), 5(g), and 5(h):

(d) The Court denied standing based on causation and redressability problems in California v. Texas, 141 S.Ct. 2104 (2021), in which the plaintiffs argued that a change in law since the Court's prior cases involving the Affordable Care Act (ACA) rendered the statute facially invalid and therefore unenforceable. In the Justices' first encounter with the ACA, National Federation of Independent Business v. Sebelius, 567 U.S. 519 (2012), a divided Court held that Congress lacked power under the Commerce Clause to enact a mandate that individuals purchase health insurance, but upheld the challenged provision under Congress's power to tax. When Congress subsequently reduced the penalty for non-purchase of insurance to $0, but did not otherwise repeal the purchase mandate, two individuals and eighteen states sought invalidation of the entire ACA on the theory that the individual mandate could no longer be characterized as a tax and that all other provisions were non-severable.

The Court, by 7–2, found that because none of the plaintiffs had standing to bring the action against the Secretary of Health and Human Services and the other federal defendants, it need not determine either the continuing validity of the now-unenforceable individual mandate or the severability of the mandate from the remainder of the ACA. Writing for the majority, Justice Breyer did not question that the individual plaintiffs had alleged injury in the form of costs for the purchase of health insurance, but he ruled that they failed to satisfy the causation prong of the standing test. "[O]ur cases have consistently spoken of the need to assert an injury that is the result of a statute's actual or threatened *enforcement*", Justice Breyer wrote. In the absence of any credible threat that the defendants would enforce the mandate to purchase insurance, any harm that the plaintiffs had suffered was not "fairly traceable" to the defendants, he reasoned. Redressability analysis pointed to the same conclusion, Justice Breyer added, because a court could grant not effectual relief. The plaintiffs had not sought an injunction against enforcement of the individual mandate, and, under the Declaratory Judgment Act, a court could not issue a declaratory judgment of unconstitutionality, either, absent the possibility of action by one of the parties that would give rise to a justiciable suit for coercive relief. (On the relevant principles governing jurisdiction under the Declaratory Judgments Act, see Note on the Jurisdictional Significance of the Declaratory Judgment Act, Seventh Edition, p. 841.) "To find standing here to attack an unenforceable statutory provision would allow a federal court to issue what would amount to 'an advisory opinion without the possibility of any judicial relief ' ", Justice Breyer ruled (citations omitted).

Justice Breyer then found that the plaintiff states, who had claimed that they suffered financial injuries from provisions of the ACA other than the individual mandate as well as indirect injuries from the mandate itself, also lacked standing to challenge the mandate's validity. He relied on causation principles to reject the states' claim that the individual mandate led state residents to enroll in state-operated insurance programs that cost the states money. "Given the[ ] benefits [that these programs provide], neither logic nor intuition suggests that the presence of the minimum essential coverage requirement would lead an individual to enroll in one of those programs that its absence would lead them to ignore", he wrote. "[W]here a causal relation between injury and challenged action depends upon the decision of an independent third party", a plaintiff must adduce more supporting facts at the summary judgments stage than the states had put into the record.

Justice Breyer acknowledged that provisions of the ACA other than the individual mandate imposed direct costs on the plaintiff states, such as those incurred in providing information to residents and furnishing information to the Internal Revenue Service. Nevertheless, he deemed it fatal to their case that all of the relevant provisions "operate independently of" the individual mandate that the plaintiffs sought to challenge. "No one claims these other provisions violate the Constitution", he emphasized.

Justice Alito, joined by Justice Gorsuch, dissented. In his view, "the individual plaintiffs' claim to standing raise[d] a novel question" that did not need to be addressed, since "the States have standing for reasons that are straightforward and meritorious." Justice Alito began with the premise that the states had suffered financial injuries from provisions of the ACA other than the individual mandate. Building on that premise, he further reasoned that if the states were correct (a) that the individual mandate was constitutionally invalid and (b) that other provisions of the ACA could not be severed from it, then the states' financial injuries were "indeed traceable to the mandate." According to Justice Alito, the Court had granted standing to plaintiffs mounting facial challenges to statutes on grounds of statutory nonseverability in a number of prior cases and then treated the question of statutory severability as a merits question. In his view, that was the correct approach.

Justice Breyer's response to Justice Alito's standing analysis, which Justice Thomas expanded upon in a concurring opinion, was that the "novel theory" that Justice Alito advanced in dissent was neither argued by the plaintiffs in the lower courts nor presented in the plaintiffs' cert petitions and that "[w]e accordingly decline to consider it." Justice Alito, by contrast, thought that the state plaintiffs had adequately presented the gist of the argument that he more fully developed.

Justice Alito appears correct in his contention that a number of the Court's prior decisions entertaining facial challenges to federal statutes implicitly rely on a standing-through-nonseverability analysis under which plaintiffs who are directly harmed by one provision of a statute seek facial invalidation based on an alleged defect in another provision. (A recent example is Seila Law LLC v. Consumer Financial Protection Bureau (CFPB), 140 S.Ct. 2183 (2020), in which a law firm that suffered harm pursuant to a statute's enforcement provisions was permitted to challenge another provision involving the appointment and removal of the CFPB's Director. Although the Court ultimately rejected the firm's argument that an invalid limitation on presidential removal was not severable from the rest of the statute, it did so only after rejecting a challenge to the firm's standing.) Justice Thomas's concurring opinion responded by noting, in addition to the Court's waiver analysis, that "this Court has not addressed standing-through-inseverability in any detail, largely relying on it through implication."

At some point the Court will need to consider the soundness of the theory that plaintiffs have standing to challenge statutory provisions that do not directly cause them injury because those provisions are non-severable from other, injury-causing provisions of the same statute. When it does so, much will undoubtedly hinge on the Court's understanding of relevant principles of statutory severability and nonseverability. For discussion, see Preliminary Note on As-Applied and Facial Challenges and the Problem of Separability, Seventh Edition p. 169. See also Fallon, *Facial Challenges, Saving Constructions, and Statutory Severability*, 99 Tex.L.Rev. 215, 245–48 (2020) (arguing that if statutes are constitutionally invalid due to the application of nonseverability principles, rule-of-law and due process principles require that adversely affected parties should be able to challenge them); Baude, *Severability First Principles*, 109 Va.L.Rev. 1, 14, 57 (2023) (arguing that inseverability is properly understood as a form of "fallback law," and if so, then "[s]uch a plaintiff has an orthodox legal injury, an orthodox claim for why that injury is illegal, and an orthodox claim for redress").

(e)　In Federal Election Commission v. Cruz, 142 S.Ct. 1638 (2022) the Court found that an incumbent candidate for Senate (and his campaign) had standing to challenge federal restrictions on the use of funds raised after election day. It rejected the argument that the plaintiffs lacked standing because this was a "self-inflicted" injury. The Court described the government's argument as "[a]t bottom . . . ask[ing] us to recognize an exception to traceability for injuries that a party purposely incurs." Citing Evers v. Dwyer, 358 U.S. 202, 204 (1958) and Havens Realty Corp. v. Coleman, 455 U.S. 363, 374 (1982), and distinguishing Clapper v. Amnesty Int'l, 568 U.S. 398 (2013), the Court rejected such a rule: "That appellees chose to subject themselves to those provisions does not change the fact that they *are* subject to them, and will face genuine legal penalties if they do not comply."

The Court also rejected an argument that the plaintiffs could challenge only the regulations implementing the statute, and not the statute itself, even though the plaintiffs had likely violated only the regulations. It concluded that the plaintiffs' injury "is, even if brought about by the agency's threatened enforcement of its regulation, traceable to the operation of Section 304 itself." Because an agency's regulatory authority must ultimately be traced to a statute, a conclusion that the statute was "invalid and unenforceable" would imply that the agency rule was too.

(f)　In Haaland v. Brackeen, 143 S.Ct. 1609 (2023), the Court rejected a set of challenges to the constitutionality of the Indian Child Welfare Act on redressability grounds. Most importantly, it rejected a claim by a group of individual non-Indian plaintiffs who argued that the Act violated equal protection principles by treating them less favorably than Indian parents seeking to adopt or foster an Indian child. The Court agreed that "[t]he racial discrimination [these plaintiffs] allege counts as an Article III injury," but it held that they "have not shown that this injury is 'likely' to be 'redressed by judicial relief.'" (quoting TransUnion LLC v. Ramirez, 141 S.Ct. 2190, 2203 (2021)). The plaintiffs sought relief (an injunction and a declaratory judgment) against various federal parties, but "enjoining the federal parties would not remedy the alleged injury, because state courts apply the placement preferences, and state agencies carry out the court-ordered placements."

The Court acknowledged the plaintiffs' argument that "state courts are likely to defer to a federal court's interpretation of federal law" and thus that "winning this case would solve their problems." But this possibility still did not satisfy the redressability prong. "[R]edressability requires that the court be able to afford relief *through the exercise of its power*, not through the persuasive or even awe-inspiring effect of the opinion *explaining* the exercise of its power." (quoting Franklin v. Massachusetts, 505 U. S. 788, 825 (1992) (Scalia, J., concurring in part and concurring in judgment) (emphasis in original)). This meant that redressability draws a hard line between judicial judgments and judicial opinions: "It is a federal court's judgment, not its opinion, that remedies an injury; thus it is the judgment, not the opinion, that demonstrates redressability. The individual petitioners can hope for nothing more than an opinion, so they cannot satisfy Article III."

(g) In United States v. Texas, 143 S.Ct. 1964 (2023) the Court rejected another claim of standing, this time Texas's and Louisiana's assertion of standing to challenge the executive branch's prioritization of certain immigration arrests. The states claimed that by not making more arrests, the federal government was imposing costs on the state, forcing them to incarcerate or provide social services to those that the government was declining to arrest. The Court rejected this claim of standing, relying heavily and extensively on "[t]he leading precedent" of Linda R.S. v. Richard D., Seventh Edition pp. 123–124. According to the Court, this case shielded some set of "challenges to the Executive Branch's exercise of enforcement discretion over whether to arrest or prosecute," The Court grounded this principle more generally in "precedents and longstanding historical practice" as well as a range of other "good reasons," such as the scope of Article II, judicial manageability, foreign policy concerns, and more.

Despite its purported reliance on Linda R.S., however, it is not clear whether the majority decided the case on the basis of redressability and traceability, or instead on the basis of lack of injury. In discussing the monetary costs imposed on the states, for example, the Court wrote: "Monetary costs are of course an injury. But this Court has 'also stressed that the alleged injury must be legally and judicially cognizable.'" (quoting Raines v. Byrd, 521 U. S. 811. 819 (1997)). It explained that this "'requires, among other things,' that the 'dispute is traditionally thought to be capable of resolution through the judicial process'—in other words, that the asserted injury is traditionally redressable in federal court," (quoting Raines, 521 U.S. at 819), and emphasized that this would be assessed on the basis of "history and tradition." In later parts of its analysis, the Court relied heavily on substantive arguments in favor of executive discretion, seeming to blend its standing analysis with the merits.

By contrast, a three-justice concurrence in the judgment by Justice Gorsuch argued more specifically that "[t]he problem here is redressability." The redressability problem that the concurrence saw, however, was also quite distinct from the Linda R.S. principle, and involved the concurrence's substantive skepticism about the reach of various federal remedies. Most notably, the concurrence questioned the power of federal courts to vacate agency rules under the Administrative Procedure Act, on the basis of the statute's text, history, and structure, as well as background principles of judicial power. Finally the concurrence argued that even if such a remedy was authorized by the APA, "faithful application of [equitable] principles suggests that an extraordinary remedy like vacatur would demand truly extraordinary circumstances to justify it. Cf. S. Bray & P. Miller, Getting Into Equity, 97 N[otre] D[ame] L. Rev. 1763, 1797 (2022) ('[I]n equity it all connects—the broader and deeper the remedy the plaintiff wants, the stronger the plaintiff's story needs to be.')."

The scope of the majority's holding is somewhat unclear. After establishing broad principles of executive discretion, the Court also listed a series of cases that might be justiciable nonetheless: "selective-prosecution claims under the Equal Protection Clause"; cases where Congress had specifically authorized judicial review; cases where "the Executive Branch wholly abandoned its statutory responsibilities"; cases where the executive also granted legal benefits or legal status; and "policies governing the continued detention of noncitizens who have already been arrested." Does United States v. Texas establish a broad principle of judicial restraint, or does it approximate a case-specific judgment on the merits that will affect few other cases?

(h) Finally, the Court's divergent standing decisions in two challenges to the Biden administration's proposed student-loan forgiveness plan further illustrate the complicated interplay between these principles. In Department of Education v. Brown, 143 S.Ct. 2343 (2023), the Court unanimously found that two individual plaintiffs lacked standing to sue. The plaintiffs' argument, in brief, was that they had been injured because their loans had not been covered, or not covered adequately, by the administration's chosen plan. But had the administration been forced to use a different statutory authority to pursue loan relief, it would have been required to use more elaborate administrative procedures, and the result of that process might have benefited the plaintiffs.

The Court expressed doubts about the plaintiffs' injury and about its redressability, but concluded that "the deficiencies of respondents' claim are clearest with respect to traceability." The two possible statutory authorities for student-loan relief were independent from another. Thus, "the Department's decision to give *other* people relief under a *different* statutory scheme did not cause respondents not to obtain the benefits they want. The cause of their supposed injury is far more pedestrian than that: The Department has simply *chosen* not to give them the relief they want."

Meanwhile, the same day, a 6–3 majority did find standing to challenge the program by a different plaintiff: the state of Missouri, which was one of the plaintiffs in a case captioned Biden v. Nebraska, 143 S.Ct. 2355 (2023). Missouri's standing came from the effects of student-loan relief on the Missouri Higher Education Loan Authority (MOHELA). It was accepted on all sides that the policy would injury MOHELA by depriving it of servicing fees it otherwise would have earned had the loans continued. The Court concluded that "[t]he plan's harm to MOHELA is also a harm to Missouri" because "MOHELA is a 'public instrumentality' of the State." By contrast, the dissenting opinion by Justice Kagan argued that because MOHELA was financially and legally independent, with statutory power to sue and be sued. it was the proper party, not Missouri. What is the nature of the dissent's objection to MOHELA's standing? Is it a problem of "third-party standing," as the dissent seemed to suggest? Or is it a problem of traceability and redressability, because even relief to MOHELA will have no effect on the state of Missouri itself?

Page 127. Add at the end of Paragraph (6):

In a survey of standing doctrine under the Roberts Court, Fallon, *The Fragmentation of Standing,* 93 Tex.L.Rev. 1061 (2015), traces standing's "fragmentation", which the author defines as "the division of standing law into multiple compartments", since the articulation of the modern, three-part (injury, causation, and redressability) test in the 1970s. In the author's view, "large generalizations" about standing, including those offered in Supreme Court opinions, are characteristically either empty or misleading. Nevertheless, he writes, the Court's decisions tend to form patterns defined by interconnections among such features as: (a) the provision under which a plaintiff brings suit, (b) the nature and sensitivity of the remedy that a plaintiff seeks, (c) whether the plaintiff sues to enforce a substantive or a procedural right, (d) whether the plaintiff is a private citizen or a governmental body or official, and (e) the presence or absence of congressional authorization. These patterns, Professor Fallon claims, "frequently exhibit an implicit normative logic" and enable predictions of future outcomes, but require scholars and judges to look behind the Court's words to "the kinds of facts that actually drive decisions in practice". Professor Fallon suggests that his "doctrinal Realist credo affords a note of hope, not despair" for those seeking ordered consistency among leading decisions. Is there any reason why the verbal formulae in which the Supreme Court couches standing doctrine should be less reliable than judicial articulations of other legal doctrines?

––––––––––

NOTE ON SPECIALIZED STANDING DOCTRINES: TAXPAYER AND LEGISLATOR STANDING

Page 132. Add at the end of footnote 4:

Compare Nash, *A Functional Theory of Congressional Standing,* 114 Mich.L.Rev. 339 (2015) (arguing that congressional standing should be based on a broader view of injury than mere vote nullification and should extend to injuries involving Congress's "constitutional functions" such as impediments to information gathering and certain diminishments of bargaining power). For further discussions of congressional standing, see Campbell, *Executive Action and Nonaction*, 95 N.C.L.Rev. 553 (2017) (arguing that Congress should have standing to challenge presidential failures to enforce the law when "congressional votes resulting in the passage of a law have been completely nullified"); Sant'Ambrogio, *Legislative Exhaustion*, 58 Wm. & Mary L.Rev. 1253 (2017) (coining the term "Legislative Exhaustion" to describe the argument that Congress ought to have standing only when it lacks nonjudicial methods of resolving a dispute with the executive branch, as when the President declines to enforce federal law based on constitutional objections); Grove, *Standing Outside of Article III*, 162 U.Pa.L.Rev. 1311 (2014) (identifying Article I and Article II as well as Article III limits on the standing of Congress and the executive branch); Jackson, *Congressional Standing to Sue: The Role of Courts and Congress in U.S. Constitutional Democracy*, 93 Ind.L.J. 845 (2018) (canvasing competing considerations and concluding that, although there should be no categorical preclusion of congressional standing, "most controversies between the branches are best addressed through political mechanisms").

Page 132. Add a new Paragraph (3)(d):

(d) In an opinion by Justice Ginsburg (joined by Justices Kennedy, Breyer, Sotomayor, and Kagan), the Court in Arizona State Legislature v. Arizona Independent Redistricting Comm'n, 576 U.S. 787 (2015) ("AIRC"), held that the Arizona State Legislature had standing to challenge a state ballot initiative that transferred to an independent commission the legislature's previous authority to redistrict Arizona's seats in the U.S. House of Representatives. The state legislature argued, *inter alia*, that this shift violated the Elections Clause, U.S. Const. art. I, § 4, cl. 1, which gives "the Legislature" of each state the power to prescribe the "Time, Places and Manner" of federal legislative elections. Although ultimately rejecting that claim on the merits, the Court found that the suit asserted a concrete and legally cognizable injury caused by the initiative's alleged infringement of the legislature's constitutionally assigned role.

The Court distinguished Raines v. Byrd, Seventh Edition, p. 131, on the ground that, in that case, "six *individual Members* of Congress" challenged the Line Item Veto Act and that neither the House nor the Senate had authorized suit by those Members. In contrast, the Arizona Legislature in AIRC sued as "an institutional plaintiff asserting an institutional injury, and * * * commenced this action after authorizing votes in both of its chambers." Quoting Coleman v. Miller, Seventh Edition, pp. 130–131, the Court in AIRC further noted that the challenged Arizona initiative would " 'completely nullif[y]' " the legislature's votes on federal redistricting. This consideration, said the Court, made the injury analogous to that of the twenty state senators who had been granted standing in Coleman to argue that their votes against ratifying a constitutional amendment were nullified, in violation of Article V, by the lieutenant governor's tie-breaking vote in favor.

In a dissenting opinion in AIRC, Justice Scalia (joined by Justice Thomas) contended that the traditional Anglo-American conception of "cases" or "controversies" does not "include suits between units of government regarding their legitimate powers." Even if such a suit was sufficiently "concrete" to permit effective adjudication, Justice Scalia concluded that the "separation of powers" precludes federal adjudication of interbranch disputes unless necessary to redress some resultant "concrete harm" to "a private party". Limiting the judicial power in this way, he added, "keeps us minding our own business." While acknowledging that Coleman seemed at odds with his position, Justice Scalia viewed that decision as an outlier whose true holding was far from clear.[5]

Would the Court's approach in AIRC justify congressional standing if Congress itself (or even a particular House) authorized Members to sue to vindicate an alleged "institutional injury" to Congress? Justice Ginsburg's opinion reserved that question, noting that "a suit between Congress and the President would raise separation-of-powers concerns absent here." Justice Scalia replied that if the Framers would have disfavored congressional standing, they presumably would have been *all the more averse* to unprecedented judicial meddling by federal courts with the branches of their state governments." How should the Court sort out such competing contentions about implied limits on federal judicial power?

[5] Grove, *Government Standing and the Fallacy of Institutional Injury*, 167 U.Pa.L.Rev. 611 (2019), also maintains that Coleman should not be followed. According to her, Coleman relied on "a now outdated rule of appellate standing" that permitted Supreme Court review of state court decisions of federal claims that a federal district court could not have entertained. Professor Grove argues more broadly that claims of standing predicated on "institutional injuries" are incompatible with a constitutional design that allocates rights to individuals, not institutions, and relies on individuals to assert their own rights. She would allow only narrow exceptions to permit government bodies to perform functions that they could not perform without resort to a court, such as imposing sanctions (including for contempt of legislative bodies).

Page 132. Add a new Paragraph (3)(e):

(e) In Virginia House of Delegates v. Bethune-Hill, 139 S.Ct. 1945 (2019), the Court held, by 5–4, that the Virginia House of Delegates lacked standing to appeal from a lower court ruling that a state redistricting plan (adopted by the state House and Senate) constituted a forbidden racial gerrymander. The issue arose when the State Attorney General, after defending the plan in the lower court, decided not to pursue an appeal, and the state House, which had previously participated as an intervenor, sought Supreme Court review. Justice Ginsburg's opinion, in which Justices Thomas, Sotomayor, Kagan, and Gorsuch joined, first ruled that the House lacked authority under Virginia law to represent the state's interests. Though Virginia could have "designated the House to represent its interests," it had not done so. Justice Ginsburg's opinion then held that a single house of a bicameral legislature suffered no sufficiently distinctive injury from the invalidation of a state law, including a districting statute, to support standing. In so ruling, the Court distinguished Sixty-seventh Minnesota State Senate v. Beens, 406 U.S. 187 (1972) (per curiam), which allowed the Minnesota Senate to challenge a lower court ruling in a malapportionment case that reduced the Senate's size from 67 to 35. "Cutting the size of the legislative chamber in half would necessarily alter its day-to-day operations" in a way that a mere change in district lines and membership would not, she reasoned: "[T]he House as an institution has no cognizable interest in the identity of its members." Justice Alito's dissenting opinion deemed it unnecessary to "address the [majority's] first" holding that "Virginia law does not authorize the House to defend the invalidated redistricting plan on behalf of the Commonwealth". In his view, it was "obvious" that the Virginia House, like "any group consisting of members who must work together to achieve the group's aims has a keen[, constitutionally cognizable] interest in the identity of its members [and] in how its members are selected." Accordingly, he thought it decisive that "neither the Court nor the Virginia Solicitor General has provided any support for the proposition that Virginia law bars the House from defending, in its own right, the constitutionality of a districting plan."

The majority and dissenting opinions appear ultimately to agree that state law is capable of controlling whether one branch of a bicameral legislature has standing to defend a state districting plan—either as a representative of the state or, according to the dissent, in its own right. To the extent that state law is controlling, which side should bear the burden of establishing a state-law authorization or prohibition?

Page 132. Add a Paragraph (5):

(5) Actions by Voters. In Gill v. Whitford, 138 S.Ct. 1916 (2018), the Supreme Court held unanimously that challengers to an alleged partisan gerrymander of the Wisconsin Legislature had failed to establish the "concrete and particularized" injury needed for standing: "We have long recognized that a person's right to vote is 'individual and personal in nature.' Reynolds v. Sims, 377 U.S. 533, 561 (1964). Thus, 'voters who allege facts showing disadvantage to themselves as individuals have standing to sue' to remedy that disadvantage. Baker v. Carr, 369 U.S. [186, 206 (1962)]. The plaintiffs in this case alleged that they suffered such injury from partisan gerrymandering, which works through 'packing' and 'cracking' voters of one party to disadvantage those voters. That is, the plaintiffs claim a constitutional right not to be placed in legislative districts deliberately designed to 'waste' their votes in elections where their chosen candidates will win in landslides (packing) or are destined to lose by closer margins (cracking). To the extent the plaintiffs' alleged harm is the dilution of their votes, that injury is district specific", and "results from the boundaries of the particular district[s] in which [they] reside[ ]. And a plaintiff's remedy must be 'limited to the inadequacy that produced [his] injury in fact.' Lewis v. Casey, 518 U.S. 343, 357 (1996). * * * For similar reasons, we have held that a plaintiff who alleges that he is the object of a racial gerrymander * * * has standing to assert only that his own district has been so gerrymandered. See United States v. Hays, 515 U.S. 737, 744–45 (1995)."[6]

Although "[f]our of the plaintiffs * * * pleaded a particularized [injury]" of having been deliberately placed in districts where their votes would be wasted, they "failed to meaningfully pursue their allegations of individual harm" and "instead rested their case at trial—and their arguments before this Court—on [a] theory of statewide injury to Wisconsin Democrats" through the wasting of Democratic votes on a statewide basis. As thus framed, the case was "about group political interests, not individual legal

---

[6] For criticism of the standing analyses in the Court's racial gerrymandering cases involving deliberate attempts to create majority-minority districts, see Issacharoff & Karlan, *Standing and Misunderstanding in Voting Rights Law*, 111 Harv.L.Rev. 2276 (1998) (arguing that the Court has failed to develop a coherent theory of what injury, if any, such districting inflicts). *Cf.* Ely, *Standing to Challenge Pro-Minority Gerrymanders*, 111 Harv.L.Rev. 576, 587 (1997) (maintaining that whites included in a majority-minority district "are being denied the opportunity to elect one of 'their own' ").

rights", and the plaintiffs' proposed measure of impermissible gerrymandering—an "efficiency gap" theory that compares each party's "wasted" votes on a statewide basis—gauged harms "to the fortunes of political parties", not the kinds of concrete injuries to individuals that are necessary for standing.

Having identified these defects in the plaintiffs' claims to standing, the Court remanded to the district court to give some of them the opportunity to adduce evidence "that would tend to demonstrate a burden on their individual votes." Justices Thomas and Gorsuch, concurring and part and concurring in the judgment, would have remanded with instructions to dismiss on the ground that the plaintiffs had already had "a more-than-ample opportunity to prove their standing under [established] principles."

Justice Kagan, joined by Justices Ginsburg, Breyer, and Sotomayor, concurred. She noted first that if the plaintiffs could establish personal injury arising from a constitutionally forbidden partisan gerrymander of their own districts, the violations "might warrant a statewide remedy": "with enough plaintiffs joined together—attacking all the packed and cracked districts in a statewide gerrymander—th[e] obligatory revisions could amount to a wholesale restructuring of the State's districting plan."

Justice Kagan also maintained that although the case had mostly been litigated on a vote-dilution theory, partisan gerrymanders may "inflict other kinds of constitutional harm" that would be cognizable under a theory alleging infringement of First Amendment rights of political association: "Justice Kennedy explained the First Amendment associational injury deriving from a partisan gerrymander in his concurring opinion in Vieth [v. Jubelirer, 541 U.S. 267 (2004)]", in which he explained that " '[r]epresentative democracy' is today 'unimaginable without the ability of citizens to band together' to advance their political beliefs. That means significant 'First Amendment concerns arise' when a State purposely 'subject[s] a group of voters or their party to disfavored treatment.' "

Justice Kagan continued: "As so formulated, the associational harm of a partisan gerrymander is distinct from vote dilution. * * * [Even if their own districts were 'left untouched' by a gerrymander, members] of the 'disfavored party' in the State, deprived of their natural political strength by a partisan gerrymander, may face difficulties fundraising, registering voters, attracting volunteers, generating support from independents, and recruiting candidates to run for office (not to mention eventually accomplishing their policy objectives)." Chief Justice Roberts' opinion for the Court responded: "We leave for another day consideration of other possible theories of harm not presented here and whether those theories might present justiciable claims giving rise to statewide remedies."

Justice Kagan's articulation of a theory of standing based on injury to associational rights, which she developed almost entirely from suggestive remarks in Justice Kennedy's opinion concurring in the judgment in Vieth, seemed clearly framed for the purpose of winning Justice Kennedy's vote, either in a future case or upon further review of the Gill case. And the standing question in partisan gerrymandering cases seems closely connected to the political question issue that the Court, in Gill, found it unnecessary to confront after holding that the plaintiffs had failed to establish standing. In Vieth, Seventh Edition p. 253, four Justices had ruled that challenges to partisan gerrymanders presented nonjusticiable political questions due to the absence of judicially manageable standards for determining when a gerrymander went "too far." Justice Kennedy, concurring, concluded only that no judicially manageable standards had yet "emerged". In Gill, the plaintiffs sought to advance a judicially manageable standard by relying on a state-wide "efficiency gap." Would it be anomalous for a voting scheme that creates a statewide efficiency gap to give rise to "concrete and particularized" injuries under the First Amendment but not the Equal Protection Clause? Justice Kagan maintained that it would not: "Standing, we have long held, 'turns on the nature and source of the claim asserted.' Warth v. Seldin, 422 U.S. 490, 500 (1975)."

NOTE ON CONGRESSIONAL POWER TO CONFER STANDING TO SUE

Page 151. Add a new Paragraph (2)(c):

(c)   In Spokeo, Inc. v. Robins, 578 U.S. 330 (2016), the Court reaffirmed the framework that it had developed in Lujan v. Defenders of Wildlife, Seventh Edition p. 133, to define congressional authority to confer standing, but divided 6–2 over how to apply that framework. The Fair Credit Reporting Act requires consumer reporting agencies to "follow reasonable procedures to assure maximum possible accuracy of" consumer reports and provides that " '[a]ny person who willfully fails to comply with any requirement [of the Act] with respect to any [individual] is liable to that [individual]' ". Robins brought suit under the Act against Spokeo, a "people search engine" that maintained an inaccurate report about him on its website. In evaluating Robins' standing, the Court, in an opinion by Justice Alito, reaffirmed that "a bare procedural violation, divorced from any concrete harm", would not satisfy the Article III injury requirement "without [harm to] some concrete interest that is affected by the deprivation". The question thus became "whether the particular procedural violations alleged in this case entail a degree of risk sufficient to meet" the requirements of Article III. According to Robins, Spokeo falsely reported, inter alia, that he was in his fifties, had a graduate degree, and was economically well off, when in fact he was out of work and seeking employment. Robins maintained that Spokeo's report damaged his employment prospects by making him appear overqualified for jobs that he might have obtained otherwise.

In appraising that claim Justice Alito emphasized that Article III requires plaintiffs to allege injuries that are both "particularized" and "concrete", which he defined as meaning " 'real, and not 'abstract.' " He then quoted Lujan's recognition that "Congress may 'elevat[e] to the status of legally cognizable injuries concrete, de facto injuries that were previously inadequate in law.' " Against this background, Justice Alito concluded that Robins had alleged an injury particularized to him, but noted that "not all inaccuracies cause harm or present any material risk of harm." As an example, the majority offered the dissemination of an incorrect zip code, which it thought unlikely to "work any concrete harm." The lower court, the majority found, had focused its standing analysis exclusively on the requirement of particularized injury and thus failed to analyze "whether the particular procedural violations alleged in this case"—which the plaintiff said resulted in the publication of misinformation about him—"entail a degree of risk sufficient to meet the concreteness requirement." Accordingly, the Court vacated and remanded for further proceedings without deciding whether Robins "adequately alleged an injury in fact". Justice Thomas, who joined the Court's opinion, also concurred separately.

Justice Ginsburg, joined by Justice Sotomayor, dissented. Although Justice Ginsburg "agree[d] with much of the Court's opinion", she would have affirmed the lower court's decision to uphold standing without a remand, based on the allegation in Robins' complaint that "Spokeo's misinformation 'cause[s] actual harm to [his] employment prospects.' "

The principal significance of Spokeo appeared to lie in the affirmation in the majority opinion—which six Justices joined and with which the dissenting Justices registered no express disagreement—that "Congress' role in identifying and elevating intangible harms does not mean that a plaintiff automatically satisfies the injury-in-fact requirement whenever a statute grants a person a statutory right and purports to authorize that person to sue to vindicate that right."[5a]

The Court then clarified and stiffened the "concrete" injury requirement in TransUnion LLC v. Ramirez, 141 S.Ct. 2190 (2021), another case under the Fair Credit Reporting Act (FCRA). The case grew out of a product marketed by TransUnion to alert its customers when consumers on whom it maintained files had names matching those of people on a U.S. government list of terrorists, drug traffickers, and other serious criminals with whom it is generally unlawful to transact business. In determining which individuals to flag as "potential match[es]" with names on the government list, TransUnion initially conducted no investigation beyond a comparison of first and last names. After a series of events that began with a rebuffed attempt to buy a car because his name was on a "terrorist list", the plaintiff Sergio Ramirez, relying on a FCRA provision that creates a cause of action for "any consumer" whose rights under the Act are violated, sued TransUnion alleging three bases for relief. First, he alleged that TransUnion "failed to follow reasonable procedures to ensure the accuracy of information in his credit file" in violation of 15 U.S.C. § 1681e(b). Second, he claimed that TransUnion violated § 1681g(a)(1), which requires credit reporting agencies to provide consumers who file requests with "all of th[e] formation" in their

---

[5a] The scholarly reaction was largely critical. For three noteworthy examples, see Hessick, *Standing and Contracts*, 89 Geo.W.L.Rev. 298 (2021) (arguing that Spokeo's logic renders many traditionally enforceable contracts unenforceable in federal court); Bennett, *The Paradox of Exclusive State-Court Jurisdiction over Federal Claims*, 105 Minn.L.Rev. 1211 (2021) (arguing that Spokeo's logic leads to the illogical conclusion that many federal claims are enforceable only in state court); Bayefsky, *Constitutional Injury and Tangibility*, 59 Wm.&MaryL.Rev. 2285 (2018) (criticizing Spokeo's focus on concreteness and tangibility). See also Baude, *Standing in the Shadow of Congress*, 2016 Sup.Ct.Rev. 197 (2017) (arguing that Justice Thomas's concurring opinion, and the Ninth Circuit decision under review in Spokeo, provided the better approach).

credit files. In response to a request from Ramirez, TransUnion's first mailing included no disclosure that it had identified him as a "potential match" for a name on a government list of terrorists and dangerous criminals. Although TransUnion included that information in a subsequent mailing, the second mailing did not include a summary of his rights under the FCRA. Ramirez's third claim was that this omission violated his right to have a summary of consumers' rights provided in connection with a disclosure to him of the contents of his file. In addition to seeking statutory damages and punitive damages, Ramirez "sought to certify a class of all people in the United States to whom TransUnion sent a mailing during the period from January 1, 2011, to July 26, 2011, that was similar in form to the second mailing that Ramirez received. * * * Before trial, the parties stipulated that the class contained 8,185 members, including Ramirez. The parties also stipulated that" the credit reports of only 1,853 members of the class (including Ramirez) were actually disseminated to TransUnion's customers during the roughly seven-month period covered by the parties' stipulation.

In an opinion by Justice Kavanaugh, the Court began with a statement of general principles that relied heavily on formulations from Spokeo, including its assertion that "Congress may 'elevate to the status of legally cognizable injuries concrete, de fact injuries that were previously inadequate in law'" and its rejection of "the proposition that 'a plaintiff automatically satisfies the injury-in-fact requirement whenever a statute grants a person a statutory right and purports to authorize that person to sue to vindicate that right.'" Justice Kavanaugh elaborated: "under Article III, an injury in law is not an injury in fact" absent a concrete harm.

Applying these principles to the plaintiffs' claim based on TransUnion's alleged failure to ensure the accuracy of information in credit files, Justice Kavanaugh held that only the 1,853 individuals about whom false or misleading information was disseminated to TransUnion's customers suffered the "concrete" injury required for Article III standing. In assessing the concreteness of alleged harms, "Spokeo v. Robins indicated that courts should assess whether the alleged injury to the plaintiff has a 'close relationship' to a harm 'traditionally' recognized as providing a basis for a lawsuit in American courts." Under that formula, the plaintiffs whose credit reports had been disseminated suffered an injury analogous to the reputational harms "traditionally recognized as providing a basis" for suits for defamation. But the other 6,332 came up short. "The mere existence of a misleading * * * alert in a consumer's internal credit file" did not constitute a concrete injury in the absence of publication or an analogue.

Nor could standing be predicated on the risk that misleading information in the plaintiffs' credit files would be disseminated in the future. Although a risk of future injury will sometimes ground standing to seek injunctive relief, "in a suit for damages, the mere risk of future harm, standing alone, cannot qualify as a concrete harm—at least unless the exposure to the risk of future harm itself causes a separate concrete harm." Finally, the Court rejected the argument that credit reports on many of the 6,332 class members who claimed standing were likely sent to creditors outside of the seven-month period for which the parties had stipulated that only 1,853 of the plaintiffs' reports were actually distributed but within the nearly four-year period during which the plaintiffs claimed that TransUnion had violated their rights under FCRA. According to the Court, speculation about probabilities would not suffice; it was the plaintiffs' "burden to prove at trial that their reports were actually sent."

Turning to the plaintiffs' claims that TransUnion had failed to provide them with their complete credit files upon request and that it had further failed to include a summary of the plaintiffs' rights when it finally disclosed the warnings included in those files, Justice Kavanaugh emphasized that TransUnion had ultimately given the plaintiffs everything to which they were entitled, albeit spread over multiple mailings: "the plaintiffs have not demonstrated that the format of TransUnion's mailings caused them a harm with a close relationship to a harm traditionally recognized as providing a basis for a lawsuit in American courts. * * * Without any evidence of harm caused by the format of the mailings", TransUnion's "bare procedural violation[s]" would not support standing (alteration in original) (quoting Spokeo,). Accordingly, "none of the 8,185 class members other than the named plaintiff Ramirez"—who testified that he was confused by the conflicting information in the two mailings and canceled a planned international trip as a result—had "suffered a concrete harm" traceable to TransUnion's initial non-disclosure of information and subsequent failure to provide a summary of consumers' rights.

Justice Thomas, joined by Justices Breyer, Sotomayor, and Kagan, dissented. His analysis, which was largely originalist, turned on a distinction between whether a plaintiff sued "based on the violation of a duty owed broadly to the whole community" or "asserts his or her own rights." Where a plaintiff sued to enforce a "public right" or a duty to the public as a whole, such as a general duty to obey or enforce the law, the existence of a justiciable case or controversy required a showing of concrete harm at the time of the Founding. But where a plaintiff sought to enforce a right or duty that was private or personal to her—such as a right to be free from trespass to her land—the plaintiff "needed only to allege the violation. * * * Courts typically did not require any showing of actual damage." According to Justice Thomas, "[t]his distinction mattered not only for traditional common-law rights, but also for newly created statutory ones," such as those created by the copyright laws that the First Congress enacted, under which copyright holders need not demonstrate monetary loss in order to sue for damages.

In the case before the Court, Justice Thomas reasoned, each of the plaintiffs had "established a violation of his or her private rights", because all of the FCRA provisions under which they sued created "duties [that] are owed to individuals, not to the community writ large." Although Justice Thomas pointedly noted that "it was not until 1970—'180 years after the ratification of Article III'—that this Court even introduced the 'injury in fact' (as opposed to injury in law) concept of standing", he thought that the Court's application of that concept to deny standing largely accorded with historical understandings of Article III in cases involving public rights, including those that Congress had created by statute. But where Congress had Article I power to confer a private right, Justice Thomas believed Congress could also authorize enforcement actions by right-holders. "Never before has this Court declared that legal injury is inherently insufficient to support standing."

"Even assuming that this Court should be in the business of second-guessing private rights," Justice Thomas continued, "TransUnion's misconduct here is exactly the sort of thing that has long merited legal redress." The withholding of information was a sufficient injury to uphold standing. Furthermore, Justice Thomas thought, the errors in TransUnion's files created a real risk of disclosure at some time other than within the seven-month period in which TransUnion had disseminated erroneous credit reports involving roughly 25 percent of the plaintiff class. "Twenty-five percent over just a 7-month period seems, to me, 'a degree of risk sufficient to meet the concreteness requirement.'" Even apart from risk of harm, TransUnion had published its credit reports when it divulged their contents to the vendors that printed and sent its mailings to the plaintiffs. "In the historical context of libel, publication even to a single other party", including a stenographer, "could be enough to give rise to suit."

Justice Thomas added: "[E]ven setting aside everything already mentioned—the Constitution's text, history, precedent, financial harm, libel, the risk of publication, and actual disclosure to a third party—one need only tap into common sense to know that receiving a letter identifying you as a potential drug trafficker or terrorist is harmful. All the more so when the information comes in the context of a credit report, the entire purpose of which is to demonstrate that a person can be trusted."

Justice Kagan also filed a separate dissent, joined by Justices Breyer and Sotomayor. She explained that she "differ[ed] with Justice Thomas on just one matter * * *. In his view, any 'violation of an individual right' created by Congress gives rise to Article III standing." By contrast, the Court had said in Spokeo, and she continued to believe, that "Article III requires a concrete injury even in the context of a statutory violation." But she thought that her view would lead to the same result as Justice Thomas's "in all but highly unusual cases" due to the deference that the courts owed to Congress in determining "when something causes a harm or risk of harm in the real world." "Subject to that qualification," Justice Kagan concluded, "I join Justice Thomas's dissent in full."

In formulating the test for Article III standing, TransUnion quotes repeatedly from the Court's prior cases, including Spokeo v. Robins. Does the TransUnion decision deviate from Spokeo, clarify it, or continue what some have long viewed as a pattern of sometimes more-demanding and sometimes less-demanding applications of standing law's stated requirements?[5b]

From a methodological perspective, the Court's approach to the standing issue in TransUnion—which relies heavily on modern judicial precedents—contrasts with its standing analysis in Uzuegbunam v. Preczewski, 141 S.Ct. 792 (2021), also discussed p. 10 *supra* and p. 44 *infra*, decided in the same Term, in which Justice Thomas's majority opinion rested

---

[5b] For a particularly emphatic denunciation of Transunion, see Cass Sunstein, *Injury in Fact, Transformed*, 2021 Sup.Ct.Rev. 349 (2022).

on an originalist theory similar to that advanced in his TransUnion dissent. The Uzuegbunam opinion, in which all members of the TransUnion majority except for the Chief Justice joined, relied on English and American common law cases to conclude that Article III permits "plaintiffs to pursue nominal damages whenever they suffer[ ] a personal legal injury", even in the absence of "continuing or threatened injury", because "every legal injury necessarily causes damage". By contrast with Uzuegbunam, the Court's opinion in TransUnion emphasized Founding-era purposes in restricting the judicial branch to the adjudication of actual cases or controversies, but it did seek to refute Justice Thomas's readings of the Founding-era cases on which he relied. What inferences should be drawn about when the Court will and will not base its standing determinations on evidence of Founding-era practices?

Justice Thomas's dissenting opinion in TransUnion complains that the majority's insistence on distinguishing "concrete" and "real" harms from those that are not sufficiently concrete or real requires an " 'inescapably value-laden' inquiry" and ultimately a " 'policy judgment' ". If so, would Justice Thomas call for any less value-laden an inquiry in determining whether plaintiffs have suffered injury in cases, such as Lujan v. Defenders of Wildlife, Seventh Edition page 133, that he would assign to the "public rights" category? See Baude, *Standing in the Shadow of Congress*, 2016 Sup.Ct.Rev. 197, 227–231 (2017) (attempting to explicate Justice Thomas's position on public and private rights).

Justices Kagan, Breyer, and Sotomayor join Justice Thomas's dissent, but Justice Kagan's separate dissent appears to question the significance of the line between congressional creation of private and public rights that forms the centerpiece of Justice Thomas's opinion when she acknowledges that standing requires injury in both kinds of cases. Although she concludes that her approach would largely overlap with Justice Thomas's in practice because of her commitment to deference to Congress in identifying injury, her approach appears to concede that some hypothetical grants of "private" rights could exceed the justiciability requirements of Article III. Justice Kavanaugh put this testing hypothetical: "Suppose, for example, that Congress passes a law purporting to give all American citizens an individual right to clean air and clean water, as well as a cause of action to sue and recover $100 in damages from any business that violates any pollution law anywhere in the United States." Is this hypothetical a problem for the dissent? But to turn it back on the majority, would the hypothetical be any different if the law denominated this right as a "property" right to a small share of jointly-owned clean air? (The majority says that "of course" there is Article III standing if "the plaintiff has suffered concrete harm to her property.")

Page 151. Add a new Paragraph (2)(d):

(d)   In Thole v. U.S. Bank N.A., 140 S.Ct. 1615 (2020), the Court held (by 5–4) that retired participants in the Bank's defined-benefit retirement plan lacked standing to challenge alleged mismanagement of the plan, despite a provision of the Employee Retirement Income Security Act (ERISA) authorizing suits by plan beneficiaries. Because the plaintiffs had been paid all benefits due in the past, and were "legally and contractually entitled to receive * * * [fixed] monthly payments for the rest of their lives", they had suffered no cognizable injury, the Court reasoned. Absent a concrete injury, the statute's attempted conferral of a right to sue failed to satisfy Article III.

Justice Sotomayor, joined by Justices Ginsburg, Breyer, and Kagan, dissented. She argued that "[b]ecause ERISA requires that retirement-plan assets be held in trust," beneficiaries had "equitable interests" in the plan's assets—analogous to those recognized by the traditional law of trusts—the alleged harms to which constituted actionable injuries.[5c] The dissent also argued, inter alia, that the statutory authorization to sue effectively assigned the plan's claims to the petitioners. By contrast, the Court emphasized that no formal assignment had occurred.

The majority did not appear to dispute that if Congress had formally assigned the claims of the retirement plan to the plan's beneficiaries or had otherwise authorized plan beneficiaries to sue as the plan's representatives, its doing so would have conferred Article III standing. Was it appropriate to require such a formal assignment when Congress had explicitly sought to endow plan beneficiaries with rights to sue?

[5c] Justice Thomas, joined by Justice Alito, concurring, criticized prior decisions' use of "the common law of trusts as 'the starting point' for interpreting ERISA."

Page 151. Add at the end of footnote 6:

But see Pfander, *Standing, Litigable Interests, and Article III's Case-or-Controversy Requirement*, 65 UCLA L.Rev. 170 (2018) (questioning the Westminster paradigm in light of early assignment to Article III courts of "noncontentious" cases arising under federal law, including naturalization petitions, and arguing that eighteenth-century Scottish practice provides a better model for understanding early American analogues to modern standing doctrine).

Page 152. Add at the beginning of footnote 9:

Pfander, *Standing, Litigable Interests, and Article III's Case-or-Controversy Requirement*, 65 UCLA L.Rev. 170 (2018), argues that Congresses and courts of the early republic distinguished between "controversies," which required parties with concretely adverse interests, and "cases," which could encompass noncontentious federal business that involved no injury, such as petitions for naturalization. According to Pfander, that practice mirrored features of Scots law, in which distinctive limitations—not unlike the statutory qualifications sometimes attached to modern citizen-suit provisions—applied to public actions involving broadly shared injuries. He argues, however, that a more historically accurate account of standing would accord Congress broader powers to confer jurisdiction in the absence of modern notions of injury in fact, "especially where Congress has taken [alternative] steps to protect the government's enforcement primacy and the defendant's interest in the avoidance of duplicative litigation." Pfander has expanded further on these and other arguments in a recent book, Pfander, Cases Without Controversies: Uncontested Adjudication in Article III Courts (2021) .

Page 152. Add at the end of footnote 9:

Young, *Standing, Equity, and Injury in Fact*, 97 Notre Dame L.Rev. 1885, 1888 (2022) ("To the extent that Court's standing jurisprudence defines Article III's requirements in line with traditional practice, longstanding practice in equity may provide a firmer ground for injury in fact than does traditional practice on the law side of the house.").

Page 156. Add at the end of footnote 15:

Beck, *Qui Tam Litigation Against Government Officials: Constitutional Implications of a Neglected History*, 93 Notre Dame L.Rev. 1235 (2018), argues that from the fourteenth through the late eighteenth centuries, the British Parliament, colonial and then state legislatures, and the U.S. Congress all enacted qui tam legislation authorizing "informers" to sue public officials—such as tax collectors—for monetary penalties for failing to perform their duties. Drawing parallels between his findings and those of Professor Louis Jaffe and Raoul Berger, Seventh Edition pp. 151–152, Professor Beck asserts that the Supreme Court has predicated standing doctrine, and particularly its demand for personalized injury, on a misapprehension of historical practices relevant to interpretation of Article III. At the same time, Beck notes important distinctions between historical qui tam actions and modern citizen suit provisions. Among them, qui tam plaintiffs had a pecuniary stake in the outcome of their legal actions, which were predicated in specific allegations of past wrongdoing. Professor Beck's article makes no claims about which historical facts should count for how much in determining whether modern standing doctrine should be overhauled. (For general discussion of the relevance of history to constitutional decisionmaking, see Fallon, *The Many and Varied Roles of History in Constitutional Adjudication*, 90 Notre Dame L.Rev. 1753 (2015).)

Page 156. Add a new footnote 17a at the end of Paragraph (5):

[17a] See also Gilles & Friedman, *The New Qui Tam: A Model for the Enforcement of Group Rights in a Hostile Era*, 98 Tex.L.Rev. 489 (2020) (assessing state utilization of qui tam statutes to enforce state protections for vulnerable groups and noting different federal challenges that differently drafted statutes would encounter).

Page 160. Add at the end of Paragraph (7):

The disputes in ASARCO and Hollingsworth occur against the background of the long-settled rule that a plaintiff suing in federal court, even on a state law claim, must satisfy federal standing rules. For a challenge to that assumption as applied to diversity cases not raising federal questions, see Hessick, *Cases, Controversies, and Diversity,* 109 Nw.L.Rev. 57 (2015), arguing that application of state justiciability rules in diversity actions "would better achieve diversity jurisdiction's goals of providing an alternative forum for resolving state claims involving out-of-state litigants." According to Professor Hessick, "the reasons underlying federal justiciability doctrines" largely involve avoidance of judicial interference with other branches under the federal separation of powers and have no application to diversity cases. Do you agree?

———

B. STANDING TO ASSERT THE RIGHTS OF OTHERS AND RELATED ISSUES INVOLVING "FACIAL CHALLENGES" TO STATUTES

NOTE ON ASSERTING THE RIGHTS OF OTHERS

Page 165. Add at the end of footnote 2:

For a suggestion that the Court should return to the traditional approach of sharply limiting third-party standing, coupled with a specific protest that the Court has gone astray in allowing doctors and abortion clinics to invoke women's abortion rights, see Whole Woman's Health v. Hellerstedt, 579 U.S. 582 (2016) (Thomas, J., dissenting); see also Whole Woman's Health v. Jackson, 142 S.Ct. 522, 539 n.1 (2021) (Thomas, J., concurring in part and dissenting in part) (reiterating this view and citing other reasons that plaintiffs lacked standing to enforce abortion rights).

Page 166. Add at the end of Paragraph (3):

The Court divided sharply about third-party standing in June Medical Services LLC v. Russo, 140 S.Ct. 2103 (2020), which invalidated a Louisiana statute that required any doctor who performs abortions to have admitting privileges at a nearby hospital. In allowing abortion doctors to assert the rights of their patients, Justice Breyer's plurality opinion for four Justices— with which the Chief Justice agreed with regard to standing—interwove several strands of argument: (1) the rule against third-party standing is prudential and therefore waivable; (2) the state had waived its objection in the lower courts; and (3) in any event, the Court "generally permitted plaintiffs to assert third-party rights where the 'enforcement of the challenged restriction against the litigant would result directly in the violation of third parties' rights'", as reflected in prior cases that had "permitted abortion providers to invoke the rights of their actual or potential patients".

Justice Alito, joined in relevant part by Justices Thomas and Gorsuch, disagreed about waiver on factual grounds. Further, he did not think that the plaintiffs qualified for third-party standing under traditional principles, due to the absence of a close relationship between the parties and the ability of women seeking abortion to assert their own rights. Additionally, Justice Alito insisted that conflict-of-interest principles, as recognized in cases including Elk Grove Unified School Dist. v. Newdow, Seventh Edition p. 158, precluded doctors from claiming third-party standing to challenge a law that the state defended as designed to protect the health of women whose rights the doctors sought to assert.

In response to the conflict-of-interest argument, Justice Breyer maintained that plaintiffs commonly are allowed to challenge statutes that were ostensibly enacted for the benefit of the parties whose rights they invoke. As examples, he cited Craig v. Boren, Seventh Edition p. 161, in which the state statute sought to protect young men from the perils of driving while intoxicated, and several prior abortion cases.

In a case of actual conflict of interest, should a challenger to a statute be able to invoke a third-party's rights? In a case in which the challenger seeks to assert the rights of a large number of absent parties, how should a court ascertain whether an actual conflict of interest exists?

Besides joining much of Justice Alito's opinion, Justice Thomas dissented separately to argue that the Court lacked subject matter jurisdiction because third-party standing was incompatible with historical understandings of Article III. With regard to third-party standing, Justice Kavanaugh, dissenting, said only that the district court should address the state's "new argument (raised for the first time in this Court)" on remand.

Most recently, in Dobbs v. Jackson Women's Health Organization, 142 S.Ct. 2228 (2022), which overruled Roe v. Wade, 410 U.S. 113 (1973), and Planned Parenthood v. Casey, 505 U.S. 833 (1992), the Court's majority opinion (written by Justice Alito) stated: "The Court's abortion cases . . . have ignored the Court's third-party standing doctrine." (citing June Medical, *supra* (Alito, J., dissenting); June Medical, *supra* (Gorsuch, J., dissenting); and Whole Woman's Health v. Hellerstedt, 579 U.S. 582, (2016) (Thomas, J., dissenting)). In so far as it may arise in future cases, does Dobbs cast doubt on the third-party standing holding of June Medical?

Page 168. Add at the end of footnote 7:

For the argument that private parties lack rights under most structural constitutional provisions and therefore should ordinarily have no standing to complain of violations, see Huq, *Standing for the Structural Constitution*, 99 Va.L.Rev. 1435 (2013). But see Barnett, *Standing for (and up to) Separation of Powers*, 91 Ind.L.J. 665 (2016) (arguing that structural challenges are analogous to "procedural" challenges for which causation and redressability requirements are relaxed and that injured parties may come within the zone of interests that structural provisions protect).

Page 168. Add a new footnote 7a at the end of Paragraph (4)(c):

[7a] Without reference to the Lexmark case, the Court applied traditional third-party standing analysis in Sessions v. Morales-Santana, 582 U.S. 47 (2017). Justice Ginsburg's majority opinion held that a party seeking to establish U.S. citizenship could assert his father's equal protection rights in challenging a statute that preferred unwed citizen mothers over unwed citizen fathers in passing on their citizenship to children born abroad.

Page 168. Add a new Paragraph (4)(d):

(d) Professors Bradley and Young argue that much of the perceived incoherence of third-party standing comes from attempting to capture several distinct legal issues into a single unitary principle. Bradley & Young, *Unpacking Third-Party Standing*, 131 Yale L.J. 1 (2021). Instead, they argue, the analysis should "unpack" the doctrine by way of two sets of distinctions. First, it should distinguish litigants who fall within the "zone of interests" of a substantive right and who are really litigating their own rights from true third-party claims. Second, it should distinguish various kinds of third parties: the directly regulated, the collaterally injured, and representatives. In particular, regulated parties should always be able to assert third-party standing when enforcement of the law against them will violate the rights of third parties. Finally, Bradley and Young challenge the "valid rule" argument made by Fallon, Seventh Edition p. 167, as over- and underinclusive.

―――――

PRELIMINARY NOTE ON AS-APPLIED AND FACIAL CHALLENGES AND THE PROBLEM OF SEPARABILITY

Page 172. Add a new Paragraph (4)(c):

(c) Whole Woman's Health v. Hellerstedt, 579 U.S. 582 (2016), held, by 5–3, that the district court had correctly upheld a facial challenge (which the Fifth Circuit subsequently rejected) to two provisions of Texas law that the Court found to constitute undue burdens on abortion rights: (1) a requirement that doctors performing abortions have admitting privileges at a hospital within 30 miles of the abortion facility, and (2) a mandate that all abortion facilities must meet "the minimum" statutory standards applicable to "ambulatory surgical centers" under state law. The Court ruled the provisions facially invalid despite a severability clause providing that "every provision, section, subsection, sentence, clause, phrase, or word in this Act, and every application of the provision [sic] in this Act, are severable from each other." The clause further directed that if "any application of any provision * * * is found by a court to be invalid, the remaining applications of that provision to all other persons and circumstances shall be severed and may not be affected." Writing for the Court, Justice Breyer reasoned that the challenged provisions "vastly increase the obstacles confronting women seeking abortions in Texas without providing any benefit to women's health capable of withstanding any meaningful scrutiny" and are therefore "unconstitutional on their face". He continued: "Including a severability provision in the law does not change that conclusion. Severability clauses, it is true, do express the enacting legislature's preference for a narrow judicial remedy. As a general matter, we attempt to honor that preference. But our cases have never required us to proceed application by conceivable application when confronted with a facially unconstitutional statutory provision. * * * Indeed, if a severability clause could impose such a requirement on courts, legislatures would easily be able to insulate unconstitutional statutes from most facial review. * * * A severability clause is not grounds for a court to 'devise a judicial remedy that * * * entail[s] quintessentially legislative work.' Ayotte v. Planned Parenthood of Northern New Eng., 546 U.S. 320, 329 (2006). * * * We reject Texas' invitation to pave the way for legislatures to immunize their statutes from facial review. * * * Texas' attempt to broadly draft a requirement to sever 'applications' does not require us to proceed in piecemeal fashion when we have found the statutory provisions at issue facially unconstitutional."

Justice Alito, joined by Chief Justice Roberts and Justice Thomas, dissented: "Federal courts have no authority to carpet-bomb state laws, knocking out provisions that are perfectly consistent with federal law, just because it would be too much bother to separate them from unconstitutional provisions. * * * By forgoing severability, the Court strikes down numerous provisions that could not plausibly impose an undue burden. For example, [under the provisions of Texas law that apply to ambulatory surgery centers,] [c]enters must maintain fire alarm and emergency communications systems, and eliminate '[h]azards that might lead to slipping, falling, electrical shock, burns, poisoning, or other trauma'. [The enforcement of these and other unexceptionable provisions is now] * * * enjoined. * * * If the Court is unwilling to undertake the careful severability analysis required, * * * [t]he proper course would be to remand to the lower courts."

Does the Court opinion effectively reject the assumption that state law determines the separability of state statutes, possibly on the ground that federal law determines facial invalidity and that total invalidation (rather than separation) is sometimes a necessary remedy, also as a matter of federal law? If so, how could the majority square that conclusion with cases such as Yazoo & Mississippi Valley R.R. v. Jackson Vinegar Co., Seventh Edition p. 168, which seem to presuppose that whether a state statute is subject to a facial challenge depends on state separability law? Does the Court impliedly hold that the particular severability clause at issue is unconstitutional in light of the challenged provisions' substantive content and effects, possibly on the ground that requiring piecemeal analysis would constitute an "undue burden" on abortion rights? If so, in what sense?

Most of the Court's substantive analysis in Whole Woman's Health rests on the ground that the challenged provisions are invalid based on their effects, but the opinion also quoted language affirming that statutes can be invalid if they have "the purpose of presenting a substantial obstacle to a woman seeking an abortion". The decision regarding facial challenges and non-severability might have fit better with seemingly settled doctrine if the

Court had concluded that the challenged provisions had the forbidden purpose of unduly burdening abortion rights and that that forbidden purpose rendered them invalid in all possible applications. Would it be tenable to interpret the decision as resting on that basis despite the absence of textual evidence that the Court intended it so to be read?

Page 173. For the third sentence of Paragraph (5)(b), substitute the following:

(In Heckler, the Court found no constitutional violation and thus no need to provide a remedy of any kind.)

Page 173. Add at the end of Paragraph (5)(b):

Sessions v. Morales-Santana, 582 U.S. 47 (2017), also discussed pp. 7, 32, *supra*, echoed Califano v. Westcott that when a federal statute unconstitutionally benefits one class in preference to another, "the preferred rule in the typical case is to extend favorable treatment". But the Court, in an opinion by Justice Ginsburg, also recognized that withdrawal of benefits from the favored class is a constitutionally permissible remedy for equal protection violations, and it affirmed that "[t]he choice between these outcomes is governed by the legislature's intent, as revealed by the statute at hand." Turning to the statutory scheme at issue, the Court concluded that Congress would not have wanted to extend a provision of the immigration laws that made it easier for unwed citizen mothers than for either unwed citizen fathers or for married couples to pass on their citizenship to children born abroad: "Put to the choice, Congress, we believe, would have abrogated [the] exception [that favors unmarried citizen mothers who have resided in the U.S. only for short periods over otherwise similarly situated unwed fathers and married couples], preferring preservation of the general rule." Until and unless Congress enacted "a uniform prescription that neither favors nor disadvantages any person on the basis of gender", the Court determined, the otherwise generally applicable rule "should apply, prospectively, to children born to unwed U.S.-citizen mothers."

Why is extension of benefits "the preferred rule" if the choice of remedies "is governed by the legislature's intent"? Is there any basis on which a presumption for extension could be supported? Are there judicially manageable standards for determining what Congress would have done in the absence of a presumption?

The Court again applied severability doctrine to redress what Justice Kavanaugh's plurality opinion termed an "equal-treatment constitutional violation" of the First Amendment's Free Speech Clause in Barr v. American Ass'n of Political Consultants, Inc., 140 S.Ct. 2335 (2020). The Telephone Consumer Protection Act of 1991 generally prohibits robocalls to cell phones but, following a 2015 amendment, excepted robocalls made to collect debts owed to or guaranteed by the United States. In a challenge brought by plaintiffs who wished to make political robocalls, six Justices—though without a majority opinion—concluded that the statute discriminated impermissibly on the basis of content. Again without a majority opinion, seven Justices agreed that the appropriate judicial response was to sever the provision that exempted robocalls involving debts owed to or guaranteed by the government.

Justice Gorsuch, joined by Justice Thomas, dissented from the severability holding. Although he agreed that the statute was invalid as applied to the challengers, he thought that they lacked standing to challenge its application to debt collectors. Believing it problematic under the separation of powers for the Court, by severing a statutory exemption, "to render unlawful conduct that Congress has explicitly made lawful", Justice Gorsuch instead would have enjoined the application of the statute to the challengers. He concluded: "[I]f this is what modern 'severability doctrine' has become, it seems to me all the more reason to reconsider our course."

As Justice Kavanaugh noted in response, Justice Gorsuch's "proposed remedy", when conjoined with stare decisis, "would in effect allow all robocalls to cell phones—notwithstanding Congress's decisive choice to prohibit most robocalls to cell phones." Justice Kavanaugh added: "[T]here is no magic solution to severability that solves every conundrum, especially in equal-treatment cases, but the Court's current approach * * * is constitutional, stable, predictable, and commonsensical."

The severability "conundrum" arose in Barr partly as a result modern First Amendment doctrine that treats all forms of content discrimination as presumptively invalid and thereby gives rise to "equal-treatment constitutional violation[s]". Dissenting on the merits, Justice Breyer proposed reconsidering past decisions that subject all forms of content discrimination to strict judicial scrutiny. Had Justice Breyer prevailed, no severability conundrum would have arisen. Do the difficulties that arise in connection with "equal-treatment constitutional violation[s]" demonstrate a general infirmity in separability doctrine, or are they distinctive? May some of those difficulties result from judicial choices in crafting substantive constitutional tests?

Page 173. Add at the end of Paragraph (5)(c):

In Murphy v. NCAA, 138 S.Ct. 1461 (2018), a majority of the Justices followed the approach of the NFIB v. Sebelius dissent by refusing to sever and uphold what they regarded as secondary statutory provisions after invalidating a central one. In an opinion by Justice Alito, the Court ruled that the Professional and Amateur Sports Protection Act (PASPA) unconstitutionally commandeered state legislatures by forbidding them to authorize gambling on sporting events. Having done so, the majority declined to sever provisions that would have (a) prohibited the States from themselves sponsoring or advertising sports gambling schemes and (b) barred private actors from operating gambling schemes pursuant to state law. Writing for a 6–3 majority, Justice Alito reasoned that if Congress had known that states could authorize gambling by private entities, it would not have "wanted" to bar state lotteries, which "were thought more benign" than private gambling, nor to prohibit only those private gambling operations that the states had authorized. Justice Ginsburg's dissenting opinion, which Justice Sotomayor joined in whole and Justice Breyer in part, complained that "[t]he Court wields an axe to cut down [the challenged statute] instead of using a scalpel to trim [it]": "Deleting the alleged 'commandeering' directions would free the statute to accomplish just what Congress legitimately sought to achieve: stopping sports-gambling regimes while making it clear that the stoppage is attributable to federal, not state, action." Is hypothesizing counterfactual intent (involving what Congress would have wanted, if an unforeseen partial invalidation were to occur) as a basis for declining to sever statutes more or less defensible than appealing to legislative intent as a basis for interpreting statutes? Concurring in Murphy, Justice Thomas raised related questions, and suggested that they had no good answers, but joined the majority in full because "no party in this case has asked us to reconsider [modern severability] precedents". Did the Court's precedents dictate Murphy's approach to severability?

Justice Kavanaugh's plurality opinion in Barr v. American Ass'n of Political Consultants, 140 S.Ct. 2335 (2020), in which Chief Justice Roberts and Justice Alito joined, took a different approach to severability. After acknowledging that "some of the Court's cases declare that courts should sever" a statute's unconstitutional provisions "unless 'the statute created in its absence is one that Congress would not have enacted'", Justice Kavanaugh immediately asserted that "this formulation often leads to an analytical dead end * * * because courts are not well equipped to imaginatively reconstruct a prior Congress's hypothetical intent." Justice Kavanaugh therefore endorsed "a strong presumption of severability" as a better, more workable alternative. In Seila Law LLC v. Consumer Financial Protection Bureau, 140 S.Ct. 2183 (2020), Justice Thomas's opinion concurring in part and dissenting in part, in which Justice Gorsuch joined, wrote that that "[a] text-based" approach to statutory interpretation, to which he subscribes, "does not allow a free-ranging inquiry into what 'Congress, faced with the limitations imposed by the Constitution, would have preferred' had it known of a constitutional issue."

Would it be fair to conclude that at least five Justices now reject the approach of Murphy v. NCAA under which statutory severability depends on counterfactual inquiries into reconstructed congressional intent? See Fallon, *Facial Challenges, Saving Constructions, and Statutory Severability*, 99 Tex.L.Rev. 215 (2020) (arguing that when Congress enacts a statute, it should be presumed to enact "all of the statute's valid parts and applications" and maintaining that to make severability depend on whether Congress would have enacted some provisions in the absence of others is incompatible with both textualist and purposivist theories of statutory interpretation).

The Court encountered a different kind of situation in which it had to choose between alternative possible responses to a constitutional violation in United States v. Arthrex, Inc., 141 S.Ct. 1970 (2021). Writing for five Justices, Chief Justice Roberts held that a statutory scheme that authorized Administrative Patent Judges (APJs) to issue decisions on behalf of the executive branch violated the Appointments Clause because the APJs were not nominated by the President and confirmed by the Senate nor were their decisions reviewable by a superior officer who was subject to presidential direction. As an analytical matter, the constitutional violation arose from the interaction of multiple provisions: the appointments provision was impermissible only insofar as other provisions granted APJs authority exceeding that which could be granted to an "inferior" officer. The respondent asked the Court to invalidate the entire scheme of APJ decisionmaking in "inter partes" patent review (involving challenges to existing patents). The Government argued that the Court should invalidate a provision making the APJs removable only for cause. Instead, seven Justices—four in an opinion by the Chief Justice and three in an opinion by Justice Breyer concurring in the judgement in part and dissenting in part—agreed that the Court should sever a statutory provision that otherwise would have limited the authority of the Director of the Patent and Trademark Office to review final decisions by APJs.

Concurring in part and dissenting in part, Justice Gorsuch complained that the Court "gift[ed] the Director a new power that he never before enjoyed." He thought the Court should have responded to the Appointments Clause violation by "setting aside" the agency decision involved in the case before the Court and leaving it to Congress to make the "policy" choice of how to cure the violation. For an insightful discussion of the issues of statutory severability that arise when a constitutional violation occurs due to the interaction of multiple provisions, see Lea, *Situational Severability*, 103 Va.L.Rev. 735 (2017). Lea identifies "the text, structure, legislative history, and purpose of the statutory scheme, as well as the practical effects of the possible fallback options", as relevant considerations. Does judicial decisionmaking based on those factors constitute a form of policy choice that the judiciary ought to eschew in the way commended by Justice Gorsuch? For a further survey of possible approaches to this problem, see Baude, *Severability First Principles*, 109 Va.L.Rev. 1 (2023) at 41–55.

Page 174. Add at the end of Paragraph (5)(d):

Fish, *Severability as Conditionality*, 64 Emory L.J. 1293 (2015), argues that courts lack the authority to hold statutes non-severable except insofar as the legislature, as a matter of statutory interpretation, has explicitly or implicitly made the continuing validity of one part of a statute—defined as one or more words—conditional on another part. According to the author, this approach would recognize that courts lack constitutional competence to make policy-based judgments concerning how statutes ought to operate following the invalidation of an isolable part. Note that issues of statutes' separability arise not only with respect to words that have no valid applications, but also with respect to words or strings of words that may be unconstitutional in some applications but constitutional in others (if invalid applications are deemed severable). For example, a statute that forbids "speaking to a woman within 50 feet of an abortion facility without her consent" would have many invalid applications, but severability doctrine determines whether it could be enforced against an abortion protestor who utters constitutionally prohibitable threats against a woman within 50 feet of an abortion facility.

See also Manheim, *Beyond Severability*, 101 Iowa L.Rev. 1833 (2016) (incisively critiquing a broad menu of approaches to severability, and advocating an approach to "flawed statutes" that would identify and implement whatever "option[ ] the legislature would prefer", but offering no specific guidance on how to discern legislative intent).

Page 175. Add at the end of footnote 4:

For a conceptual survey of judicial approaches to separability and defense of a methodology aimed at preserving statutory purposes, see Fish, *Choosing Constitutional Remedies*, 63 UCLA L.Rev. 322 (2016).

Fish, *Judicial Amendment of Statutes*, 84 Geo.Wash.L.Rev. 563 (2016), argues that when courts find statutes unconstitutional, they often remedy the identified defects through judicial amendment, rather than mere severance of invalid language. As examples, the author cites United States v. Booker, Seventh Edition p. 174, and Heckler v. Mathews, Seventh Edition p. 173. Even if Fish were correct in his analysis of the Supreme Court's rulings in cases such as Booker and Heckler, would it follow, as Fish suggests, that courts have a general power to amend otherwise invalid statutes, rather than that the Court has overstepped its constitutional role in some past cases?

NOTE ON THE SCOPE OF THE ISSUE IN FIRST AMENDMENT CASES AND RELATED PROBLEMS INVOLVING "FACIAL CHALLENGES"

Page 180. Add at the end of Paragraph (4):

The issue of how to gauge the substantiality of a statute's overbreadth poses puzzles along another dimension, involving the relationship between First Amendment overbreadth doctrine and other tests of statutes' validity under the First Amendment. See Monaghan, *Overbreadth*, 1981 Sup.Ct.Rev. 1. In Americans for Prosperity Foundation v. Bonta, 141 S.Ct. 2373 (2021), the Court, in an opinion by Chief Justice Roberts, held that a California requirement that charities disclose the names and addresses of their major donors impermissibly burdened the First Amendment right to freedom of association because it was not "narrowly tailored to the government's" asserted regulatory interests. After ruling that the compelled disclosure rule failed the narrow tailoring requirement, the Court, in a separate section of its opinion, asserted that its "foregoing discussion ma[de] clear why a facial challenge [was] appropriate" under the First Amendment overbreadth test, which establishes that "a law may be invalidated as overbroad if a substantial number of its applications are unconstitutional, judged in relation to the statute's plainly legitimate sweep" (quoting United States v. Stevens, 559 U.S. 460, 473 (2010)). If the challenged California regulation failed to satisfy a substantive First Amendment requirement of "narrow tailoring", did the Court need to conduct a further inquiry into whether the regulation was substantially overbroad before adjudging it facially invalid? See Isserles, *Overcoming Overbreadth: Facial Challenges and the Valid Rule Requirement*, 48 Am.U.L.Rev. 359 (1998) (distinguishing overbreadth facial challenges from "valid rule facial challenges," which assert that statutes fail a test of constitutional validity other than the overbreadth test). Justice Sotomayor, joined by Justices Breyer and Kagan, dissented, principally because she thought that the challenged disclosure requirement imposed no "actual First Amendment burden" in most cases and that the Court's demand for narrow tailoring was therefore misplaced.

Page 184. Add at the end of the carryover paragraph:

Expressions Hair Design v. Schneiderman, 581 U.S. 37 (2017), reiterated that "a plaintiff whose speech is clearly proscribed cannot raise a successful vagueness claim" even in a First Amendment case.

––––––––––

NOTE ON FACIAL CHALLENGES AND OVERBREADTH BEYOND THE FIRST AMENDMENT

Page 185. Add a new footnote * at the end of the first full paragraph:

*   Distinct from whether a court can adjudicate a facial challenge is whether a lower federal court, in upholding one, can issue a universal injunction barring a statute's enforcement against other parties in other districts and other circuits. In a concurring opinion in Trump v. Hawaii, 138 S.Ct. 2392 (2018), Justice Thomas characterized universal injunctions as "a recent development, emerging for the first time in the 1960s and dramatically increasing in popularity only very recently." He questioned whether federal courts have either statutory or constitutional jurisdiction to issue universal injunctions. Justice Gorsuch, joined by Justice Thomas, took up similar themes in an opinion concurring in the Supreme Court's grant of a stay of a universal injunction in Dep't of Homeland Security v. New York, 140 S.Ct. 599 (2020). (The injunction barred the enforcement of a Department of Homeland Security rule defining "public charge" under a federal statute that denied noncitizens admission into the United States if, "in the opinion of" the Attorney General, the noncitizen is "likely at any time to become a public charge." 8 U.S.C. § 1182(a)(4)(A); see 84 Fed.Reg. 41,292 (Aug. 14, 2019) (Rule).) In calling for the Court to "take up some of the underlying equitable and constitutional questions raised by the rise of nationwide injunctions," Justice Gorsuch noted that such remedies can preclude the percolation of issues through multiple circuits. But he also stressed that the stakes for the parties to a suit seeking nationwide relief are asymmetric: "Because plaintiffs generally are not bound by adverse decisions in cases to which they were not a party, there is a nearly boundless opportunity to shop for a friendly forum to secure a win nationwide." (By contrast, if a lower court upheld a constitutional challenge to a rule or statute but did not issue a nationwide injunction, nonmutual offensive issue preclusion would not normally apply against the government. See United States v. Mendoza, 464 U.S. 154 (1984), Seventh Edition p. 1370.)

The opinions by Justices Thomas and Gorsuch both relied in part on two recent articles: Bray, *Multiple Chancellors: Reforming the National Injunction*, 131 Harv.L.Rev. 417 (2017) (arguing that universal injunctions were rare if not nonexistent until recent times and concluding that the Article III "judicial Power" is solely "a power to decide a case for a particular claimant"); and Morley, *De Facto Class Actions? Plaintiff- and Defendant-Oriented Injunctions in Voting Rights, Election Law, and Other Constitutional Cases*, 39 Harv.J.L. & Pub.Pol'y 487 (2016) (mounting a multifaceted attack on the casual issuance of nationwide injunctions against the enforcement of federal statutes, orders, and regulations); see also Siddique, *Nationwide Injunctions*, 117 Colum.L.Rev. 2095 (2017) (arguing that federal courts should, and normally do, adhere to the principle that an injunction should extend no further than necessary to provide "complete relief to the plaintiffs" and proposing an amendment to Rule 65 of the FRCP to codify this requirement).

Responding to the argument that universal injunctions are a recent innovation, Sohoni, *The Lost History of the "Universal" Injunction*, 133 Harv.L.Rev. 920 (2020), offers historical evidence that "Article III courts have issued injunctions that extend beyond just the plaintiff for well over a century." Sohoni's article complements an earlier argument by Frost, *In Defense of Nationwide Injunctions*, 93 N.Y.U.L.Rev. 1065 (2018), that nationwide injunctions lie within the Article III judicial power and that district courts should be able to issue them "in three categories of cases: when they are the only method of providing the plaintiff with complete relief; when they are the only means of preventing irreparable injury to individuals similarly situated to plaintiffs; and when they are the only practical remedy because a more limited injunction would be chaotic to administer and would impose significant costs on the courts or others." Although highly critical of proposals "to outright strip the federal courts of the substantive power to grant" universal injunctions, Professor Sohoni acknowledges that universal injunctions often pose distinctive problems and should rarely issue. She also points out that the Congress of an earlier era responded to perceived abuses of federal equitable powers by channeling suits seeking federal injunctions against state statutes to three-judge district courts. For discussion of a variety of limitations on the award of federal equitable relief—including some imposed by Congress and others crafted by the Supreme Court—see the Seventh Edition, Chapter X.

Page 185. Add at the end of Paragraph (2):

City of Los Angeles v. Patel, 576 U.S. 409 (2015), upheld a facial challenge under the Fourth Amendment to a provision compelling hotel operators to keep records containing specified information about their guests and to make those records available to police on demand. In doing so, Justice Sotomayor's majority opinion noted that the Court had allowed facial challenges "under a diverse array of constitutional provisions" including the Second Amendment, the Due Process Clause, and the Foreign Commerce Clause, as well as the First Amendment. Justice Sotomayor described the formula of United States v. Salerno, Seventh Edition p. 184, under which a statute will be invalidated facially only if it is unconstitutional in all of its applications, as "the most exacting standard that the Court has prescribed for facial challenges". But she found even that standard to be satisfied by reasoning that the challenged provision was "irrelevant" to any case in which the Fourth Amendment itself permitted warrantless searches. Given the provision's irrelevancy in most cases, its only practical effect came when it purported to permit searches that the Fourth Amendment forbade, and it was therefore unconstitutional as applied to all cases in which it mattered.

Writing in dissent, Justice Scalia, joined by Chief Justice Roberts and Justice Thomas, argued that the challenged ordinance constituted a legislative authorization of warrantless searches of historically closely regulated businesses and that it had many valid applications. Justice Alito's separate dissenting opinion, in which Justice Thomas joined, offered a series of hypothetical cases in which the penalty provisions of the challenged ordinance might coerce hotel owners and personnel to cooperate with otherwise valid searches. These cases, he argued, demonstrated that the challenged ordinance was not invalid in all applications in which it had practical effect. For the majority, Justice Sotomayor parried that "[a]n otherwise facially unconstitutional statute cannot be saved from invalidation based solely on the existence of a penalty provision that applies when searches are not actually authorized by the statute." Why not?

Page 192. Add at the end of Paragraph (7):

Johnson v. United States, 576 U.S. 591 (2015), held a penalty-enhancing provision of the Armed Career Criminal Act (ACCA) to be constitutionally invalid on its face due to vagueness. The challenged provision provided enhanced punishment for defendants convicted of being felons in possession of a firearm if they had three or more previous convictions for a "violent felony". The ACCA defines "violent felony" to include certain enumerated crimes such as burglary and arson and any other felony that "involves conduct that presents a serious potential risk of physical injury to another." To apply the ACCA's penalty-enhancement provisions, a prior Court decision had prescribed a "categorical" approach, which "requires a court to picture the kind of conduct that [a prior] crime involves in 'the ordinary case,' and to judge whether that abstraction presents a serious potential risk of physical injury." Against the background of that holding, "[t]wo features of the [challenged] clause conspire[d] to make it unconstitutionally vague." It left "grave uncertainty about how to estimate the risk posed by a [type of] crime." And it created a comparable "uncertainty about how much risk it takes for a crime to qualify as a violent felony." Justice Scalia, speaking for the Court, concluded that because the resulting indeterminacy "both denies fair notice to defendants and invites arbitrary enforcement by judges", the statute violated the demand for clarity that due process imposes in criminal cases. In reaching that conclusion, Justice Scalia rejected an argument, pressed by Justice Alito in dissent, that a facial challenge must fail "because some crimes clearly pose a serious risk of physical injury to another" and the statute therefore must have some valid applications. "[A]lthough statements in some of our opinions could be read to suggest otherwise, our *holdings* squarely contradict the theory that a vague provision is constitutional merely because there is some conduct that clearly falls within the provision's grasp", Justice Scalia wrote. The Court's holding, he insisted, did not threaten the validity of criminal statutes that "use terms like 'substantial risk'" but do not "require[ ] application of the 'serious potential risk' standard to an idealized ordinary case of the crime."

Justices Kennedy and Thomas, in separate opinions concurring only in the judgment, both concluded that the petitioner's conviction for possession of a short-barreled shotgun did not qualify as a violent felony. Justice Alito dissented. He would have interpreted the ACCA to avoid vagueness problems by holding that it requires conduct-specific determinations of whether a defendant's own prior felonies posed a serious risk of physical injury to another. But he contended that even if a categorical approach were used, vagueness challenges not involving the First Amendment had to be addressed "on an as-applied basis" and that some felonies (such as attempted rape) certainly would pose a serious potential risk of physical injury in the ordinary case.

The most obvious significance of Johnson lies in its rejection of the premise that a facial challenge based on vagueness grounds must fail if a statute has any valid applications—a premise that Justice Alito described as "an application of the broader rule", asserted in United States v. Salerno, Seventh Edition p. 184, "that, except in First Amendment cases, we will hold that a statute is facially unconstitutional only if 'no set of circumstances exists under which the Act would be valid.'" Sessions v. Dimaya, 138 S.Ct. 1204 (2018), extended the Johnson rationale from a criminal to a civil case, though Justice Kagan's plurality opinion spoke narrowly on this point by emphasizing the severity of the penalty—the removal from the United States of a lawfully present non-citizen—that was at stake.[6a]

[6a] Sessions v. Dimaya turned on a provision of the Immigration and Naturalization Act that virtually mandated removal of any non-citizen convicted of a "crime of violence" while in the U.S. Finding close similarities to the statute in Johnson, which also required courts to determine whether a crime was likely to be violent in most cases, the plurality rejected suggestions that a more permissive void-for-vagueness standard should apply in civil removal actions than in criminal cases. Concurring in part and in the judgment, Justice Gorsuch agreed that robust void-for-vagueness analysis applied, but he saw no good reason why Congress should need to "speak more clearly when it seeks to deport a lawfully resident alien than when it wishes to subject a citizen to indefinite civil commitment, strip him of a business license essential to his family's living, or confiscate his home." Chief Justice Roberts, joined by Justices Kennedy, Thomas, and Alito, dissented, finding the statute materially less vague than that in Johnson. Justice Thomas filed a separate dissent in which he questioned whether modern vagueness

doctrine could be justified as consistent with the original meaning of the Due Process Clause. (Justice Gorsuch's concurring opinion agreed with Justice Thomas about the importance of that question. He concluded, however, that "the vagueness doctrine enjoys a secure footing in the original understanding".)

In United States v. Davis, 139 S.Ct. 2329 (2019), the Court, in an opinion by Justice Gorsuch, found that a statute imposing heightened penalties for felonies "that by [their] nature, involv[e] a substantial risk that physical force * * * may be used" referred to an imagined ordinary instance of the crime and was therefore unconstitutionally vague under Johnson. Justice Kavanaugh, in an opinion that three other Justices joined, dissented on statutory interpretation grounds, insisting that the challenged statute called for a permissible, case-specific calculation of the risk posed by a particular defendant's unlawful conduct.

Page 193. Add at the end of Paragraph (8):

Fallon, *Facial Challenges, Saving Constructions, and Statutory Severability*, 99 Tex.L.Rev. 215 (2020), argues for a sharp conceptual distinction between saving constructions, which are statutory interpretations that should be disciplined by canons of construction, and statutory severances, which should occur following a determination that a statute is invalid. In cases in which courts give narrowing constructions to avoid mere constitutional doubts about a statute's validity, Professor Fallon worries that "reliance on the vocabulary of 'narrowing' constructions can result in courts producing outcomes that they could not achieve by severing invalid applications." According to Fallon, "the conflation of narrowing constructions with severing can [also] lead to confusion and mistake in cases in which the Supreme Court, after rejecting a proposed narrowing construction as insupportable, then fails to ask the classic severability question of whether a statute that could not be sustained as written could nevertheless be severed such that some parts or applications could still be enforced."

————

4. MOOTNESS

NOTE ON MOOTNESS: ITS RATIONALE AND APPLICATIONS

Page 201. Add at the end of the first full paragraph:

Consider a very recent example: in Moore v. Harper, 143 S.Ct. 2065 (2023), the Court decided a case on certiorari from the Supreme Court of North Carolina, even though the Supreme Court of North Carolina had reconsidered crucial parts of the case while the case was pending before the U.S. Supreme Court. In brief: the North Carolina Supreme Court had concluded that the North Carolina General Assembly had violated the state constitution in gerrymandering districts for federal congressional elections, and had ordered the maps to be redrawn. It had both written a precedential opinion and entered a judgment to that effect ("Harper I") and litigation about the proper remedy continued in the state courts. The U.S. Supreme Court then granted certiorari to decide whether the North Carolina Supreme Court's decision violated Article I, Section 4's Elections Clause. While that part of the case was pending before the U.S. Supreme Court, the North Carolina Supreme Court issued an additional decision on the remedial issues ("Harper II") and then (after a change in membership on the North Carolina

Supreme Court) granted a petition for rehearing that both eliminated its remedial decision and "overruled" its original gerrymandering decision, which was on review at the U.S. Supreme Court.

But the Supreme Court decided that the case was not moot, because the court below had not tried to and could not disturb the *judgment* in Harper I, even as it overruled the *precedent*: "In other words, although partisan gerrymandering claims are no longer viable under the North Carolina Constitution, the North Carolina Supreme Court has done nothing to alter the effect of the judgment in Harper I enjoining the use of the 2021 maps. As a result, the legislative defendants' path to complete relief runs through this Court." Justice Thomas, joined on this point by Justice Alito and Justice Gorsuch, dissented, arguing that the distinction on which the Court relied lacked any substance: "our jurisdiction requires a case, and this case is over no matter what becomes of the empty husk of *Harper I*'s interlocutory judgment." Is the majority opinion an example of this functional approach to mootness? For additional discussion, see pp. 87–88, *infra*.

Page 201. Add at the end of footnote 3:

In Fisher v. University of Texas, 579 U.S. 365 (2016), the Court, without noticing any mootness issue, ruled on an equal protection challenge to affirmative action policies in place in 2008, even though "[p]etitioner long since has graduated from another college, and the University's policy—and the data on which it first was based—may have evolved or changed in material ways."

Page 203. Add new Paragraphs (3)(d), (3)(e), and (3)(f):

(d)   New York State Rifle & Pistol Ass'n, Inc. v. City of New York, 140 S.Ct. 1525 (2020), arose when the petitioners sought declaratory and injunctive relief from a New York City ordinance that barred possessors of licenses to keep handguns in their homes from transporting their weapons anywhere besides seven firing ranges within the City. The challengers' complaint maintained that the Second Amendment requires "unrestricted access to gun ranges and shooting events." After two lower courts upheld the ordinance and the Supreme Court granted certiorari, the New York Legislature enacted legislation abrogating any local regulation that prevented the holders of "premises licenses" from transporting their guns "directly to or from" an authorized range, competition, or second home. Nearly contemporaneously, the City amended its regulation to conform to the new state law.

The Supreme Court vacated the lower court's decision upholding the original New York ordinance in a brief *per curiam* opinion that held the petitioners' claim to declaratory and injunctive relief to be moot. Following the changes in New York State and City law, the Court reasoned, "petitioners may now transport firearms to a second home or shooting range outside the city, which is the precise relief that [they] requested." The Court then declined to consider whether mootness might be averted based on a request for damages that the petitioners raised for the first time in the Supreme Court. Instead, it remanded the case for the lower courts to consider whether the petitioners "may still add a claim for damages in this lawsuit."

Justice Alito dissented, joined by Justice Gorsuch in full and Justice Thomas in part. He maintained that New York's newly enacted rule continued to burden the petitioners' asserted right of "unrestricted access" to gun ranges by limiting them to traveling "directly" to and from their homes. Accordingly, he reasoned, they had not received the complete relief that they sought, and their claim to injunctive relief therefore was not moot. Justice Alito concluded that the petitioners' claim to damages relief also sufficed to save the case from mootness. Reaching the merits, he found that the amended New York ordinance violated the Second Amendment.

With regard to mootness, the core disagreement between the *per curiam* opinion and Justice Alito's dissent appeared to lie in divergent understandings of what would constitute a continuing, live claim to judicial "relief" in the absence of damages. The Court's cryptic observation that New York's change of law gave the petitioners "the precise relief that [they] requested" seems not strictly correct. The petitioners sought an injunction against the enforcement of what they maintained was an invalid statute, not a voluntarily enacted change of law that fell short of granting "unrestricted" rights to transport licensed weapons to shooting ranges and gun shows. By contrast, the dissent's conception of the "relief" sought by the petitioners— the absence of which kept the dispute alive—encompassed protection against any regulation, whenever enacted, that denied the broad rights to transport licensed weapons that they claimed under the Second Amendment.

The Justices' divergent understandings of what constitutes a live, continuing claim to injunctive and declaratory "relief" seem likely to matter only in cases on appeal. In the district court, the plaintiffs would undoubtedly have standing to challenge the newly enacted New York City ordinance, in a new action if not through an amendment of their complaint. But if the arguments bearing on the validity of the amended ordinance might differ in material respects from those concerning the original ordinance—for example, if it is arguable that the new ordinance is valid under the Second Amendment even if the old one was not—it is a different question whether the Supreme Court should be the first court to address those arguments. Does mootness doctrine furnish an apt analytical framework for resolving that question? Note, too, that if the Court had deemed the dispute between the parties justiciable based on a damages claim, it presumably would have had to determine the constitutionality of the original New York ordinance, whereas a determination that the plaintiffs suffered a continuing injury would have had to focus on the revised New York ordinance. Under these circumstances, how should the Court have responded to New York's deliberate efforts to render the case moot? Given the complexity of the entwined issues of justiciability and orderly appellate procedure, is the Court fairly subject to criticism for disposing of the case in a terse and sometimes opaque *per curiam* opinion?

(e)   Uzuegbunam v. Preczewski, 141 S.Ct. 792 (2021), also discussed p. 27 *supra*, held that a suit for nominal damages sufficed to avoid mootness in a case in which the plaintiff challenged the enforcement against him of the policies of a public college that (he claimed) violated his free speech rights. By the time the case reached the Supreme Court, the plaintiff was no longer a student at the college and the college had withdrawn the rules from which he had initially sought injunctive, as well as nominal monetary, relief. In an opinion by Justice Thomas, the Court held that the plaintiff's claim to nominal damages sufficed for standing and thus forestalled any mootness objection to the adjudication of his claim on the merits that might have arisen otherwise. Chief Justice Roberts dissented on the ground that the plaintiff's suit for damages failed to satisfy the "redressability" requirement of standing doctrine and that the case was therefore moot.

Does Uzuegbunam v. Preczewski deprive mootness doctrine of any continuing force in barring adjudication of the substantive merits of a constitutional claim in any case in which the plaintiff seeks nominal damages for as well as injunctive relief from a past constitutional violation? Chief Justice Roberts suggested that the effect of the decision might "admit of a sweeping exception: Where a plaintiff asks only for a dollar, the defendant should be able to end the case by giving him a dollar, without the court needing to pass on the merits of the plaintiff's claims. Although we recently reserved the question whether a defendant can moot a case by depositing the full amount requested by the plaintiff, Campbell-Ewald Co. v. Gomez, 577 U.S. 153, 166 (2016), our cases have long suggested that he can, see, e.g., California v. San Pablo & Tulare R. Co., 149 U.S. 308, 313–314 (1893)." Would the "exception" contemplated by the Chief Justice, which Justice Kavanaugh also endorsed in a concurring opinion, be a desirable one? For discussion of the Campbell-Ewald case, see below.

(f)   West Virginia v. EPA, 142 S.Ct. 2587 (2022), found jurisdiction to review the legality of the Clean Power Plan, despite a lower court ruling and change in agency position that meant that the plan was unlikely to be enforced in the future. In doing so, the Court emphasized the difference between standing and mootness analysis. Though the government framed its argument in standing terms, the Court responded: "It is the doctrine of *mootness*, not standing, that addresses whether 'an intervening circumstance [has] deprive[d] the plaintiff of a personal stake in the outcome of the lawsuit' " (emphasis in original, quoting Genesis HealthCare Corp. v. Symczyk, 569 U.S. 66, 72 (2013)).

The mootness label meant that the government bore a "heavy" burden of proving that it was " 'absolutely clear that the allegedly wrongful behavior could not reasonably be expected to recur' " (quoting Parents Involved in Community Schools v. Seattle School Dist. No. 1, 551 U.S. 701, 719 (2007)). Because the government still maintained that the Clean Power Plan had been legal, and did not disavow similar using legal arguments to support rulemaking in the future, it could not prove mootness.

Justice Kagan (joined by Justices Breyer and Sotomayor) dissented on the merits, and also described the Court's opinion as "really an advisory opinion," but she also conceded that "[t]he Court may be right that [exercising jurisdiction] does not violate Article III mootness rules (which are notoriously strict)." Because West Virginia v. EPA relied so heavily on the distinction between mootness and standing, it puts additional pressure on the relationship between the two discussed in paragraph (1).

Page 203. Add at the end of footnote 6:

A unanimous Court applied the mootness exception for cases capable of repetition, yet evading review in Kingdomware Technologies, Inc. v. United States, 579 U.S. 162 (2016), in which a business owned by a service-disabled veteran challenged the Government's failure to award it short-term contracts pursuant to a narrow interpretation of a statute mandating preferences for service-disabled or other veteran-owned businesses. The contracts whose award Kingdomware Technologies sought to challenge were performed in less than two years, a period "too short to complete judicial review of the lawfulness of the procurement," and Kingdomware had "shown a reasonable likelihood that it would be awarded a future contract if its interpretation" prevailed.

Page 205. Add a new footnote 10a at the end of the last full paragraph:

[10a] In Chapman v. Doe, 143 S.Ct. 857 (2023), the Court granted, vacated, and remanded under Munsingwear in response to the joint request of the parties as part of an agreement to dismiss the case. Justice Jackson, however, dissented, expressing her "concern[ ] that contemporary practice related to so-called "Munsingwear vacaturs' has drifted away from the doctrine's foundational moorings." She noted that the petitioner had contributed to the mootness through her agreement, but also argued "more fundamentally" that the Court ought to reserve Munsingwear vacaturs for "extraordinary" circumstances for both formal and practical reasons.

Page 207. Add a new footnote 13 at the end of the second paragraph:

[13] In MOAC Mall Holdings v. Transform Holdco LLC, 143 S.Ct. 927 (2023), the Court applied Chafin to reject an analogous argument for mootness in a bankruptcy case—that the Court's ruling would not matter because other legal provisions would foreclose relief on remand: "Chafin forecloses this kind of argument. Here, as elsewhere, we decline to act as a court of 'first view,' plumbing the Code's complex depths in 'the first instance' to assure ourselves that Transform is correct about its contention that no relief remains legally available."

NOTE ON MOOTNESS IN CLASS ACTIONS

Page 211. Add at the end of footnote 2:

The Court adopted the theory of Justice Kagan's dissent in Genesis Healthcare Corp. v. Symczyk, Seventh Edition p. 210, in Campbell-Ewald Co. v. Gomez, 577 U.S. 153 (2016). Gomez filed a class action complaint in which he alleged that the defendant violated his rights under the Telephone Consumer Protection Act by sending him unauthorized text messages and sought $1,500 in damages, the maximum that he could recover under the Act. Campbell-Ewald made a settlement offer of the full amount, which Gomez refused. Campbell-Ewald then argued that its offer had mooted the case. Writing for five Justices, Justice Ginsburg held that "under basic principles of contract law" the "unaccepted offer" was "a legal nullity, with no operative effect" and that both parties thus "retained the same stake in the litigation they had at the outset." In a potentially important passage at the end of her opinion, however, Justice Ginsburg reserved the question "whether the result would be different if a defendant deposits the full amount of the plaintiff's individual claim in an account payable to the plaintiff, and the court then enters judgment for the plaintiff in that amount." Is there any reason why a defendant who wished to forestall a class action by offering to pay the named plaintiff's claim prior to class certification would not make such a deposit? (If not, has Justice Ginsburg suggested that the defendant may moot any such class action simply by taking one additional step with respect to the named plaintiff?) Justice Thomas concurred on the ground that the defendant had not satisfied the common law standard for a "tender" of complete relief, which required an admission of liability. Chief Justice Roberts, joined by Justices Scalia and Alito, dissented.

Again emphasizing the significance of Rule 23, United States v. Sanchez-Gomez, 138 S.Ct. 1532 (2018), unanimously held that the rationale of Gerstein and Geraghty did not extend to challenges, raised on motions in criminal actions, to a U.S. Marshall Service policy of shackling in-custody defendants for some court appearances. Although the court of appeals had viewed the challenges by four defendants as a "functional class action", the Court found all of the individual cases to be moot on appeal in the absence of any formal mechanism for class certification.

---

5. RIPENESS

NOTE ON "RIPENESS" IN PUBLIC LITIGATION CHALLENGING THE
VALIDITY OR APPLICATION OF STATUTES AND REGULATIONS

Page 221. Add at the end of Paragraph (2)(c):

Trump v. New York, 141 S.Ct. 530 (2020), also discussed p. 11 *supra*,
found that a challenge to a presidential memorandum directing the
Secretary of Commerce to take steps facilitating the President's intended
exclusion of unlawful immigrants from the population count used to
apportion congressional representation and disburse certain federal funds
was unripe. There were too many contingencies, the Court reasoned in a per
curiam opinion, involving how many undocumented immigrants the
Secretary might identify and the President might exclude, as well as what
adverse effects the plaintiff states might suffer. Justice Breyer, joined by
Justices Sotomayor and Kagan, dissented with respect to justiciability and
would have ruled that relevant statutes required the counting of all persons
without regard to immigration status. President Trump's term expired
before the Commerce Department produced the data required to implement
the exclusion policy, and President Biden issued an executive order revoking
the memorandum in January 2021. See Exec. Order No. 13986, 86 Fed. Reg.
7015 (Jan. 20, 2021).

Page 225. Add at the end of Paragraph (3)(b):

In Knick v. Township of Scott, 139 S.Ct. 2162 (2019), also discussed p.
161, *infra*, the Court, by 5 to 4, partially overruled Williamson County,
Seventh Edition p. 224, as based on a substantive misinterpretation of the
Takings Clause. Under a proper interpretation, the Court ruled in an opinion
by Chief Justice Roberts, a property owner suffers a constitutional violation
as soon as "the government takes his property without just compensation,
and therefore may bring his claim in federal court under § 1983 at that time."
The requirement that the plaintiff pursue compensation in state court first
constituted an impermissible requirement to exhaust state remedies that is
incompatible with § 1983, the Chief Justice reasoned. The Court did not
question Williamson County's alternative holding that a takings claim does
not become ripe until a property owner has pursued opportunities for
administrative relief from regulatory burdens (such as seeking a variance
from a zoning ordinance).

Dissenting, Justice Kagan defended the aspect of Williamson County
that the Court overruled as "rooted in" a correct "understanding of the Fifth
Amendment's Takings Clause stretching back to the late 1800s." Like the
Chief Justice, Justice Kagan appeared to view Williamson County's
reference to ripeness as inseparable from its conclusions about the scope of
the Taking Clause's substantive guarantee.

NOTE ON "RIPENESS" AND RELATED ISSUES IN PUBLIC ACTIONS CHALLENGING PATTERNS OR PRACTICES IN THE ADMINISTRATION OF THE LAW

Page 234. For the first paragraph of Paragraph (3), substitute the following:

The Court treated Lyons as a standing case and reasoned that he lacked the requisite injury-in-fact to sue for an injunction. No one disputed Lyons' standing to seek damages. Why shouldn't his past injury have established the existence of a case or controversy focused largely on the appropriateness of equitable relief? Was the problem that a forward-looking injunction would not redress the harm that had suffered in the past?

————

6. POLITICAL QUESTIONS

NOTE ON POLITICAL QUESTIONS

Page 249. Add at the end of Paragraph (1):

Fallon, *Political Questions and the Ultra Vires Conundrum*, 87 U.Chi.L.Rev. 1481 (2020), argues that the political question doctrine should not apply to any case in which the branch whose decision the judiciary is asked to review acted ultra vires. (For example, imagine that the Senate, after convicting Judge Nixon of high crimes and misdemeanors, had purported to impose a punishment of criminal incarceration.) If political questions are by definition ones that lie within the jurisdiction of a branch other than the judiciary, must the courts resolve the jurisdictional question that claims of ultra vires action present—or might other branches have non-reviewable jurisdiction to determine whether they have jurisdiction in some cases?

Page 249. Add at the end of footnote 3:

Grove, *The Lost History of the Political Question Doctrine*, 90 N.Y.U.L.Rev. 1908 (2015), argues that the modern political question doctrine is a twentieth-century invention. Under the "traditional" doctrine that applied throughout the nineteenth century, Professor Grove writes, "political questions were *factual* determinations made by the political branches that courts treated as conclusive in the course of resolving cases." Based on Professor Grove's evidence, the line between law and fact does not appear sharp, and she acknowledges that the Court breached it, at least in dictum, in Luther v. Borden, Seventh Edition p. 258. Nevertheless, she maintains, the traditional doctrine was not jurisdictional: the Court exercised its jurisdiction to apply the determination of another branch. According to Professor Grove, the modern, jurisdictional doctrine had its first flowering in 1912, in Pacific States Tel. & Tel. Co. v. Oregon, Seventh Edition p. 259, but even the reasoning of that decision was arguably limited to the Guarantee Clause. After gaining traction in some plurality opinions, the modern, general, jurisdictional doctrine emerged only in 1962 in Baker v. Carr, Seventh Edition p. 250. Professor Grove attributes the rise of the modern doctrine largely to casebook authors in the "legal process" school, beginning with then-Professor Felix Frankfurter and later including Henry Hart and Herbert Wechsler, who, she writes, sought more generally to limit the range of properly judicial authority with jurisdictional doctrines that they ascribed to Article III. In Professor Grove's view, the modern political question doctrine is vulnerable to criticism both because it lacks historical foundations and because it gives the Supreme Court too much power, not too little: by reserving "for itself the power to decide which institution decides any constitutional question * * * the Court has most often used its modern political question cases * * * as a vehicle to assert its supremacy over various areas of constitutional law." However one judges a number of Professor Grove's specific claims, the article offers a fascinating study in the possibility of historically evolving understandings of a concept and of the use of that concept to serve shifting agendas.

Page 253. Substitute the following for the second paragraph of Paragraph (4) and the remainder of Paragraph (4) entirely:

In Rucho v. Common Cause, 139 S.Ct. 2484 (2019), which follows immediately in this Supplement, a majority of the Justices found that challenges to partisan gerrymanders present nonjusticiable political questions due to an absence of judicially manageable standards.

Page 257. After Paragraph (7), add the following principal case and accompanying Notes:

Rucho v. Common Cause

___ U.S. ___, 139 S.Ct. 2484, 204 L.Ed.2d 931 (2019).
Appeal from the United States District Court
for the Middle District of North Carolina.

■ CHIEF JUSTICE ROBERTS delivered the opinion of the Court.

Voters and other plaintiffs in North Carolina and Maryland challenged their States' congressional districting maps as unconstitutional partisan gerrymanders. The North Carolina plaintiffs complained that the State's districting plan discriminated against Democrats; the Maryland plaintiffs complained that their State's plan discriminated against Republicans. The plaintiffs alleged that the gerrymandering violated the First Amendment, the Equal Protection Clause of the Fourteenth Amendment, the Elections Clause, and Article I, § 2, of the Constitution. * * *

I

[All agree that the partisan gerrymanders at issue in the two cases were deliberate and at least initially highly effective. In Rucho, the case from North Carolina,] one of the two Republicans chairing the redistricting committee * * * explained that the map was drawn with the aim of electing ten Republicans and three Democrats because he did "not believe it [would be] possible to draw a map with 11 Republicans and 2 Democrats." One Democratic state senator objected that entrenching the 10–3 advantage for Republicans was not "fair, reasonable, [or] balanced" because, as recently as 2012, "Democratic congressional candidates had received more votes on a statewide basis than Republican candidates." * * * In November 2016, North Carolina conducted congressional elections using the 2016 Plan [at issue in the litigation], and Republican candidates won 10 of the 13 congressional districts. * * *

The second case before us is Lamone v. Benisek. In 2011, the Maryland Legislature—dominated by Democrats—undertook to redraw the lines of that State's eight congressional districts. The Governor at the time, Democrat Martin O'Malley, * * * appointed a redistricting committee to help redraw the map * * *. The Governor later testified that his aim was to "use the redistricting process to change the overall composition of Maryland's congressional delegation to 7 Democrats and 1 Republican by flipping" one district. * * * The 2011 Plan accomplished that by moving roughly 360,000 voters out of the Sixth District and moving 350,000 new voters in. Overall, the Plan reduced the number of registered Republicans in the Sixth District by about 66,000 and increased the number of registered Democrats by about 24,000. The map was adopted by a party-line vote. It was used in the 2012 election and succeeded in flipping the Sixth District. A Democrat has held the seat ever since.

II

A

* * * In these cases we are asked to decide an important question of constitutional law. "But before we do so, we must find that the question is presented in a 'case' or 'controversy' that is, in James Madison's words, 'of a Judiciary Nature.' " DaimlerChrysler Corp. v. Cuno, 547 U.S. 332, 342 (2006) (quoting 2 Records of the Federal Convention of 1787, p. 430 (M. Farrand ed. 1966)). * * * The question here is whether there is an "appropriate role for the Federal Judiciary" in remedying the problem of partisan gerrymandering—whether such claims are claims of *legal* right, resolvable according to *legal* principles, or political questions that must find their resolution elsewhere.

B

Partisan gerrymandering is nothing new. Nor is frustration with it. * * * The Framers addressed the election of Representatives to Congress in the Elections Clause. Art. I, § 4, cl. 1. That provision assigns to state legislatures the power to prescribe the "Times, Places and Manner of holding Elections" for Members of Congress, while giving Congress the power to "make or alter" any such regulations. * * * [The Court here cited historical examples of congressional regulation before recognizing that only a requirement that states use single-member districts remains in place today.] * * *

Appellants suggest that, through the Elections Clause, the Framers set aside electoral issues such as the one before us as questions that only Congress can resolve. We do not agree. In two areas—one-person, one-vote and racial gerrymandering—our cases have held that there is a role for the courts with respect to at least some issues that could arise from a State's drawing of congressional districts. See Wesberry v. Sanders, 376 U.S. 1 (1964); Shaw v. Reno, 509 U.S. 630 (1993).

But the history is not irrelevant. The Framers were aware of electoral districting problems and considered what to do about them. * * * At no point was there a suggestion that the federal courts had a role to play. Nor was there any indication that the Framers had ever heard of courts doing such a thing.

C

* * * Partisan gerrymandering claims have proved far more difficult to adjudicate [than one-person, one-vote cases and cases involving racial discrimination]. The basic reason is that, while it is illegal for a jurisdiction to depart from the one-person, one-vote rule, or to engage in racial discrimination in districting, "a jurisdiction may engage in constitutional political gerrymandering." Hunt v. Cromartie, 526 U.S. 541, 551 (1999) (citing Bush v. Vera, 517 U.S. 952, 968 (1996); [further citations omitted].

To hold that legislators cannot take partisan interests into account when drawing district lines would essentially countermand the Framers' decision to entrust districting to political entities. The "central problem" is not determining whether a jurisdiction has engaged in partisan gerrymandering. It is "determining when political gerrymandering has gone too far." Vieth [v. Jubelirer, 541 U.S. 267, 296 (2004) (plurality opinion)]. [The Court here recounted its prior confrontations will challenges to political gerrymandering. In Davis v. Bandemer, 478 U.S. 109 (1986)), a majority thought the case was justiciable but splintered over the proper standard to apply. Four Justices (White, Brennan, Marshall, and Blackmun) would have required proof of "intentional discrimination against an identifiable political group and an actual discriminatory effect on that group." Two Justices (Powell and Stevens) would have focused on "whether the boundaries of the voting districts have been distorted deliberately and arbitrarily to achieve illegitimate ends." But Justice O'Connor, joined by Chief Justice Burger and Justice Rehnquist, would have held that partisan gerrymandering claims pose political questions because the Equal Protection Clause simply "does not supply judicially manageable standards for resolving" them.

[Eighteen years later, in Vieth, Justice Scalia's plurality opinion also would have held challenges to gerrymanders nonjusticiable due to an absence of judicially manageable standards.] Justice Kennedy, concurring in the judgment, noted "the lack of comprehensive and neutral principles for drawing electoral boundaries [and] the absence of rules to limit and confine judicial intervention." He nonetheless left open the possibility that "in another case a standard might emerge." Four Justices dissented. * * *

III

[The] question [in appraising political gerrymandering claims] is one of degree: How to "provid[e] a standard for deciding how much partisan dominance is too much." League of United Latin American Citizens v. Perry, 548 U.S. 399, 420 (2006) (opinion of Kennedy, J.). And it is vital in such circumstances that the Court act only in accord with especially clear standards: "With uncertain limits, intervening courts—even when proceeding with best intentions—would risk assuming political, not legal, responsibility for a process that often produces ill will and distrust." Vieth, 541 U.S., at 307 (opinion of Kennedy, J.). * * *

* * * Partisan gerrymandering claims invariably sound in a desire for proportional representation. * * * "Our cases, however, clearly foreclose any claim that the Constitution requires proportional representation * * *." * * * Unable to claim that the Constitution requires proportional representation outright, plaintiffs inevitably ask the courts to make their own political judgment about how much representation particular political parties *deserve*—based on the votes of their supporters—and to rearrange the challenged districts to achieve that end. But federal courts are not equipped to apportion political power as a matter of fairness, nor is there any basis for concluding that they were authorized to do so. * * *

The initial difficulty in settling on a "clear, manageable and politically neutral" test for fairness is that it is not even clear what fairness looks like in this context. * * * Fairness may mean a greater number of competitive districts. * * * On the other hand, perhaps the ultimate objective of a "fairer" share of seats in the congressional delegation is most readily achieved by yielding to the gravitational pull of proportionality and engaging in cracking and packing, to ensure each party its "appropriate" share of "safe" seats. * * * Or perhaps fairness should be measured by adherence to "traditional" districting criteria, such as maintaining political subdivisions, keeping communities of interest together, and protecting incumbents. * * *

Deciding among just these different visions of fairness (you can imagine many others) poses basic questions that are political, not legal. There are no legal standards discernible in the Constitution for making such judgments, let alone limited and precise standards that are clear, manageable, and politically neutral. * * *

Even assuming the court knew which version of fairness to be looking for, there are no discernible and manageable standards for deciding whether there has been a violation. * * * Appellees contend that if we can adjudicate one-person, one-vote claims, we can also assess partisan gerrymandering claims. * * * [But] "vote dilution" in the one-person, one-vote cases refers to the idea that each vote must carry equal weight. * * * That requirement does not extend to political parties. It does not mean that each party must be influential in proportion to its number of supporters.

IV

Appellees and the dissent propose a number of "tests" for evaluating partisan gerrymandering claims, but none meets the need for a limited and precise standard that is judicially discernible and manageable. And none provides a solid grounding for judges to take the extraordinary step of reallocating power and influence between political parties. * * *

A

[The District Court in the North Carolina case used a test that involved a "predominant" legislative purpose coupled with a demand for] a showing "that the dilution of the votes of supporters of a disfavored party in a particular district * * * is likely to persist in subsequent elections such that an elected representative from the favored party in the district will not feel a need to be responsive to constituents who support the disfavored party." * * *

The District Court's "predominant intent" prong is borrowed from the racial gerrymandering context. * * * If district lines were drawn for the purpose of separating racial groups, then they are subject to strict scrutiny because "race-based decisionmaking is inherently suspect." But determining that lines were drawn on the basis of partisanship does not indicate that the districting was improper. A permissible intent— securing partisan advantage—does not become constitutionally impermissible, like racial discrimination, when that permissible intent "predominates."

The District Court tried to limit the reach of its test by requiring plaintiffs to show, in addition to predominant partisan intent, that vote dilution "is likely to persist" to such a degree that the elected representative will feel free to ignore the concerns of the supporters of the minority party. But "[t]o allow district courts to strike down apportionment plans on the basis of their prognostications as to the outcome of future elections . . . invites 'findings' on matters as to which neither judges nor anyone else can have any confidence." Bandemer, 478 U.S., at 160 (opinion of O'Connor, J.). * * *

B

The District Courts also found partisan gerrymandering claims justiciable under the First Amendment, coalescing around a basic three-part test: proof of intent to burden individuals based on their voting history or party affiliation; an actual burden on political speech or associational rights; and a causal link between the invidious intent and actual burden. * * * To begin, there are no restrictions on speech, association, or any other First Amendment activities in the districting plans at issue. * * * The plaintiffs' argument is that partisanship in districting should be regarded as simple discrimination against supporters of the opposing party on the basis of political viewpoint. * * * [But that test] simply describes the act of districting for partisan advantage. It provides no standard for determining when partisan activity goes too far.

As for actual burden, the slight anecdotal evidence found sufficient by the District Courts in these cases shows that this too is not a serious standard for separating constitutional from unconstitutional partisan gerrymandering. * * * How much of a decline in voter engagement is enough to constitute a First Amendment burden? How many door knocks must go unanswered? How many petitions unsigned? How many calls for volunteers unheeded? * * *

C

The dissent proposes using a State's own districting criteria as a neutral baseline from which to measure how extreme a partisan gerrymander is. The dissent would have us line up all the possible maps drawn using those criteria according to the partisan distribution they would produce. Distance from the "median" map would indicate whether a particular districting plan harms supporters of one party to an unconstitutional extent.

As an initial matter, it does not make sense to use criteria that will vary from State to State and year to year as the baseline for determining whether a gerrymander violates the Federal Constitution. The degree of partisan advantage that the Constitution tolerates should not turn on criteria offered by the gerrymanderers themselves. * * *

Even if we were to accept the dissent's proposed baseline, it would return us to "the original unanswerable question (How much political motivation and effect is too much?)." Vieth, 541 U.S., at 296–297 (plurality opinion). Would twenty percent away from the median map be okay? Forty percent? Sixty percent? Why or why not? * * *

The dissent argues that there are other instances in law where matters of degree are left to the courts. True enough. But those instances typically involve constitutional or statutory provisions or common law confining and guiding the exercise of judicial discretion. * * * Here, on the other hand, the Constitution provides no basis whatever to guide the exercise of judicial discretion. * * * The only provision in the Constitution that specifically addresses the matter assigns it to the political branches. See Art. I, § 4, cl. 1. [The Court next dismissed arguments based on the Elections Clause and Article I, § 2.]

V

Excessive partisanship in districting leads to results that reasonably seem unjust. But the fact that such gerrymandering is "incompatible with democratic principles," Arizona State Legislature [v. Arizona Independent Redistricting Comm'n, 576 U.S. 787 (2015)], does not mean that the solution lies with the federal judiciary. * * * Federal judges have no license to reallocate political power between the two major political parties, with no plausible grant of authority in the Constitution, and no legal standards to limit and direct their decisions. * * *

Our conclusion does not condone excessive partisan gerrymandering. Nor does our conclusion condemn complaints about districting to echo into a void. The States, for example, are actively addressing the issue on a number of fronts. * * * [The Court here described state legislation, state ballot initiatives, and state constitutional amendments to limit partisan gerrymandering.] * * *

As noted, the Framers gave Congress the power to do something about partisan gerrymandering in the Elections Clause. * * * [The Court here described several bills introduced in Congress.] * * * We express no view on any of these pending proposals. We simply note that the avenue for reform established by the Framers, and used by Congress in the past, remains open. * * *

■ JUSTICE KAGAN, with whom JUSTICES GINSBURG, BREYER, and SOTOMAYOR join, dissenting.

For the first time ever, this Court refuses to remedy a constitutional violation because it thinks the task beyond judicial capabilities. * * * The partisan gerrymanders in these cases deprived citizens of the most fundamental of their constitutional rights: the rights to participate equally in the political process, to join with others to advance political beliefs, and to choose their political representatives. * * * If left unchecked, gerrymanders like the ones here may irreparably damage our system of government.

And checking them is *not* beyond the courts. The majority's abdication comes just when courts across the country, including those below, have coalesced around manageable judicial standards to resolve partisan gerrymandering claims. * * *

I

* * * [The] majority concedes (really, how could it not?) that gerrymandering is "incompatible with democratic principles." * * * That recognition would seem to demand a response. The majority offers two ideas * * *. One is that the political process can deal with the problem—a proposition so dubious on its face that I feel secure in delaying my answer for some time. The other is that political gerrymanders have always been with us. To its credit, the majority does not frame that point as an originalist constitutional argument. After all (as the majority rightly notes), racial and residential gerrymanders were also once with us, but the Court has done something about that fact. The majority's idea instead seems to be that if we have lived with partisan gerrymanders so long, we will survive.

That complacency has no cause. * * * While bygone mapmakers may have drafted three or four alternative districting plans, today's mapmakers can generate thousands of possibilities at the touch of a key—and then choose the one giving their party maximum advantage (usually while still meeting traditional districting requirements). The effect is to make gerrymanders far more effective and durable than before, insulating politicians against all but the most titanic shifts in the political tides. * * *

Partisan gerrymandering of the kind before us not only subverts democracy (as if that weren't bad enough). It violates individuals' constitutional rights as well. * * * Th[e] practice implicates the Fourteenth Amendment's Equal Protection Clause. * * * And partisan gerrymandering implicates the First Amendment too. That Amendment gives its greatest protection to political beliefs, speech, and association. Yet partisan gerrymanders subject certain voters to "disfavored

treatment"—again, counting their votes for less—precisely because of
"their voting history [and] their expression of political views." Vieth, 541
U.S., at 314 (opinion of Kennedy, J.). * * *

[The] majority never disagrees; it appears to accept the "principle
that each person must have an equal say in the election of
representatives." And indeed, without this settled and shared
understanding that cases like these inflict constitutional injury, the
question of whether there are judicially manageable standards for
resolving them would never come up.

II

So the only way to understand the majority's opinion is as follows:
In the face of grievous harm to democratic governance and flagrant
infringements on individuals' rights—in the face of escalating partisan
manipulation whose compatibility with this Nation's values and law no
one defends—the majority declines to provide any remedy. * * * I'll give
the majority this one—and important—thing: It identifies some dangers
everyone should want to avoid. Judges should not be apportioning
political power based on their own vision of electoral fairness, whether
proportional representation or any other. And judges should not be
striking down maps left, right, and center, on the view that every
smidgen of politics is a smidgen too much. Respect for state legislative
processes—and restraint in the exercise of judicial authority—counsels
intervention in only egregious cases.

But in throwing up its hands, the majority misses something under
its nose: What it says can't be done *has* been done. Over the past several
years, federal courts across the country—including, but not exclusively,
in the decisions below—have largely converged on a standard for
adjudicating partisan gerrymandering claims (striking down both
Democratic and Republican districting plans in the process). * * *

A

Start with the standard the lower courts used. * * * [B]oth courts
(like others around the country) used basically the same three-part test
to decide whether the plaintiffs had made out a vote dilution claim. As
many legal standards do, that test has three parts: (1) intent; (2) effects;
and (3) causation. First, the plaintiffs challenging a districting plan must
prove that state officials' "predominant purpose" in drawing a district's
lines was to "entrench [their party] in power" by diluting the votes of
citizens favoring its rival. [See Common Cause v. Rucho, 318 F. Supp. 3d
777, 805–806 (M.D.N.C. 2018).] Second, the plaintiffs must establish that
the lines drawn in fact have the intended effect by "substantially"
diluting their votes. [See Benisek v. Lamone, 348 F. Supp. 3d 493, 498
(D. Md. 2018).] And third, if the plaintiffs make those showings, the State
must come up with a legitimate, non-partisan justification to save its
map. If you are a lawyer, you know that this test looks utterly ordinary.
It is the sort of thing courts work with every day. * * *

The majority's response to the District Courts' purpose analysis is discomfiting. The majority does not contest the lower courts' findings; how could it? Instead, the majority says that state officials' intent to entrench their party in power is perfectly "permissible," even when it is the predominant factor in drawing district lines. But that is wrong. * * * [W]hen political actors have a specific and predominant intent to entrench themselves in power by manipulating district lines, that goes too far. * * *

On to the second step of the analysis, where the plaintiffs must prove that the districting plan substantially dilutes their votes. * * * Consider the sort of evidence used in North Carolina first. There, the plaintiffs demonstrated the districting plan's effects mostly by relying on what might be called the "extreme outlier approach." * * * The approach—which also has recently been used in Michigan and Ohio litigation—begins by using advanced computing technology to randomly generate a large collection of districting plans that incorporate the State's physical and political geography and meet its declared districting criteria, *except for* partisan gain. * * * The further out on the tail, the more extreme the partisan distortion and the more significant the vote dilution.

Using that approach, the North Carolina plaintiffs offered a boatload of alternative districting plans—all showing that the State's map was an out-out-out-outlier. One expert produced 3,000 maps, adhering in the way described above to the districting criteria that the North Carolina redistricting committee had used, other than partisan advantage. To calculate the partisan outcome of those maps, the expert also used the same election data (a composite of seven elections) that [a North Carolina expert] had employed when devising the North Carolina plan in the first instance. * * * Every single one of the 3,000 maps would have produced at least one more Democratic House Member than the State's actual map, and 77% would have elected three or four more. * * * Based on those and other findings, the District Court determined that the North Carolina plan substantially dilutes the plaintiffs' votes.

Because the Maryland gerrymander involved just one district, the evidence in that case was far simpler—but no less powerful for that. * * * In the old Sixth [District], 47% of registered voters were Republicans and only 36% Democrats. But in the new Sixth, 44% of registered voters were Democrats and only 33% Republicans. That reversal of the district's partisan composition translated into four consecutive Democratic victories, including in a wave election year for Republicans (2014). In what was once a party stronghold, Republicans now have little or no chance to elect their preferred candidate. The District Court thus found that the gerrymandered Maryland map substantially dilutes Republicans' votes. * * *

By substantially diluting the votes of citizens favoring their rivals, the politicians of one party had succeeded in entrenching themselves in office. They had beat democracy.

B

The majority's broadest claim, as I've noted, is that this is a price we must pay because judicial oversight of partisan gerrymandering cannot be "politically neutral" or "manageable." * * * Consider neutrality first. Contrary to the majority's suggestion, the District Courts did not have to—and in fact did not—choose among competing visions of electoral fairness. That is because they did not try to compare the State's actual map to an "ideally fair" one (whether based on proportional representation or some other criterion). Instead, they looked at the difference between what the State did and what the State would have done if politicians hadn't been intent on partisan gain. Or put differently, the comparator (or baseline or touchstone) is the result not of a judge's philosophizing but of the State's own characteristics and judgments. * * *

The majority's sole response misses the point. According to the majority, "it does not make sense to use" a State's own (non-partisan) districting criteria as the baseline from which to measure partisan gerrymandering because those criteria "will vary from State to State and year to year." But that is a virtue, not a vice—a feature, not a bug. * * *

The majority's "how much is too much" critique fares no better than its neutrality argument. How about the following for a first-cut answer: This much is too much. By any measure, a map that produces a greater partisan skew than any of 3,000 randomly generated maps (all with the State's political geography and districting criteria built in) reflects "too much" partisanship. Think about what I just said: The absolute worst of 3,001 possible maps. The *only one* that could produce a 10–3 partisan split even as Republicans got a bare majority of the statewide vote. And again: How much is too much? This much is too much: A map that without any evident non-partisan districting reason (to the contrary) shifted the composition of a district from 47% Republicans and 36% Democrats to 33% Republicans and 42% Democrats. A map that in 2011 was responsible for the largest partisan swing of a congressional district in the country.

And if the majority thought that approach too case-specific, it could have used the lower courts' general standard—focusing on "predominant" purpose and "substantial" effects—without fear of indeterminacy. I do not take even the majority to claim that courts are incapable of investigating whether legislators mainly intended to seek partisan advantage. * * * Nor is there any reason to doubt, as the majority does, the competence of courts to determine whether a district map "substantially" dilutes the votes of a rival party's supporters from the everything-but-partisanship baseline described above. * * * As this Court recently noted, "the law is full of instances" where a judge's decision rests on "estimating rightly ... some matter of degree"— including the "substantial[ity]" of risk or harm. * * *

III

This Court has long understood that it has a special responsibility to remedy violations of constitutional rights resulting from politicians' districting decisions. * * * [T]he need for judicial review is at its most urgent in cases like these. "For here, politicians' incentives conflict with voters' interests, leaving citizens without any political remedy for their constitutional harms." [Gill v. Whitford, 138 S.Ct. 1916, 1941 (2018),] (Kagan, J., concurring). Those harms arise because politicians want to stay in office. No one can look to them for effective relief.

[Here Justice Kagan argued that Congress and state political processes were unlikely to provide an effective remedy. After noting that the majority had also recognized state courts as a possible source of relief—since the federal political question doctrine does not apply to claims brought under their states' constitutions—she asked:] But what do those courts know that this Court does not? If they can develop and apply neutral and manageable standards to identify unconstitutional gerrymanders, why couldn't we? * * *

The practices challenged in these cases imperil our system of government. Part of the Court's role in that system is to defend its foundations. None is more important than free and fair elections. With respect but deep sadness, I dissent.

NOTE ON NONJUSTICIABILITY DUE TO THE ABSENCE OF JUDICIALLY MANAGEABLE STANDARDS

(1) Varieties of Political Questions. In Nixon v. United States, Seventh Edition p. 237, the Supreme Court appeared to contemplate that the plaintiff had a right to be "tr[ied]" by the Senate before being convicted and removed from office, but ruled that the Impeachment Trial Clause, Art. I, § 3, cl. 6, constituted a "textually demonstrable constitutional commitment" of authority to the Senate to determine what "the word 'try'" required. In Rucho, by comparison, the Court does not appear to think that any branch, institution, or official other than the judiciary has constitutional responsibility for identifying and protecting the federal rights that the plaintiffs claimed, including under the Equal Protection Clause and the First Amendment.

The Court takes note of efforts by Congress and the states to restrict partisan vote dilution as a matter of federal statutory or state constitutional law. But suppose that Congress were to enact legislation specifically aimed at protecting constitutional rights under the Equal Protection Clause or the First Amendment. After Rucho, could such legislation pass muster as "enforcing" rather than "interpreting" the Constitution under City of Boerne v. Flores, Seventh Edition p. 188? Legislation enacted under the Elections Clause, Art. I, § 4, cl. 1, would not be subject to review under Boerne, but recall that the Court in Rucho specifically rejects a suggestion that that

Clause constituted Congress as the authoritative arbiter of voting rights under the Equal Protection Clause in congressional districting cases.

If there are no judicially manageable standards for defining the constitutional right that the plaintiffs claim, and if the Constitution does not commit responsibility for defining and enforcing it to another branch, then in what sense does the Court recognize the existence of a constitutional right at all? Dissenting, Justice Kagan insists that the majority acknowledges that gerrymandering that goes "too far" violates rights: "[W]ithout this settled and shared understanding * * *, the question of whether there are judicially manageable standards for resolving [partisan gerrymandering cases] would never come up." Compare Chief Justice Roberts's framing of the question before the Court as whether the plaintiffs' claims "are claims of *legal* right, resolvable according to *legal* principles, or political questions that must find their resolution elsewhere" (emphasis in original). Is the majority as committed as Justice Kagan suggests to the proposition that the Constitution forbids gerrymanders that "go too far" and that the only problem is determining which gerrymanders violate that vague standard? Suppose the Court had ruled on the merits that the plaintiffs had not pleaded the violation of any rights cognizable under the Equal Protection Clause, the First Amendment, or any other provision of the Constitution. Would a ruling of that kind have practical consequences that differed in any way from those of the Court's actual ruling? See generally Harrison, *The Political Question Doctrines*, 67 Am.U.L.Rev. 457 (2017) (denying that the political question doctrine is jurisdictional in character).

(2) Judicially Manageable Standards. Consider the suggestion of Fallon, *Judicially Manageable Standards and Constitutional Meaning*, 119 Harv.L.Rev. 1274 (2006), that the term judicially manageable standards is ambiguous. In one usage, it refers to "inputs" to judicial deliberations, such as the First Amendment and the Equal Protection Clause. But when viewed as inputs, many constitutional provisions are too vague to serve as judicially manageable standards. To render them serviceable, the Supreme Court routinely devises tests and formulas of the kind that clutter the landscape of constitutional law, including strict scrutiny, rational basis review, the test for permissible restrictions on speech in a public forum, the test for forbidden racial gerrymanders (as discussed in Rucho), and so forth. In a second sense, the term judicially manageable standards thus refers to the *outputs* of constitutional adjudication or to the products of the Court's own efforts to devise tests or standards that pass muster as judicially manageable. In Rucho, the problem was that no one, in the view of the majority, had devised a constitutionally adequate judicially manageable standard in the output sense. When the Court says that it cannot find or discern judicially manageable standards (in the output sense) to gauge when gerrymanders go too far, does it confess a judicial failure (in comparison with the Court's success in devising tests to identify violations of other constitutional norms)?

(3) Standards for Judging the Judicial Manageability of Standards. Does the Supreme Court have a judicially manageable standard to guide its determinations about which proposed standards of constitutional validity— such as the tests proposed by the lower courts and the dissenting opinion in

Rucho—are judicially manageable? At some point, the demand for further meta-standards must surely come to an end. But how would you reconstruct the Court's reasoning process in concluding that the standards proposed by the Rucho dissenters were not good enough? How would you reconstruct the Court's reasoning processes in concluding—as seems implicit in its conclusion that all challenges to partisan gerrymandering present nonjusticiable political questions—that no judicially manageable standard could possibly emerge in the future? Compare the position taken by Justice Kennedy, concurring in Vieth, finding no judicially manageable standard with which to resolve the case at bar but acknowledging that "in another case a standard might emerge."

In Zivotofsky v. Clinton, Seventh Edition p. 256, the Court determined that problems involving judicially manageable standards that would arise if the judiciary were asked to "decide the political status of Jerusalem" (as part of Israel or not) "dissipate when the issue is recognized to be the more focused one of the constitutionality of" a federal statute that identified Jerusalem as part of Israel. In elaboration, the Court summarized some of the parties' competing arguments of text, history, and precedent, then concluded: "Recitation of these arguments—which sound in familiar principles of constitutional interpretation—is enough to establish that this case does not 'turn on standards that defy judicial application'" (quoting Baker v. Carr, Seventh Edition p. 250). Based on that conclusion, the Court, in an opinion by Chief Justice Roberts, remanded the case to the lower court for decision of the constitutional question on the merits. It did so without pausing to specify the precise test of constitutional validity that the lower court should apply. Why was the Chief Justice so confident that the court could identify a judicially manageable standard in Zivotofsky but equally convinced that no judicially manageable standard could ever emerge in a constitutional challenge to a partisan gerrymander?

(4) Legitimacy. Part of the Court's explanation for its refusal to craft a test for identifying gerrymanders that go too far lies in a role-based aversion to entering what Justice Frankfurter, in Colegrove v. Green, Seventh Edition p. 250, described as a "political thicket." In a familiar articulation of this concern, the Supreme Court would put its legitimacy at risk, by raising questions about whether it is a neutral arbiter, if it were to seek to resolve politically charged disputes without clear criteria for decision. Compare this passage from Chief Justice Roberts' majority opinion, quoting an earlier opinion by Justice Kennedy: "With uncertain limits, intervening courts—even when proceeding with best intentions—would risk assuming political, not legal, responsibility for a process that often produces ill will and distrust." By contrast, Justice Kagan seems more concerned with what might be viewed as the legitimacy of American democratic institutions if incumbent politicians can virtually determine the outcome of future elections by gerrymandering voting districts.

The concept of legitimacy is an elusive one, which can mean different things in different contexts. Should the Justices have made calculations concerning legitimacy (in its various senses) a part of their decisionmaking process? If so, which kinds of legitimacy, and the legitimacy of which institutions, should they weigh most heavily? See generally Fallon, Law and Legitimacy in the Supreme Court (2018) (distinguishing among legal, sociological, and moral legitimacy).

(5) The Division of the Justices. In Rucho v. Common Cause, the five Justices in the majority were all appointed by Republican presidents. The four dissenters were all appointed by Democrats. Should a Justice who was troubled by the possible appearance of partisan division within the Court in a case with such obvious partisan political implications have considered changing his or her vote, otherwise contrary to his or her conscientious beliefs about proper constitutional adjudication, just to avoid that appearance? See Grove, *The Supreme Court's Legitimacy Dilemma*, 132 Harv.L.Rev. 2240 (2019) (discussing considerations that arise when Justices are urged to "vote[ ] in a way that they deem[ ] legally incorrect in order to safeguard the Court's public reputation"). See generally Charles & Fuentes-Rohwer, *Judicial Intervention as Judicial Restraint*, 132 Harv.L.Rev. 236, 271–75 (2018) (arguing that perceptions of the courts as political institutions are seeping from elites to the general public; that abstention from gerrymandering disputes will be viewed "through the lens of partisan polarization"; that gerrymandering is part of the dynamic that produces deepening partisan division and suspicion; and that the Court should intervene to break the cycle).

————

NOTE ON SPECIFIC SUBJECT MATTER AREAS IMPLICATING THE POLITICAL QUESTION DOCTRINE

Page 259. Add at the end of Paragraph (2):

See also Williams, *The "Guarantee" Clause*, 132 Harv.L.Rev. 602 (2018) (maintaining that the "guarantee" language echoed eighteenth-century treaty formulations that would not have been judicially enforceable and concluding that "available evidence regarding the [Guarantee Clause's] original meaning strongly supports" treating disputes under the provision as nonjusticiable).

CHAPTER III

The Original Jurisdiction of the Supreme Court

Introductory Note on the Power of Congress to Regulate the Original Jurisdiction of the Supreme Court

Page 271. Eliminate the last paragraph of Paragraph (4) in light of Franchise Tax Board of California v. Hyatt, 139 S.Ct. 1485 (2019), which overruled Nevada v. Hall, 440 U.S. 410 (1979).

Note on the Original Jurisdiction as an Inappropriate Forum

Page 275. Add at the end of Paragraph (4):

In recent years, Justice Alito and Justice Thomas have challenged the Court's practice of exercising discretion to decline to decide cases within its exclusive original jurisdiction under 28 U.S.C. § 1251(a). See Texas v. California, 141 S.Ct. 1469 (2021) (Alito, J., dissenting, joined by Justice Thomas); Texas v. Pennsylvania, 141 S.Ct. 1230 (2020) (statement by Alito, J., joined by Justice Thomas); Arizona v. California, 140 S.Ct. 684 (2020) (Thomas, J., dissenting, joined by Justice Alito); Nebraska v. Colorado, 577 U.S. 1211 (2016) (Thomas, J., dissenting, joined by Justice Alito). Their opinions together offer four arguments that jurisdiction under § 1251(a) should be viewed as mandatory. First, § 1251(a) states that the Court "*shall have*" exclusive original jurisdiction over all controversies between states, and in no way implies discretion to decline to exercise review. By contrast, when Congress defined the Court's discretionary appellate jurisdiction under § 1254(1) and 28 U.S.C. § 1257(a), it did so clearly by stating that controversies from federal and state courts "*may* be reviewed". Second, 28 U.S.C. § 1332 states that the lower federal courts "shall have original jurisdiction" over certain diverse-party controversies, and lower federal courts in general lack discretion to decline to exercise such jurisdiction on policy grounds. The similar phrase in § 1251(a) should receive a similar construction. Third, since the Court's original jurisdiction over controversies between states is exclusive, the Court's denial of a state's motion for leave to file a bill of complaint under § 1251(a) often leaves the state without any judicial forum to vindicate its claims. Fourth, the concern that mandatory jurisdiction under § 1251(a) would "crowd out considerations of more important matters on [the Court's] appellate docket" is legally irrelevant and, in any case, rests on "a dubious factual premise". Texas v. California, 141 S.Ct. at 1472.

NOTE ON THE SCOPE OF JURISDICTION OVER CASES IN WHICH A STATE IS A PARTY: JURISDICTION ONLY WHEN INDEPENDENTLY CONFERRED BY STATE PARTY STATUS

Page 277. Add at the end of footnote 2:

For a defense and reconciliation of the Court's decisions, see Shelfer, *The Supreme Court's Original Jurisdiction Over Disputes Between the United States and a State*, 66 Buff.L.Rev. 193 (2018). Shelfer argues that Texas v. ICC correctly ruled that original jurisdiction over suits in which a State is a party is bounded by the party status heads of jurisdiction in the first paragraph of Article III, Section 2. But he further contends that disputes between the United States and a State fall within the Court's original jurisdiction because the constitutional framers and ratifiers understood the phrase "Controversies to which the United States shall be a Party" (in the first Paragraph of Section 2, which defines the judicial power generally) to entail "two separate provisions: one over controversies between the United States and a state, and one over other controversies between the United States and an individual or foreign state." The author squares this interpretation with United States v. Texas by arguing that it is best understood to base original jurisdiction not on the presence of a federal question but rather on the implicit grant of jurisdiction over a controversy between a State and the United States.

Page 278. Add a new footnote 3a at the end of the penultimate paragraph of Paragraph (5):

[3a] In Texas v. New Mexico, 138 S.Ct. 954 (2018), the Court allowed the United States to intervene in a case between states to assert a claim under an interstate compact even though the compact conferred on it no right to sue. Texas brought the original jurisdiction suit against New Mexico for alleged violations of the Rio Grande Compact, an agreement among Colorado, New Mexico, and Texas. In a unanimous opinion by Justice Gorsuch, the Court sustained the United States' exception to the Special Master's recommendation that its claim under the compact be dismissed. The Court reasoned that its "unique authority to mold original actions" enabled it to allow the United States to pursue claims that a "normal litigant might not be permitted to pursue in traditional litigation" at least when the government seeks to defend "distinctively federal interests." The United States could assert a claim under the compact, the Court concluded, because of its responsibilities closely related to the compact, because a breach of the compact could jeopardize treaty obligations with Mexico, and because the United States was intervening in an existing action and sought basically the same relief as Texas.

NOTE ON A STATE'S STANDING TO SUE AND ON PARENS PATRIAE STANDING

Page 279. Add a new footnote * at the end of the last paragraph of Section A:

[*] For a recent symposium on state standing that addresses many of the issues in this Note, see Symposium, *Federal Courts, Practice & Procedure: State Standing*, 94 Notre Dame L.Rev. 1883–2158 (2019). Grove, *Foreword: Some Puzzles of State Standing*, 94 Notre Dame L.Rev. 1883 (2019), is a good introduction to the literature on state standing. And Huq, *State Standing's Uncertain Stakes*, 94 Notre Dame L.Rev. 2127 (2019), analyzes the practical consequences of various resolutions of the doctrinal uncertainty in state standing outlined in this Note.

Page 286. Add at the end of footnote 5:

Professor Grove challenges this argument in *When Can a State Sue the United States?*, 101 Cornell L.Rev. 851 (2016). Grove maintains that states are entitled to "special solicitude" in standing analysis only when they "challenge federal action that preempts, or otherwise undermines the enforceability of, state law", but lack standing in cases that question the federal executive branch's compliance with federal law. Professor Nash responds that in areas where other actors lack standing to challenge Executive branch underenforcement, states should have standing under their *parens patriae* authority to protect their constituents. Nash, *Sovereign Preemption State Standing*, 112 Nw.U.L.Rev. 201 (2017). He argues for "sovereign preemption state standing", which would permit states to sue the federal government when it preempts state law in an area but the Executive branch allegedly underenforces the federal law that Congress enacted to address that area.

For other recent commentary on state standing in suits against the federal government, see Woolhandler & Collins, *Reining in State Standing*, 94 Notre Dame L.Rev. 2015 (2019) (arguing that state standing should presumptively be limited to suits involving the state as the object of federal regulation); Mikos, *Standing for Nothing*, 94 Notre Dame L.Rev. 2033 (2019) (arguing against "special solicitude" in standing analysis for states seeking to protect state law and warning that it risks making states "roving constitutional watchdogs" over the federal government); Crocker, *An Organizational Account of State Standing*, 94 Notre Dame L.Rev. 2057 (2019) (arguing for state standing by analogy to organizational plaintiffs); Hessick, *Quasi-Sovereign Standing*, 94 Notre Dame L.Rev. 1927 (2019) (explaining why states should be able to assert their quasi-sovereign interests against the U.S. government, but arguing that Congress should enact prudential limits on state standing); Young, *State Standing and Cooperative Federalism*, 94 Notre Dame L.Rev. 1893 (2019) (defending state standing in federal court lawsuits that challenge national policy as an attractive way for a competent and accountable party to aggregate diffuse claims); Mank & Solimine, *State Standing and National Injunctions*, 94 Notre Dame L.Rev. 1955 (2019) (arguing that state *parens patriae* standing to sue the federal government should be subject to "somewhat relaxed criteria" and proposing several factors that courts should account for before granting nationwide injunctions sought by states); Nash, *State Standing for Nationwide Injunctions Against the Federal Government*, 94 Notre Dame L.Rev. 1985 (2019) (arguing that if standing doctrine generally limits the availability of nationwide injunctions, states typically should not have "special solicitude" to seek such injunctions against the federal government); Davis, *The Private Rights of Public Governments*, 94 Notre Dame L.Rev. 2091 (2019) (mapping private rights model of standing onto state standing and arguing that courts should address questions about special solicitude only in cases where a state lacks standing under rules applicable to private parties); Davis, *The New Public Standing*, 71 Stan.L.Rev. 1229 (2019) (suggesting that courts should be wary of affording states special solicitude to sue the federal government based on financial injuries).

Page 286. Add at the end of Paragraph (4):

The Supreme Court seemed to signal that it was taking an uncertain step away from Massachusetts v. EPA in United States v. Texas, 143 S.Ct. 1964 (2023). In that case, Texas and Louisiana challenged immigration-enforcement guidelines promulgated by the Secretary of the Department of Homeland Security on the ground that they resulted in underenforcement of the Department's duty under two federal statutes to arrest certain criminal noncitizens. The Court rejected the states' standing argument that they suffered financial injury due, for example, to expenditures incurred in incarcerating and supplying healthcare to noncitizens whom the federal government should have arrested. As discussed in greater detail in Chapter 2, p. 16 *supra*, the Court did so based on the principle "that a citizen lacks standing to contest the policies of the prosecuting authority when he himself is neither prosecuted nor threatened with prosecution." 143 S.Ct. at 1970 (quoting Linda R. S. v. Richard D., 410 U.S. 614, 619 (1973)).

The Court did not purport to limit Massachusetts v. EPA. But without mentioning "special solicitude," it stated that "federal courts must remain mindful of bedrock Article III constraints in cases brought by States against an executive agency or officer", and added that "when a State asserts * * * that a federal law has produced only [indirect effects on state revenues or state spending], the State's claim for standing can become more attenuated", *id.* at 1972 n.3. It also distinguished Massachusetts v. EPA on the ground that it involved "a challenge to the denial of a statutorily authorized petition for rulemaking, not a challenge to an exercise of the Executive's enforcement discretion", *id.* at 1975 n.6. Are these propositions fully consistent with Massachusetts v. EPA? Both the concurring and dissenting opinions thought not. See *id.* at 1977 (Gorsuch, J., concurring in the judgment) (noting that "it's hard not to wonder why the Court says nothing about 'special solicitude' in this case"); *id.* at 1997 (Alito, J., dissenting) (arguing that the "reasoning in [Massachusetts v. EPA] applies with at least equal force in the case at hand").

————

NOTE ON THE WAR CRIMES CASES

Page 294. Replace Paragraph (5) with the following:

(5) Review of Military Tribunals and of Other Non-Article III Federal Tribunals. The Supreme Court clarified some of these issues in Ortiz v. United States, 138 S.Ct. 2165 (2018), p. 76, *infra*, which held that Article III permits direct Supreme Court review of the decisions of the United States Court of Appeals for the Armed Forces (CAAF). The CAAF is a "court of record" that reviews decisions of the four appellate courts for the armed services, which, in turn, review decisions by trial-level courts martial. The CAAF is not an Article III court because its members lack tenure and salary protections. Rather, it is located within the Executive branch.

In an opinion by Justice Kagan, the Court acknowledged that review of CAAF decisions cannot rest on its original jurisdiction because the CAAF does not resolve cases that affect ambassadors, public ministers or consuls, or that involve a State party, as Article III, § 2, cl. 2, requires. But the Court ruled that such review is an exercise of appellate jurisdiction because it involves a federal question and satisfies (in Marbury's words) the "essential criterion of appellate jurisdiction" since "it revises and corrects the proceedings in a cause already instituted, and does not create that cause." The Court rejected an argument by an amicus that courts located in the Executive branch are akin to Secretary of State James Madison, over whose decision the Court in Marbury held it lacked appellate jurisdiction. In contrast with Madison, the CAAF's "essential character" is "judicial" and thus is similar to the other non-Article III courts—state courts, territorial courts and District of Columbia courts—over which the Court has long exercised appellate jurisdiction. The Court distinguished Ex parte Vallandigham, 68 U.S. 243 (1864), which held that neither section 14 of the First Judiciary Act nor Article III permitted the Supreme Court to entertain a petition for a writ of certiorari directly from a military commission that had convicted a prisoner of disloyalty during the Civil War. In contrast with the CAAF, that commission lacked "judicial character" because it was created and controlled entirely by a Union general and thus was "more an adjunct to a general than a real court". Justice Alito, joined by Justice Gorsuch, dissented.

What are Ortiz's implications for the Supreme Court's appellate jurisdiction over other types of military courts? Does Ortiz provide a clearer rationale for Hirota, Seventh Edition p. 292, since the International Military Tribunal of the Far East, similar to the commission in Vallandigham but unlike the CAAF, was "set up by General MacArthur as the agent of the Allied Powers"? What if General MacArthur had established an appellate court independent of his command to review Tribunal decisions?

CHAPTER IV

CONGRESSIONAL CONTROL OF THE DISTRIBUTION OF JUDICIAL POWER AMONG FEDERAL AND STATE COURTS

---

1. CONGRESSIONAL REGULATION OF FEDERAL JURISDICTION

INTRODUCTORY NOTE ON CONGRESSIONAL POWER OVER THE JURISDICTION OF THE ARTICLE III COURTS

Page 298. Add at the end of footnote 9:

Recent public deliberations on jurisdiction stripping align with Grove's view that such proposals are likely to face political headwinds. In 2021, President Joseph R. Biden Jr. established a Presidential Commission on the Supreme Court of the United States to consider the "role and operation of the Supreme Court in our constitutional system" and to analyze arguments "for and against Supreme Court reform, including an appraisal of the merits and legality of particular reform proposals." See Presidential Commission on the Supreme Court of the United States, Final Report *i* (2021) (https://www.whitehouse.gov/wp-content/uploads/2021/12/SCOTUS-Report-Final-12.8.21-1.pdf). Declining to take a position on prominent jurisdiction stripping proposals and noting disagreement among its members, the Commission argued that withdrawing Supreme Court jurisdiction over particular issues—such as the validity of a wealth tax or abortion legislation—would risk creating disuniformity in the definition of federal rights or might effectively leave the determination of such rights to a single lower court (given the availability of nationwide injunctions). See *id.* at 161–62, The Commission added that limiting jurisdiction stripping to the Supreme Court (as opposed to also stripping jurisdiction from lower courts, federal and state) would do relatively little to enhance democratic participation in rights definition. See *id.* at 160. The Commission also concluded that jurisdiction-stripping legislation "would likely trigger constitutional challenges," some of which the Court might deem meritorious. *Id.* at 169. The likelihood of success of such challenges, the Commission further stated, would diminish if Congress left open alternative avenues of judicial review, adding that this approach would then raise the concerns noted above. See *id.* For an article defending jurisdiction stripping and other "disempowering" measures as a means of advancing progressive constitutional ends, see Doerfler & Moyn, *Democratizing the Supreme Court*, 109 Cal.L.Rev. 1703 (2021).

Page 300. Add at the end of footnote 15:

For a broad critique of existing empirical studies of parity, see McBride, *Parity as Comparative Capacity: A New Empirics of the Parity Debate*, 90 U.Cin.L.Rev. 68 (2021).

Page 303. Add a new footnote 25 at the end of the carryover paragraph:

25 Echoing some of these concerns about elected state judges, the Court in Williams-Yulee v. Florida Bar, 575 U.S. 433 (2015) (5–4), rejected a First Amendment challenge to Florida's ban on the solicitation of campaign funds by candidates for state judicial office. Distancing the Court from its earlier decision in Republican Party of Minnesota v. White, Seventh Edition p. 302, Chief Justice Roberts' opinion for the Court in Williams-Yulee applied strict scrutiny and held

(a) that Florida has a compelling governmental interest in preserving public confidence in the neutrality of the state's judicial officers and (b) that the state's limit on personal solicitation is narrowly tailored to that interest.

In a separate opinion, Justice Ginsburg reiterated her position that, in light of the institutional differences between politicians and judges, states should generally have broader latitude to regulate judicial elections and that the Court should not apply strict scrutiny to such regulation. In a dissent joined by Justice Thomas, Justice Scalia assumed that the state had a compelling interest in the appearance of judicial neutrality but argued that the personal solicitation ban was insufficiently tailored to that interest. In a separate dissent, Justice Kennedy emphasized the dangers of treating a judicial election differently from other elections for First Amendment purposes. Justice Alito also dissented, arguing that the ban was not narrowly tailored.

NOTE ON THE POWER OF CONGRESS TO LIMIT THE JURISDICTION OF FEDERAL COURTS

Page 307. Add at the end of footnote 1:

See also Dow, *Is the "Arising Under" Jurisdictional Grant in Article III Self-Executing?*, 25 Wm. & Mary Bill Rts.J. 1, 10 (2016) (arguing that Professor Bator's argument is "perfectly question-begging" and that "such evidence as there is of original intent on this question reveals that the Framers themselves did not believe Congress would enjoy the power Bator" ascribed to the Madisonian Compromise).

Page 312. Add a new footnote 9a at the end of the third paragraph of Paragraph (5):

[9a] For a critical reading of Lauf, see Redish, *Constitutional Remedies as Constitutional Law*, 62 B.C.L.Rev. 1865 (2021).

Page 314. Add at the end of the first paragraph in footnote 15:

Further, based on his survey of English constitutional practice, Professor Birk found that when Parliament made "exceptions" or "exemptions" to the jurisdiction of English and Scottish "supreme courts" at common law, it did not divest the courts of power to correct major interpretive errors, denials of due process, or transgressions of jurisdictional limits. Consistent with that history, Birk infers that the Founders' understanding of the power granted Congress by the Exceptions Clause would not readily have accommodated exceptions denying the Supreme Court of the United States power to exercise such supervisory authority over inferior courts. See Birk, *The Common-Law Exceptions Clause: Congressional Control of Supreme Court Appellate Jurisdiction in Light of British Precedent*, 63 Vill.L.Rev. 189 (2018).

Page 315. Add a new footnote 15a at the end of the penultimate paragraph:

[15a] For another elaboration and defense of Hart's view, see Monaghan, *Jurisdiction Stripping Circa 2020: What the Dialogue (Still) Has to Teach Us*, 69 Duke L.J. 1 (2020). Monaghan proposes that the Court should "excise subject-matter limitations on its appellate jurisdiction when a substantial, undefended purpose of such jurisdiction-stripping legislation is to limit the Court's ability to consider a properly preserved constitutional claim." He grounds this conclusion in "Marbury v. Madison's emphasis on limited government and rule-of-law principles", arguing that "the line of our constitutional development" has given the Court a "unique and essential role in maintaining the idea of the limited government contemplated by the written 1789 Constitution." Responding to Monaghan, Sprigman, *Congress's Article III Power and the Process of Constitutional Change*, 95 N.Y.U.L.Rev. 1778 (2020), argues that Congress's explicit and extensive "Article III power" over federal court jurisdiction enables it, in effect, to "prescribe, by ordinary legislation, constitutional rules in areas where the meaning of the Constitution is unsettled" or even to "displace otherwise settled constitutional rules by ordinary legislation." Thus, "the real barriers to Congress's exercise of its power . . . are not constitutional but rather political and prudential."

Page 315. Add at the end of the second paragraph in footnote 16:

Grove, *Article III in the Political Branches*, 90 Notre Dame L.Rev. 1835 (2015), shows that, at least since McCardle, Congress and the President have fairly consistently rejected proposals under the Exceptions Clause to strip Supreme Court jurisdiction over specific subject areas. Professor Grove argues, however, that the political branches' decisions *not* to enact legislation may shed little light on the validity of jurisdiction stripping because it is difficult to know whether and to what extent such decisions reflect political rather than constitutional judgments about jurisdiction stripping. She adds that "the different institutional makeup and capacities of the courts" may position them better than the political branches to protect the "individual and minority rights" that jurisdiction stripping puts at risk. If constitutional text and history are as inconclusive as Frost and Grove suggest, would the judicial branch ever be justified in displacing a legislative judgment to strip Supreme Court jurisdiction? What role if any should an accumulated historical gloss on the meaning of Article III or the development of uncodified constitutional conventions about judicial independence play in analyzing such questions? See, *e.g.*, Bradley & Siegel, *Historical Gloss, Constitutional Conventions, and the Judicial Separation of Powers*, 105 Geo.L.J. 255 (2017) (arguing that such considerations have importantly influenced the political defeat or rejection of important jurisdiction-stripping proposals in the past century). For an argument that the Exceptions Clause responded to significant concerns that the grant of appellate jurisdiction would authorize the Court to revisit jury verdicts and that the clause thus provided robust constitutional authority to limit appellate review, see Lee, *Article IX, Article III, and the First Congress: The Original Constitutional Plan for the Federal Courts, 1787–1792*, 89 Fordham L.Rev. 1895, 1935–36 (2021).

Page 318. Add a new footnote 20a at the end of the first sentence in Paragraph (5):

[20a] In contrast, Huq, *The Constitutional Law of Agenda Control*, 104 Cal.L.Rev. 1401 (2016), argues that, "in the absence of a definitive statement to the contrary from the Court, it would seem that the text of Article III vests the legislature with tolerably broad authority to determine which constitutional questions of national import end up on the judiciary's agenda."

Page 321. Add the following at the end of footnote 26:

Finally, Professor Walsh identifies yet another potentially significant gap in Section 25's coverage, arguing that the text of Section 25, read in its historical context, does not reach criminal cases. See Walsh, *In the Beginning There Was None: Supreme Court Review of State Criminal Prosecutions*, 90 Notre Dame L.Rev. 1867 (2015). How heavy is Professor Walsh's burden of persuasion, given the contrary view about Section 25 expressed by Chief Justice Marshall's opinion for the Court in Cohens v. Virginia, 19 U.S. (6 Wheat.) 264 (1821)?

Page 324. Add in place of the last paragraph in Paragraph (D)(2):

To similar effect is Bank Markazi v. Peterson, 578 U.S. 212 (2016) (6–2), in which the Court rejected a challenge under United States v. Klein, Seventh Edition p. 323, to a federal statute that sought to resolve a dispute over the availability of assets for the execution of certain judgments. Bank Markazi arose out of judgments entered against the Republic of Iran for terrorism-related harms under a "terrorism exception" to the Foreign Sovereign Immunities Act (FSIA). Sixteen groups of respondents, consisting of more than 1,000 plaintiffs, moved to enforce those judgments in consolidated proceedings in the U.S. District Court in the Southern District of New York. Pursuant to a 2002 statute that provides for the execution of judgments obtained under the terrorism exception, the enforcement proceedings focused on certain assets in a New York bank account that, according to respondents, was owned by Bank Markazi, Iran's central bank. Petitioners contested the claim that the assets in question belonged to the Bank. In light of that dispute, a provision in the Iran Threat Reduction and Syria Human Rights Act of 2012, 22 U.S.C. § 8772, provided that, if the district court made several specified findings, it could enforce respondents' underlying judgments against the financial assets "that are identified in and the subject of * * * Case No. 10 Civ. 4518 (BSJ) (GWG)."

Petitioners, invoking Klein, argued that § 8772 violated the separation of powers. They contended, in relevant part, that Congress invaded the judicial function by imposing a rule of decision on the district court in a pending case. Relying on Robertson v. Seattle Audubon Soc'y, Seventh Edition p. 324, Justice Ginsburg's opinion for the Court rejected petitioners' contention, drawing a distinction between prescribing rules of decision and " 'amend[ing] applicable law.' " The Court stressed that " 'congressional power to make valid statutes retroactively applicable to pending cases has often been recognized' " (quoting the Seventh Edition p. 324). In this instance, the Court held, Congress had merely amended existing law. That conclusion, moreover, was unaffected by the fact that Congress specified the docket number of the proceedings to which its new policy applied.

In a dissent joined by Justice Sotomayor, Chief Justice Roberts argued that Congress rather than the judiciary had, in reality, decided the case. The dissent reasoned that if the legislature "targeted [the] specific case and eliminated [one party's] specific defenses so as to ensure [the other's] victory," then the judiciary "presided over [a] *fait accompli*" rather than actually deciding the case. To the dissent, § 8772 was not different from "a law saying 'respondents win.' " Such a statute, according to the Chief Justice, contradicted the historical context and purpose of the Founders' decision to establish an independent judiciary.

In Patchak v. Zinke, 138 S.Ct. 897 (2018), the Court divided (4–2–3) again over Klein's implications for statutory questions. The case arose out of Patchak's challenge to a decision by the Secretary of the Interior under the Indian Reorganization Act (IRA), 25 U.S.C. § 5108, to acquire a tract of land, known as the Bradley Property, to be held in trust for the Match-E-Be-Nash-She-Wish Band of Pottawatomi Indians. The Band had requested that the Secretary take into trust the Bradley Property so that the Band could build a casino on the site. In Match-E-Be-Nash-She-Wish Band of Pottawatomi Indians v. Patchak, 567 U.S. 209, 224–28 (2012), the Supreme Court had held that Patchak, who owns nearby land that would be affected by the use to which the land in question was to be put, had prudential standing to challenge the Secretary's decision under the Administrative Procedure Act.

Subsequently, Congress passed the Gun Lake Trust Land Reaffirmation Act (Gun Lake Act), Pub.L.No. 113–179, 128 Stat. 1913 (2014), to settle the status of the Bradley Property. Section 2(a) of the Act stated that the Bradley Property "is reaffirmed as trust land, and the actions of the Secretary of the Interior in taking that land into trust are ratified and confirmed." Section 2(b) stated that, "[n]otwithstanding any other provision of law, an action (including an action pending in a Federal court as of the date of enactment of this Act) relating to the land described [herein] shall not be filed or maintained in a Federal court and shall be promptly dismissed."

In a plurality opinion, Justice Thomas, joined by Justices Breyer, Alito, and Kagan, rejected Patchak's claim that the Gun Lake Act violated Article III. Invoking Robertson v. Seattle Audubon Society, Seventh Edition p. 324, the plurality concluded that jurisdiction-stripping statutes run afoul of Article III if they seek to "compel[ ] . . . findings or results under old law", but not if they create new law. The plurality ruled that the Gun Lake Act *changed* the law respecting federal jurisdiction, a permissible exercise of legislative power under Article I, § 8, and Article III, § 1. The plurality then distinguished United States v. Klein, Seventh Edition p. 323, on the ground that the statute at issue there had sought to use jurisdiction to produce an outcome indirectly that Congress could not produce directly. In Klein, the plurality explained, "Congress had no authority to declare that pardons are not evidence of loyalty, so it could not achieve the same result by stripping jurisdiction whenever claimants cited pardons as evidence of loyalty." The Gun Lake Act, by contrast, permissibly "create[d] new law for suits relating to the Bradley Property".

In an opinion concurring in the judgment, Justice Ginsburg, joined by Justice Sotomayor, reasoned that the Gun Lake Act reflected a permissible decision by Congress to retract a previously granted waiver of sovereign immunity by the United States.

In dissent, Chief Justice Roberts, joined by Justices Kennedy and Gorsuch, analogized the Gun Lake Act to a statute "directing that, in the hypothetical pending case of Smith v. Jones, 'Smith wins.' " Noting that the Framers designed Article III in reaction to the familiar state practice of legislative revision of judgments, the dissent deemed it dispositive that, in its view, Congress had enacted the Gun Lake Act in order to direct an outcome in the pending case. "Because the Legislature has no authority to direct entry of judgment for a party," the Chief Justice stated, "it cannot achieve the same result by stripping jurisdiction over a particular proceeding."[29a]

The plurality expressed doubt that the constitutionality of jurisdiction-stripping should turn upon the number of cases to which a statute applied when enacted or upon concerns about an "unexpressed [legislative] motive[ ]" to resolve a particular piece of litigation. In any case, the plurality found it sufficient that the Gun Lake Act applied to all potential suits relating to the Bradley Property, and not just the case before it.

Does Klein now stand largely (or only) for the proposition that Congress cannot use jurisdiction to achieve indirectly a disposition that it could not achieve directly under the Constitution?

[29a] To similar effect, see, for example, Redish, *Federal Judicial Independence: Constitutional and Political Perspectives*, 46 Mercer L.Rev. 697, 718–21 (1995) (arguing that Congress should not be able to dictate the outcome of a case without changing applicable law).

Page 325. Add at the end of footnote 31:

For a somewhat different take on Klein, see Zoldan, *The Klein Rule of Decision Puzzle and the Self-Dealing Solution*, 74 Wash. & Lee L.Rev. 2133 (2017), which argues that Klein is best understood as the instantiation of the background constitutional principle that Congress may not engage in self-dealing—in this case, by gerrymandering jurisdiction to favor the government and disfavor a claimant against the public fisc.

NOTE ON PRECLUSION OF ALL JUDICIAL REVIEW AND ON THE RIGHT TO SEEK JUDICIAL REDRESS

Page 329. Add at the end of Paragraph (2):

Cf. Cuozzo Speed Technologies, LLC v. Lee, 579 U.S. 261, (2016) (reserving the question whether a statute barring judicial review of certain decisions by the Director of the Patent Office applies to constitutional questions).

Page 334. Add a new footnote 6a at the end of the first paragraph of Paragraph (6):

[6a] In light of Whole Woman's Health v. Jackson, 142 S.Ct. 522 (2021) (see pp. 126–139, *infra*), Armstrong v. Exceptional Child Center, Inc., 575 U.S. 320 (2015) (see Seventh Edition pp. 745, note 12, & pp. 845, 934, 1012–1013), and other Roberts Court decisions, Professor Fallon argues that the Court has shown "increased skepticism about the constitutional necessity of remedies for constitutional violations." See Fallon, *Constitutional Remedies: In One Era and Out the Other*, 136 Harv.L.Rev. 1300, 1325 (2023). Fallon argues that this apparent development runs counter to longstanding constitutional practice and the founding generation's assumption that it was adopting constitutional rights against a rich remedial backdrop.

Page 335. Add a new footnote 8 at the end of Paragraph (6):

[8] Bracketing the question of due process constraints, Professor Dorf suggests that the Necessary and Proper Clause may give Congress power to strip state and federal court jurisdiction over the constitutionality of federal but not state statutes. See Dorf, *Congressional Power to Strip State Courts of Jurisdiction*, 97 Tex.L.Rev. 1 (2018).

Page 335. Add at the end of Paragraph (7):

For the argument that Congress's greater power to forgo creating federal statutory rights altogether includes the lesser power to create such rights but omit a judicial enforcement mechanism, see Dorf, n. 8, *supra*, at 16–22.

FURTHER NOTE ON PRECLUSION OF ALL JUDICIAL REVIEW AND ON THE RIGHT TO SEEK JUDICIAL REDRESS: HABEAS CORPUS AND THE SUSPENSION CLAUSE

Page 337. Add at the end of footnote 2:

In response to the St. Cyr decision, Congress added a "limited review provision" to the INA that restricted judicial review of removal orders in certain cases to "constitutional claims or questions of law". 8 U.S.C. § 1252(a)(2)(D). In Guerrero-Lasprilla v. Barr, 140 S.Ct. 1062 (2020), the Court, per Justice Breyer, held that the phrase "questions of law" permits judicial review of "the application of a legal standard to undisputed or established facts." The Court reached this conclusion based on textual interpretation, the "strong presumption" favoring judicial review of administrative action, and legislative history suggesting that Congress intended to provide an adequate substitute for habeas review. This analysis elicited a strong dissent by Justice Thomas, joined in part by Justice Alito, who argued that "the majority effectively nullifies a jurisdiction-stripping statute, expanding the scope of judicial review well past the boundaries set by Congress."

In an opinion for a 5–4 Court in Patel v. Garland, 142 S.Ct. 1614 (2022), Justice Barrett concluded that Section 1252(a)(2)(D) did not disturb the statute's underlying preclusion of review of questions of fact by immigration judges in petitions for discretionary relief from removal. See 8 U.S.C. § 1252(a)(2)(B). Treating the question as a straightforward one of statutory interpretation, Justice Barrett emphasized that by excluding "constitutional claims or questions of law" from the preclusion provision, subsection (D) "must have left *something* within the rule [of preclusion]" and that the "remaining category is questions of fact." In a dissent joined by Justices Breyer, Sotomayor, and Kagan, Justice Gorsuch disagreed with the majority's reading of the statute, arguing that the Court's analysis did not sufficiently credit the presumption of reviewability of administrative action. This failure, Justice Gorsuch said, negated "the law's general rule guaranteeing individuals the chance to seek judicial review to correct obvious bureaucratic missteps."

If precluding review of questions of law in removal cases raises constitutional concerns, why doesn't preclusion of review of questions of fact raise similar questions? Should it matter, for these purposes, whether the petitioner alleges an "egregious" error of fact?

Page 338. Strike the second paragraph of footnote 5.

Page 338. Add at the end of Paragraph (2):

In Department of Homeland Security v. Thuraissigiam, 140 S.Ct. 1959 (2020), the Supreme Court rejected Suspension Clause and due process challenges to restrictions on the ability of an asylum seeker to obtain review of expedited administrative removal proceedings. Petitioner crossed the border clandestinely, and a border patrol agent apprehended him within 25 yards of the border. Once in government custody, petitioner sought asylum in the administrative proceedings that Congress prescribed, but he failed to convince various immigration officials that he had a "credible fear of persecution" upon return to his native country. A different finding on the "credible fear" determination would have spared him "expedited removal" and afforded him additional procedural opportunities to seek asylum in the United States. After an Immigration Judge approved petitioner's removal from the country, petitioner sought a writ of habeas corpus in federal court, contending that he satisfied the credible fear test and that he had been denied a fair hearing. Challenging the various provisions in IIRIRA that purported to restrict federal court review of his case,[5a] petitioner requested a new opportunity to present his asylum claim before administrative officials.

Justice Alito's opinion for the Court (joined by Chief Justice Roberts and Justices Thomas, Gorsuch, and Kavanaugh) analyzed the Suspension Clause claim against the backdrop of the understanding of the Clause that existed in 1789. The Court reasoned that habeas at the time of the Founding was "a means to secure *release* from unlawful detention" and did not extend to an invocation of the writ, like petitioner's, "to achieve an entirely different end, namely, to obtain additional administrative review of his asylum claim and ultimately to obtain authorization to stay in this country."[5b] The Court explained that the principle embraced by St. Cyr—that "the writ could be invoked by aliens already in the country who were held in custody pending

---

[5a] Section 1252(e)(2) provides for habeas review in limited circumstances: first, to ascertain "whether the petitioner is an alien"; second, "whether the petitioner was ordered removed"; and third, whether the petitioner has already been granted lawful entry to the United States. 8 U.S.C. §§ 1252(e)(2)(A)–(C). Section 1252(a)(2)(A)(iii) otherwise provides that "[n]otwithstanding any other provision of law (statutory or nonstatutory), including section 2241 of Title 28, or any other habeas corpus provision * * * no court shall have jurisdiction to review * * * [a] determination made [with respect to a credible fear claim]".

[5b] How does the Court's emphasis on the relief sought by Thuraissigiam compare to the Court's treatment of the remedy sought in Boumediene v. Bush, Seventh Edition pp. 338–341, 1224–1236, 1249–1258? There, the Court remanded the habeas cases to the lower courts for expanded proceedings within which detainees held at Guantanamo Bay could challenge their classifications as enemy combatants in the War on Terror. And how does the Court's methodology compare in the two cases? In Boumediene, the Court said that it "has been careful not to foreclose the possibility that the protections of the Suspension Clause have expanded along with post-1789 developments" (citing St. Cyr, 533 U.S. at 300–01). For further discussion, see pp. 159–162, *infra.*

deportation"—could not help petitioner, who was seeking *entry* into the United States. As for petitioner's due process argument, the Court noted that "[w]hile aliens who have established connections in this country have due process rights in deportation proceedings, the Court long ago held that Congress is entitled to set the conditions for an alien's lawful entry into this country and that, as a result, an alien at the threshold of initial entry cannot claim any greater rights under the Due Process Clause (citing Nishimura Ekiu v. United States, 142 U.S. 651, 660 (1892))." Because petitioner had "attempted to enter the country illegally and was apprehended just 25 yards from the border", the Court held, he "has no entitlement to procedural rights other than those afforded by statute." That he was actually taken into custody on United States soil, accordingly, was of no moment to the Court's analysis in light of Congress's "plenary authority to decide which aliens to admit" (citing Nishimura Ekiu, 142 U.S. at 659), and earlier holdings providing that "even those paroled elsewhere in the country for years pending removal * * * are 'treated' for due process purposes 'as if stopped at the border' " (quoting Shaughnessy v. United States ex rel. Mezei, 345 U.S. 206, 215 (1953)).

Justice Thomas wrote a concurring opinion "to address the original meaning of the Suspension Clause". He argued that the expedited removal procedures bore "little resemblance to a suspension as that term was understood at the founding", since they did "not allow the executive to detain based on mere suspicion of a crime or dangerousness." Justice Breyer, joined by Justice Ginsburg, concurred in the judgment. The concurring Justices concluded that the statutory scheme was constitutional as applied to petitioner. They emphasized petitioner's "status" as akin to one stopped at the border and opined that "[t]o interpret the Suspension Clause as insisting upon habeas review of these claims would require, by constitutional command, that the habeas court make indeterminate and highly record-intensive judgments on matters of degree." Finding no precedent "suggesting that the Suspension Clause demands parsing procedural compliance at so granular a level", they concluded that the expedited removal procedures were constitutional as applied here.

Justice Sotomayor, joined by Justice Kagan, dissented. The dissent maintained that the Court had long heard "claims indistinguishable from those" raised by petitioner. Characterizing petitioner's claims as raising both mixed questions of law and fact and legal challenges to "procedural defects" in the administrative procedures Congress prescribed, the dissent argued that the Constitution required judicial review. More generally, the dissent took issue with the majority's fixation upon 1789 to frame its analysis, pointing out that no analogous immigration restrictions were then in existence. Finally, in analyzing petitioner's claims under the Due Process Clause, Justice Sotomayor emphasized that he "was actually within the territorial limits of the United States" when captured, a fact that in her view raised a host of questions as to just how far the majority's holding would sweep in future cases.

For additional discussion of Thuraissigiam, see pp. 168, 171–174., *infra*.

2. CONGRESSIONAL AUTHORITY TO ALLOCATE JUDICIAL POWER TO NON-ARTICLE III FEDERAL TRIBUNALS

NOTE ON CROWELL V. BENSON AND ADMINISTRATIVE ADJUDICATION

Page 354. Add at the end of footnote 5:

Recent scholarship, including a subsequent article by Professor Nelson, have introduced new complexities to this dichotomy. See, *e.g.*, Ablavsky, *Getting Public Rights Wrong: The Lost History of the Private Land Claims*, 74 Stan.L.Rev. 277 (2022) (arguing that early historical practice contemplated the permissibility of administrative adjudication of certain private land claims); Nelson, *Vested Rights, "Franchises", and the Separation of Powers*, 169 U.Pa.L.Rev. 1429 (2021) (explaining that his earlier article had defined the category of "privileges" too broadly by including certain franchises that could not be challenged without judicial process).

Page 356. Add a new footnote 5a at the end of Paragraph (5)(a):

[5a] Justice Thomas has suggested that, in cases of private right, administrative agencies may not make factual findings if subject only to deferential judicial review. See Axon Enter., Inc. v. FTC, 143 S.Ct. 890, 910 (2023) (Thomas, J., concurring) (arguing that factual finding lies "at the core of judicial power"). See also B & B Hardware, Inc. v. Hargis Industries, Inc., 575 U.S. 138, 171 (2015) (Thomas, J., dissenting) ("Because federal administrative agencies are part of the Executive Branch, it is not clear that they have power to adjudicate claims involving core private rights."). How significantly would acceptance of Justice Thomas's position alter the work of the administrative state? Do private rights constitute much of the agencies' business?

Page 357. Add at the end of footnote 6:

In recent years, moreover, several of the Justices have questioned whether the Chevron doctrine comports with the requirements of separation of powers and with the judiciary's law declaration function. See PDR Network, LLC v. Carlton & Harris Chiropractic, Inc., 139 S.Ct. 2051, 2057 (2019) (Thomas, J., concurring in the judgment); BNSF Railway Co. v. Loos, 139 S.Ct. 893, 908–09 (2019) (Gorsuch, J., dissenting); Pereira v. Sessions, 138 S.Ct. 2105, 2121 (2018) (Kennedy, J., concurring); Michigan v. EPA, 576 U.S. 743, 760–764 (2015) (Thomas, J., concurring). See also Buffington v. McDonough, 143 S.Ct. 14 (2022) (Gorsuch, J., dissenting in the denial of certiorari). Near the end of October Term 2022, the Court granted certiorari on a petition presenting the following question: "Whether the Court should overrule Chevron or at least clarify that statutory silence concerning controversial powers expressly but narrowly granted elsewhere in the statute does not constitute an ambiguity requiring deference to the agency." Loper Bright Enterprises v. Raimondo, 45 F.4th 359 (D.C.Cir.2022), cert. granted, 143 S.Ct. ___ (May 1, 2023) (No. 22-451).

Page 358. Add a new footnote 6a at the end of Paragraph (5)(c):

[6a] For the argument that due process and Article III considerations justify the judiciary's exercise of meaningful constitutional fact review of administrative decisions, see Redish & Gohl, *The Wandering Doctrine of Constitutional Fact*, 59 Ariz.L.Rev. 289 (2017).

INTRODUCTORY NOTE ON LEGISLATIVE COURTS

Page 362. Add at the end of Paragraph (2)(a):

For an article contending that Canter provides an inapt analogy for the historically and constitutionally unique status of the District of Columbia, see Durling, *The District of Columbia and Article III*, 107 Geo.L.J. 1205 (2019).

Page 362. Add at the end of footnote 3:

For an article questioning the textual and historical basis for the Court's broad acceptance of military tribunals, see Vladeck, *Military Courts and Article III*, 103 Geo.L.J. 933 (2015) (proposing a limiting principle that authorizes military courts only in contexts in which "established norms of foreign and international practice" justify their use).

Page 363. Add in place of Paragraph (3):

(3) The Constitutional Status of Non-Article III Courts. How court-like are legislative courts despite their lack of Article III status? Certainly, legislative courts sometimes handle Article III business. Territorial courts (and the D.C. local courts), for example, hear diversity and federal question cases, and American Ins. Co. v. Canter, Seventh Edition p. 362, was an admiralty case. Territorial courts, the D.C. local courts, and courts martial adjudicate criminal cases—matters that only a court, and not an administrative agency, could properly hear. Indeed, the Court has long acknowledged that, where historical exceptions to Article III govern, legislative courts can properly hear Article III business even though their judges do not have life tenure and salary protection. See Glidden Co. v. Zdanok, 370 U.S. 530, 549–51 (1962) (opinion of Harlan, J.).

In Ortiz v. United States, 138 S.Ct. 2165 (2018), the Court made clear that when legislative courts hear such cases, they operate as courts for purposes of Supreme Court review. At issue was whether the Supreme Court could exercise appellate jurisdiction over the final judgment of the Court of Appeals for the Armed Forces (CAAF)—a non-Article III tribunal that reviews judgments of courts-martial in criminal cases. In Marbury v. Madison, Seventh Edition p. 59, Chief Justice Marshall's opinion for the Court established that "the essential criterion of appellate jurisdiction" is "that it revises and corrects the proceedings in a cause already instituted, and does not create that cause." In Ortiz, an amicus contended that, because the CAAF is in reality an adjudicative body within the Executive Branch—and not an Article III court—appellate jurisdiction did not lie under the criterion set forth in Marbury.

In an opinion for a divided (7–2) Court, Justice Kagan noted that courts-martial and military courts possess a judicial "character" that gives them a certain "*court*-likeness", even if they are not Article III courts. She reasoned that military courts exercise a "vast swath" of jurisdiction over criminal offenses that overlaps with the jurisdiction of federal and state courts; impose "terms of imprisonment and capital punishment" upon service members; render judgments that carry res judicata effect; and feature an appellate process that functions much like that of ordinary courts. Although military judges lack life tenure and salary protection, Justice Kagan emphasized that the tradition of non-Article III courts-martial goes back to the beginning of the Republic. She noted, moreover, that in United States v. Coe, 155 U.S. 76 (1894), the Court upheld its appellate jurisdiction over the judgments of territorial courts, even though they are not Article III tribunals. In other cases, moreover, the Court had uncontroversially exercised appellate jurisdiction over judgments of the non-Article III D.C. local courts. In her view, the petition for a writ of certiorari to the CAAF was appellate because it asked the Court to revise the judgment in a case instituted "in a judicial system recognized since the founding as competent to render the most serious decisions."

In dissent, Justice Alito, joined by Justice Gorsuch, concluded that Article III authorized the Court to exercise appellate review only of an exercise of the judicial power. In the dissent's view, courts-martial "have always been understood to be Executive Branch entities that help the President, as Commander in Chief, to discipline the Armed Forces." According to Justice Alito, "Executive Branch adjudications . . . do not give rise to 'cases' that Article III grants us appellate jurisdiction to review, precisely because officers of the Executive Branch cannot lawfully be vested with judicial power." The dissent distinguished courts-martial from territorial and D.C. local courts on the ground that the latter reflect Congress's "unique authority to create governments for the Territories and the District of Columbia and to confer on the various branches of those governments powers that are distinct from the legislative, executive, and judicial power of the United States."[8]

If Congress restyled the NLRB as the National Labor Relations Court, could Congress provide for direct Supreme Court review of the resulting adjudications? And if the Supreme Court could review directly a decision of the NLRB, could it also review directly a decision made by a single federal official, as when Secretary of State Madison "adjudicated" Marbury's claim that he was entitled to his commission?

[8] Justice Alito's dissent finds support in Baude, *Adjudication Outside Article III*, 133 Harv.L.Rev. 1511 (2020). Baude argues that whether a tribunal's exercise of power is consistent with Article III's vesting of "judicial power" in the Supreme Court and lower federal courts should not turn on the form of adjudication, since adversary presentation of issues, and the application of law to fact, are not processes limited to Article III courts. Instead, the relevant inquiry should focus on the type of power the tribunal possesses, and whether it purports to exercise the "judicial Power of the United States". Applying this framework, Baude concludes that the majority in Ortiz was wrong, and Justice Alito was right, because "[m]ilitary tribunals may have judicial *character*," but they exercise executive rather than "judicial *power*."

FURTHER NOTE ON LEGISLATIVE COURTS

Page 384. Add at the end of footnote 4:

Baude, *Adjudication Outside Article III*, 133 Harv.L.Rev. 1511 (2020), argues that the public rights framework was inappropriate in Stern and Northern Pipeline for a different reason: "The public rights doctrine is a principle of executive power. But today's bankruptcy courts have not been vested with executive power. Their judges are appointed by Article III courts, supervised by Article III courts, and 'constitute[d]' as 'a unit of the district court.' " Baude concludes that bankruptcy courts must be sustained, if at all, as adjuncts to Article III courts.

Page 385. Add in place of the final paragraph of Paragraph (5):

Oil States Energy Servs., LLC v. Greene's Energy Group, LLC, 138 S.Ct. 1365 (2018), cast some light on the definition of a public right by suggesting that both the government's status as a party and the historical practice surrounding a particular type of claim remain relevant to determining whether a claim is a "public right." At issue was a procedure established by the Leahy-Smith America Invents Act, 125 Stat. 284, pursuant to which the Patent and Trademark Office (PTO) conducts "inter partes review" of a patent's validity. Under this procedure, a party other than the patent holder may petition the PTO to determine whether to cancel a patent on the ground that it fails the novelty or nonobviousness criteria for patentability.

Although the inter partes review arguably involves adjudication between private parties—the patent challenger and the patent holder—the Court held (7–2) that the adjudication concerned public rights properly assigned to a non-Article III tribunal. In his opinion for the Court, Justice Thomas explained that the PTO's granting a patent itself involves a public right—a matter between the government and a patent applicant seeking a public franchise. From that starting point, the Court reasoned that inter partes review merely seeks "reconsideration of that grant". Justice Thomas also relied on the fact that, under the common law of England, the Privy Council—an executive body—had concurrent jurisdiction with the courts to revoke a patent, suggesting that patent challenges would have been seen as a permissible executive function at the time of the founding. In a dissent joined by Chief Justice Roberts, Justice Gorsuch disagreed not with the Court's reliance on history, but rather with its reading of the historical record, which he took to establish that patent challenges had become an exclusive judicial function at common law prior to the founding and that they continued to be treated as such in subsequent U.S. practice. See United States v. Arthrex, Inc., 141 S.Ct. 1970, 1988 (2021) (Gorsuch, J., concurring in part and dissenting in part) (reiterating the view that Oil States upset a "traditional understanding" that "an issued patent was considered a vested property right that could be taken from an individual only through a lawful process before a court").

Should the concept of public rights be limited to situations, like those in the Oil States case, in which the claim can be resolved exclusively by the executive—whether by reason of history or because sovereign immunity shields the government from judicial process in cases to which the government is a party (as, for example, when an agency denies an individual's claim for monetary benefits)?[5] Put another way, does the greater power to forgo judicial process include the lesser power to provide something less than the full Article III process? On such a view, much agency adjudication, including matters in which the government imposes a sanction against an individual, would have to be rerationalized on a different basis— perhaps on an adjunct theory or some variant of it. Indeed, note that Justice Breyer's dissent in Stern v. Marshall, Seventh Edition p. 364, fears that the Court's decision calls into question the validity of a range of longstanding administrative agencies like the NLRB, CFTC, and HUD, while the majority in Stern simply says that those tribunals are distinguishable without necessarily blessing them; and Justice Scalia injects a note of skepticism when he mentions "certain adjudications by federal administrative agencies, which are governed (for better or worse) by our landmark decision in Crowell v. Benson".

---

[5]   Sovereign immunity would not necessarily bar a claim against a federal official involving the same matter in dispute, but that claim differs from one against the government itself.

The explicitly historical approach used by both the Court and the dissent in Oil States has given rise to a new round of historical scholarship raising questions about the public rights/private rights framework used in that case. See, *e.g.*, Ablavsky, *Getting Public Rights Wrong: The Lost History of the Private Land Claims*, 74 Stan.L.Rev. 277 (2022) (arguing that the administrative adjudication of certain private land claims in newly acquired territory in the nineteenth century muddies the public rights inquiry and casts doubt on the Oil States test); Pfander & Borrasso, *Public Rights and Article III: Judicial Oversight of Agency Action*, 82 Ohio St.L.J. 493 (2021) (arguing that early doctrine distinguished between "constitutive authority" to establish new rights or obligations, which could be handled administratively, and retrospective adjudication of disputed matters, which could not); Nelson, *Vested Rights, "Franchises", and the Separation of Powers*, 169 U.Pa.L.Rev. 1429 (2021) (reconsidering an earlier article treating franchises as privileges and contending that, historically, patents had taken on a contractual character and, once granted, could be challenged only through judicial process). But see Golden & Lee, *Congressional Power, Public Rights, and Non-Article III Adjudication*, 98 Notre Dame L.Rev. 1113, 1167–1168 (2023) (arguing that, while English law was "in a state of flux" at the time of the founding, the majority properly relied on deeply rooted English practice permitting executive adjudication of patent rights, a reading that supports present congressional flexibility to rely on non-Article III adjudicators).

Page 386. Add a new footnote 5a at the end of Paragraph (6)(a)(ii):

[5a] For the argument that the salience of state common law claims in the analysis reflects the federalism value of preserving state adjudicative authority against federal encroachment, see Golden & Lee, *Federalism, Private Rights, and Article III Adjudication*, 108 Va.L.Rev. 1547 (2022).

Page 388. Add a new Subparagraph (7)(c):

(c) The Implications of Consent. In Wellness International Network, Limited v. Sharif, 575 U.S. 665 (2015), Justice Sotomayor's opinion for the Court held that Article III permits bankruptcy judges to adjudicate Stern claims when both parties consent. Justice Sotomayor explained that, since the early days of the Republic, federal courts have often referred matters to special masters, arbitrators, and referees when the parties have given their consent. The Court added that consent played an important role in sustaining (a) agency adjudication of common law counterclaims in CFTC v. Schor, Seventh Edition p. 383, and (b) magistrates' authority to oversee jury selection in various cases. See Seventh Edition p. 393.

The Court in Wellness International held that a litigant may waive his or her "personal" right to an Article III tribunal. Citing Schor, the Court explained that, with such a waiver, the proper question was what " 'practical effect' " non-Article III adjudication would have on the " 'constitutionally assigned role of the federal judiciary.' " In the bankruptcy context, the Court found such effects to be minimal because bankruptcy judges are appointed and removable by Article III judges and function as judicial officers within the district court. In addition, the bankruptcy courts' jurisdiction over Stern claims encompasses only a " 'narrow class' " of common law matters that are incidental to the primary jurisdiction over bankruptcy. Finally, the Court concluded that Congress had no evident purpose "to aggrandize itself or humble the Judiciary" by assigning Stern claims to bankruptcy judges. Rather, Congress merely sought to "supplement[ ] the capacity of district courts through the able assistance of bankruptcy judges."

In a dissent joined by Justice Scalia and, in part, by Justice Thomas, Chief Justice Roberts criticized the majority for reviving a functionalist approach that put efficiency, convenience, and utility ahead of the prophylactic protections that an independent judiciary assures. Casting the right to an Article III forum as central to liberty and accountability, the dissent argued that "an individual may not consent away the institutional interest protected by the separation of powers." Justice Thomas also dissented separately.

Read together, do Stern and Wellness International suggest that the Court will apply (a) a strict, formalist approach to cases that do not involve party consent and (b) a more forgiving, functionalist approach when consent is present? If litigants cannot consent to the adjudication of non-Article III business heard in Article III courts, should they be able to consent to the adjudication of Article III business in non-Article III courts? For analysis questioning the relationship between party consent and the permissibility of non-Article III adjudication, see Dodge, *Reconceptualizing Non-Article III Tribunals*, 99 Minn.L.Rev. 905 (2015); Hessick, *Consenting to Adjudication Outside Article III Courts*, 71 Vand.L.Rev. 715 (2018).

———

NOTE ON MAGISTRATE JUDGES

Page 393. Add in place of footnote 8:

8   At least five federal circuits have upheld § 636(c) consent jurisdiction in class actions, based on the consent of the class representative(s) and defendant(s), rejecting the view that unnamed class members are "parties" whose consent is required. See McAdams v. Robinson, 26 F.4th 149, 155 (4th Cir.2022); Koby v. ARS Nat'l Servs., Inc. 846 F.3d 1071, 1076 (9th Cir.2017); Day v. Persels & Associates, LLC, 729 F.3d 1309, 1324–25 (11th Cir.2013); Dewey v. Volkswagen Aktiengesellschaft, 681 F.3d 170, 180–81 (3d Cir.2012); Williams v. Gen. Elec. Capital Auto Lease, Inc. 159 F.3d 266, 268–70 (7th Cir.1998).

———

NOTE ON MILITARY TRIBUNALS OR COMMISSIONS

Page 409. Add in place of footnote 10:

10   In Bahlul v. United States, 840 F.3d 757 (D.C.Cir.2016) (en banc), cert. denied, 138 S.Ct 313. (2017), a badly splintered en banc decision of the D.C. Circuit affirmed a military tribunal's conviction of Bahlul for conspiracy to commit war crimes. Bahlul, who was a Pakistani national, argued that, under Articles I and III, the government could invoke non-Article III military commissions only to try offenses against "the *international* law of war" and that conspiracy was not such an offense.

In a brief per curiam opinion, the court affirmed Bahlul's conviction. The nine participating judges, however, produced five separate opinions (two of which concluded that Bahlul's conviction could be affirmed without reaching the constitutional question). Judge Kavanaugh, joined by two other judges, concurred on the ground that nothing in the Constitution or the Court's precedents requires Congress to restrict military tribunals only to offenses against the international laws of war. In addition, he concluded, "Congress's longstanding practice strongly supports the conclusion that international law is not a constitutional constraint on Congress's authority to [invoke a] . . . military commission." (A separate concurrence by Judge Henderson took a similar position). In a joint dissent, Judges Rogers, Tatel, and Pillard argued that Article III establishes a strong default rule of adjudication by judges with life-tenure and salary protection and that military commissions represent a limited historical exception for cases involving (a) courts in areas under martial law, (b) courts in areas of temporary military occupation, and (c) cases involving enemy combatants charged with violations of the international laws of war.

In a case such as Bahlul, how conclusive should historical practice be in determining the constitutionality of Congress's decision to assign adjudication of an offense such as conspiracy to a military commission? For the view that judges have done a poor job of capturing the historical complexities that surround the use of military commissions over the course of more than two centuries, see Lederman, *The Law(?) of the Lincoln Assassination*, 118 Colum.L.Rev. 323 (2018) (suggesting that divisions of opinion among Civil War-era officials and the Court's post-war decision in Ex parte Milligan, Seventh Edition p. 405, complicate modern reliance on Civil War-era practices relating to military commissions); and Lederman, *Of Spies, Saboteurs, and Enemy Accomplices: History's Lessons for the Constitutionality of Wartime Military Tribunals*, 105 Geo.L.J. 1529 (2017) (arguing that, without deep immersion in prior common law practice, it is easy for judges to overread Revolutionary War-era and early congressional practices relating to the use of military tribunals to try spies and those accused of giving aid and comfort to the enemy).

Page 410. Add a new footnote 11 at the end of Paragraph (7):

[11]   Based on a comprehensive historical analysis of the writ starting with its codification in England's Habeas Corpus Act of 1679, Professor Tyler argues that the privilege protects citizens and individuals in allegiance with the sovereign against being detained outside the formal criminal process, even in wartime, absent Congress's suspension of the writ for one of the reasons enumerated in the Suspension Clause. See Tyler, Habeas Corpus in Wartime: From the Tower of London to Guantanamo Bay (2018). To what extent should historical practice determine the present content of the habeas guarantee? Should it at least furnish a baseline below which the government may not go? For further discussion, see *infra* pp. 168–171.

---

3.   FEDERAL AUTHORITY AND STATE COURT JURISDICTION

NOTE ON THE POWER OF CONGRESS TO PROVIDE FOR REMOVAL FROM STATE TO FEDERAL COURTS

Page 426. Add a new footnote 4 at the end of the second sentence of the final paragraph of Paragraph (2)(c):

[4]   Goldman, *The Neglected History of State Prosecutions for State Crimes in Federal Courts*, 52 Tex.Tech.L.Rev. 783, 786 (2020), questions Mesa's federal defense requirement on historical grounds, arguing that earlier "officer-removal provision did not implicitly require any assertion of substantive federal law" and that "contemporary legislators and courts generally understood such cases to arise validly under federal law, even without such a requirement."

NOTE ON THE OBLIGATION OF STATE COURTS TO ENFORCE FEDERAL LAW

Page 441. Add a new footnote 3a at the end of the second sentence of Paragraph (2)(b):

[3a]   For an argument that the Testa line of cases cannot be justified by the Supremacy Clause, and may actually undermine enforcement of federal law by diminishing the role of the states in fashioning different remedies, see Woolhandler & Collins, *State Jurisdictional*

Independence and Federal Supremacy, 72 Fla.L.Rev. 73, 93–105, 119–125 (2020). In response, Vázquez and Vladeck argue that the Madisonian Compromise and the structures built around it reflect a default expectation of state court enforcement of federal rights, see Vázquez & Vladeck, *Testa, Crain, and the Constitutional Right to Collateral Relief*, 72 Fla.L.Rev. 10, 13 (2021).

Page 445. Add a new footnote 6a at the end of Paragraph (4):

[6a] Though in a different context, Montgomery v. Louisiana, 577 U.S. 190 (2016), further suggests that state courts may have a duty to hear federal claims for reasons other than avoiding discrimination against such claims. At issue was whether a state court conducting collateral review of a state conviction may preclude retroactive application of a new rule of substantive federal constitutional law. In 1970, a Louisiana court sentenced Henry Montgomery to life without parole for a crime he committed while under the age of 18. More than four decades later, Miller v. Alabama, 567 U.S. 460 (2012), held that states may not, consistent with the Eighth Amendment, impose a life sentence without the possibility of parole for a crime committed by a juvenile. Montgomery brought a claim for relief under Miller through a state collateral review procedure that allows prisoners to challenge the legality of their sentences on Eighth Amendment grounds. As a matter of state practice, however, the state court held that Miller does not apply retroactively on state collateral review.

In a 6–3 decision, Justice Kennedy wrote for the Court that, as a matter of federal constitutional law, state collateral proceedings must give retroactive effect to new substantive constitutional rules—those "that place certain criminal laws and punishments altogether beyond the State's power to impose." The Court relied on the fact that while Teague v. Lane, Seventh Edition p. 1295, barred the retroactive application of new law in collateral federal habeas corpus proceedings, that same decision had made an exception for new substantive rules of constitutional law. Although Teague itself purported only to interpret the jurisdictional statutes governing collateral federal habeas review, Justice Kennedy's opinion in Montgomery held that the relevant Teague exception was "best understood as resting upon constitutional premises." In particular, Montgomery reasoned that "when a State enforces a proscription or penalty barred by the Constitution, the resulting conviction or sentence is, by definition, unlawful." To buttress its conclusion, the Court cited "a long tradition" of its giving retroactive effect to substantive constitutional rules on collateral review.

Justice Scalia, joined by Justices Thomas and Alito, dissented on the ground that the Teague exception for new rules of substantive constitutional law was not constitutionally compelled. In a separate dissent, Justice Thomas argued that nothing in the text of the Constitution or historical practice creates a right to collateral relief, either in state or federal court. According to Justice Thomas, the retroactivity requirement would not apply if the state eliminated state collateral review of all federal claims or perhaps even just Eighth Amendment claims. "Only when state courts have chosen to entertain a federal claim," he wrote, "can the Supremacy Clause conceivably command a state court to apply federal law." This conclusion, he added, reflects the idea that "the Constitution leaves the initial choice to entertain federal claims up to state courts, which are 'tribunals over which the government of the Union has no adequate control, and which may be closed to any claim asserted under a law of the United States'" (quoting Osborn v. Bank of the United States, 22 U.S. (9 Wheat.) 738, 821 (1824)).

Can Justice Thomas's position about state courts be squared with the majority's reasoning? The majority seems to say that the U.S. Constitution prohibits a state court from keeping a prisoner in confinement when his or her conviction or sentence contravenes substantive constitutional rules limiting the state's power. Does that conclusion suggest that states have a constitutional duty to provide some form of collateral relief in such cases? Does your answer depend on whether federal habeas corpus relief is available to such a prisoner? For further discussion of Montgomery v. Louisiana, see pp. 107–108, 182, 187–204, *infra*.

Page 448. Add in place of Paragraph (6)(d):

(d) **The Murphy Decision.** In Murphy v. National Collegiate Athletic Ass'n, 138 S.Ct. 1461 (2018), the Court (6–3) reaffirmed and extended its anticommandeering doctrine. The Professional and Amateur Sports Protection Act of 1992 (PASPA), 106 Stat. 4227, in relevant part made it unlawful for states to "authorize by law or compact" various forms of gambling on competitive sporting events. In the Court's view, this statute precluded a state from partially repealing any existing state legislation that barred such gambling. In effect, therefore, PASPA put state legislatures "under the direct control of Congress"—"as if federal officers were installed in state legislative chambers and were armed with the authority to stop legislators from voting on any offending proposals." This result, the Court said, constituted a "direct affront to state sovereignty" under the system of dual sovereignty affirmed by the Tenth Amendment.

(e) The Brackeen Decision. In Haaland v. Brackeen, 143 S.Ct. 1609 (2023), the Court rejected an anticommandeering challenge to a provision of the Indian Child Welfare Act requiring state courts to apply a complex set of federal rather than state-law preferences for child placement in state custody proceedings involving any child who is the member of an Indian tribe. See 25 U.S.C. § 1915(a), (b). Though acknowledging that "Congress can require state courts, unlike state executives and legislatures, to enforce federal law," petitioners drew "a distinction between requiring state courts to entertain federal causes of action and requiring them to apply federal law to state causes of action." In an opinion written by Justice Barrett and joined by the Chief Justice and Justices Sotomayor, Kagan, Gorsuch, Kavanaugh, and Jackson, the Court held that petitioners' anticommandeering argument "runs headlong into . . . [t]he Supremacy Clause," reasoning that a federal statute's preemptive effect is unaffected by the fact that it "modifies a state cause of action."

(f) The Import of the Decisions. Do concerns with state autonomy expressed in New York, Printz, and Murphy provide a basis for the Justices, in an appropriate case, to limit congressional power to require unwilling state courts to hear federal claims? For an affirmative answer, see Blackman, *State Judicial Sovereignty*, 2016 U.Ill.L.Rev. 2033. Does Brackeen help clarify the scope of federal power in state courts?

CHAPTER V

REVIEW OF STATE COURT DECISIONS BY THE SUPREME COURT

_____

1. THE ESTABLISHMENT OF THE JURISDICTION

DEVELOPMENT OF THE STATUTORY PROVISIONS

Page 463. Add at the end of footnote 14:

Johnson, *The Origins of Supreme Court Question Selection*, 122 Colum.L.Rev. 793 (2022), observes that in the wake of the Judges' Bill, Court members transformed certiorari review from a vehicle for deciding "the whole case" into a means of selecting specific questions for resolution (sometimes suggested by the Justices themselves), doing so, he contends, in contravention of jurisdictional statutes.

Page 463. Add at the end of the last paragraph of Paragraph (3):

More recently, in the 2019 Term, the Court decided 11 cases arising out of state courts with full opinions. In the 2020 Term in which the COVID-19 pandemic led the Court to decide few cases overall, the drop in review of cases from state courts was especially pronounced, with the Court only deciding 3 such cases with full opinions. That number rose to 5 in the 2021 Term. See *The Supreme Court, 2021 Term—The Statistics*, 136 Harv.L.Rev. 500, 510 (2022); *The Supreme Court, 2020 Term—The Statistics*, 135 Harv.L.Rev. 491, 500 (2021); *The Supreme Court, 2019 Term—The Statistics*, 134 Harv.L.Rev. 610, 620 (2020).

_____

NOTE ON THE ATTACKS UPON THE JURISDICTION

Page 475. Add a new footnote 4a at the end of the first sentence in Paragraph (2):

  [4a] James v. City of Boise, 577 U.S. 306 (2016) (per curiam), summarily reversed a decision of the Idaho Supreme Court refusing to follow the Supreme Court's interpretation of a federal statute. In civil rights cases brought in state court pursuant to 42 U.S.C. § 1983, state court judges may "allow the prevailing party * * * a reasonable attorney's fee." *Id.* § 1988. Notwithstanding the fact that § 1988 refers to "the prevailing party" without qualification, the Court in Hughes v. Rowe, 449 U.S. 5 (1980) (per curiam), held that a prevailing *defendant* may recover fees only if the court finds that the plaintiff filed a frivolous lawsuit. In James, the Idaho Supreme Court held that the Supreme Court of the United States lacked " 'the authority to limit the discretion of state courts where such limitation is not contained in the statute.' " In a two-page per curiam opinion, the Supreme Court reversed. Quoting Justice Story's opinion for the Court in Martin v. Hunter's Lessee, Seventh Edition p. 464, the Court wrote that "if state courts were permitted to disregard this Court's rulings on federal law, 'the laws, the treaties, and the constitution of the United States would be different in different states, and might, perhaps,

never have precisely the same construction, obligation, or efficacy, in any two states. The public mischiefs that would attend such a state of things would be truly deplorable.' "

Did the Idaho Supreme Court technically contradict Martin when it refused to follow a precedent rather than a judgment of the Supreme Court? Given the modern Court's sharply limited capacity to review cases, would the refusal of state courts to acquiesce in the Court's interpretation of federal law compromise federal uniformity almost as much?

———

2. THE RELATION BETWEEN STATE AND FEDERAL LAW

A. SUBSTANTIVE LAW

NOTE ON REVIEW OF STATE DECISIONS UPHOLDING CLAIMS OF FEDERAL RIGHT

Page 503. Add a new Paragraph (5):

(5) The Debate Renewed. In Kansas v. Carr, 577 U.S. 108 (2016), the Court revisited the debate over whether it should hear cases in which state courts "overprotect" federal rights. In its modern incarnation, the debate takes the form of asking whether the Court should exercise its discretion to deny certiorari in such cases, and not whether there is an adequate and independent state ground per se. Petitioner sought review of a Kansas Supreme Court decision vacating respondents' capital sentences on the ground that the trial court violated the Eighth Amendment by (a) giving the jury unclear instructions about mitigating circumstances and (b) declining to sever sentencing proceedings for respondents, who had been jointly tried. In his final opinion for the Court, Justice Scalia held that the state supreme court's opinion left "no room for doubt that it was relying on the Federal Constitution."

In a dissent that echoed some of the concerns voiced by Justice Stevens in Michigan v. Long, Seventh Edition p. 499, Justice Sotomayor argued that the Court should grant certiorari only when "the benefits of hearing a case outweigh the costs of so doing." In her view, reviewing state court cases that grant relief to criminal defendants imposes several systemic costs: First, Supreme Court's review "may have little effect if a lower court is able to reinstate its holding as a matter of state law." Second, in cases involving "no suggestion" that the state court "violated any [individual's] federal constitutional right", federal review "intervene[s] in an intrastate dispute between the State's executive and its judiciary rather than entrusting the State's structure of government to sort it out." Third, granting review interferes with federalism interests in "state experimentation with how best to guarantee a fair trial." In this case, moreover, Justice Sotomayor saw few benefits to Supreme Court review because the key issues were hard to generalize beyond the particular state sentencing scheme or even the facts of the case. Finally, Justice Sotomayor stressed that the state court's rulings neither "indicate[d] a hostility to applying federal precedents" nor granted relief that was "particularly likely to destabilize or significantly interfere with federal policy." In that light, she concluded that "the Court should not have granted certiorari".

Justice Scalia's opinion for the Court responded that Supreme Court review was appropriate because the state court held that "the Federal Constitution *requires*" vacation of the state sentences. The Court emphasized that "state courts may experiment all they want with their own constitutions, and often do in the wake of this Court's decisions." The Court added that "what a state court cannot do is experiment with our federal Constitution and expect to elude this Court's review so long as victory goes to the criminal defendant." Such an approach, in Justice Scalia's view, undermined uniformity while "enabl[ing] state courts to blame the unpopular death-sentence reprieve of the most horrible criminals upon the Federal Constitution when it is in fact their own doing."

Does shifting the debate to one about the appropriateness of granting certiorari alter the competing interests at stake? When, if ever, should the Court allow the posture of the parties to influence its decisions to grant or deny certiorari?

NOTE ON AMBIGUOUS STATE DECISIONS AND TECHNIQUES FOR CLARIFYING THEM

Page 507. Add at the end of the penultimate paragraph of Paragraph (5):

See also Wilson v. Sellers, 138 S.Ct. 1188 (2018) (holding that for purposes of assessing whether an unexplained state court decision "unreasonabl[y]" applied federal law or determined questions of fact, a federal habeas court should presume that the decision rested on the same grounds as the last reasoned state court decision in the case); Foster v. Chatman, 578 U.S. 488, 498 n.3 (2016) (affirming the Court's practice of reviewing "a lower [state] court decision * * * in order to ascertain whether a federal question may be implicated in an unreasoned summary order from a higher court").

Page 509. Add at the end of the penultimate paragraph of Paragraph (7):

Shapiro, *An Incomplete Discussion of "Arising Under" Jurisdiction*, 91 Notre Dame L.Rev. 1931 (2016) (contribution to symposium in honor of Dan Meltzer), elaborates thoughtfully on the evolution of doctrinal and scholarly positions concerning the Supreme Court's authority to hear cases that turn on state incorporation of federal law.

NOTE ON FEDERAL PROTECTION OF STATE-CREATED RIGHTS

Page 522. Add a new Paragraph (3) and renumber existing Paragraph (3) as Paragraph (4):

(3) Moore v. Harper. Two decades after Bush v. Gore, a group of state legislators challenged the authority of the North Carolina Supreme Court to reject legislatively drawn voting districts as inconsistent with the state constitution. In so doing, the legislators argued that the federal Elections Clause, which expressly assigns to "the Legislature" of each State the power to prescribe "[t]he Times, Places and Manner of" federal elections, Art. I, § 4, cl. 1, precludes state courts from rejecting legislative maps based on state constitutional principles because doing so interferes with the federal Constitution's delegation of exclusive power in this area to the legislature. In Moore v. Harper, 143 S.Ct. 2065 (2023), the Supreme Court rejected the argument, concluding that "[t]he Elections Clause does not insulate state legislatures from the ordinary exercise of state judicial review." This result followed, Chief Justice Roberts wrote for the majority, because "[w]hen a state legislature carries out its constitutional power to prescribe rules regulating federal elections, the 'commission under which' it exercises authority is twofold" (citing The Federalist No. 78, at 467). First, he observed, "[t]he legislature acts both as a lawmaking body created and bound by its state constitution". Second, it acts "as the entity assigned particular authority by the Federal Constitution." "Both constitutions", he concluded, "restrain the legislature's exercise of power."

The Court reiterated Murdock's principle that " 'State courts are the appropriate tribunals . . . for the decision of questions arising under their local law, whether statutory or otherwise" (citing Murdock, 20 Wall. at 626). But, "[a]t the same time, the Elections Clause expressly vests power to carry out its provisions in 'the Legislature' of each State, a deliberate choice that this Court must respect." It followed, Chief Justice Roberts opined, that "[a]s in other areas where the exercise of federal authority or the vindication of federal rights implicates questions of state law, we have an obligation to ensure that state court interpretations of that law do not evade federal law." Referencing the debate in Bush v. Gore between Chief Justice Rehnquist and Justice Souter over how to carry out that obligation—that is, how to review state court interpretations of state law—the Moore v. Harper Court declined to adopt any test governing state court decisions respecting state law in Elections Clause disputes. Instead, the Court's opinion held "only that state courts may not transgress the ordinary bounds of judicial review such that they arrogate to themselves the power vested in state legislatures to regulate federal elections."

In dissent, Justice Thomas feared that the majority had improperly extended Bush v. Gore's review of state court determinations of state statutory law to state court determinations of state *constitutional* law. "When 'it is a constitution [courts] are expounding,' not a detailed statutory scheme, the standards to judge the fairness of a given interpretation are typically fewer and less definite" (quoting McCulloch, 17 U.S. (4 Wheat.) 316, 407 (1819)). The result, he feared, would be to "invest[ ] potentially large swaths of state constitutional law with the character of a federal question not amenable to meaningful or principled adjudication by federal courts."

Page 522. Add at the end of new Paragraph (4):

Does Moore v. Harper add to this debate or just further prolong resolution whether federal court review of state court determinations of state law will depend on the context in which they arise? Chief Justice Roberts writes in his opinion for the Court that "[t]he questions presented in this area are complex and context specific", suggesting that the latter is the case. Separately, is Justice Thomas right to fear that reviewing state court interpretations of state constitutional (as opposed to statutory) law to ensure that they do "not transgress the ordinary bounds of judicial review" (the Court's phrase) will present special challenges?

B. PROCEDURAL REQUIREMENTS

NOTE ON THE ADEQUACY OF STATE PROCEDURAL GROUNDS

Page 538. Insert a new paragraph after the third paragraph of Paragraph (5)(a):

The Supreme Court has made clear that "[t]he question whether a state procedural ruling is adequate is itself a question of federal law." Beard v. Kindler, 558 U.S. 53, 60 (2009). And although it is only in "exceptional cases" that the Court will find a state ground inadequate, Lee v. Kemna, 534 U.S. 362, 376 (2002), it continues to do so on occasion. Cruz v. Arizona, 143 S.Ct. 650 (2023), is a good example. In Cruz, the Court held that a capital defendant's federal due process claim was subject to its appellate review despite a holding by the Arizona Supreme Court that the claim was procedurally barred from state post-conviction review because the claim did not rely upon a "significant change in the law" as required under Arizona Rule of Criminal Procedure 32.1(g). Writing for the Court, Justice Sotomayor emphasized that the state court had interpreted Rule 32.1(g) in a manner that was "entirely new and in conflict with prior Arizona case law." Id. 659 (holding that Lynch v. Arizona, 578 U.S. 613 (2016) (per curiam), which rejected Arizona's application of the Court's earlier precedent in Simmons v. South Carolina, 512 U.S. 154 (1994) (requiring that capital juries be informed when a life sentence does not afford possibility of parole), constituted a "significant change in the law" under settled state practice). The Court concluded by reiterating the principle that "[i]n exceptional cases where a state-court judgment rests on a novel and unforeseeable state-court procedural decision lacking fair or substantial support in prior state law, that decision is not adequate to preclude review of a federal question." The Court then disposed of the case as follows: "[T]he judgment of the Supreme Court of Arizona is vacated, and the case is remanded for further proceedings not inconsistent with this opinion."

On remand, can the state court hold fast to its prior application of Rule 32.1(g) in the case? Given that the adequate and independent state ground doctrine is aimed at determining whether the Supreme Court has jurisdiction to review an underlying federal question on appeal, it is curious that the Court declined to review the due process claim at issue and instead sent the case back to the state courts. On remand, are the Arizona courts obligated either to change their interpretation of state law or review the federal question?

Page 539. Add at the end of Paragraph (5)(b):

Should the federal courts analyze the adequacy of state procedural grounds one by one, as in the previous cases, or focus more systematically on the fairness of the complex procedural mazes that criminal defendants must often clear before they can assert their federal claims in state court? See Primus, *Federal Review of State Criminal Convictions: A Structural Approach to Adequacy Doctrine*, 116 Mich.L.Rev. 75 (2017) (advancing the latter view).

Page 542. Add in place of the final sentence of the penultimate paragraph of Paragraph (6):

For decisions reaffirming Kindler's approach to discretion and procedural default in habeas, see Johnson v. Lee, 578 U.S. 605 (2016) (per curiam); Walker v. Martin, 562 U.S. 307 (2011).

Page 546. Add in place of the final sentence of Paragraph (10):

Subsequent decisions have tried more nuanced approaches to deciphering unreasoned state court decisions. See Wilson v. Sellers, 138 S.Ct. 1188 (2018) (applying the presumption, in the context of federal habeas corpus, that an unexplained state court decision rests on the same grounds as the last reasoned state court decision in the same case); Foster v. Chatman, 578 U.S. 488, 498 n.3 (2016) (employing a similar framework); Ylst v. Nunemaker, Seventh Edition p. 507 (same); Coleman v. Thompson, Seventh Edition p. 507 (relying in part on the content of the motion to dismiss as a means to decode an ambiguous state court decision). *Cf.* Capital Cities Media, Inc. v. Toole, Seventh Edition p. 506 (instead of presuming one way or the other, vacating and remanding to the state court for clarification).

———

3. FINAL JUDGMENTS AND THE HIGHEST STATE COURT

NOTE ON THE FINAL JUDGMENT RULE AND THE HIGHEST STATE COURT REQUIREMENT

Page 555. Add a new footnote 1a at the end of Paragraph (3):

[1a] Recently, in Moore v. Harper, 143 S.Ct. 2065 (2023), the Court held that despite the existence of ongoing state court proceedings, it enjoyed jurisdiction under the second Cox category to review the first round of a state supreme court's review of a federal Elections Clause challenge because that court had "finally decided" the relevant "federal issue" in a way that bound the parties. Also relevant to the Court's conclusion was the fact that the Court's decision had the potential to reverse the judgment of the state court and require implementation of legislative districting maps that the state supreme court had rejected. Accordingly, the Court ruled that it enjoyed "jurisdiction under both Article III and § 1257(a)." For further discussion, see p. 87–89, *supra*.

Page 557. Add at the end of Paragraph (8):

In Atlantic Richfield Co. v. Christian, 140 S.Ct. 1335 (2020), the Supreme Court reviewed a state supreme court's determination that a federal environmental statute did not displace various common law claims notwithstanding the state's highest court having remanded the case to proceed to trial. The state supreme court had exercised review through a writ of supervisory control, which under state law presents "a self-contained case, not an interlocutory appeal" and "initiates a separate lawsuit." Under such circumstances, the Court held, "[i]t is the nature of the [state] proceeding, not the issues the state court reviewed, that establishes our jurisdiction."

CHAPTER VI

THE LAW APPLIED IN CIVIL ACTIONS IN THE DISTRICT COURTS

1. PROCEDURE

NOTE ON THE HISTORICAL DEVELOPMENT OF THE STATUTES AND RULES OF COURT

Page 563. Add at the end of footnote 4:

Justice Barrett elaborated on these themes in a concurring opinion in United States v. Tsarnaev, 142 S.Ct. 1024 (2022). She argued that, while the Supreme Court plausibly possesses the authority to proscribe uniform procedural rules for lower federal courts, the courts of appeals likely lack supervisory authority to impose procedural rules on district courts. In dissent, Justice Breyer disagreed, arguing that Supreme Court precedents "clearly recognize the existence of such a power."

Page 565. Add at the end of the first paragraph of Paragraph (2):

In a few words appearing in Rule 2 of the new rules (which, slightly changed, now reads "There is one form of action—the civil action"), the rulemakers both specifically rejected use of the common-law forms of action (then still operative in a number of states) and effectuated, with respect to the rules of procedure, the merger of law and equity referred to at Seventh Edition p. 560."[7a]

[7a] Bray, *The System of Equitable Remedies*, 63 UCLA L.Rev. 530 (2016), argues that despite the merger of procedural rules eight decades ago, "there has been remarkably little merger of law and equity" for remedies. Challenging the "reigning view in the American legal academy" that the separation of legal and equitable remedies is irrational, the author argues that the "surviving equitable remedies and related doctrines work together as a system" to give courts the capacity to manage ongoing relief when damages at law are inadequate. The system, Bray maintains, has three components: (1) the equitable remedies themselves, which serve the need of compelling action or inaction; (2) equitable managerial devices, such as contempt, which enable courts to "manag[e] the parties and ensur[e] compliance"; and (3) equitable constraints, such as equitable ripeness requirements and equitable defenses, that serve as "frictions against the abuse of equitable remedies and managerial devices." Assuming the soundness of Bray's thesis, is there any reason for a court in a merged system not to resort to "equitable" methods or techniques when they would be of use in an action that would have been purely one "at law" before merger?

Page 566. Add a new footnote 8a at the end of the first sentence in Paragraph (4):

[8a] Leib, *Are the Federal Rules of Evidence Unconstitutional?*, 71 Am.U.L.Rev. 911 (2022), argues that the Rules Enabling Act as applied to the Federal Rules of Evidence is unconstitutional because it authorizes the Supreme Court to revise, repeal, and amend a federal statute (which is how the Federal Rules of Evidence were promulgated) in violation of INS v. Chadha, 462 U.S. 919 (1983), Clinton v. City of New York, 524 U.S. 417 (1998), and the non-delegation doctrine.

Page 566. Add at the end of Paragraph (4):

See generally Richard Marcus, *Rulemaking's Second Founding*, 169 U.Pa.L.Rev. 2519 (2021) (reviewing background to and significance of 1988 revision).

Page 567. Add at the end of footnote 10:

For a very critical history of the rulemaking process for the Supreme Court Rules from the 1980s to 2022 that emphasizes the process's secrecy and insularity, see Dodson, *The Making of the Supreme Court Rules*, 90 Geo.Wash.L.Rev. 866 (2022).

Page 568. Add a new footnote 13a after the semi-colon in the second line:

     [13a] David Marcus, *The Collapse of the Federal Rules System*, 169 U.Pa.L.Rev. 2485 (2021).

―――――

NOTE ON CHALLENGES TO THE VALIDITY OF THE FEDERAL RULES

Page 573. Add at the end of footnote 1:

For additional reflection on the relationship between Rule 4 and amenability to suit, see Spencer, *The Territorial Reach of Federal Courts*, 71 Fla.L.Rev. 979 (2019) (arguing that Rule 4(k) exceeds the rulemaking authority conferred by the Rules Enabling Act and should be revised to permit nationwide service of process); Woolley, *Rediscovering the Limited Role of the Federal Rules in Regulating Personal Jurisdiction*, 56 Hous.L.Rev. 565 (2019) (arguing that the Rules Enabling Act generally does not permit the Court to regulate amenability to suit and that Murphree is not to the contrary, but that Rule 4(k) is valid because it merely restates otherwise applicable law); Sachs, *The Unlimited Jurisdiction of the Federal Courts*, 106 Va.L.Rev. 1703 (2020) (defending Rule 4's validity, arguing that rules defining the scope of a federal court's service of process do not directly alter the court's jurisdiction and thus are authorized by the Rules Enabling Act, and further arguing that Congress has ratified Murphree's interpretation of the Rules Enabling Act).

Page 575. Add the following at the end of footnote 5:

See also Spencer, *Substance, Procedure, and the Rules Enabling Act*, 66 UCLA L.Rev. 654 (2019) (reading the Rules Enabling Act's authorization to prescribe "rules of practice and procedure" to be an independent constraint on rulemaking beyond the prohibition on rules that "abridge, enlarge or modify any substantive right", and explaining implications).

―――――

2. THE POWERS OF THE FEDERAL COURTS IN DEFINING PRIMARY LEGAL OBLIGATIONS THAT FALL WITHIN THE LEGISLATIVE COMPETENCE OF THE STATES

NOTE ON THE RATIONALE OF THE ERIE DECISION

Page 591. Add at the end of footnote 4:

For more recent views, see Sherry, *Normalizing Erie*, 69 Vand.L.Rev. 1161 (2016) (arguing that the Court has exaggerated Erie's constitutional concerns and should apply "ordinary federalism" principles found in doctrines like the dormant commerce clause and implied preemption to vertical choice-of-law questions); Young, *Erie as a Way of Life*, 10 ConLawNOW 175 (2018–2019) (maintaining that Erie appropriately "enlisted the national separation of powers in the cause of federalism" by affirming the "interstitial" character of federal law without categorically limiting federal legislative power).

Page 591. Add at the end of footnote 5:

In *Finding Law*, 107 Cal.L.Rev. 527 (2019), Professor Sachs seeks to revive the view, supposedly rejected in Erie, "that unwritten law can be found, rather than made." He argues that judges might plausibly "find" customary rules of law by analogizing them to "dictionary authors" who identify customary rules of language. He further argues that court decisions might carry precedential effect without becoming instances of judicial lawmaking; a legal system might use prior precedents to resolve particular cases "as if" they were the law, much the way preclusion doctrines treat prior judgments as resolving disputes without altering the underlying law on which the judgments are based. Sachs describes Erie as a "blunder" that distorted states' efforts to adopt a general common law as their own law, and that unduly encouraged federal courts to recognize a category of "so-called" federal common law.

————

NOTE ON THE KLAXON DECISION AND PROBLEMS OF HORIZONTAL CHOICE OF LAW IN CASES INVOLVING STATE-CREATED RIGHTS

Page 594. Add at the end of footnote 2:

Wolff, *Choice of Law and Jurisdictional Policy in the Federal Courts*, 165 U.Pa.L.Rev. 1847 (2017), offers a concise but rich historical analysis of the "multiple lines of doctrine that intersect" in Klaxon in order to emphasize the narrowness of its holding and to argue that it "does not foreclose the development of a federal rule of decision in resolving conflicts between the local policies of interested states".

Page 596. Replace footnote 6 with the following:

[6] In Atlantic Marine Constr. Co. v. United States Dist. Court, 571 U.S. 49 (2013), the Court recognized a significant exception to the Van Dusen choice-of-law principle. Atlantic Marine held that when a transfer of venue under § 1404 is made on the basis of a valid forum selection clause, the transferee court should apply the choice-of-law rules of the state in which it sits. The Court explained that the "policies motivating our exception [in Van Dusen] to the Klaxon rule for § 1404(a) transfers" did not apply because, in contrast with Van Dusen, a plaintiff who files suit in violation of a valid forum selection clause enjoys no "venue privilege" and thus is not entitled to concomitant "state-law advantages." Atlantic Marine assumed that the forum selection clause was valid and thus left open what law governs that question when the underlying claim is based on state law. Most courts of appeals have concluded that federal common law should govern, see, *e.g.*, Albemarle Corp. v. AstraZeneca UK Ltd., 628 F.3d 643, 650 (4th Cir.2010), though one has held that state law controls, see Jackson v. Payday Fin., LLC, 764 F.3d 765, 774–75 (7th Cir.2014). For academic treatments of the issue, compare Adam Steinman, *Atlantic Marine Through the Lens of Erie*, 66 Hastings L.J. 795, 804–19 (2015) (suggesting that Erie and Klaxon compel application of state law), with Sachs, *The Forum Selection Defense*, 10 Duke J.Const.L. & Pub.Pol'y 1, 14–26 (2014) (arguing that a range of federal interests justifies development of federal common law). For an argument that courts administering multidistrict litigation proceedings under 28 U.S.C. § 1407 should apply the choice-of-law rules of transferor courts notwithstanding the presence of a forum selection clause and the holding of Atlantic Marine, see Bock, *All Disputes Must Be Brought Here: Atlantic Marine and the Future of Multidistrict Litigation*, 106 Cal.L.Rev. 1657 (2018).

Page 596. Replace Paragraph (7)(b) with the following:

Scholars and some lower courts have questioned the applicability of the Klaxon rule to state-law issues that arise in bankruptcy, see, *e.g.*, Cross, *State Choice of Law Rules in Bankruptcy*, 42 Okla.L.Rev. 531 (1989), in cases under the Class Action Fairness Act of 2005 (CAFA), see, *e.g.*, Wolff, *Choice of Law and Jurisdictional Policy in the Federal Courts*, 165 U.Pa.L.Rev. 1847 (2017), and in cases subject to the multidistrict litigation statute, see, *e.g.*, Atwood, *The Choice of Law Dilemma in Mass Tort Litigation: Kicking Around Erie, Klaxon, and Van Dusen*, 19 Conn.L.Rev. 9 (1986). For a robust defense of the Klaxon rule in these and other special contexts, see Clopton, *Horizontal Choice of Law in Federal Court*, 169 U.Pa.L.Rev. 2193 (2021).

Page 597. Add at the end of Paragraph (7)(c):

In Cassirer v. Thyssen-Bornemisza, 142 S.Ct. 1502 (2022), a unanimous Supreme Court, in an opinion by Justice Kagan, held that under Section 1606 of the Foreign Sovereign Immunities Act, state choice-of-law rules determine which non-federal property law governs the dispute. The Court "expresse[d] no view" on whether or when federal law might limit the application of state choice-of-law rules in an "unusual" case where their application "created foreign relations concerns."

––––––––––

NOTE ON THE WAYS OF ASCERTAINING STATE LAW

Page 598. Add at the end of Paragraph (2):

Professors Issacharoff and Marotta-Wurgler argue that federal courts are steering the evolution of the common law of contracts in novel legal contexts such as browsewrap, clickwrap, and shrinkwrap due to a combination of the federalization of class action law under the Class Action Fairness Act and the influence of federal court predictions about state law. Though federal court decisions do not bind state courts, Issacharoff and Marotta-Wurgler observe that the law often "settles on one or a few influential decisions" by federal appellate courts that are "followed by subsequent courts, including state high courts." Issacharoff & Marotta-Wurgler, *The Hollowed Out Common Law*, 67 UCLA L.Rev. 600 (2020).

Page 598. Add at the end of footnote 1:

But see Bruhl, *Interpreting State Statutes in Federal Court*, 98 Notre Dame L.Rev. 61 (2022) (challenging some of Gluck's findings and arguing that federal courts do and should (with a few exceptions) employ state methods of interpretation when interpreting state statutes).

––––––––––

3. ENFORCING STATE-CREATED OBLIGATIONS— EQUITABLE REMEDIES AND PROCEDURE

NOTE ON STATE LAW AND FEDERAL EQUITY

Page 604. Add at the end of footnote 2:

Morley, *The Federal Equity Power*, 59 B.C.L.Rev. 217 (2018), comprehensively analyzes Erie's application to equity and concludes that "the equitable principles a court must apply to a claim arise from the source of law giving rise to that cause of action." On this view, federal equitable principles govern federal claims but federal courts must look to the equitable principles of the state in deciding whether to grant equitable relief for claims arising under state law. Is it a bug or a feature of this elegant proposal that when a plaintiff presents multiple claims in a diversity or supplemental jurisdiction case, "a plaintiff may be able to obtain an injunction for her federal claims, but not her state ones, or vice versa"?

Page 605. Replace the last sentence of footnote 3 with the following:

The Court held, in the context of a contracting party's effort to compel arbitration, that the FAA preempts a California state rule that treats class action waivers as unconscionable in certain consumer contracts of adhesion. The Court subsequently explained that Concepcion establishes an "equal-treatment principle" that requires preemption of "any state rule discriminating on its face against arbitration". Kindred Nursing Centers Ltd. v. Clark, 581 U.S. 246 (2017) (holding that the FAA preempts a Kentucky judge-made rule that a power of attorney does not entitle a representative to enter into an arbitration agreement unless the power of attorney expressly grants that authority); see also DIRECTV, Inc. v. Imburgia, 577 U.S. 47 (2015) (applying equal-treatment principle in a case where parties had conditionally chosen pre-Concepcion California law to govern waiver of class arbitration, reasoning that construction of parties' choice to allow waiver would not put arbitration contracts on an "equal footing with all other contracts" under California law).

Page 606. Add at the end of footnote 4:

Pfander and Formo, *The Past and Future of Equitable Remedies: An Essay for Judge Frank Johnson*, 71 Ala.L Rev. 723 (2020), argue that, because equity adjusts in light of changes in the scope of common law remedies over time, Grupo Mexicano's emphasis on equity's past may make equity incapable of responding to intervening changes in the law. In any case, the authors contend that early decisions of the Supreme Court grant pre-judgment asset freeze injunctive relief of the kind the Grupo Mexicano Court described as historically unprecedented. In a different vein, Bray, *The Supreme Court and the New Equity*, 68 Vand.L.Rev. 997 (2015), argues that Grupo Mexicano and Great-West were the first of a line of eleven recent Supreme Court decisions that together establish a "new equity" jurisprudence. The defining features of this jurisprudence, Bray maintains, include a focus on history and tradition to define the scope of equitable relief, a reaffirmation of the "no adequate remedy at law" prerequisite for such relief, and an insistence that equitable remedies are exceptional and discretionary. After acknowledging the historical and doctrinal errors in many of the "new equity" decisions (including Grupo Mexicano and Great-West), the author offers a qualified defense of the jurisprudence that emerges from the decisions on the grounds that it (a) is "well suited to judicial decisionmaking", and (b) constitutes a reasonable response to the challenge of making sense of equitable doctrines in a world without courts of equity. Do you agree with the author that the Court's historical analysis in the "new equity" decisions, though "not good as historians' history", can be "good as history for legal purposes because its very artificiality makes it more suited to the judicial resolution of cases", at least so long as this "artificial history" is a "sensible interpretation" of statutes that authorize "equitable relief" and is "largely consistent with traditional equitable principles"?

———

NOTE ON HANNA AND ITS AFTERMATH

Page 625. Add at the end of footnote 15:

Professor Erbsen argues that Hanna's twin aims test wrongly focuses on "whether federal law has priority" rather than the "more salient" questions whether the federal law in issue (a statute, Rule, or federal common law) is valid, and "whether it encompasses the disputed issue." He contends that his proposed reorientation would better serve Erie's concerns about separation of powers and federalism. Erbsen, *A Unified Approach to Erie Analysis for Federal Statutes, Rules, and Common Law*, 10 UC Irvine L.Rev. 1101 (2020).

CHAPTER VII

FEDERAL COMMON LAW

---

1. DEFINING PRIMARY OBLIGATIONS

A. CRIMINAL PROSECUTIONS

NOTE ON FEDERAL COMMON LAW CRIMES

Page 640. Add a new footnote 2a at the end of Paragraph (1):

[2a] For cautionary notes about relying on the early history of federal courts law, see Fallon, *The Many and Varied Roles of History in Constitutional Adjudication*, 90 Notre Dame L.Rev. 1753, 1775 (2015) ("[P]erhaps the safest conclusion is that all agree that historical inquiries are necessary and appropriate to determine whether historical practice has 'liquidated' the meaning of otherwise vague or ambiguous constitutional provisions, and if so how, but that a number of questions about the nature and conditions of liquidation remain unsettled."); Tyler, *Assessing the Role of History in the Federal Courts Canon: A Word of Caution*, 90 Notre Dame L.Rev. 1739, 1741–42 (2015) (noting that in the history of "the early years following ratification of the Constitution, one tends to find both examples of major principles that remained the subject of disagreement as well as examples of early legislation and practices that today we would reject as plainly inconsistent with the constitutional separation of powers").

B. CIVIL ACTIONS

NOTE ON THE EXISTENCE, SOURCES, AND SCOPE OF FEDERAL COMMON LAW

Page 652. Add a new footnote 7a at the end of the penultimate paragraph of Paragraph (6):

[7a] In recent years, the Court has moved away from the broad implied delegation theory epitomized by Justice Jackson's D'Oench Duhme concurrence. Consider Rodriguez v. Federal Deposit Insurance Corporation, 140 S.Ct. 713 (2020), where the unanimous Court declined to adopt a federal common law rule that several circuits had used to resolve disputes over the distribution of joint tax refunds among affiliated corporations, and held instead that state law should govern. The Court explained that "[j]udicial lawmaking in the form of federal common law plays a necessarily modest role under a Constitution that vests the federal government's 'legislative Powers' in Congress and reserves most other regulatory authority to the States." It recognized "limited areas" (such as admiralty and interstate disputes) where judges "may appropriately craft the rule of decision", but emphasized that "strict conditions must be satisfied" before "federal judges may claim a new area for common lawmaking". One of the "most basic" conditions, the need "to protect uniquely federal interests," was missing in the case. Federal regulations specified a government interest in receiving taxes from corporate groups and in delivering refunds to such groups, but were silent on the issue at hand: the distribution of such refunds among group members. That was enough for the Court to conclude that it lacked the authority to make federal common law even though the issue arose in the context of a federal tax dispute in a federal bankruptcy proceeding.

Page 652. Add in place of the last sentence in Paragraph (6):

If, in some cases "in which no state's law controls, and to which no federal statute or treaty provides an answer," federal judges can and do "find law" that is grounded in settled principles of common law, equity, or the law of nations, why must the resulting rule of decision be understood as *federal* common law? For the argument that it should not be so understood, see Sachs, *Finding Law*, 107 Cal.L.Rev. 527, 578 (2019).

Page 656. Add a new footnote 12 at the end of Paragraph (7)(c):

[12] Professor Pojanowski argues that those who claim that American judges should exercise common law powers in the interpretation of statutes underestimate the historical similarities between the common law and legislative traditions from which the U.S. legal system emerged. See Pojanowski, *Reading Statutes in the Common Law Tradition*, 101 Va.L.Rev. 1357 (2015). He argues, in particular, that "classical common lawyers saw legislation as a central component in a common law *system* that sought to internalize the general customs and ways of the realm." To the extent that the common law itself originated in custom, moreover, it was also "possible to claim that this positive law grew up from the community." And, much like the process of common law adjudication, English parliamentary procedures were designed to arrive at a community judgment about disputed matters. Hence, Professor Pojanowski concludes that those who today invoke (or resist) common law reasoning as a model for interpreting legislation do so based on an ahistorical view of the distinctions between the two. Assuming that Professor Pojanowski correctly identifies overlooked historical similarities between the common law and legislation, how does that insight affect the role of the courts in a constitutional system that departs in important ways from its common law antecedents?

NOTE ON FEDERAL PREEMPTION OF STATE LAW

Pages 680–81. Substitute the following for Paragraph (5):

(5) Express Preemption Clauses. In theory, an express preemption clause presents a standard question of statutory interpretation. Recent decisions interpreting such clauses, however, have suggested that they do not preclude consideration of implied preemption as well, and some decisions find implied preemption without even reaching the question of express preemption. See generally Geier v. American Honda Motor Co., 529 U.S. 861, 869–74 (2000); Jordan, *The Shifting Preemption Paradigm: Conceptual and Interpretive Issues*, 51 Vand.L.Rev. 1149 (1998). Compare, *e.g.*, Boggs v. Boggs, 520 U.S. 833 (1997) (ignoring ERISA's broad and explicit preemption clause and holding instead that applying Louisiana community property law to determine the disposition of a decedent's ex-spouse's undistributed pension benefits would conflict with the purpose of particular substantive ERISA provisions), with Egelhoff v. Egelhoff, 532 U.S. 141 (2001) (holding that ERISA's express preemption clause displaced state law establishing a default provision that the designation of a spouse as the beneficiary of a pension and life insurance policy was automatically revoked upon divorce). If Congress takes the trouble to enact an express preemption clause, does the Court threaten to disrupt the balance that Congress struck if it invokes implied preemption principles as well? *Cf.* Gobeille v. Liberty Mut. Ins. Co., 577 U.S. 312, 329 (2016) (Thomas, J., concurring) (approvingly noting that in some "cases involving express pre-emption provisions, the [statutory] text has been the beginning and often the end of our analysis").

In interpreting express preemption clauses, the Court has articulated two competing views about whether the presumption against preemption applies. In one line of authority, the Court has said that "when the text of a pre-emption clause is susceptible of more than one plausible reading, courts ordinarily 'accept the reading that disfavors pre-emption.'" See Altria Group, Inc. v. Good, 555 U.S. 70, 77 (2008) (quoting Bates v. Dow Agrosciences LLC, 544 U.S. 431, 449 (2005)). In another, the Court has said that when a "statute 'contains an express pre-emption clause,' we do not invoke any presumption against pre-emption but instead 'focus on the plain wording of the clause, which necessarily contains the best evidence of Congress' pre-emptive intent.'" Puerto Rico v. Franklin California Tax-Free Trust, 579 U.S. 115 (2016) (quoting Chamber of Commerce v. Whiting, 563 U.S. 582, 594 (2011)).[7] Does the Court have sound reasons to apply the presumption against preemption, rather than ordinary rules of construction, when Congress has expressed an explicit intention to preempt, leaving only the question of scope to be decided by the courts? If principles of federalism counsel against preemption in cases of doubt, should the same federalism policies govern in cases in which Congress has spoken unclearly about its intention to preempt?

[7] For a decision in which the Court broadly interpreted an awkwardly worded preemption clause without any mention of the presumption against preemption, see Bruesewitz v. Wyeth LLC, 562 U.S. 223 (2011). See also Coventry Health Care of Mo., Inc. v. Nevils, 581 U.S. 87, 95–96 (2017) (holding that an express preemption clause of the Federal Employees Health Benefits Act preempts a given state law despite the availability of a "plausible" nonpreemptive interpretation).

Pages 681–82. Add in place of the final paragraph of Paragraph (6):

Several of the Court's most textually inclined Justices have sharply questioned "obstacle" preemption. For example, describing the Court's "entire body of 'purposes and objectives' pre-emption jurisprudence [as] inherently flawed", Justice Thomas' separate opinion in Wyeth v. Levine, 555 U.S. 555, 594 (2009) (Thomas, J., concurring in the judgment), argued that obstacle preemption cases "improperly rely on legislative history, broad atextual notions of congressional purpose, and even congressional inaction in order to pre-empt state law." To find preemption based on those indicia of unenacted statutory purpose, he reasoned, contradicts the safeguards of federalism found in the Supremacy Clause, U.S. Const. Art. VI, cl. 2, which "gives 'supreme' status only to those [laws] that are 'made in Pursuance' of '[t]his Constitution.'" To respect that condition, he said, the Court may find preemption only when a state law conflicts with a statutory text (or a regulation authorized by such a text) that has cleared the hurdles of bicameralism and presentment set forth by Article I, § 7. How convincing is Justice Thomas' reading of the Supremacy Clause?

Expressing similar concerns, a recent plurality opinion by Justice Gorsuch, joined by Justices Thomas and Kavanaugh, concluded that finding preemption based on asserted interference with the "purposes and objectives" of a federal statute "risk[s] displacing the legislative compromises actually reflected in the statutory text—compromises that sometimes may seem irrational to an outsider coming to the statute cold, but whose genius lies in having won the broad support our Constitution demands of any new law." Virginia Uranium, Inc. v. Warren, 139 S.Ct. 1894, 1908 (2019); see also AT & T Mobility LLC v. Concepcion, 563 U.S. 333, 353 (2011) (Thomas, J., concurring) (reiterating his concerns about "purposes-and-objectives preemption"); Williamson v. Mazda Motor of America, Inc., 562 U.S. 323, 341–43 (2011) (Thomas, J., concurring in the judgment) (same).[8] This position aligns with views about legislative compromise and bicameralism that the Court has embraced in some of its recent opinions. See Seventh Edition pp. 654–655, *supra*.[9]

In view of the challenges Congress would face if it were to try to anticipate, specify, and accurately express the proper resolution to all of the preemption questions that would arise in the lifetime of even a moderately complex regulatory statute, can textualism plausibly supply a workable approach to preemption questions? See Meltzer, *Textualism and Preemption*, 112 Mich.L.Rev. 1 (2013) (arguing that the answer is no). For an essay situating Professor Meltzer's critique in a broader theory of purposive interpretation, see Fallon, *On Viewing the Courts as Junior Partners of Congress in Statutory Interpretation Cases: An Essay Celebrating the Scholarship of Daniel J. Meltzer*, 91 Notre Dame L.Rev. 1743 (2016) (contribution to symposium in honor of Dan Meltzer).

[8] Williamson highlights the judicial lawmaking discretion inherent in obstacle preemption. In that case, the Court held that a Department of Transportation regulation giving auto manufacturers the choice to install lap or shoulder belts in certain rear positions in a vehicle did not preempt a state tort action alleging that Mazda acted negligently by using a shoulder rather than a lap belt in such a position. By contrast, the Court in Geier v. American Honda Motor Co., *supra*, had previously held that, by giving manufacturers the choice between airbags or passive restraints, a prior version of the same regulation *did* preempt a state tort action alleging that an auto manufacturer had negligently failed to equip its vehicles with airbags. In Williamson, the majority distinguished Geier on the ground that both the drafting history and subsequent agency interpretations of the amended regulation revealed no agency intent to give manufacturers an *affirmative* choice between shoulder and lap belts. In his opinion concurring in the judgment in Williamson, Justice Thomas argued that the Court's reasoning, which he described as free-ranging "psychoanalysis" of the agency's goals, confirmed that "[p]urposes-and-objectives pre-emption" necessarily "roams beyond statutory or regulatory text" and "is thus wholly illegitimate."

[9] In contrast with his views on "obstacle" preemption, Justice Thomas would not hesitate to find preemption in a case resting on a true conflict—one in which a party cannot simultaneously comply with state and federal law. See Seventh Edition pp. 679–680. In a plurality opinion in PLIVA, Inc. v. Mensing, 564 U.S. 604 (2011), Justice Thomas (joined by Chief Justice Roberts and Justices Scalia and Alito) relied on historical analysis found in Nelson, *supra*, to conclude that the Supremacy Clause was modeled on *non obstante* clauses that eighteenth century legislatures had inserted into statutes to signal their intention to repeal earlier statutes on the same subject. In particular, legislatures used *non obstante* clauses to signal the inapplicability of the traditional strong presumption against implied repeal—a presumption that required interpreters to strain to read potentially conflicting statutes as being in harmony. From that starting point, the plurality concluded that the *non obstante* language in the Supremacy Clause meant that courts should not strain to find ways to avoid an evident conflict between state and federal law. See also Merck Sharp & Dohme Corp. v. Albrecht, 139 S.Ct. 1668, 1681 (2019) (Thomas, J., concurring) (arguing that founding-era evidence suggests that a federal law preempts a state law when "the two are in logical contradiction").

Page 685. Add a new footnote 10a at the end of the penultimate paragraph of Paragraph (9):

[10a] One commentator has suggested that the Court's readiness to find field or obstacle preemption in a case like Arizona v. United States, Seventh Edition p. 685, compromises the states' ability to address perceived underenforcement of federal law by the Executive Branch of the federal government. See Morley, *Reverse Nullification and Executive Discretion*, 17 U.Pa.J.Const.L. 1283 (2015). How should the Court balance the executive's interest in exercising

prosecutorial discretion against the states' interests in enforcing federal norms they think important? Does it depend on whether the question at issue implicates an area of special national concern such as foreign relations? On a perceived need for federal uniformity?

Page 685. Add a new footnote 13 at the end of the last paragraph of Paragraph (9):

13 In Kansas v. Garcia, 140 S.Ct. 791 (2020), the Court considered whether the Immigration Reform and Control Act (IRCA) preempted Kansas from using information on an alien's fraudulent W-4 and K-4 forms as the basis for a state law identity theft prosecution. The four-Justice dissent, written by Justice Breyer, argued that Arizona v. United States "demonstrates that IRCA impliedly preempts state laws that trench on Congress's detailed and delicate design" for policing fraud committed in the process of demonstrating federal work authorization. The majority, however, per Justice Alito, distinguished Arizona on the ground that "federal law does not create a comprehensive and unified system regarding the information that a State may require employees to provide." The Court emphasized that "[f]rom the beginning of our country, criminal law enforcement has been primarily a responsibility of the States," and it argued that the "federal system would be turned upside down if we were to hold that federal criminal law preempts state law whenever they overlap".

NOTE ON FEDERAL COMMON LAW IMPLIED BY JURISDICTIONAL GRANTS

Page 694. Add at the end of footnote 10:

See also Air & Liquid Sys. Corp. v. DeVries, 139 S.Ct. 986, 992 (2019) ("In maritime tort cases, we act as a common-law court, subject to any controlling statutes enacted by Congress.").

Page 694. Add in place of footnote 11:

11 In some tension with its earlier position in Moragne, the Court in Atlantic Sounding Co. v. Townsend, 557 U.S. 404 (2009), held that the common law of admiralty authorizes the recovery of punitive damages when a shipowner willfully denies a crew member maintenance and cure after an injury. See Seventh Edition p. 686 n.*, *supra* (defining maintenance and cure). In so holding, the Court (5–4, per Justice Thomas) concluded that the punitive damages remedy traditionally available in maintenance and cure actions remained so despite the fact that such damages would *not* be recoverable in an action brought pursuant to the Jones Act, 46 U.S.C. § 30104, which allows someone in the plaintiff's position to elect between a common law and statutory remedy. In contrast with its approach in Moragne, the Court in Townsend did not use the policy reflected in a federal statute to define a parallel common law admiralty claim. A dissent written by Justice Alito and joined by the Chief Justice and Justices Scalia and Kennedy would have followed the Jones Act's policy in determining the availability of punitive damages under the common law of admiralty.

In contrast, in The Dutra Group v. Batterton, 139 S.Ct. 2275 (2019), the Court (6–3, per Justice Alito) followed the Jones Act's policy to hold that a seaman could not recover punitive damages on a claim of unseaworthiness. In so doing, the Court reaffirmed its position that " 'an admiralty court should look primarily to . . . legislative enactments for policy guidance' " (quoting Miles v. Apex Marine Corp., Seventh Edition p. 693). While acknowledging that Atlantic Sounding had deviated from the policy of the Jones Act based on established maritime law tradition, the Court in Dutra found that, "unlike maintenance and cure, [the maritime law of] unseaworthiness did not traditionally allow recovery of punitive damages." In light of that history, the Court thought it inappropriate to recognize a novel remedy that would create disuniformity between the common law of unseaworthiness and the statutory remedy for personal injury available under the Jones Act.

Why should the Court apply the "policy" of a statute to common law cases that the statute does not govern directly? For an argument that courts possessing common law authority may properly use that power to broaden a statute's reach to new cases that text itself does not reach, see Pojanowski, *Statutes in Common Law Courts*, 91 Tex.L.Rev. 479 (2013).

Page 697. Add before the penultimate sentence of Paragraph (2):

The Supreme Court now seems to have accepted, at least in dicta, the structural reading of Hinderlider, concluding that "implicit alterations to the

States' relationships with each other" at the time of the founding opened the door for application of a federal rule of decision to interstate disputes. Franchise Tax Bd. v. Hyatt, 139 S.Ct. 1485, 1497–98 (2019).

NOTE ON FEDERAL COMMON LAW RELATING TO FOREIGN AFFAIRS

Page 709. Add a new footnote 1a at the end of the first paragraph of Paragraph (2)(a):

[1a] Harrison, *The American Act of State Doctrine*, 47 Geo.J.Int'l L. 507, 533–37 (2016), argues that the act of state doctrine, properly understood, originally served a choice of law function directing American courts to accept as binding the legal judgments of a foreign sovereign. Does that understanding of the act of state doctrine, if correct, clarify the source of the Supreme Court's authority to develop and apply that doctrine?

Page 715. Add at the end of footnote 11:

For a history of the debate and an argument that modern technological and economic changes support the revisionist position, see Stephan, *One Voice in Foreign Relations and Federal Common Law*, 60 Va.J.Int'l L. 1 (2019).

Page 716. Add at the end of the penultimate paragraph in Paragraph (4)(c):

See generally Bellia & Clark, The Law of Nations and the United States Constitution (2017) (elaborating on the ways in which the law of nations informs the allocation of U.S. constitutional power respecting relations with foreign sovereigns). For further analysis of Bellia & Clark's structural and historical contentions, see Symposium, *The Law of Nations and the United States Constitution*, 106 Geo.L.J. 1558 (2019).

Page 716. Add at the end of footnote 13:

Born, *Customary International Law in United States Courts*, 92 Wash.L.Rev. 1641 (2017), purports to "reject[ ] central elements of both the modernist and revisionist positions" in the course of arguing that CIL should be treated as federal law but "will be directly applicable in U.S. courts only when the federal political branches have expressly or impliedly provided for judicial application of a particular rule." Compare Howard, *A Revised Revisionist Position in the Law of Nations Debate*, 15 Duke J.Const.L. & Pub.Pol'y 53 (2020), who concludes that "the traditional law of nations is exclusively within the domain of federal law, while modern CIL can be adopted by either the federal or state political branches", and that "the law of nations only becomes domestic law if either (a) the Constitution permits or requires the law of nations in interpretation of its provisions; or (b) the political branches adopt a certain custom or give the judiciary jurisdiction to decide questions regarding the law of nations." How, if at all, do these positions differ from the revisionist position?

NOTE ON THE ALIEN TORT STATUTE AND CUSTOMARY INTERNATIONAL LAW

Page 720. Add a new footnote 8a at the end of Paragraph (2):

[8a] The Court moved in the direction of Justice Scalia's Sosa dissent in Jesner v. Arab Bank, PLC, 138 S.Ct. 1386 (2018), a suit by foreign nationals against a Jordanian financial institution for its alleged financing of terrorist attacks on them or their families in the Middle East. In an opinion written by Justice Kennedy, the Court held, 5–4, that a cause of action is not available under the ATS in a suit against a foreign corporation. The Court relied on precedents that "cast doubt on the authority of courts to extend or create private causes of action even in the realm of domestic law." Those precedents included two decisions that refused to imply constitutional

causes of action: Ziglar v. Abbasi, 582 U.S. 120 (2017), also discussed on pp. 108–109, 148, 212, *infra*, which emphasized that " 'the Legislature is in the better position to consider if the public interest would be served by imposing a new substantive legal liability' "; and Correctional Services Corp. v. Malesko, Seventh Edition p. 774, which extended the Court's reluctance to imply constitutional causes of action to the question of corporate liability. The Court in Jesner concluded that "[n]either the language of the ATS nor the precedents interpreting it support an exception to these general principles". It further noted that lower-court ATS litigation against foreign corporate defendants had sparked diplomatic tensions that disserved the aims of the ATS and that underscored the wisdom of declining to imply a cause of action here. In a portion of the opinion that garnered only a plurality, Justice Kennedy, joined by Chief Justice Roberts and Justice Thomas, expressed doubt whether corporate liability for human rights violations was well enough established in international law to satisfy Sosa's requirement "of a norm that is specific, universal, and obligatory."

Justices Alito and Gorsuch joined the parts of the opinion that garnered a majority but filed separate concurring opinions. Justice Gorsuch emphasized that when the ATS was enacted in 1789, a federal court case between aliens would have been impermissible because alien-alien suits in non-federal question cases were (and remain) inconsistent with Article III, see Mossman v. Higginson, 4 Dall. 12 (1800), and because a suit under the law of nations did not arise under federal law in 1789 since the law of nations was then part of general law.

In a dissenting opinion joined by Justices Ginsburg, Breyer, and Kagan, Justice Sotomayor contended that the Sosa test went only to the question of what tort "violations" were well enough recognized under the law of nations, and not to which defendants might be called to account in a civil action to remedy recognized violations. The dissent also questioned whether Justice Gorsuch's separate opinion sufficiently accounted for the broad and dynamic language of the ATS, which in the dissent's view authorized the recognition of federal rights of action under the Sosa test. Finally, the dissent concluded that categorically rejecting corporate liability was too overinclusive and underinclusive an instrument for addressing diplomatic concerns arising out of the ATS's application.

Can Jesner's strict approach to implying causes of action, which led the Court to note that "a proper application of Sosa" might "preclude courts from ever recognizing any new causes of action under the ATS", be squared with the approach in Sosa itself, which refused to "close the door to further independent judicial recognition of actionable international norms"?

Page 722. Add a new footnote 10 at the end of the penultimate paragraph of Paragraph (5):

[10] Legal scholars have expressed a range of views on Kiobel. See, *e.g.*, Vázquez, *Things We Do With Presumptions: Reflections on Kiobel v. Royal Dutch Petroleum*, 89 Notre Dame L.Rev. 1719 (2014) (arguing, *inter alia*, that the presumption against extraterritoriality does not apply to a jurisdictional statute purporting to give courts power to adjudicate universal norms); Weinberg, *What We Don't Talk About When We Talk About Extraterritoriality: Kiobel and the Conflict of Laws*, 99 Cornell L.Rev. 1471 (2014) (contending that Kiobel's facts fall within the literal terms of the ATS's jurisdictional grant and that the national interest in having U.S. courts hear a case like Kiobel lies in the "mutual, reciprocal interest" of all nations in "protecting human rights"); Young, *Universal Jurisdiction, the Alien Tort Statute, and Transnational Public-Law Litigation After Kiobel*, 64 Duke L.J. 1023, 1100 (2015) (arguing that Kiobel "was a particularly appropriate case for judicial caution about the extraterritorial reach of American law" because of the foreign relations implications of recognizing an implied right of action in wholly extraterritorial cases).

Page 722. Add a new footnote 11 at the end of the last paragraph of Paragraph (5):

[11] In Nestle USA, Inc. v. Doe, 141 S.Ct. 1931 (2021), plaintiffs alleged in an ATS suit that two U.S. corporations aided and abetted child slavery when they provided resources to, and bought cocoa from, farms in Ivory Coast to which plaintiffs were trafficked as children. Applying Kiobel, the Court in an opinion by Justice Thomas ruled, by a vote of 8–1, that plaintiffs' claims were impermissibly extraterritorial. The Court reasoned that "[n]early all the conduct that they say aided and abetted forced labor * * * occurred in Ivory Coast," and that plaintiffs' allegation that "every major operational decision by both companies is made in or approved in the U.S." did not render the claims domestic for ATS purposes. On the latter point, the Court explained that "[b]ecause making 'operational decisions' is an activity common to most corporations, generic allegations of this sort do not draw a sufficient connection between the cause of action respondents seek—aiding and abetting forced labor overseas—and domestic conduct." Justice Thomas added, in an opinion joined only by Justices Gorsuch and Kavanaugh, that the Court

lacked authority to recognize aiding and abetting liability "because federal courts should not recognize private rights of action for violations of international law beyond the three historical torts identified in Sosa." Justice Gorsuch wrote a concurring opinion to emphasize that while corporations enjoy no immunity from ATS actions, the Court should "jettison the misguided notion that courts have discretion to create new causes of action under the ATS". Justice Alito joined this opinion on the first point, and Justice Kavanaugh joined it on the second point. Justice Sotomayor, joined by Justices Breyer and Kagan, concurred in part and concurred in the judgment. Her opinion argued that corporations were not immune from ATS liability and took issue with Justice Thomas's argument that the Court should never recognize ATS causes of action beyond the three historical ones identified in Sosa. Finally, Justice Alito in the lone dissent argued that domestic corporations were not immune under the ATS and that the Court should remand the case for further legal development before reaching the extraterritoriality issue.

Nestle clarifies what plaintiffs must allege about domestic corporate contacts to defeat the presumption against extraterritoriality in the ATS context. Five Justices across three opinions also agreed that the *domestic* corporations in this case can be sued in ATS cases. None of these opinions explained how this latter conclusion is consistent with the Court's holding in Jesner, *supra* note 8a, that the judiciary should not extend ATS liability to *foreign* corporations due to separation of powers concerns. Can one reconcile Nestle and Jesner on this point?

---

2. ENFORCING PRIMARY OBLIGATIONS

A. CIVIL ACTIONS

NOTE ON IMPLIED RIGHTS OF ACTION

Page 739. Add a new footnote 1a at the end of the first sentence in Paragraph (1):

[1a] Bellia & Clark, *The Original Source of the Cause of Action in Federal Courts: The Example of the Alien Tort Statute*, 101 Va.L.Rev. 609 (2015), argues that the issue of implied rights of action is a relatively modern one because federal courts had little reason, prior to the twentieth century, to consider the question. The reason, according to Bellia and Clark, is that the Process Acts of 1789 and 1792 and the Conformity Acts enacted beginning in 1872 authorized federal courts to apply state forms of proceeding in actions at law. Because federal courts could therefore apply state "forms of action," as appropriate, to address federal statutory violations, the question whether federal courts had inherent power to recognize implied rights of action simply did not arise. Conceptual and statutory developments in the twentieth century—including the Rules Enabling Act's elimination of the use of state forms of action—did away with off-the-rack rights of action and put into play the federal judiciary's inherent power to provide a remedy when Congress has not done so expressly. See Bellia, *Article III and the Cause of Action*, 89 Iowa L.Rev. 777 (2004).

Page 745. Add a new footnote 10a at the end of Paragraph (4)(c):

[10a] The Court held in Cummings v. Premier Rehab Keller, 142 S.Ct. 1562 (2022), that emotional distress damages are not available for implied causes of action under two Spending Clause statutes, the Rehabilitation Act of 1973 and the Patient Protection and Affordable Care Act of 2010. The Court emphasized that Barnes requires damages to be "traditionally available in suits for breach of contract" so that the funding recipient receives "clear notice" of the possibility of damages. It determined that such notice did not exist for emotional distress damages, which are "highly unusual" for breach of contract, and which do not reflect "the consensus rule among American jurisdictions." In a concurring opinion, Justice Kavanaugh, joined by Justice Gorsuch, argued that the contract-law analogy deployed by the majority and dissent, and in the prior Spending Clause cases, should be replaced by a separation-of-powers approach which counsels that, "with respect to existing implied causes of action, Congress, not this Court, should extend those implied causes of action and expand available remedies."

Page 746. Add the following in place of the last sentence of footnote 12:

Should the Court presume, in the absence of specification to the contrary, that traditional principles of equity are generally available to remedy violations of federal statutes? See Morley, *The Federal Equity Power*, 59 B.C.L.Rev. 217 (2018).

For further discussion of Armstrong, see Seventh Edition pp. 845, 934, & 1012–1013.

Page 747. Add a new footnote 13a at the end of the first sentence of the second paragraph of Paragraph (8):

[13a] In 2021, the United States invoked these cases, most prominently Debs, in a lawsuit to enjoin the Texas Heartbeat Act, 87th Leg., Reg. Sess., also known as S. B. 8. The Act prohibits physicians from performing an abortion on a pregnant woman after approximately six weeks of pregnancy, in violation of Roe v. Wade, 410 U.S. 959 (1973) and Planned Parenthood of Southeastern Pa. v. Casey, 505 U.S. 833 (1992). See discussion *supra* at p. 12 and *infra* pp. 126–139. After the United States Court of Appeals for the Fifth Circuit in a private-party challenge to S. B. 8 rejected a request for an injunction pending appeal, largely on sovereign immunity grounds, the United States sued Texas on the premise that it has no immunity in a suit by the federal government. The United States relied primarily on Debs to argue that it could seek equitable relief against S. B. 8's threats to its sovereign interests in protecting the supremacy of the Constitution, even absent an express statutory cause of action. The Supreme Court granted certiorari to determine the propriety of the United States' suit, but later dismissed the writ as improvidently granted. United States v. Texas, 142 S.Ct. 522 (2021). For a comprehensive analysis of Debs and its continuing significance that reads the decision narrowly to authorize the federal government to seek an injunction to protect rights of U.S. citizens connected to some kind of proprietary interest, see Bamzai & Bray, Debs *and the Federal Equity Jurisdiction*, 98 Notre Dame L.Rev. 699 (2022).

B. REMEDIES FOR CONSTITUTIONAL VIOLATIONS

NOTE ON REMEDIES FOR FEDERAL CONSTITUTIONAL RIGHTS

Page 757. Add a new footnote 4a at the end of Paragraph (3)(c):

[4a] In Nelson v. Colorado, 581 U.S. 128 (2017), the Court held that it violated due process for a state law to require a defendant who is acquitted on appeal to prove his innocence by "clear and convincing" evidence in order to recover costs, fees, and restitution paid by virtue of the subsequently vacated conviction. In so holding, the Court in Nelson invoked the due process balancing test prescribed by Mathews v. Eldridge, 424 U.S. 319 (1976). Does that approach implicitly underlie the frameworks used to require meaningful tax refund remedies in Ward, McKesson, and Reich?

Page 759. Add at the end of Paragraph (4):

The Court's decision in Montgomery v. Louisiana, 577 U.S. 190 (2016), confirms that there is a constitutional law of retroactivity that stands apart from and, in some cases, limits courts' remedial discretion. At issue was whether, and in what circumstances, a state court must apply a new rule of constitutional law on state collateral review of a state court criminal conviction. The Court's reasoning was framed by earlier decisions governing the retroactive application of new rules of law in collateral federal habeas proceedings. When the plurality in Teague v. Lane, Seventh Edition p. 1295, announced a general proscription against applying a new rule of federal law retroactively in collateral federal habeas proceedings, it also articulated an exception allowing a federal habeas court to provide relief if a new rule imposes a substantive limitation on the state's very authority to criminalize the conduct at issue. Subsequent decisions held that this "first exception" to

Teague "cover[s] not only rules forbidding criminal punishment but also rules prohibiting a certain category of punishment of certain primary conduct for a class of defendants because of their status or offense." Penry v. Lynaugh, 492 U.S. 302, 330 (1989).

Nothing in Teague suggested that its rules governing retroactivity were constitutionally required. Indeed, the plurality had made clear that its framework was an interpretation of the jurisdictional statutes governing collateral federal habeas proceedings. In a subsequent case, the Court further held that state courts may apply retroactivity rules that differ from those prescribed by Teague. See Danforth v. Minnesota, 552 U.S. 264, 266 (2008). In Montgomery, however, the Court held that state courts exercising collateral review may not deny retroactive application of new rules involving substantive limitations that would fall under Teague's first exception. The Court thus explained: "Substantive rules[ ] * * * set forth categorical constitutional guarantees that place certain criminal laws and punishments altogether beyond the State's power to impose. It follows that when a State enforces a proscription or penalty barred by the Constitution, the resulting conviction or sentence is, by definition, unlawful." From that starting point, the Court derived "a general principle" that a state court "has no authority to leave in place a conviction or sentence that violates a substantive rule, regardless of whether the conviction or sentence became final before the rule was announced."

Since the Court imposed this new rule of retroactivity in the teeth of contrary state remedial law, the Court's position on retroactivity must be one of constitutional dimension. What is the source of the constitutional law of retroactivity? Is there one? See Montgomery v. Louisiana, 577 U.S. at 220 (Scalia, J., dissenting) (calling the Court's decision an "ipse dixit" and ruling out due process and equal protection as the sources of the principle). For further discussion of Montgomery v. Louisiana, see p. 82, *supra*; pp. 182, 187–199 *infra*.

———

NOTE ON BIVENS AND THE FORMULATION OF REMEDIES IN CONSTITUTIONAL CASES

Pages 774–75. Replace the second and third paragraphs of Paragraph (7) with the following:

In three recent decisions, the Court has moved away from case-specific judicial balancing, heightened the importance of separation of powers, and in the process raised the bar yet higher to the recognition of a new Bivens cause of action.

Ziglar v. Abbasi, 582 U.S. 120 (2017) gave new emphasis to the "special factors" analysis developed in prior cases. The case arose out of the post-9/11 detention of six individuals who were arrested on immigration charges and then held without bail in a maximum security facility under a "hold-until-cleared policy"—a policy that applied to detainees whom the FBI deemed of potential interest to the investigation of terrorism. Respondents—all of

whom were of Arab or South Asian descent and five of whom were Muslim—
filed a Bivens action against three officials of the U.S. Department of Justice
and two wardens of the federal facility at which respondents had been held.
Respondents sought damages on that grounds that the petitioners had (1)
held them in "harsh pretrial conditions for a punitive purpose," in violation
of substantive due process; (2) singled them out because of their "race,
religion, or national origin," contrary to the equal protection component of
the Fifth Amendment; (3) subjected them to strip searches "without any
legitimate penological interest," in contravention of the Fourth and Fifth
Amendments; and (4) knowingly permitted the guards to abuse them, again
in violation of due process.

In an opinion for the Court (joined by Chief Justice Roberts and Justices
Thomas and Alito),[4] Justice Kennedy concluded that a Bivens action did not
lie for respondents' claims. Noting that Bivens was the product of a time in
which the Court more freely recognized implied rights of action, Justice
Kennedy deemed it "a significant step under separation-of-powers principles
for a court" to create an implied damages action against federal officials for
a constitutional violation. While not overruling Bivens in the contexts to
which it already applied, the Court made clear that "expanding the Bivens
remedy is now a 'disfavored' judicial activity" (quoting Iqbal, 556 U.S. at
675). It held that when asked to extend Bivens to a new context, it would ask
"whether the Judiciary is well suited, absent congressional action or
instruction, to consider and weigh the costs and benefits of allowing a
damages action to proceed." In this case, even though the claims were at
some level related to those recognized under Bivens and its progeny, the
Court reasoned that the challenged actions—undertaken "pursuant to a
high-level executive policy created in the wake of a major terrorist attack on
American soil"—in fact bore "little resemblance" to previously recognized
Bivens claims. More generally, the Court concluded that "special factors"
counseled hesitation against extending Bivens to respondents' claims
against large-scale executive policy concerning "sensitive issues of national
security."[5] Indeed, the Court found it "telling" that Congress has not
prescribed liability for post-9/11 detention policy even though the USA
PATRIOT Act required the Department of Justice to provide Congress with
periodic reports on civil rights and civil liberties abuses in the fight against
terrorism.

In dissent, Justice Breyer (joined by Justice Ginsburg) reasoned that
respondents' claims were not novel because Bivens, Davis v. Passman,
Seventh Edition p. 770, and Carlson v. Green, Seventh Edition p. 771, had
recognized implied rights of action, respectively, for unlawful searches and
seizures, invidious discrimination, and unconstitutional conditions of

---

[4]   Justices Sotomayor, Kagan, and Gorsuch took no part in the consideration or decision
of the case.

[5]   Although the Court itself concluded that the "special factors" analysis foreclosed almost
all of respondents' claims, it remanded the case to the court of appeals to apply the "special
factors" analysis to the particular allegation that one of the wardens had allowed the guards to
abuse respondents. That claim, in the Court's view, involved a more "modest extension" of
Bivens and thus warranted its own analysis. In a separate concurrence, Justice Thomas
explained that he would apply Bivens only to the "precise circumstances" of that case.

confinement. Justice Breyer further argued that, although the Constitution vests "primary power" over national security in the political branches, it "also delegates to the Judiciary the duty to protect an individual's fundamental constitutional rights." It followed, in his view, that the judiciary had a proper "role to play" in crafting remedies when national security interests and individual rights conflict. The Court, he added, could rely on doctrines of qualified immunity, heightened pleading, and tailored discovery to mitigate potential intrusions upon national security interests.

The second decision, Hernandez v. Mesa, 140 S.Ct. 735 (2020), involved a Bivens claim that arose out of a cross-border shooting incident in which a U.S. border patrol agent fired two shots across the U.S.-Mexico border that killed a Mexican national on Mexican soil. In an opinion by Justice Alito (joined by Chief Justice Roberts and Justices Thomas, Gorsuch, and Kavanaugh), the Court described its jurisprudence on whether to extend Bivens as a "two-step inquiry": (1) whether the claim arises in a new context or involves a new category of defendants; and, if so, (2) whether any special factors counsel hesitation about granting the extension. The Court ruled that a cross-border shooting presented a "new context, *i.e.*, one that is meaningfully different" from the three cases recognizing a Bivens remedy. It then identified three "special factors" that counseled hesitation in extending Bivens to that context. First, a Bivens remedy for cross-border shootings could affect foreign relations and undermine the executive branch's "lead role in foreign policy". Second, "the risk of undermining border security provides reason to hesitate before extending Bivens into this field." Finally, the Court took guidance from "what Congress has done in statutes addressing related matters." Examining 42 U.S.C. § 1983, the Westfall Act, and the Torture Victim Protection Act, the Court noted that "Congress has repeatedly declined to authorize the award of damages for injury inflicted outside our borders".[5a]

Justice Ginsburg dissented, joined by Justices Breyer, Sotomayor, and Kagan. Justice Ginsburg disputed the Court's view that a cross-border shooting presented a "new context". Because "the purpose of Bivens is to deter the *officer*" from using unjustified force, "the fortuity that the bullet happened to strike Hernandez on the Mexican side of the embankment . . . should not matter one whit." She further argued that the Bivens remedy should be available even if the cross-border shooting did present a new context. In contrast to the plaintiffs in Abassi, the plaintiffs here have no access to alternative remedies, and they challenge "the rogue action of a rank-and-file law enforcement officer" rather than government policies or policymakers. Moreover, the Court "does not home in on how a Bivens suit for an unjustified killing would in fact undermine security at the border", and recognizing Bivens liability here would aid, not impair, foreign relations.

[5a] Justice Thomas, joined by Justice Gorsuch, concurred but wrote separately to argue that Bivens should be overruled. In light of the Court's sharp retrenchment in implying both constitutional and statutory causes of action, its refusal to extend Bivens liability for nearly four decades, and the majority's recognition that "it is doubtful" that the Court would reach the same result if Bivens were decided today, he concluded that the Court had repudiated Bivens' foundation and that "continued adherence to even a limited form of the Bivens doctrine appears to 'perpetuate a usurpation of the legislative power.' " (Citation omitted.)

In the third decision, Egbert v. Boule, 142 S.Ct. 1793 (2022), respondent, a federal informant, alleged that a U.S. Border Patrol Agent unlawfully entered his property (an inn abutting the U.S.-Canada border often used by smugglers) and threw him against a vehicle in the midst of an enforcement action, and later retaliated by, among other things, prompting the Internal Revenue Service to audit him. Respondent brought Bivens claims against the agent under the Fourth Amendment for excessive force and the First Amendment for unlawful retaliation. In an opinion by Justice Thomas (joined by Chief Justice Roberts and Justices Alito, Kavanaugh, and Barrett), the Court rejected the Fourth Amendment claim for two independent reasons. First, after reducing the two-step test from Hernandez to the question "whether there is *any* rational reason (even one) to think that *Congress* is better suited" to decide whether a damages action is appropriate, the Court concluded that Congress was better suited here because the case involved border security and, by extension, national security.[5b] Second, the Court explained that courts may not fashion a Bivens remedy "if Congress has already provided, or authorized the Executive to provide," an alternate remedial scheme. Here the executive branch's investigation of Egbert's actions and its provision of a grievance procedure sufficed to preclude a cause of action even though respondent claimed the grievance procedure lacked adequate process. The Court also ruled that a Bivens action can never lie for First Amendment retaliation because Congress is better suited than courts to weigh the social costs of such an action.[5c]

Justice Sotomayor, in an opinion joined by Justices Breyer and Kagan, dissented on the Fourth Amendment excessive force claim but concurred in the judgment on the First Amendment retaliation claim. Relying on the two-step inquiry from Hernandez, she concluded that the Fourth Amendment claim should be recognized because the context was materially indistinguishable from Bivens, and in event, there was no special factor because the case's mere proximity to the border raised no national security issue. But she agreed with the First Amendment ruling, albeit on the different ground that a First Amendment retaliation claim presents a special factor because it "raises line-drawing concerns similar to those identified in Wilkie." More broadly, Justice Sotomayor criticized as contrary to Ziglar and Hernandez—decisions that themselves had circumscribed the Bivens inquiry in new ways—the Court's holding that only Congress, not the courts, may weigh the costs and benefits of a new cause action. She further argued that the Court's "alternative remedies" analysis was flawed because the internal executive branch grievance procedure provided "no remedy at all." While bemoaning the Court's relentless narrowing of viable Bivens claims,

---

[5b] The primary national security issues related to Bivens prior to Hernandez and Boule grew out of the post-9/11 environment. See Pfander, Constitutional Torts and the War on Terror (2017); Kent, *Are Damages Different?: Bivens and National Security*, 87 S.Cal.L.Rev. 1123 (2014); Litman, *Remedial Convergence and Collapse*, 106 Cal.L.Rev. 1477 (2018); Marguiles, *Curbing Remedies for Official Wrongs: The Need for Bivens Suits in National Security Cases*, 68 Case W.Res.L.Rev. 1153 (2018).

[5c] Justice Gorsuch concurred in the judgment. He agreed with the majority's new formulation of the Bivens test, but argued that because Congress is always better situated than courts "to weigh the value of a new cause of action', the Court should "return the power to create new causes of action" to Congress.

Justice Sotomayor stated that "lower courts should not read [the majority opinion] to render Bivens a dead letter."

The Court has not extended Bivens to new fact situations since Carlsen v. Green was decided more than four decades ago, and the successively stricter tests announced in Ziglar, Hernandez, and Boule give rise to serious doubt whether it ever will. Should the Court go further and overrule Bivens and the two subsequent decisions recognizing implied constitutional causes of action, as Justices Thomas and Gorsuch have argued, see *supra* notes 5a and 5c? As recently as Ziglar, the Court noted that it did "not inten[d] to cast doubt on the continued force, or even necessity, of Bivens in the search-and-seizure context in which it arose", and added that the "settled law of Bivens in this common and recurrent sphere of law enforcement, and the undoubted reliance upon it as a fixed principle in the law, are powerful reasons to retain it in that sphere."

Moreover, as Justice Sotomayor noted in dissent in Boule, Congress "has recognized and relied on the Bivens cause of action in creating and amending other remedies, including the FTCA." One such recognition is the Westfall Act, Pub.L.No. 100–694, 102 Stat. 4563 (1988), which made the FTCA the exclusive remedy for certain nonconstitutional torts by federal officials but expressly stated that that remedy did not extend to civil actions against a federal governmental employee "brought for a violation of the Constitution of the United States." See 28 U.S.C. § 2679(b)(2)(A). The Court in Hernandez noted that "[b]y enacting this provision, Congress made clear that it was not attempting to abrogate Bivens," but rather "simply left Bivens where it found it." Pfander & Baltmanis, *Rethinking Bivens: Legitimacy and Constitutional Adjudication*, 98 Geo.L.J. 117 (2009), have gone further and claimed that the Westfall Act "ratified" Bivens. See also Vázquez & Vladeck, *State Law, the Westfall Act, and the Nature of the Bivens Question*, 161 U.Pa.L.Rev. 509 (2013) (drawing similar inferences from the Westfall Act). How do these varying interpretations of the Westfall Act's impact on Bivens affect the Court's discretion to overrule Bivens? If the Westfall Act affirmatively "ratified" the Bivens framework, should the Court assume that the Act ratified the framework as of 1971, when Bivens was decided, or as of 1988 when the Court had already begun its retrenchment in cases such as Bush v. Lucas, Seventh Edition pp.771–772; Chappell v. Wallace, Seventh Edition p. 773; and United States v. Stanley, Seventh Edition p. 773?

For a symposium that analyzes Bivens and many other issues in this Chapter, see Symposium, *Federal Courts: Practice & Procedure: The Fiftieth Anniversary of Bivens*, 96 Notre Dame L.Rev. 1755–2005 (2021). Kent, *Lessons for Bivens and Qualified Immunity Debates from Nineteenth-Century Damages Litigation Against Federal Officers*, 96 Notre Dame L.Rev. 1755 (2021), questions conventional wisdom about how officer damages suits operated in the early republic by showing that they were often endorsed by the political branches and that the Supreme Court in some contexts crafted immunity doctrines to shield federal officers from such suits. Sisk, *Recovering the Tort Remedy for Federal Official Wrongdoing*, 96 Notre Dame L.Rev. 1789 (2021), argues that Congress should repeal the FTCA's intentional tort exception and that the Supreme Court should clarify that the FTCA's discretionary function exception protects only genuine policymaking deliberations. Schwartz, Reinert, & Pfander, *Going Rogue: The Supreme Court's Newfound Hostility to Policy-Based Bivens Claims*, 96 Notre Dame L.Rev. 1835 (2021), contend that the Court's reluctance in Ziglar, *supra*, to grant a Bivens claims against federal officers making large-scale national policy determinations runs counter to longstanding doctrine and is sowing confusion in the lower courts. Vladeck, *The Inconsistent Originalism of Judge-Made Remedies Against Federal Officials*, 96 Notre Dame L.Rev. 1869 (2021), argues, largely on historical grounds, "that the same principles that drive the ability of judges to fashion constitutional remedies for prospective relief ought to drive their ability to fashion such remedies for retrospective relief." Woolhandler & Collins, *Was Bivens Necessary?*, 96 Notre Dame L.Rev. 1893 (2021), defend Bivens within a restrictive framework of the federal courts' common law powers. Vázquez, *Bivens and the Ancien Régime*, 96 Notre Dame L.Rev. 1923 (2021), argues that the Court's reluctance to imply statutory causes of action does not justify a similar reluctance with respect to damages remedies for constitutional violations. Crocker, *A Scapegoat Theory of Bivens*, 96 Notre Dame L.Rev. 1943 (2021), suggests that Bivens was a response "to public scapegoating of vulnerable populations through swaths of the criminal justice system," and that "the Bivens regime in turn bred the scapegoat of its own ridicule and rejection by the later Supreme Court". And Kozel, *Stare Decisis as Authority and Aspiration*, 96 Notre Dame L.Rev. 1971 (2021), explores Bivens as a case study about the continuing power of stare decisis in the Supreme Court.

Page 777. Add a new Paragraph (10):

(10) Bivens, Erie, and Federalism. In Hernandez v. Mesa, 140 S.Ct. 735, 742 (2020), the Court invoked Erie to argue that "federal courts today cannot fashion new claims in the way that they could before 1938. With the demise of federal general common law, a federal court's authority to recognize a damages remedy must rest at bottom on a statute enacted by Congress, and no statute expressly creates a Bivens remedy." Is Bivens at odds with Erie? Compare Fallon, *Bidding Farewell to Constitutional Torts*, 107 Calif.L.Rev. 933, 987–88 (2019): "Bivens lay well within the federal judiciary's traditional, common lawmaking power. The analogy to Ex Parte Young is strong, as are analogies to the exclusionary rule and other judge-made remedies for constitutional violations, including mandates to state courts to entertain damages actions against state officials. Insistence that separation-of-powers concerns preclude federal judicial lawmaking also ignores, and would leave unjustified, the role the Court has assumed in shaping official immunity law."

Note also that the Westfall Act, passed in 1988, precludes state-law tort actions against federal officers for actions taken in the scope of their employment. See Pfander & Baltmanis, *Rethinking* Bivens: *Legitimacy and Constitutional Adjudication*, 98 Geo. L.J. 117 (2009) (arguing that the Westfall Act changes the nature of the Bivens inquiry). Thus, in a case like Hernandez, the "traditional" route to damages—a state-law tort suit where the constitutional issue is litigated as part of the officer's defense—is now unavailable. Should the absence of a state court remedy change the way federal courts approach Bivens claims? For affirmative answers, see Fallon, *supra*, at 989 ("With the Westfall Act creating a substantially broadened category of victims of constitutional lawbreaking for whom it is Bivens actions or nothing, the historically well-grounded principle that damages remedies should normally be available to victims of constitutional misconduct ought to control."); Vladeck, *Constitutional Remedies in Federalism's Forgotten Shadow*, 107 Calif.L.Rev. 1043 (2019) (similar).

CHAPTER VIII

THE FEDERAL QUESTION JURISDICTION OF THE DISTRICT COURTS

---

1. INTRODUCTION

NOTE ON THE STATUTORY DEVELOPMENT OF THE JURISDICTION

Page 783. Replace footnote 38 with the following:

   38 In Merrill Lynch, Pierce, Fenner & Smith Inc. v. Manning, 578 U.S. 374 (2016), the Court held that interpretive doctrines governing subject matter jurisdiction under § 1331 also apply to § 27 of the Securities Exchange Act of 1934, which grants federal district courts exclusive jurisdiction "of all suits in equity and actions at law brought to enforce any liability or duty created by [the Exchange Act] or the rules or regulations thereunder." 15 U.S.C. § 78aa(a). The Court further noted that wording similar to § 27 "appears in nine other federal jurisdictional provisions—mostly enacted, like § 27, as part of New Deal-era regulatory statutes."

---

2. THE SCOPE OF THE CONSTITUTIONAL GRANT OF FEDERAL QUESTION JURISDICTION

NOTE ON THE SCOPE OF THE CONSTITUTIONAL GRANT

Page 800. Add at the end of Paragraph (7):

The Court recently clarified the Red Cross rule. The federal corporate charter of the Federal National Mortgage Association (Fannie Mae) grants Fannie Mae the power "to sue and to be sued, and to complain and to defend, in any court of competent jurisdiction, State or Federal." 12 U.S.C. § 1723(a). In Lightfoot v. Cendant Mortgage Corp., 580 U.S. 82 (2017), the Court held that this provision established Fannie Mae's capacity to bring suit and be sued but did not grant federal jurisdiction over cases involving Fannie Mae. The Court acknowledged that the specific reference to federal court, taken alone, pointed toward federal jurisdiction. But the Court further reasoned that the phrase "any court of competent jurisdiction" required an extant, independent source of subject-matter jurisdiction. The Court concluded that Fannie Mae's corporate charter permits suit by or against Fannie Mae only in a "state or federal court already endowed with subject-matter jurisdiction over the suit."

The Court has now interpreted a "sue and be sued" clause in six federal corporate charters stretching back to the charter of the first Bank of the

United States at issue in Deveaux. While members of Congress may not have been aware of the jurisdictional consequences of the specific language on which they voted in all of these charters, does Lightfoot imply that future legislators drafting a "sue and be sued" clause should be guided by the following interpretive principle? A specific reference in the clause to federal court will confer federal jurisdiction unless some other provision in the clause indicates a need for an independent basis of jurisdiction.

———

3. THE SCOPE OF THE STATUTORY GRANT OF FEDERAL QUESTION JURISDICTION

A. THE STRUCTURE OF "ARISING UNDER" JURISDICTION UNDER THE FEDERAL QUESTION STATUTE

NOTE ON THE MOTTLEY CASE AND THE WELL-PLEADED COMPLAINT RULE

Page 815. Add at the end of Section (5):

(6) Jurisdiction over Actions to Confirm or Vacate Arbitral Awards. In Badgerow v. Walters, 142 S. Ct. 1310 (2022), the Court refused to extend the look-through method of jurisdictional assessment to actions brought to confirm or vacate arbitral awards. As noted in section (5) above, the Vaden Court applied the look-through method to actions to compel arbitration under § 4 of the Federal Arbitration Act (FAA). But in a decision by Justice Kagan for eight Justices, the Badgerow Court held that the look-through approach was necessitated by and limited to the specific language of § 4. Because Congress had not included the same language in §§ 9 and 10 of the FAA, dealing with confirmation and vacatur of arbitral awards, Justice Kagan held that it did not intend courts to follow a similar look-through approach to the jurisdictional analysis of those proceedings.

The employment dispute arose from Badgerow's termination—after which she invoked a contractual right to arbitration and sought compensation for a discharge that was said to violate state and federal law. (Had there been an action to compel arbitration under Vaden, the federal questions would have conferred look-through jurisdiction.) After losing the arbitration, Badgerow sued in state court to vacate the award, contending it was tainted by fraud. The employer removed the action to federal court, arguing that the federal-law nature of the original dispute over Badgerow's discharge meant that a claim to vacate or confirm the resulting award would also arise under federal law.

In rejecting use of the look-through method, the Court based its decision on the contrasting language of the applicable sections of the FAA. Section 4 provides for jurisdiction in a federal district court that, "save for [the arbitration] agreement, would have jurisdiction" over "the controversy between the parties." Section 4 thus looked to the underlying controversy between the parties, rather than to the claim stated in the petition to compel arbitration. By contrast, the sections that govern petitions to confirm or vacate an award do not contain the "save for" language and do not confer jurisdiction on the district courts. The Court regarded the textual difference as decisive; the district courts were to apply standard jurisdictional analysis, looking either for diversity or for a federal question on the face of the well-pleaded complaint to confirm or vacate an award. Rejecting policy arguments, the Court found that extending the look-through method would not materially simplify the jurisdictional analysis. Nor did the Court see signs of a congressional desire to broaden federal judicial engagement with arbitral matters, many of which Congress left to state courts. Justice Breyer dissented for himself alone.

Page 815. Renumber as (7) The Standard for Congressional Divestment of § 1331 Jurisdiction.

Page 815. Add at the bottom of renumbered paragraph (7):

Questions of implied displacement also arise when Congress creates appellate-style judicial review of agency action. In Axon Enterprise, Inc. v. Federal Trade Comm'n, 143 S.Ct. 890 (2023), the Supreme Court unanimously rejected the government's implied displacement claims as to the appellate-style review of the FTC and SEC. In both instances, the agency brought enforcement proceedings against individuals that were to be heard initially before an administrative law judge (ALJ) subject to further review within the agency and then by federal appellate courts. In both instances, the targets sued in federal district court under 28 U.S.C. § 1331 to enjoin the enforcement proceeding on the ground that agency ALJs were insufficiently accountable to the President. District courts in Texas and Arizona dismissed the suits on the government's motion, remitting the plaintiffs to defensive litigation before the agencies.

On review of conflicting decisions by the Fifth and Ninth Circuits, the Court in an opinion by Justice Kagan found that the three factors identified in Thunder Basin Coal Co. v. Reich, 510 U.S. 200 (1994) cut against implied displacement. First, denying district court jurisdiction might foreclose "meaningful judicial review" by forcing the plaintiffs to appear before a structurally problematic ALJ. Second, the plaintiffs' separation-of-powers challenge was said to be "wholly collateral" to the statute's review provisions. Third, and finally, the plaintiffs' claims implicated issues of constitutional law that fell outside the agency's expertise. Justice Thomas concurred in the opinion but wrote separately to question the constitutionality of all agency adjudication of private enforcement actions. Concurring in the judgment, Justice Gorsuch viewed the Thunder Basin factors as an improper judicial gloss on section 1331's straightforward grant of statutory jurisdiction.

———

NOTE ON "ARISING UNDER" JURISDICTION AND THE CAUSE OF ACTION TEST

Page 819. Replace footnote 2 with the following:

² For decisions taking a narrow view of when a federal question is so insubstantial as to provide a basis for federal question jurisdiction, see Shapiro v. McManus, 577 U.S. 39 (2015); Hagans v. Lavine, 415 U.S. 528 (1974). The Court has indicated that the Bell v. Hood "nonfrivolous-argument" pleading standard for statutory federal question jurisdiction does not necessarily apply to other bases of statutory federal jurisdiction. In Bolivarian Republic of Venezuela v. Helmerich & Payne International Drilling Co., 581 U.S. 170 (2017), the Court considered what averments must be made in a case asserting jurisdiction under 28 U.S.C. § 1605(a)(3). This provision creates an exception to foreign sovereign immunity, and thus statutory federal jurisdiction, in a "case * * * in which rights in property taken in violation of international law are in issue." Relying on the language and purpose of § 1605(a)(3), the Court rejected the Bell v. Hood standard and instead required the plaintiff to make out and maintain a legally valid claim that property rights are in issue and that the relevant property was taken in violation of international law. The Court also noted that under the diversity jurisdiction statute, 28 U.S.C. § 1332, parties must in fact be diverse, and not merely arguably so. Are there good reasons to have a relatively lenient pleading standard for statutory federal question jurisdiction but not for other forms of statutory federal jurisdiction?

NOTE ON THE SCOPE OF "ARISING UNDER" JURISDICTION UNDER 28 U.S.C. § 1331

Page 836. Add a new Paragraph (3)(c) just before Paragraph (4):

(c)   In Merrill Lynch, Pierce, Fenner & Smith Inc. v. Manning, 578 U.S. 374 (2016), the Court held that the "arising under" test of 28 U.S.C. § 1331 applies to § 27 of the Securities Exchange Act of 1934, which grants federal district courts exclusive jurisdiction "of all suits in equity and actions at law brought to enforce any liability or duty created by [the Exchange Act] or the rules or regulations thereunder." Manning sued several financial institutions in New Jersey state court under New Jersey law for allegedly illegal "naked short sales" of stock that, according to the complaint, also violated a Securities and Exchange Commission regulation. The defendants removed the case to federal court but the court of appeals remanded. It ruled that the district court lacked subject matter jurisdiction under § 1331 because Manning's claims were "brought under state law" and none "necessarily raised" a federal issue. This ruling decided the question of subject matter jurisdiction under § 27, which, the court held, was co-extensive with § 1331. The Supreme Court reviewed only the § 27 issue, and affirmed.

In explaining why it was appropriate for § 27 to include the "federal element" component of § 1331's jurisdictional test, the Court noted that a state-law action could be brought in federal court to enforce an Exchange Act duty under § 27 if it "necessarily depends on a showing that the defendant breached the Exchange Act". The Court offered this hypothetical:

"Suppose, for example, that a state statute simply makes illegal 'any violation of the Exchange Act involving naked short selling.' A plaintiff seeking relief under that state law must undertake to prove, as the cornerstone of his suit, that the defendant infringed a requirement of the federal statute. (Indeed, in this hypothetical, that is the plaintiff's *only* project.) Accordingly, his suit, even though asserting a state-created claim, is also 'brought to enforce' a duty created by the Exchange Act."

The Court then noted that such a claim, whose "very success depends on giving effect to a federal requirement", is like a claim for federal jurisdiction under § 1331 when the state-law claim " 'necessarily raise[s] a stated federal issue, actually disputed and substantial, which a federal forum may entertain without disturbing any congressionally approved balance' of federal and state power" (quoting Grable, 545 U.S., at 314).

Justice Thomas, in a concurrence in the judgment joined by Justice Sotomayor, rejected the assimilation of the "federal element" prong of the § 1331 test to § 27. He argued that the better reading of § 27 would be to allow federal jurisdiction over all state-law claims that necessarily raise an Exchange Act issue without importing the "arising under" test's additional inquiries about substantiality, disputedness, and the federal-state balance. The Court responded:

"[T]his Court has not construed any jurisdictional statute, whether using the words 'brought to enforce' or 'arising under' (or for that matter, any other), to draw the concurrence's line. For as long as we have contemplated exercising federal jurisdiction over state-law claims necessarily raising federal issues, we have inquired as well into whether those issues are 'really and substantially' disputed. See, *e.g.*, Hopkins v. Walker, 244 U.S. 486, 489 (1917); Shulthis v. McDougal, 225 U.S. 561, 569 (1912). And similarly, we have long emphasized the need in such circumstances to make 'sensitive judgments about congressional intent, judicial power, and the federal system.' Merrell Dow Pharmaceuticals Inc. v. Thompson, 478 U.S. 804, 810 (1986). At this late juncture, we see no virtue in trying to pull apart these interconnected strands of necessity and substantiality-plus. Indeed, doing so here—and thus creating a gap between our 'brought to enforce' and 'arising under' standards—would conflict with this Court's precedent and undermine important goals of interpreting jurisdictional statutes."

The Court acknowledged the oddity of construing the very different language in § 1331 and § 27 to mean the same thing. But it said that the test for "arising under" jurisdiction has never been based on the statute's "particular phrasing", and noted that that § 1331 was given a narrower construction than the identical words in Article III due to the statute's "history[,] the demands of reason and coherence, and the dictates of sound judicial policy" (quoting Romero v. Int'l Terminal Operating Co., 358 U.S. 354, 379 (1959)). Because the "arising under" test does not turn on § 1331's text, "there is nothing remarkable in its fitting as, or even more, neatly a differently worded statutory provision."[5a]

[5a] Does the Manning Court in downplaying the text take adequate account of the role of Congress? Consider Mulligan, *28 U.S.C. § 1331 Jurisdiction in the Roberts Court: A Rights-Inclusive Approach*, 51 Stetson L.Rev. 201 (2022). Mulligan identifies in recent cases a more rights-inclusive approach to federal question jurisdiction—one that departs from the Holmes cause-of-action test and aligns more closely with Mulligan's own understanding of what Congress meant to accomplish when the statute became law in the nineteenth century. For a similar approach, rejecting the Holmes test and more generally defending a faithful agent role for the federal courts in interpreting jurisdictional statutes, see Redish, et al., *Federal*

The Court insisted that the extension of the scope of § 1331's "arising under" jurisprudence to § 27 promoted administrative simplicity because "judges and litigants are familiar with the 'arising under' standard and how it works", the test "[f]or the most part * * * provides ready answers to jurisdictional questions", and "an existing body of precedent gives guidance whenever borderline cases crop up." Do the decisions studied in this Section support this happy assessment? Or is it more accurate to say, with Justice Thomas, that the "arising under" standard "is anything but clear" and "involves numerous judgments about matters of degree that are not readily susceptible to bright lines"?

Page 837. Add the following at the end of Paragraph (4):

For further reflections in this context on the virtues and vices of clear and determinate rules versus refined but less determinate ones, and on how this casebook and two of its authors have approached this issue over the years, see Shapiro, *An Incomplete Discussion of "Arising Under" Jurisdiction*, 91 Notre Dame L.Rev. 1931 (2016) (contribution to symposium in honor of Dan Meltzer).

———

5. SUPPLEMENTAL (PENDENT) JURISDICTION

NOTE ON SUPPLEMENTAL JURISDICTION IN FEDERAL QUESTION AND OTHER NONDIVERSITY CASES

Pages 870–71. Replace the text of Paragraph (7)(b) with the following:

(b) Tolling the Statute of Limitations. Section 1367(d) specifies the time period in which an asserted supplemental claim that is later dismissed may be refiled in state court. It provides that the state-law period of limitations for any such claim "shall be tolled while the claim is pending [in federal court] and for a period of 30 days after it is dismissed unless State law provides for a longer tolling period." In Artis v. District of Columbia, 138 S.Ct. 594 (2018), the Court, in an opinion by Justice Ginsburg for five Justices, rejected the view that Section 1367(d) permits the state limitation period to run during the pendency of the supplemental claim but imposes a 30-day grace period to refile. It instead held that Section 1367(d) "stops the clock" on the state limitations period during the claim's pendency in federal court, thus giving the plaintiff whatever time remained under state law on the stopped clock, plus 30 days, to refile. The Court reasoned that this conclusion best comported with the language of subsection (d) and the dominant usage of the term "tolled".

———

Jurisdiction As Statutory Interpretation: A Majordomo Purposivist Perspective, 74 SMU L.Rev. 303 (2021). Whatever one might say about the proper judicial role in interpreting § 1331, should the Court evaluate the jurisdictional implications of subsequent statutes, such as the 1934 federal securities law implicated in Manning, by reference to the congressional intent surrounding the 1875 enactment of the precursor to § 1331?

The Court rejected the argument that Section 1367(d), so interpreted, exceeds Congress' enumerated powers. Relying on Jinks v. Richland County, 538 U.S. 456 (2003) (rejecting constitutional objections to Section 1367(d)'s 30-day grace period for claim refiled in state court and otherwise time-barred there), it ruled that the subsection was "necessary and proper" for carrying out Congress' power to establish inferior federal courts in a fair and efficient manner because it provides an alternative to the unsatisfactory options that federal courts otherwise faced when deciding whether to retain jurisdiction over supplemental claims that might be time barred in state court. The Court further ruled that the provision does not unduly infringe state sovereignty. It acknowledged that the rejected "grace period" interpretation of Section 1367(d) might be less intrusive on state authority, but ruled that the Constitution did not limit Congress' discretion to that degree. Justice Gorsuch, joined by Justices Kennedy, Thomas, and Alito, dissented. He disagreed with the Court's interpretation of Section 1367(d) and expressed particular concern about its impact on state authority to define time limitations on state-law claims.

CHAPTER IX

SUITS CHALLENGING OFFICIAL ACTION

1. SUITS CHALLENGING FEDERAL OFFICIAL ACTION

PRELIMINARY NOTE ON THE SOVEREIGN IMMUNITY OF THE UNITED STATES AND THE ENFORCEMENT OF THE LAW AGAINST FEDERAL OFFICIALS AND FEDERAL AGENCIES

Page 879. Add at the end of footnote 6:

See also Brettschneider & McNamee, *Sovereign and State: A Democratic Theory of Sovereign Immunity,* 93 Tex.L.Rev. 1229 (2015) (arguing that the state is rightly immune from suit when it acts with democratic legitimacy, but insisting that it ceases to act with democratic legitimacy, and that sovereign immunity should not apply, in cases involving violations of "fundamental" rights)

Page 880. Add a footnote 6a at the end of Paragraph (2)(d):

[6a] For contending views about whether sovereign immunity applies in actions under the Takings Clause, compare Brauneis, *The First Constitutional Tort: The Remedial Revolution in Nineteenth-Century State Just Compensation Law,* 52 Vand.L.Rev. 57, 135–40 (1999) (yes), with Berger, *The Collision of the Takings and State Sovereign Immunity Doctrines,* 63 Wash. & Lee L.Rev. 493 (2006) (no).

Page 880. Add at the end of Paragraph (2)(d):

Note, 129 Harv.L.Rev. 1068 (2016), argues that if the Constitution creates a cause of action against the states in takings and tax refund cases, then the Fourteenth Amendment alters any element of the constitutional plan that otherwise would have afforded the states sovereign immunity in such cases.

Page 881. Add a footnote 7a at the end of the first full paragraph:

[7a] For a comparative appraisal of the nineteenth-century framework that subjected government officials to the same common-law liability rules as private individuals, even for actions taken in wartime, see Pfander, *Dicey's Nightmare: An Essay on the Rule of Law,* 107 Calif.L.Rev. 737 (2019). According to Professor Pfander, that strategy better realized rule-of-law ideals than does modern law that creates distinctive liabilities but also establishes special immunity rules for officials sued for constitutional violations. But see Fallon, *Bidding Farewell to Constitutional Torts,* 107 Cal.L.Rev. 933 (2019), maintaining that "[e]ven if we could return to a common law regime in which governmental officials were subject to the same liability rules as ordinary citizens, we should not." On the one hand, Professor Fallon argues, officials cloaked with public authority pose distinctive threats, including to interests that the common law did not protect. On the other hand, public interests might sometimes require recognition of distinctive official immunities from damages liability.

NOTE ON STATUTORILY AUTHORIZED REVIEW OF FEDERAL OFFICIAL ACTION AND ON LEGISLATION WAIVING THE SOVEREIGN IMMUNITY OF THE UNITED STATES

Page 901. Add at the end of Paragraph (2)(c)(ii):

See also Daniel v. United States, 139 S.Ct. 1713 (2019) (Thomas, J., dissenting from denial of certiorari) (calling for reconsideration of Feres). (Justice Ginsburg also noted that she would grant the petition, but she did not expressly join Justice Thomas's opinion.)

Page 902. Add at the end of Paragraph (2)(d):

In Brownback v. King, 141 S.Ct. 740 (2021), a unanimous Court noted but did not resolve the question whether a district court's dismissal of an FTCA claim on a motion under Rule 12(b)(6) operates to bar a Bivens claim predicated on the same actions by the same defendants and included in the same lawsuit. On its facts, Brownback held that even though proper pleading of jurisdiction over an FTCA claim requires pleading of all the elements of a valid FTCA cause of action, and dismissal for failure to state a claim therefore entails a failure of subject matter jurisdiction, dismissal for failure to state a claim remains a judgment on the merits capable of precluding a subsequent Bivens action.

Page 902. Substitute for the first sentence of Paragraph (3)(a):

According to Kovacs, *Scalia's Bargain*, 77 Ohio St.L.J. 1155 (2016), the circuits are split over whether the waiver of sovereign immunity is limited to suits under the APA and is constrained by its "final agency action" requirement. The majority position is no: though codified in the APA, the waiver applies to any suit, whether or not brought under the APA.

Page 904: Insert New Paragraph (6):

(6) Immunity of Federal Territories and Indian Tribes. The United States has the power both to regulate commerce with the Indian tribes and to regulate federal territories. These powers of regulation have been thought to authorize Congress to subject both Indian tribes and territories to suit, notwithstanding any sovereign immunity they would enjoy if sued as defendants in state or federal court court—provided Congress does so in a clear statutory statement. In Lac du Flambeau Band of Lake Superior Chippewa Indians v. Coughlin, 143 S.Ct. 1689 (2023), the Supreme Court held that the federal bankruptcy statute clearly expressed Congress's intent to override tribal immunity. By contrast, in Financial Oversight and Management Board v. Centro de Periodismo de Investigativo, 143 S.Ct. 1176 (2023), the Court ruled that the federal statute in question did not include the clear statement needed to override Puerto Rico's assumed sovereign immunity.

The Court has frequently confirmed the background norm of tribal sovereign immunity. See Michigan v. Bay Mills Indian Community, 572 U.S. 782, 788 (2014). By contrast, the Court has yet to clarify the extent of any sovereign immunity enjoyed by Puerto Rico. See Financial Oversight and Management Board, 143 S.Ct. at 1183 n.3 (assuming without deciding that

Puerto Rico enjoys sovereign immunity). In that case, Justice Thomas dissented for himself alone, arguing that the Court could not "logically" reject the suit against an arm of the Puerto Rican government for want of a clear statement without first deciding that the territory has sovereign immunity, which he believed the record did not support. *Id.* at 1186.

_____

2. SUITS CHALLENGING STATE OFFICIAL ACTION

A. THE ELEVENTH AMENDMENT AND STATE SOVEREIGN IMMUNITY

INTRODUCTORY NOTE ON STATE SOVEREIGN IMMUNITY AND THE ELEVENTH AMENDMENT

Page 905. Add a new footnote * at the end of Paragraph (1):

   * Clark & Bellia, *The International Law Origins of American Federalism*, 120 Colum.L.Rev. 835 (2020), argue that the term "State" as it appears in Article III was a "term of art," drawn from international law, and presupposed that the states retained all of the powers and prerogatives of international law sovereigns—including immunity from unconsented suit— unless they "clearly and expressly" surrendered their sovereign rights. According to the authors, early debates about state sovereign immunity are best understood against this international law background.

_____

NOTE ON THE ORIGIN, MEANING, AND SCOPE OF THE ELEVENTH AMENDMENT

Page 918. Add at the end of Paragraph (5):

   Based on a close examination of text and history, Baude & Sachs, *The Misunderstood Eleventh Amendment*, 169 U.Pa.L.Rev. 609 (2021), argue for a literal interpretation of the Eleventh Amendment, according to which it bars federal subject matter jurisdiction over all actions prosecuted against states by citizens of other states, including appeals to the Supreme Court from state court judgments, but reaches no farther. Professors Baude and Sachs also argue, however, that the Eleventh Amendment did nothing to displace the common law sovereign immunity that states retained at the time of the Amendment's ratification. According to the authors, most of the Supreme Court's leading cases on the Eleventh Amendment and state sovereign immunity reach the correct results. But the Court's reasoning repeatedly goes awry, they maintain, either by mixing up the immunity conferred by the Eleventh Amendment with the states' common law immunity or by postulating that a constitutional immunity inheres in the constitutional plan.

Page 920. Add at the end of footnote 15:

   Note, *Waiver by Removal? An Analysis of State Sovereign Immunity*, 102 Va.L.Rev. 549 (2016), reports that the circuits are split on whether a state's removal of a suit from state to federal court waives its immunity from claims against which it would have possessed sovereign immunity in state court.

———

NOTE ON EX PARTE YOUNG AND SUITS AGAINST STATE OFFICERS

Page 927. Add at the end of footnote 3:

For a valuable study of Ex parte Young's historical and doctrinal context, including its situation in the Lochner era and its subsequent embrace by jurists and commentators "of all political stripes", see Barry Friedman, *The Story of Ex parte Young: Once Controversial, Now Canon*, in Federal Courts Stories (Jackson & Resnik eds. 2010), at 247.

Page 933. Add at the end of the first paragraph of Paragraph (5)(a):

In response to Professor Harrison, Pfander & Dwinell, *A Declaratory Theory of State Accountability*, 102 Va.L.Rev. 153 (2016), argue that "[e]quity did not recognize routine antisuit injunctions" (although it did authorize some) and, in particular, that equity "had no jurisdiction over criminal matters, a gap that explains the frequent dictum that equity has no power to stay criminal proceedings." Accordingly, the authors conclude, "[t]he Court * * * broke new ground in Ex parte Young, authorizing a new kind of injunction that was untethered to established antisuit forms", and was recognized by commentators at the time as having done so.

Pfander & Wentzel, *The Common Law Origins of Ex parte Young*, 72 Stan.L.Rev. 1269 (2020), trace the deep origins of Ex parte Young not to the traditions of equity, but to common law writs of mandamus, certiorari, and prohibition that functioned in English and early American practice as tools for oversight of the administrative state. According to the authors, nineteenth- and early twentieth-century courts of equity increasingly assumed the functions originally performed by common law writs, partly in response to perceived gaps and partly in response to rule-of-law norms embodied in the Fourteenth Amendment. In the account offered by Pfander & Wentzel, the process of "equitable substitution" was well under way, but not complete, at the time of the decision in Ex parte Young. In a prescriptive vein, the authors conclude that "historically minded scholars and jurists should consult both the equitable and common law traditions when assessing the scope of Article III judicial power" to recognize causes of action and furnish remedies for constitutional violations.

———

Page 935. Add the following principal case and accompanying Notes after Paragraph (5):

Whole Woman's Health v. Jackson

___ U.S. ___, 142 S.Ct. 522, 211 L.Ed 2d 316 (2021).
Certiorari to the United States Court of Appeals for the Fifth Circuit.

■ JUSTICE GORSUCH announced the judgment of the Court, and delivered the opinion of the Court except as to Part II-C.

The Court granted certiorari before judgment in this case to determine whether, under our precedents, certain abortion providers can pursue a pre-enforcement challenge to a recently enacted Texas statute.

We conclude that such an action is permissible against some of the named defendants but not others.

I

[In 2021, Texas enacted the Texas Heartbeat Act, also known as S. B. 8, prohibiting physicians (with limited exceptions) from "knowingly perform[ing] or induc[ing] an abortion on a pregnant woman if the physician detected a fetal heartbeat for the unborn child." Tex. Health & Safety Code, §§ 171.204–205 (West Cum. Supp. 2021). In pegging its prohibition to a fetal heartbeat that physicians can detect six weeks into the pregnancy, the Texas statute defied the 23-week viability standard of *Planned Parenthood v. Casey*, 505 U.S. 833 (1992). In an acknowledged effort to avoid federal court pre-enforcement challenges to the law's constitutionality, the Texas statute does not authorize or direct state officials to bring criminal prosecutions or civil enforcement actions. Instead, S. B. 8 authorizes "any person" to enforce the law by bringing a private civil action to collect a penalty of $10,000 or more from anyone who performs or assists in a prohibited abortion. Tex. Health & Safety Code, §§ 171.207, 208. In addition, S. B. 8 confers a state-wide venue privilege on plaintiffs, protects plaintiffs from any award of costs or fees if they pursue frivolous enforcement claims, and invites plaintiffs to pursue duplicative litigation by foreclosing non-mutual claim and issue preclusion. *Id.* §§ 171.208(a), 208(i), 208(e)(5).

In their complaint, petitioners alleged that S. B. 8 violates the Federal Constitution and sought an injunction barring the following defendants from taking any action to enforce the statute: a state-court judge (Jackson); a state-court clerk (Clarkston); the Texas attorney general (Paxton); the executive directors of Texas medical, nursing, and pharmacy licensing boards (Carlton, Thomas, and Benz); the director of Texas human services (Young); and a single private party (Dickson). Shortly after the petitioners filed their federal complaint, the State-employed individual moved to dismiss, mainly on sovereign immunity grounds. The sole private defendant also moved to dismiss, claiming that the petitioners lacked standing to sue him. The District Court denied the motions.

On interlocutory review, the Fifth Circuit Court of Appeals stayed proceedings in the district court pending its resolution of the defendants appeals and rejected the petitioners' request for an injunction suspending S. B. 8's enforcement. On an emergency petition to stay enforcement of S. B. 8 before it took effect two days later, the Court denied relief. See *Whole Woman's Health v. Jackson*, 141 S. Ct. 2494 (2021) (*Whole Woman's Health I*).

Petitioners filed a second emergency request, asking the Court to grant certiorari before judgment to resolve the Texas defendants' interlocutory appeals in the first instance, without awaiting the views of the Fifth Circuit. The Court granted the petitioners' request and set the case for expedited briefing and argument.]

II

Because this Court granted certiorari before judgment, we effectively stand in the shoes of the Court of Appeals. * * * In this preliminary posture, the ultimate merits question—whether S. B. 8 is consistent with the Federal Constitution—is not before the Court. Nor is the wisdom of S. B. 8 as a matter of public policy.

A

Turning to the matters that are properly put to us, we begin with the sovereign immunity appeal involving the state-court judge, Austin Jackson, and the state-court clerk, Penny Clarkston. While this lawsuit names only one state-court judge and one state-court clerk as defendants, the petitioners explain that they hope eventually to win certification of a class including all Texas state-court judges and clerks as defendants. In the end, the petitioners say, they intend to seek an order enjoining all state-court clerks from docketing S. B. 8 cases and all state-court judges from hearing them.

Almost immediately, however, the petitioners' theory confronts a difficulty. Generally, States are immune from suit under the terms of the Eleventh Amendment and the doctrine of sovereign immunity. See, *e.g.*, Alden v. Maine, 527 U.S. 706, 713 (1999). To be sure, in Ex parte Young, this Court recognized a narrow exception grounded in traditional equity practice—one that allows certain private parties to seek judicial orders in federal court preventing state executive officials from enforcing state laws that are contrary to federal law. 209 U.S. 123, 159–60 (1908). But as Ex parte Young explained, this traditional exception does not normally permit federal courts to issue injunctions against state-court judges or clerks. Usually, those individuals do not enforce state laws as executive officials might; instead, they work to resolve disputes between parties. If a state court errs in its rulings, too, the traditional remedy has been some form of appeal, including to this Court, not the entry of an *ex ante* injunction preventing the state court from hearing cases. As Ex parte Young put it, "an injunction against a state court" or its "machinery" "would be a violation of the whole scheme of our Government." *Id.* at 163.

Nor is that the only problem confronting the petitioners' court-and-clerk theory. Article III of the Constitution affords federal courts the power to resolve only "actual controversies arising between adverse litigants." * * * Private parties who seek to bring S. B. 8 suits in state court may be litigants adverse to the petitioners. But the state-court clerks who docket those disputes and the state-court judges who decide them generally are not. Clerks serve to file cases as they arrive, not to participate as adversaries in those disputes. Judges exist to resolve controversies about a law's meaning or its conformance to the Federal and State Constitutions, not to wage battle as contestants in the parties' litigation. As this Court has explained, "no case or controversy" exists "between a judge who adjudicates claims under a statute and a litigant who attacks the constitutionality of the statute." Pulliam v. Allen, 466 U.S. 522, 538 n.18 (1984).

Then there is the question of remedy. Texas Rule of Civil Procedure 24 directs state-court clerks to accept complaints and record case numbers. The petitioners have pointed to nothing in Texas law that permits clerks to pass on the substance of the filings they docket—let alone refuse a party's complaint based on an assessment of its merits. Nor does Article III confer on federal judges some "amorphous" power to supervise "the operations of government" and reimagine from the ground up the job description of Texas state-court clerks. Raines v. Byrd, 521 U.S. 811, 829 (1997) (internal quotation marks omitted).

Troubling, too, the petitioners have not offered any meaningful limiting principles for their theory. If it caught on and federal judges could enjoin state courts and clerks from entertaining disputes between private parties under *this* state law, what would stop federal judges from prohibiting state courts and clerks from hearing and docketing disputes between private parties under *other* state laws? And if the state courts and clerks somehow qualify as "adverse litigants" for Article III purposes in the present case, when would they not? * * *

* * * Under the petitioners' theory, would clerks have to assemble a blacklist of banned claims subject to immediate dismissal? What kind of inquiry would a state court have to apply to satisfy due process before dismissing those suits? How notorious would the alleged constitutional defects of a claim have to be before a state-court clerk would risk legal jeopardy merely for filing it? Would States have to hire independent legal counsel for their clerks—and would those advisers be the next target of suits seeking injunctive relief? When a party hales a state-court clerk into federal court for filing a complaint containing a purportedly unconstitutional claim, how would the clerk defend himself consistent with his ethical obligation of neutrality? See Tex. Code of Judicial Conduct Canon 3(B)(10) (2021) (instructing judges and court staff to abstain from taking public positions on pending or impending proceedings). Could federal courts enjoin those who perform other ministerial tasks potentially related to litigation, like the postal carrier who delivers complaints to the courthouse? Many more questions than answers would present themselves if the Court journeyed this way. * * *

[In dissent, our] colleagues point to *Pulliam*. But that case had nothing to do with state-court clerks, injunctions against them, or the doctrine of sovereign immunity. Instead, the Court faced only the question whether the suit before it could proceed against a judge consistent with the distinct doctrine of judicial immunity. * * *

If anything, the remainder of our colleagues' cases are even further afield. *Mitchum v. Foster* did not involve state-court clerks, but a judge, prosecutor, and sheriff. When it came to these individuals, the Court held only that the Anti-Injunction Act did not bar suit against them. Once more, the Court did not purport to pass judgment on any sovereign immunity defense, let alone suggest any disagreement with Ex parte Young. * * * Simply put, nothing in any of our colleagues' cases supports their novel suggestion that we should allow a pre-enforcement action for injunctive relief against state-court clerks, all while simultaneously holding the judges they serve immune.

B

Perhaps recognizing the problems with their court-and-clerk theory, the petitioners briefly advance an alternative. They say they seek to enjoin the Texas attorney general from enforcing S. B. 8. Such an injunction, the petitioners submit, would also automatically bind any private party who might try to bring an S. B. 8 suit against them. But the petitioners barely develop this back-up theory in their briefing, and it too suffers from some obvious problems.

Start with perhaps the most straightforward. While Ex parte Young authorizes federal courts to enjoin certain state officials from enforcing state laws, the petitioners do not direct this Court to any enforcement authority the attorney general possesses in connection with S. B. 8 that a federal court might enjoin him from exercising. * * *

Even if we could overcome this problem, doing so would only expose another. Supposing the attorney general did have some enforcement authority under S. B. 8, the petitioners have identified nothing that might allow a federal court to parlay that authority, or any defendant's enforcement authority, into an injunction against any and all unnamed private persons who might seek to bring their own S. B. 8 suits. The equitable powers of federal courts are limited by historical practice. "A court of equity is as much so limited as a court of law." Alemite Mfg. Corp. v. Staff, 42 F.2d 832 (2d Cir. 1930) (L. Hand, J.). Consistent with historical practice, a federal court exercising its equitable authority may enjoin named defendants from taking specified unlawful actions. But under traditional equitable principles, no court may "lawfully enjoin the world at large," *Alemite*, or purport to enjoin challenged "laws themselves." Whole Woman's Health I, 141 S.Ct. at 2495 (citing California v. Texas, 141 S. Ct. 2104, 2115–16 (2021)). * * *

C

While this Court's precedents foreclose some of the petitioners' claims for relief, others survive. The petitioners also name as defendants Stephen Carlton, Katherine Thomas, Allison Benz, and Cecile Young. On the briefing and argument before us, it appears that these particular defendants fall within the scope of Ex parte Young's historic exception to state sovereign immunity. Each of these individuals is an executive licensing official who may or must take enforcement actions against the petitioners if they violate the terms of Texas's Health and Safety Code. Accordingly, we hold that sovereign immunity does not bar the petitioners' suit against these named defendants at the motion to dismiss stage. * * *

Justice THOMAS suggests that the licensing-official defendants lack authority to enforce S. B. 8 because that statute says it is to be "exclusively" enforced through private civil actions "[n]otwithstanding . . . any other law." * * * Of course, Texas courts and not this one are the final arbiters of the meaning of state statutory directions. See Railroad Comm'n of Texas v. Pullman Co., 312 U.S. 496, 500 (1941). But at least based on the limited arguments put to us at this stage of the litigation, it appears that the licensing defendants do have authority to enforce S. B. 8. * * *

D

[Without objection from any Justice, the Court dismissed the claims against the private defendant for want of standing, accepting Mr. Dickson's sworn statement that he did not plan to sue the petitioners to enforce S. B. 8.]

III

While this should be enough to resolve the petitioners' appeal, a detour is required before we close. Justice SOTOMAYOR charges this Court with "shrink[ing]" from the task of defending the supremacy of the Federal Constitution over state law. That rhetoric bears no relation to reality.

The truth is, many paths exist to vindicate the supremacy of federal law in this area. Even aside from the fact that eight Members of the Court agree sovereign immunity does not bar the petitioners from bringing this pre-enforcement challenge in federal court, everyone acknowledges that other pre-enforcement challenges may be possible in state court as well. In fact, 14 such state-court cases already seek to vindicate both federal and state constitutional claims against S. B. 8—and they have met with some success at the summary judgment stage. Separately, any individual sued under S. B. 8 may pursue state and federal constitutional arguments in his or her defense. Still further viable avenues to contest the law's compliance with the Federal Constitution also may be possible; we do not prejudge the possibility. * * *

The truth is, too, that unlike the petitioners before us, those seeking to challenge the constitutionality of state laws are not always able to pick and choose the timing and preferred forum for their arguments. This Court has never recognized an unqualified right to pre-enforcement review of constitutional claims in federal court. In fact, general federal question jurisdiction did not even exist for much of this Nation's history. And pre-enforcement review under the statutory regime the petitioners invoke, 42 U.S.C. § 1983, was not prominent until the mid-20th century. See Monroe v. Pape, 365 U.S. 167 (1961); see also R. Fallon, J. Manning, D. Meltzer, & D. Shapiro, Hart and Wechsler's The Federal Courts and the Federal System 994 (7th ed. 2015). To this day, many federal constitutional rights are as a practical matter asserted typically as defenses to state-law claims, not in federal pre-enforcement cases like this one.* * *

Finally, Justice SOTOMAYOR contends that S. B. 8 "chills" the exercise of federal constitutional rights. If nothing else, she says, this fact warrants allowing further relief in this case. Here again, however, it turns out that the Court has already and often confronted—and rejected—this very line of thinking. As our cases explain, the "chilling effect" associated with a potentially unconstitutional law being " 'on the books' " is insufficient to "justify federal intervention" in a pre-enforcement suit. *Younger* v. *Harris*, 401 U. S. 37, 42, 50–51 (1971). Instead, this Court has always required proof of a more concrete injury and compliance with traditional rules of equitable practice. See *Muskrat*, 219 U.S. at 361; *Ex parte Young*, 209 U.S. at 159–160. The Court has consistently applied these requirements whether the challenged law in question is said to chill the free exercise of religion, the freedom of speech, the right to bear arms, or any other right. The petitioners are not entitled to a special exemption. * * *

The order of the District Court is affirmed in part and reversed in part, and the case is remanded for further proceedings consistent with this opinion. *So ordered.*

■ JUSTICE THOMAS, concurring in part and dissenting in part.

I join all but Part II-C of the Court's opinion. In my view, petitioners may not maintain suit against any of the governmental respondents under Ex parte Young. I would reverse in full the District Court's denial of respondents' motions to dismiss and remand with instructions to dismiss the case for lack of subject-matter jurisdiction. [Justice Thomas interpreted Texas law to foreclose enforcement of S. B. 8 by state licensing officials. He also viewed the likely enforcement of S. B. 8 as too remote to satisfy the standard of imminently threatened enforcement that he saw as essential to bringing traditional equity powers into play.]

■ CHIEF JUSTICE ROBERTS, with whom JUSTICE BREYER, JUSTICE SOTOMAYOR, and JUSTICE KAGAN join, concurring in the judgment in part and dissenting in part.

[S. B. 8.] is contrary to this Court's decisions in *Roe* and *Casey*. It has had the effect of denying the exercise of what we have held is a right protected under the Federal Constitution.

Texas has employed an array of stratagems designed to shield its unconstitutional law from judicial review. * * *

These provisions, among others, effectively chill the provision of abortions in Texas. Texas says that the law also blocks any pre-enforcement judicial review in federal court. On that latter contention, Texas is wrong. As eight Members of the Court agree, petitioners may bring a pre-enforcement suit challenging the Texas law in federal court under Ex parte Young, because there exist state executive officials who retain authority to enforce it. Given the ongoing chilling effect of the state law, the District Court should resolve this litigation and enter appropriate relief without delay.

In my view, several other respondents are also proper defendants. First, under Texas law, the Attorney General maintains authority coextensive with the Texas Medical Board to address violations of S. B. 8. * * * Under Texas law, then, the Attorney General maintains authority to "take enforcement actions" based on violations of S. B. 8. He accordingly also falls within the scope of Ex parte Young's exception to sovereign immunity.

The same goes for Penny Clarkston, a court clerk. Court clerks, of course, do not "usually" enforce a State's laws. But by design, the mere threat of even unsuccessful suits brought under S. B. 8 chills constitutionally protected conduct, given the peculiar rules that the State has imposed. Under these circumstances, the court clerks who issue citations and docket S. B. 8 cases are unavoidably enlisted in the scheme to enforce S. B. 8's unconstitutional provisions, and thus are sufficiently "connect[ed]" to such enforcement to be proper defendants. Ex parte Young, 209 U.S. at 157. The role that clerks play with respect to S. B. 8 is distinct from that of the judges. Judges are in no sense adverse to the parties subject to the burdens of S. B. 8. But as a practical matter clerks are—to the extent they "set[ ] in motion the machinery" that imposes these burdens on those sued under S. B. 8.

The majority contends that this conclusion cannot be reconciled with Ex parte Young, pointing to language * * * that suggests it would be improper to enjoin courts from exercising jurisdiction over cases. Decisions after Ex parte Young, however, recognize that suits to enjoin state court proceedings may be proper. See Mitchum v. Foster, 407 U.S. 225, 243 (1972); see also Pulliam v. Allen, 466 U.S. 522, 525 (1984). And this conclusion is consistent with the entire thrust of Ex parte Young itself. Just as in Ex parte Young, those sued under S. B. 8 will be "harass[ed] . . . with a multiplicity of suits or litigation generally in an endeavor to enforce penalties under an unconstitutional enactment." Under these circumstances, where the mere "commencement of a suit," and in fact just the threat of it, is the "actionable injury to another," the principles underlying Ex parte Young authorize relief against the court officials who play an essential role in that scheme. Any novelty in this remedy is a direct result of the novelty of Texas's scheme. * * *

The clear purpose and actual effect of S. B. 8 has been to nullify this Court's rulings. It is, however, a basic principle that the Constitution is the "fundamental and paramount law of the nation," and "[i]t is emphatically the province and duty of the judicial department to say what the law is." Marbury v. Madison, 5 U.S. 137, 177 (1803). Indeed, "[i]f the legislatures of the several states may, at will, annul the judgments of the courts of the United States, and destroy the rights acquired under those judgments, the constitution itself becomes a solemn mockery." United States v. Peters, 9 U.S. 115, 136 (1809). The nature of the federal right infringed does not matter; it is the role of the Supreme Court in our constitutional system that is at stake.

■ JUSTICE SOTOMAYOR, with whom JUSTICE BREYER and JUSTICE KAGAN join, concurring in the judgment in part and dissenting in part.

For nearly three months, the Texas Legislature has substantially suspended a constitutional guarantee: a pregnant woman's right to control her own body. * * * The chilling effect has been near total, depriving pregnant women in Texas of virtually all opportunity to seek abortion care within their home State after their sixth week of pregnancy. Some women have vindicated their rights by traveling out of State. For the many women who are unable to do so, their only alternatives are to carry unwanted pregnancies to term or attempt self-induced abortions outside of the medical system.

The Court should have put an end to this madness months ago, before S. B. 8 first went into effect. It failed to do so then, and it fails again today. * * * By foreclosing suit against state-court officials and the state attorney general, the Court effectively invites other States to refine S. B. 8's model for nullifying federal rights. The Court thus betrays not only the citizens of Texas, but also our constitutional system of government.

I

I have previously described the havoc S. B. 8's unconstitutional scheme has wrought for Texas women seeking abortion care and their medical providers. [Citing Whole Woman's Health I, 141 S.Ct. at 2498–2499 (SOTOMAYOR, J., dissenting).] * * *

As a whole, these provisions go beyond imposing liability on the exercise of a constitutional right. If enforced, they prevent providers from seeking effective pre-enforcement relief (in both state and federal court) while simultaneously depriving them of effective post-enforcement adjudication, potentially violating procedural due process. To be sure, state courts cannot restrict constitutional rights or defenses that our precedents recognize, nor impose retroactive liability for constitutionally protected conduct. * * * Unenforceable though S. B. 8 may be, however, the threat of its punitive measures creates a chilling effect that advances the State's unconstitutional goals.

II

This Court has confronted State attempts to evade federal constitutional commands before, including schemes that forced parties to expose themselves to catastrophic liability as state-court defendants in order to assert their rights. Until today, the Court had proven equal to those challenges.

In 1908, this Court decided Ex parte Young. In Ex parte Young, the Court considered a Minnesota law fixing new rates for railroads and adopting high fines and penalties for failure to comply with the rates.

The law purported to provide no option to challenge the new rates other than disobeying the law and taking "the risk . . . of being subjected to such enormous penalties." Because the railroad officers and employees "could not be expected to disobey any of the provisions . . . at the risk of such fines and penalties," the law effectively resulted in "a denial of any hearing to the company." *Id.* at 146.

The Court unequivocally rejected this design. Concluding that the legislature could not "preclude a resort to the courts . . . for the purpose of testing [the law's] validity," the Court decided the companies could obtain pre-enforcement relief by suing the Minnesota attorney general based on his "connection with the enforcement" of the challenged act. The Court so held despite the fact that the attorney general's only such connection was the "general duty imposed upon him, which includes the right and the power to enforce the statutes of the State, including, of course, the act in question." * * *

Like the stockholders in Ex parte Young, abortion providers face calamitous liability from a facially unconstitutional law. To be clear, the threat is not just the possibility of money judgments; it is also that, win or lose, providers may be forced to defend themselves against countless suits, all across the State, without any prospect of recovery for their losses or expenses. * * *

Under normal circumstances, providers might be able to assert their rights defensively in state court. These are not normal circumstances. S. B. 8 is structured to thwart review and result in "a denial of any hearing." * * *

[Justice Sotomayor argued that state court clerks are proper defendants by analogy to Shelley v. Kraemer, 334 U.S. 1, 14 (1948).] In *Shelley*, private litigants sought to enforce restrictive racial covenants designed to preclude Black Americans from home ownership and to preserve residential segregation. The Court explained that these ostensibly private covenants involved state action because "but for the active intervention of the state courts, supported by the full panoply of state power," the covenants would be unenforceable. * * *

* * * Modern cases, however, have recognized that suit may be proper even against state court judges, including to enjoin state-court proceedings. [Citing Mitchum v. Foster; Pulliam v. Allen.] The Court responds that these cases did not expressly address sovereign immunity or involve court clerks. If language in Ex parte Young posed an absolute bar to injunctive relief against state-court proceedings and officials, however, these decisions would have been purely advisory.

Moreover, the Court has emphasized that "the principles undergirding the Ex parte Young doctrine" may "support its application" to new circumstances, "novelty notwithstanding." [Virginia Office for Protection and Advocacy v. Stewart, 563 U. S. 247, 261 (2011)] No party has identified any prior circumstance in which a State has delegated an enforcement function to the populace, disclaimed official enforcement authority, and skewed state-court procedures to chill the exercise of constitutional rights. Because S. B. 8's architects designed this scheme to evade Ex parte Young as historically applied, it is especially perverse for the Court to shield it from scrutiny based on its novelty. * * *

Finally, the Court raises "the question of remedy." For the Court, that question cascades into many others about the precise contours of an injunction against Texas court clerks in light of state procedural rules. Vexing though the Court may find these fact-intensive questions, they are exactly the sort of tailoring work that District Courts perform every day. * * *

III

My disagreement with the Court runs far deeper than a quibble over how many defendants these petitioners may sue. The dispute is over whether States may nullify federal constitutional rights by employing schemes like the one at hand. The Court indicates that they can, so long as they write their laws to more thoroughly disclaim all enforcement by state officials, including licensing officials. This choice to shrink from Texas' challenge to federal supremacy will have far-reaching repercussions. I doubt the Court, let alone the country, is prepared for them. * * *

[B]y foreclosing suit against state-court officials and the state attorney general, the Court clears the way for States to reprise and perfect Texas' scheme in the future to target the exercise of any right recognized by this Court with which they disagree.

This is no hypothetical. New permutations of S. B. 8 are coming. In the months since this Court failed to enjoin the law, legislators in several States have discussed or introduced legislation that replicates its scheme to target locally disfavored rights. * * *

In its finest moments, this Court has ensured that constitutional rights "can neither be nullified openly and directly by state legislators or state executive or judicial officers, nor nullified indirectly by them through evasive schemes . . . whether attempted 'ingeniously or ingenuously.'" Cooper v. Aaron, 358 U.S. 1, 17 (1958). Today's fractured Court evinces no such courage. While the Court properly holds that this suit may proceed against the licensing officials, it errs gravely in foreclosing relief against state-court officials and the state attorney general. By so doing, the Court leaves all manner of constitutional rights more vulnerable than ever before, to the great detriment of our Constitution and our Republic.

———

NOTE ON WHOLE WOMAN'S HEALTH AND PRIVATE ENFORCEMENT

(1) Subsequent Proceedings. Following the Court's decision, the Fifth Circuit did not return the case to the district court (as dissenting Justices assumed it would). Instead, that court certified to the Texas Supreme Court questions specific to the authority of state licensing officials to enforce S. B. 8. See Whole Woman's Health v. Jackson, 23 F.4th 380 (5th Cir. 2022). The Texas Supreme Court ruled that the relevant statutes conferred no such authority. See Whole Woman's Health v. Jackson, 642 S.W.3d 569 (Tex. 2022). With one judge dissenting, the Fifth Circuit then remanded the case to the district court with instructions to dismiss all claims. Whole Woman's Health v. Jackson, 31 F.4th 1004 (2022). Having granted review before judgment, the Supreme Court described itself as standing in the shoes of the Fifth Circuit. Should its remand have gone, as the petitioners urged in reliance on past practice, to the district court?

(2) United States v. Texas. After the Supreme Court denied the petition for an emergency stay of the Texas law in September 2021, the United States sued Texas in federal district court to block the State from enforcing S. B. 8. After the district court granted relief, the Fifth Circuit stayed that order and the Court granted certiorari, consolidating the matter with Whole Woman's Health II for expedited review. The Court dismissed the petition as improvidently granted on the same day it decided Whole Woman's Health v. Jackson. United States v. Texas, 142 S. Ct. 522 (2021).

The Supreme Court has stated that states cannot invoke sovereign immunity as a bar to suits by the United States. See, *e.g.*, Alden v. Maine, 527 U.S. 706, 755–56 (1999) (dicta), Seventh Edition p. 437; United States v. Texas, 143 U.S. 621, 646 (1892). But the Court has not addressed whether the United States has standing and an implied right to sue the states to prevent violations of the Fourteenth Amendment rights of state citizens. See Yackle, *A Worthy Champion for Fourteenth Amendment Rights: The United States in Parens Patriae*, 92 Nw.U.L.Rev. 111 (1997) (acknowledging the absence of clear supporting authority but urging courts to authorize such suits by the United States); Davis, *Implied Public Rights of Action*, 114 Colum.L.Rev. 1 (2014) (questioning whether United States may sue to vindicate the rights of state citizens without statutory authority).

In its S. B. 8 litigation, the government relied on In re Debs, 158 U.S. 564 (1895), Seventh Edition p. 747. There, acting without any explicit legislative authority, the Court approved a lower federal court's issuance of an injunction to end the Pullman railway strike. In re Debs and the labor injunction it spawned were criticized in part because they empowered federal judges to regulate industrial relations without legislative guidance and to impose criminal contempt sanctions on striking workers. See Frankfurter & Greene, The Labor Injunction (1930). The government's S. B. 8 litigation, by contrast, sought to enjoin violation of constitutional rights that were regarded as settled law at the time of the suit's initiation. Should federal courts more readily recognize the government's right to sue when it seeks to protect settled constitutional rights than when it invites, as in In re Debs, the creation of new judge-made rules to govern a labor dispute?

(3) The Future of Ex Parte Young. In limiting the issuance of injunctive relief to suits against officers with enforcement authority, Whole Woman's Health v. Jackson relies upon Ex parte Young. There, the Court explained:

> If, because they were law officers of the state, a case could be made for the purpose of testing the constitutionality of the statute, by an injunction suit brought against them, then the constitutionality of every act passed by the legislature could be tested by a suit against the governor and the attorney general, based upon the theory that the former, as the executive of the state, was, in a general sense, charged with the execution of all its laws, and the latter, as attorney general, might represent the state in litigation involving the enforcement of its statutes.

209 U.S. at 157. A state official "must have some connection with the enforcement of the act," otherwise, the suit is making the official "a party as a representative of the state, and thereby attempting to make the state a party." *Id.*

In viewing Texas state judicial officials as proper defendants, were the Whole Woman's Health dissenters urging an application of the Ex parte Young exception or its further expansion? Was an expansion justified to address the concerns posed by S. B. 8's evident desire to foreclose pre-enforcement federal judicial review?

(4) Constitutional Right to Pre-Enforcement Review. Writing for the majority in Whole Woman's Health, Justice Gorsuch proceeded on the assumption that doctors and clinics named as defendants in Texas state court enforcement proceedings can defend by challenging the constitutionality of the Texas restrictions. Yet S. B. 8 was drafted to burden the defensive assertion of constitutional rights; success in defeating one enforcement proceeding would not prevent similar proceedings or resolve the uncertainty as to the legality of abortions. Pre-enforcement review addresses that uncertainty. As the Court has recognized in such cases as Steffel v. Thompson, 415 U.S. 452 (1974), Seventh Edition pp. 1144–1158, litigants often seek to clarify their legal rights before taking action that could lead to the imposition of criminal or other sanctions.

Leading cases on the constitutional right to a remedy do not directly address such a right to anticipatory relief. See Seventh Edition pp. 752–761. One might read the dissenting Justices in Whole Woman's Health to suggest that the traditional availability of pre-enforcement Ex parte Young relief has ripened, over time, into a due process right. Alternatively, one might read the dissenting Justices to suggest that the factors governing preliminary injunctive relief—a clear constitutional violation, a threat of irreparable harm, and the absence of adequate remedies at law—create a strong case for equitable relief from the enforcement of S. B. 8. With the authority to fashion equitable relief in urgent matters, the Court may have fewer occasions to address the issue of constitutional entitlement.

(5) Defensive State Court Litigation. Apart from suits seeking affirmative relief, those targeted by S. B. 8 can defend in state court, raising state and federal defenses. The Whole Woman's Health majority left open the possibility of anticipatory review (by suit against licensing officials), but it also suggested that defendants' right to raise constitutional defenses affords adequate protection against the enforcement of an unconstitutional law.

In evaluating that assertion, should the majority have given greater weight to the many ways in which the Texas statute was designed to foreclose access to court for those threatened by private enforcement? S. B. 8's provisions, taken as a whole, pose severe challenges for defendants. By foreclosing any award of costs or attorney's fees for frivolous litigation, Texas law subjects defendants to the prospect of repeat litigation. Further, S. B. 8 allows suit in any court in Texas, a venue generosity that threatens defendants with the prospect of litigation throughout the state. Finally, by apparently limiting the claim preclusive effect of litigation to those who have paid a judgment, the statute denies defendants repose even if they secure a defense judgment in an initial proceeding.

(6) Continuing Relevance. Does the decision in Dobbs v. Jackson Women's Health Organization, p. 31 *supra*, lessen the significance of Whole Woman's Health? One might understand Whole Woman's Health as a temporizing decision, designed to avoid the merits while the Court worked out its view of the continuing vitality of Roe/Casey.

Yet many states have adopted laws like S. B. 8 in the past few years, some that authorize popular enforcement of anti-abortion laws, some that target other issues (such as the rights of transgender people and the way teachers discuss race in public schools). State legislatures may more broadly rely on these novel enforcement mechanisms to avoid pre-enforcement review. In addition, the Court's emphasis on enforcement authority may take on significance as lower courts consider expanding state sovereign immunity into new contexts, such as voting rights litigation, where state laws may not clearly define official enforcement authority. See Texas Alliance for Retired Americans v. Scott, 28 F.4th 669 (5th Cir.2022) (holding that a suit to contest the constitutionality of state voting laws was barred by the Eleventh Amendment when brought against a state official with ambiguous enforcement authority).

In Reed v. Goertz, 143 S. Ct. 955 (2023), the Court matter-of-factly rejected a claim by Texas that the Eleventh Amendment blocked a suit to challenge on due process grounds the state's refusal to authorize DNA testing in connection with litigation to invalidate a criminal conviction and death sentence. Justice Thomas, dissenting for himself alone, argued that the state official was named as a nominal defendant and lacked the enforcement role necessary to trigger the Ex parte Young exception. *Id.* at 972 & n.7 (Thomas, J., dissenting) (arguing that the issue presented was one of reviewing the state court's interpretation of the statute for fairness rather than blocking its enforcement by the district attorney).

———

NOTE ON CONGRESSIONAL POWER TO ABROGATE STATE IMMUNITY

Page 958. Add at the end of footnote 4:

Jackson & Resnik, *Sovereignties—Federal, State and Tribal: The Story of Seminole Tribe of Florida v. Florida*, in Federal Courts Stories (Jackson & Resnik eds. 2010), at 329, locates the decision in its evolving doctrinal context and provides interesting background on the litigation itself, including its origins in tension between state and tribal sovereigns.

Page 960. Add a new footnote 8a at the end of Paragraph (4)(a):

[8a] In Allen v. Cooper, 140 S.Ct. 994 (2020), the Court relied on Florida Prepaid to hold that Congress lacked authority to abrogate the states' sovereign immunity from suit for copyright infringement.

Page 966. Add at the end of footnote 12:

The Court unanimously rebuffed an invitation to extend Central Virginia Community College v. Katz beyond the bankruptcy power in Allen v. Cooper, 140 S.Ct. 994 (2020), which involved a suit against a state for copyright infringement. Justice Breyer, joined by Justice Ginsburg, concurred in the judgment. Although he continued to believe that the Court "went astray in Seminole Tribe of Fla. v. Florida," Seventh Edition p. 940, he "recognize[ed] that my longstanding view has not carried the day, and that the Court's decision in Florida Prepaid [Postsecondary Educ. Expense Bd. v. College Savings Bank, Seventh Edition p. 959, from which he had also dissented,] controls this case."

Page 967. Add a Paragraph (7)(c):

(c)   In PennEast Pipeline Co. v. New Jersey, 141 S.Ct. 2244 (2021), the Court held that when the states surrendered their immunity from suit by the federal government as an aspect of the constitutional plan, they also surrendered their immunity from suits by private parties to whom the federal government has delegated its eminent domain power. The case arose when the Federal Energy Regulatory Commission granted PennEast a certificate of public convenience and necessity to construct a natural gas pipeline that included an authorization to acquire necessary property by exercising "the right of eminent domain in the district court of the United States for the district in which such property may be located." When PennEast sought to exercise that authority in a suit against New Jersey, the state claimed sovereign immunity. In an opinion by Chief Justice Roberts, the Court disagreed. Relying heavily on precedent, the majority emphasized that Congress has always enjoyed the power of eminent domain and that Congress has long delegated that power to private parties to advance public purposes. Given this historical background, the Chief Justice concluded that the states had surrendered their sovereign immunity from eminent domain actions by the United States when they ratified the Constitution, and he further inferred that the surrender extended to "condemnation proceedings brought by private delegatees" such as PennEast.

Justice Barrett dissented in an opinion joined by Justices Thomas, Kagan, and Gorsuch. In her view, the Chief Justice's opinion mischaracterized the issue before the Court. Acting pursuant to its Article I power to regulate commerce, Congress had sought to authorize a private company to take property for a public purpose through the exercise of a delegated power of eminent domain. But it was well settled, Justice Barrett argued, that Congress, acting pursuant to Article I, could not authorize private suits against nonconsenting states.

Justice Gorsuch also dissented separately, in an opinion joined by Justice Thomas, to point out that the action by PennEast, a Delaware citizen, against New Jersey was barred by the literal language of the Eleventh Amendment, which he thought controlling. In support of that conclusion, he cited Baude & Sachs, *The Misunderstood Eleventh Amendment*, 169 U.Pa.L.Rev. 609 (2021), discussed p. 125 *supra*. (The Court responded that under precedents that no party had asked the Court to reconsider, the Eleventh Amendment immunity was waivable, and consent to actions such as the one before it was implicit in the constitutional plan.)

The central dispute in the PennEast case, as framed by the majority opinion and Justice Barrett's dissent, appears to hinge on whether "the eminent domain power", as the Chief Justice characterized it, uniquely entails a surrender of state sovereign immunity that extends to cases in which the federal government has delegated a power to sue to private parties. As the Chief Justice noted, if Congress can delegate to private parties the power to take private property for public use, the most efficient mechanism for effecting a taking of property may be a suit against the property owner, even when the property owner is a state. But there is also force to Justice Barrett's argument in dissent: under the Court's precedents, "[s]tate sovereign immunity indisputably makes it harder for Congress to accomplish its goals, as we have recognized many times before", and it is not obvious why the logic of efficiency should apply distinctively to suits involving delegated powers of eminent domain.

Page 967. Add a Paragraph (7)(d):

(d) In Torres v. Texas Department of Public Safety, 142 S. Ct. 2455 (2022), the Court extended PennEast in finding that the states waived their immunity from suit in the plan of the convention as to legislation adopted pursuant to Congress's Article I power to raise and support a military force. The case arose when Torres returned from active duty in Iraq with a bronchial condition that made him unable to perform his former job as a Texas state trooper. Torres invoked the Uniformed Services Employment and Reemployment Rights Act of 1994 (USERRA), which gives servicemembers the right to return to their former employer and, as necessary, request a disability accommodation. When Texas refused to allow Torres to transfer to a different position, Torres sued his state employer in Texas state court for damages. USERRA authorizes such suits to proceed in a "state court of competent jurisdiction" and supersedes any conflicting state law. See 38 U.S.C. §§ 4302(b), 4323(b)(2).

In a majority opinion for five Justices, Justice Breyer ruled that the suit could proceed in state court despite the state's assertion of a sovereign immunity defense. Relying on PennEast and emphasizing the breadth of the war powers in Article I, the Court found that the states waived their sovereign immunity when they entered the Union. The Court devoted much of its opinion to a discussion of constitutional structure and the scope of Congress's war powers, identifying several provisions that established federal preeminence and deprived states of the power to engage in war, enter into treaties, and keep troops in peacetime. By combining broad federal power and constraints on state authority, the war powers were said to meet the "complete in itself" standard from PennEast.

The majority acknowledged that the plan-of-convention waivers in PennEast (for eminent domain) and Central Virginia Community College v. Katz, Seventh Edition pp. 963–966 (for proceedings in bankruptcy), were based in part on the in rem character of those proceedings. Treating the form of contemplated proceedings as a technical matter, Justice Breyer emphasized instead what he described as the "broader" point: that the conferral of complete power put all remedial tools at the disposal of Congress, including provision for suits against the states as such. Addressing the argument that plan-of-convention waivers in PennEast and Katz allowed suit to proceed in federal court, rather than state court as under USERRA, the Court cited Testa v. Katt, Seventh Edition pp. 437–440, to argue that this was a distinction without a difference. Justice Kagan's brief concurrence explained that, having dissented in PennEast, she now accepted that decision as controlling and regarded the case for waiver under the war powers as far more straightforward.

Justice Thomas dissented in an opinion joined by Justices Alito, Barrett, and Gorsuch. Justice Thomas accepted the majority's premise that abrogation differed from plan-of-convention waiver. He nonetheless read Alden v. Maine, Seventh Edition pp. 967–976, as a plan-of-convention waiver case that directly controlled the issue of state suability in state court under legislation enacted pursuant to Article I. Justice Thomas also viewed the scope of plan-of-convention waiver as more narrowly circumscribed than did the majority. It was not enough to identify broad, preemptive federal authority; instead, Justice Thomas argued, it takes evidence that suits against the states were a predictable part of war powers enforcement under the constitutional plan. Justice Thomas surveyed history and found nothing to support that conclusion. He also criticized the majority's "complete in itself" test as one that contradicted Seminole Tribe and failed to provide a workable standard for state suability. For his part, Justice Alito did not explain why he joined the majority in PennEast and the dissent in Torres.

In considering the impact of the decision on the Seminole/Alden framework, one might ask how well Congress and the lower courts can predict when powers conferred on Congress in Article I will qualify as "complete" enough to vitiate state sovereign immunity. Some powers (commerce, intellectual property) have been previously addressed within the abrogation framework. Article I also confers arguably exclusive powers on Congress to enter treaties, coin money, and establish post offices and post roads but any such regulations seem unlikely to entail provision for state suability. The "no-state-shall" provisions of Article I, § 10 bear some resemblance to the due process and equal protection provisions of the Fourteenth Amendment. But at least some of those Article I prohibitions do not correspond to other provisions conferring "complete" powers on Congress. Nonetheless, one might argue from a plan-of-convention perspective that explicit prohibitions on state action present a stronger claim for enforcement through suits against the states than grants of regulatory power, however complete, to Congress.

———

NOTE ON ALDEN V. MAINE AND STATE IMMUNITY FROM SUIT ON FEDERAL CLAIMS IN STATE COURT

Page 976. Add at the end of Paragraph (6)(c):

The prediction that the Court would overrule Nevada v. Hall came to fruition (by 5 to 4) in Franchise Tax Board of California v. Hyatt, 139 S.Ct. 1485 (2019). In an opinion by Justice Thomas, the Court ruled that "Hall's determination that the Constitution does not contemplate sovereign immunity for each State in a sister State's courts misreads the historical record and misapprehends the 'implicit ordering of relationships within the federal system necessary to make the Constitution a workable governing charter' " (quoting Hall, 440 U.S. 410, 433 (1979) (Rehnquist, J., dissenting)). Hall had rested on the premise that the interstate sovereign immunity that prevailed at the time of the Founding existed as a matter of "comity", not legal obligation. According to Justice Thomas, even if comity provided the basis for interstate sovereign immunity, abundant evidence showed that "the Founders believed that both 'common law sovereign immunity' and 'law-of-nations sovereign immunity' prevented States from being amenable to process in any court without their consent". In addition, he argued, "the Constitution affirmatively altered the relationships between the States, so that they no longer relate to each other solely as foreign sovereigns", and "embeds interstate sovereign immunity within the constitutional design." Dissenting, Justice Breyer found Hall's reading of the historical record more persuasive than the majority's: "[W]here the Constitution alters the authority of States vis-à-vis other States, it tends to do so explicitly." Justice Breyer also emphasized that "stare decisis requires us to follow Hall" in the absence of a "special justification" that the majority had not identified: "While reasonable jurists might disagree about whether Hall was correct, that very fact—that Hall is not obviously wrong—shows that today's majority is obviously wrong to overrule it." The majority found support for its ruling in Hall's status as "an outlier in our sovereign-immunity jurisprudence, particularly when compared to more recent decisions", including Alden v. Maine. How relevant should it have been that Alden found Nevada v. Hall to be distinguishable?

Distinguishing Alden v. Maine, the Court held in Torres v. Texas Department of Public Safety, 142 S. Ct. 2455 (2022), that Congress validly authorized suit against the state in state court. See pp. 141–142 *supra*.

Page 976. Add at the end of footnote 2:

Baude, *Sovereign Immunity and the Constitutional Text*, 103 Va.L.Rev. 1 (2017), argues that Nevada v. Hall, Seventh Edition p. 975, was rightly decided under a theory that sovereign immunity is a kind of common law doctrine that is constitutionally protected against most federal, but not state, efforts to override it. Baude maintains that his theory fits both the text of the Constitution and most of the leading Supreme Court decisions. But he offers little historical or explicitly normative support beyond the constitutional text. Compare Hoffheimer, *The New Sister-State Sovereign Immunity*, 92 Wash.L.Rev. 1771 (2017) (arguing largely on original historical grounds that a state should enjoy sovereign immunity in the courts of other states only for acts committed within its own territory).

Page 981. Add at the end of Paragraph (9):

Pfander & Dwinell, *A Declaratory Theory of State Accountability*, 102 Va.L.Rev. 153 (2016), call upon states to adopt a "cooperative approach" to constitutional accountability by authorizing plaintiffs who have secured federal injunctions or declaratory judgments in suits against state officials to follow up with suits for damages against the states themselves pursuant to "the ordinary processes of state law." The earlier federal judgments would have issue preclusive effect in subsequent state law actions, but the authors emphasize that states that otherwise waived their sovereign immunity could protect their coffers by imposing damages caps or other limitations on monetary relief. How likely are the states to accept the authors' proposal? Are there any good reasons for a state not to accept it?

————

C. FEDERAL STATUTORY PROTECTION AGAINST STATE OFFICIAL ACTION: HEREIN OF 42 U.S.C. § 1983

NOTE ON 42 U.S.C. § 1983: AN OVERVIEW

Page 996. Add a new footnote 8a at the end of the first paragraph of Paragraph (2):

[8a] Lewis v. Clarke, 581 U.S. 155 (2017), similarly held that in a suit against an employee of a Native American tribe in his individual capacity, tribal sovereign immunity does not apply, even if the tribe has agreed to indemnify the employee.

Page 997. Add at the end of Paragraph (2)(b):

According to Evans, *Supervisory Liability in the Fallout of Iqbal*, 65 Syracuse L.Rev. 103 (2014), the courts of appeals are confused and divided in their interpretation of Iqbal, with most refusing to accept that it has abolished supervisory liability entirely and with some circuits either limiting Iqbal to its facts or essentially ignoring it.

Page 997. Add a footnote 8b at the end of Paragraph (2):

[8b] Reinert, *Supervisory Liability and Ashcroft v. Iqbal*, 41 Cardozo L.Rev. 945 (2020), maintains that theories of supervisory liability remain viable in the lower federal courts as long as the supervisor's causal responsibility for wrongdoing is alleged in non-conclusory terms and is predicated on a theory of the supervisor's constitutional obligations, such as an obligation to remedy ongoing patterns of misconduct of which the supervisor has clear notice. Professor Reinert also notes that "the Court permitted a classic supervisory liability claim to go forward without so much as citing Iqbal" in Ortiz v. Jordan, 562 U.S. 180 (2011), which identified the "deliberate indifference" standard for supervisory liability as "clearly established" for purposes of qualified immunity.

Page 1001. Add at the end of Paragraph (5):

In a subsequent article, *How Governments Pay: Lawsuits, Budgets, and Police Reform*, 63 UCLA L.Rev. 1144 (2016), Professor Schwartz finds the evidence inconclusive on whether liability for officials' misconduct led police departments to alter their supervisory or training practices. Her survey of 100 law enforcement agencies reveals that well over half felt no direct budgetary implications from judgments and settlements (because the costs were absorbed, for example, by insurance or by jurisdiction-wide risk-management funds). In addition, interviews with a small sample of officials in agencies that do bear financial costs out of their own budgets elicited mixed messages, with some reporting that liability "does not influence their risk management efforts because they are already highly motivated to train and supervise their officers and reduce risk whenever possible."

Another empirical study, Rappaport, *How Private Insurers Regulate Public Police*, 130 Harv.L.Rev. 1539 (2017), advances partly divergent findings. Based largely on interviews with thirty-three people connected with the police liability insurance industry, Professor Rappaport reports that insurers frequently impose training and oversight obligations on police departments as conditions of coverage or pricing. He concludes unequivocally that "insurance companies can and do shape police behavior" in jurisdictions that purchase liability insurance (rather than self-insuring, as cities and counties with populations larger than 500,000 commonly do).

Page 1003. Add at the end of footnote 15:

Wells, *The Role of Fault in Sec. 1983 Municipal Liability*, 71 S.C.L.Rev. 293 (2019), proposes an objective test for municipal liability, modeled on common law negligence standards, under which "[l]iability would not depend on proof of a policymaker's conscious disregard of obvious risks but on whether policymakers should have known of constitutional risks, whether they acted reasonably in the circumstances to diminish those risks, and whether the breach of the duty of reasonable care was the proximate cause of the plaintiff's constitutional injury." According to Professor Wells, this "middle-ground approach" would better accommodate competing values than either "the Court's largely incoherent current case law" or "vicarious liability for all constitutional torts committed by government employees in the course of their employment."

Smith, *Local Sovereign Immunity*, 116 Colum.L.Rev. 409 (2016), argues that current barriers to suits against municipalities, including the causation requirement, endow municipalities with a de facto form of sovereign immunity. To narrow the resulting right-remedy gap while simultaneously respecting some of the values that underlie sovereign immunity, Professor Smith proposes making municipalities more readily suable, but permitting damages caps or limitations on the execution of judgments against them. Does the desirability of these suggested reforms depend on whether current obstacles to suing municipalities should be viewed as forms of sovereign immunity?

Page 1005. Add at the end of Paragraph (2):

The Supreme Court decided two cases involving procedural doctrine in § 1983 actions during its 2018 Term. Nieves v. Bartlett, 139 S.Ct. 1715 (2019), held that a plaintiff asserting a First Amendment retaliatory-arrest claim must ordinarily prove absence of probable cause. (The Court recognized an exception for cases in which a plaintiff can prove that other people engaging in similar speech or conduct were not arrested). Parts of Chief Justice Roberts's opinion suggested that the Court's ruling addressed the problems of "causation" that, as prior decisions had recognized, can arise in determining when a First Amendment violation has occurred: a plaintiff must ordinarily prove absence of probable cause in order to establish that retaliation for speech was the but-for cause of an arrest. But the Chief Justice also drew on § 1983: "When defining the contours of a claim under § 1983, we look to 'common-law principles that were well settled at the time of its enactment.'" At common law, the Chief Justice found, the most analogous precedents—involving false imprisonment and malicious prosecution— either required proof of the absence of probable cause or made probable cause a complete defense. Justice Gorsuch, concurring in part and dissenting in part, and Justice Sotomayor, dissenting, both argued that the decisive question should be whether the plaintiff had adequately alleged a violation of his First Amendment rights. If so, then neither thought that the common-law background to the enactment of § 1983 could justify denying him a remedy. (Justice Thomas concurred in part and concurred in the judgment. Justice Ginsburg concurred in the judgment in part and dissented in part.)

Are issues involving the pleading and proof of constitutional violations in § 1983 actions for damages better analyzed as pure constitutional questions, or as ones involving statutory requirements for recovery that the common law might illuminate? With neither § 1983 nor the First Amendment making specific reference to probable cause, should any practical consequences hinge on how the Court answers that question?

McDonough v. Smith, 139 S.Ct. 2149 (2019), presented a question about when the statute of limitations for § 1983 claims alleging the fabrication of evidence begins to run. In an opinion joined by five other Justices, Justice Sotomayor began by stating the generally governing rule: "Although courts look to state law for the length of the limitations period, the time at which a § 1983 claim accrues 'is a question of federal law,' 'conforming in general to common-law tort principles' " (quoting Wallace v. Kato, 549 U.S. 384, 388 (2007)). Pursuant to that rule, Justice Sotomayor concluded that "the most natural common-law analogy" was the tort of malicious prosecution. Based on that analogy and on "practical considerations that have previously led this Court to defer accrual of claims that would otherwise constitute an untenable collateral attack on a criminal judgment," the Court concluded that the statute of limitations for fabricated evidence claims did not "begin to run until the criminal proceedings against the defendant (*i.e.*, the § 1983 plaintiff) have terminated in his favor." Justice Thomas, joined by Justices Kagan and Gorsuch, dissented. The petitioner McDonough had "declined to take a definitive position on" the particular constitutional provision on which his fabricated-evidence claim was based. Believing this to be a necessary antecedent question to the statute-of-limitations issue, the dissenters would have dismissed the petition as improvidently granted. For an application of McDonough, see Reed v. Goertz,143 S. Ct. 955 (2023) (concluding that the petitioner's section 1983 procedural due process challenge to the denial of state DNA testing was complete for statute-of-limitations purposes not "when the deprivation occurs" but only when "the State fails to provide due process") (citing Zinermon v. Burch, 494 U.S. 113, 126 (1990)).

Thompson v. Clark, 142 S.Ct. 1332 (2022), held that a Section 1983 plaintiff in a malicious prosecution claim for an unreasonable seizure under the Fourth Amendment need only show, for purposes of satisfying the favorable termination element, that his prosecution ended without a conviction. In an opinion by Justice Kavanaugh for six Justices, the Court relied heavily on the common law elements of the tort at the time Section 1983 was enacted, rejecting the argument that the plaintiff must show some affirmative evidence of innocence. Justice Alito, in a dissent joined by Justices Thomas and Gorsuch, objected that the Court had wrongly conjoined the tort of malicious prosecution with a Fourth Amendment unreasonable seizure claim—two claims that were said to have "almost nothing in common."

Justice Alito later wrote for a six-Justice majority in Vega v. Tekoh, 142 S.Ct. 2095 (2022), holding that the failure of a sheriff's deputy to provide Miranda warnings is not actionable in a suit for damages under Section 1983. Tekoh was acquitted at trial, despite the admission of what he challenged as an un-Mirandized statement taken by the defendant during a criminal investigation. He sued for damages, arguing that the statement's wrongful admission violated the Fifth Amendment. Characterizing Miranda as a prophylactic rule rather than a constitutional right, the Court applied a cost-benefit analysis in refusing to allow the suit to proceed. What little would be gained in terms of preventing self-incrimination was outweighed in the majority's view by the costs of allowing duplicative federal litigation of issues the state court had addressed in denying a suppression motion. Consider the implications of the Court's approach for the continued vitality of Withrow v. Williams, Seventh Edition p. 1287, treating Miranda issues as cognizable in habeas for those who, unlike Tekoh, were convicted at trial. For additional discussion, see *infra* p. 179.

———

NOTE ON § 1983 AS A REMEDY FOR THE VIOLATION OF A FEDERAL STATUTE

Page 1011: Add at the end of Paragraph (i):

Applying the general approach of Gonzaga v. Doe, the Court ruled 7–2 in Health and Hospital Corp. of Marian County v. Talevski, 143 S.Ct. 1444 (2023), that rights conferred by the Federal Nursing Home Reform Act (FNHRA) were enforceable in suits under 42 U.S.C. § 1983. The plaintiff sought damages, arguing that a county-owned nursing home violated federal statutory rights to freedom from chemical restraints and from procedurally improper transfers and discharges. Writing for the majority, Justice Jackson found that the statute unambiguously conferred the rights in question and contained nothing that would indicate congressional intent to foreclose a section 1983 remedy. Significantly, the Court rejected the petitioner's argument that federal Spending Clause statutes, like the FNHRA, were incapable of conferring rights enforceable under section 1983. Justice Alito dissented, joined by Justice Thomas, arguing that any section 1983 remedy for the rights in question was impliedly displaced by other elements of the FNHRA. In a lengthy dissent for himself alone, Justice Thomas argued more broadly that rights conferred by Spending Clause legislation may not be privately enforced through section 1983.

———

NOTE ON THE PARRATT DOCTRINE: ITS RATIONALE, IMPLICATIONS, AND AFTERMATH

Page 1027. Add at the end of footnote 2:

Kingsley v. Hendrickson, 576 U.S. 389 (2015), held, by 5 to 4, that a pretrial detainee asserting a Fourteenth Amendment due process claim for use of excessive force by jail officers need only show that the force was objectively unreasonable, not that the officers were subjectively aware of its unreasonableness.

————

3. OFFICIAL IMMUNITY

NOTE ON OFFICERS' ACCOUNTABILITY IN DAMAGES FOR OFFICIAL MISCONDUCT

Page 1040. Add a new footnote * at the end of the second paragraph of Paragraph (2)(b):

* Ziglar v. Abbasi, 582 U.S. 120 (2017), also discussed at pp. 108–110, *supra*, and p. 212, *infra*, held that officials sued for conspiracy to violate equal protection rights under 42 U.S.C. and § 1985(3) were entitled to qualified immunity under the same formula that applies to Bivens and § 1983 cases.

Page 1041. Add at the end of Paragraph (2)(d):

See generally Crocker, *Qualified Immunity and Constitutional Structure*, 117 Mich.L.Rev. 1405 (2019) (offering a historical explanation of Harlow's qualified immunity framework as an attempted corrective for the perceived excesses of Bivens, and maintaining that the Court extended the Harlow rule to section 1983 actions for federalism-related reasons, but concluding that the resulting doctrine lacks normative justification).

Page 1041. Add at the end of Paragraph (2)(e):

In Ziglar v. Abbasi, 582 U.S. 120 (2017), Justice Thomas concurred in the Court's judgment granting qualified immunity under the standard of Harlow v. Fitzgerald, Seventh Edition p. 1030, but he called for reconsidering "our qualified immunity jurisprudence" in "an appropriate case": "We apply this 'clearly established' standard 'across the board' and without regard to 'the precise nature of the various officials' duties or the precise character of the particular rights alleged to have been violated'" [quoting Anderson v. Creighton, Seventh Edition p. 1048]. * * * Because our analysis is no longer grounded in the common-law backdrop against which Congress enacted the 1871 Act, we are no longer engaged in 'interpret[ing] the intent of Congress' * * *. Our qualified immunity precedents instead represent precisely the sort of 'free-wheeling policy choice[s]' that we have previously disclaimed the power to make."

Baude, *Is Qualified Immunity Unlawful?*, 106 Calif.L.Rev. 45 (2018), marshals formidable arguments that modern qualified immunity doctrine "is so far removed from ordinary principles of legal interpretation" that it "lacks legal justification." With regard to suggestions that the Court begins its modern inquiries by looking at the traditional common law of immunity as it existed in 1871, Baude demonstrates that: (1) "[T]here was no well-established good-faith defense in suits about constitutional violations when Section 1983 was enacted, nor in Section 1983 suits early after its enactment"; (2) "the good faith defense that did exist in some common law suits" arose from the elements of some common law torts, "not a general immunity"; and (3) the qualified immunity standard formulated in Harlow v. Fitzgerald "is much broader than a good faith defense." Baude concludes: "If qualified immunity is unlawful it can be overruled. And even if the Court does not overrule it, it can stop expanding the legal error."

In defending qualified immunity, Keller, *Qualified Immunity and Absolute Immunity at Common Law*, 73 Stan.L.Rev. 1337 (2021), argues that common law doctrines in place at the time Section 1983 was enacted in 1871 extended immunity-like protections to government officials. Keller bases this claim on his review of nineteenth-century treatises on the law of torts and the law of public officers, all of which, he maintains, recognize a form of qualified immunity through the protection accorded to discretionary official actions. While Keller acknowledges that the nineteenth century approach to official liability differs in various respects from the contemporary approach, he urges its recovery both to legitimate and to refine qualified immunity today. For doubts about Keller's thesis, see Baude, *Is Quasi-Judicial Immunity Qualified Immunity?*, 74 Stan.L.Rev. Online 115 (2022) (explaining that Keller's authorities describe a quasi-judicial immunity for discretionary acts that differs markedly from today's qualified immunity); Pfander, *Zones of Discretion at Common Law*, 116 Nw.U.L.Rev. Online 148 (2021) (arguing that, during the period Keller emphasizes, constitutional restrictions on government action operated as a firm limit on official discretion, depriving officers of any protection for invasions of constitutional rights). If Baude and Pfander rightly describe the formal operation of quasi-judicial discretion at common law, might Keller's work nonetheless deserve consideration as decision-makers evaluate the wisdom of an immunity-free model of constitutional tort litigation? Or would use of Keller's framework result in some double-counting, in light of the Court's reliance on the nineteenth century common law as it defines the elements of constitutional tort liability under Section 1983?

Near the end of the 2019 Term, the Supreme Court denied certiorari in Baxter v. Bracey, 140 S.Ct. 1862 (2020), in which the petitioner asked the Court to reconsider its qualified immunity precedents as applied to § 1983 actions. Only Justice Thomas recorded a dissent from the denial of certiorari.[1a]

[1a] For a reply to Professor Baude and a defense of qualified immunity on stare decisis grounds, see Nielson & Walker, *A Qualified Defense of Qualified Immunity*, 93 Notre Dame L.Rev. 1853 (2018) (noting, inter alia, that Congress amended section 1983 in 1996 without questioning qualified immunity and has provided for immunity in other modern-era statutes). For a more general defense of the Harlow standard as initially articulated (but with criticism of its recent, more defendant-protective reformulation), see Fallon, *Bidding Farewell to Constitutional Torts*, 107 Calif.L.Rev. 933 (2019).

If the Supreme Court's qualified immunity cases have paid little heed to "ordinary principles of legal interpretation", could the same be said of the Court's decisions developing forum non conveniens and abstention doctrines and interpreting a number of other federal jurisdictional statutes, including those conferring "arising under" jurisdiction and Supreme Court appellate jurisdiction over state court judgments? See generally Fallon *Why Abstention Is Not Illegitimate: An Essay on the Distinction Between 'Legitimate' and 'Illegitimate' Statutory*

Interpretation and Judicial Lawmaking, 107 Nw.U.L.Rev. 847 (2013). Can a longstanding pattern of free-wheeling interpretive decisions provide legally adequate justification for extensions of the pattern? Do the Court's recent expansions of qualified immunity pose issues of legal justification that purposivist interpretation in earlier eras did not?

Page 1042. Substitute the following for the first two sentences of footnote 3:

By contrast, Schwartz, *After Qualified Immunity*, 120 Colum.L.Rev. 309 (2020), predicts that the abolition of qualified immunity would have at most a "modest" effect on the scope of recognized constitutional rights. Moreover, any such loss would be offset, Professor Schwartz anticipates, by the swifter clarification of substantive constitutional rights that the abolition of qualified immunity defenses would promote.

Nielson & Walker, *Qualified Immunity and Federalism*, 109 Geo.L.J. 229 (2020), largely embrace Professor Schwartz's findings about indemnification and further argue that qualified immunity promotes federalism interests by allowing states to determine when to authorize compensation for constitutional torts above the federal "floor" of liability for violation of clearly established rights. (They note that California makes no provision for qualified immunity in state-law tort suits against state officials or state civil rights claims and that a number of other states' liability schemes for state-law violations give defendant officials less protection than the Harlow standard). In light of what the authors portray as state and local governments' reliance interests in the qualified immunity doctrine, the authors maintain that pleas to alter current doctrine should be addressed to Congress, not the courts. For a critical rejoinder, see Schwartz, *Qualified Immunity and Federalism All the Way Down*, 109 Geo.L.J. 305 (2020) (arguing, inter alia, that the abolition of qualified immunity would leave state and local governments free to adjust their indemnification policies).

Page 1047. Add at the end of footnote 9:

Trump v. Vance, 140 S.Ct. 2412 (2020), held that a sitting President has no absolute immunity from state court subpoenas issued in conjunction with a criminal investigation. Chief Justice Roberts' majority opinion emphasized, however, that the President, "like any other citizen", can "raise subpoena-specific constitutional challenges," including objections "that compliance with a particular challenge would impede his constitutional duties", "in either a state or federal forum." See also Trump v. Mazars USA, LLP, 140 S.Ct. 2019 (2020) (holding that courts must weigh separation-of-powers principles in assessing whether a congressional subpoena "directed at the President's personal information" is valid and enforceable).

Page 1048. Substitute for the last sentence of the third paragraph of Paragraph (7)(a):

Cf. City of Escondido v. Emmons, 139 S.Ct. 500 (2019) (per curiam), in which the Court "[a]ssum[ed] without deciding that a court of appeals decision may constitute clearly established law for purposes of qualified immunity".

Page 1049. Add at the end of Paragraph (7)(b):

The Court quoted and applied Reichle v. Howard's broad formulation of the qualified immunity standard in Taylor v. Barkes, 575 U.S. 822 (2015) (per curiam). It similarly continued the trend of emphasizing qualified immunity's protective sweep in City and County of San Francisco, California v. Sheehan, 575 U.S. 600 (2015), in Mullenix v. Luna, 577 U.S. 7 (2015) (*per curiam*), and in a unanimous per curiam opinion in White v. Pauly, 580 U.S. 73 (2017), a case involving allegations that a police officer unreasonably used deadly force. Pointedly noting that "[i]n the last five years, this Court has issued a number of opinions reversing federal courts in qualified immunity cases", the opinion reiterated the importance of qualified immunity to "society as a whole" and emphasized that its prior cases on deadly force "do not by themselves create clearly established law outside an obvious case" (internal quotations omitted).

The trend continued into the 2017 Term with a per curiam reversal in Kisela v. Hughes, 138 S.Ct. 1148 (2018), yet another police-shooting case involving the allegedly unreasonable use of potentially lethal force in a fact situation that the majority deemed distinguishable from those in cited precedents: "This Court has repeatedly told courts—and the Ninth Circuit in particular—not to define clearly established law at a high level of generality" (internal quotations omitted). The Court quoted that language from Kisela in City of Escondido v. Emmons, 139 S.Ct. 500 (2019) (per curiam), in which it unanimously reversed the Ninth Circuit for denying a qualified immunity defense against a claim that police officers used excessive force. Although many of the recent decisions overturning denials of qualified immunity have been unanimous, in Kisela, Justice Sotomayor, joined by Justice Ginsburg, dissented, objecting that "this Court routinely displays an unflinching willingness 'to summarily reverse courts for wrongly denying officers the protection of qualified immunity' but 'rarely intervene[s] where courts wrongly afford officers the benefit of qualified immunity in these same cases.'" She added: "Such a one-sided approach to qualified immunity transforms the doctrine into an absolute shield for law enforcement officers. * * * It tells officers that they can shoot first and think later, and it tells the public that palpably unreasonable conduct will go unpunished."

Cf. Taylor v. Riojas, 141 S.Ct. 52 (2020) (per curiam) (reversing a grant of qualified immunity to prison officials who allegedly confined an inmate "in a pair of shockingly unsanitary cells" teeming with human waste; despite the absence of specifically on-point authority, "no reasonable correctional officer" could have thought the defendants' alleged conduct constitutionally permissible "under the extreme circumstances of this case").

In a per curiam decision at the end of the 2021 Term, Lombardo v. City of St. Louis, 141 S.Ct. 2239 (2021), the Court revived but postponed any final decision in a case presenting sensitive issues of alleged police use of excessive force and qualified immunity that arose when a person died after being held face down in shackles for a prolonged a period. Without expressing any view on the merits, the Court granted the petition for certiorari, vacated a decision granting summary judgment to the defendants, and remanded the case to the Eighth Circuit to clarify an opinion that the Court thought might have misunderstood its excessive force precedents. Dissenting, Justice Alito, joined by Justices Thomas and Gorsuch, objected that the Court's decision evaded "the choice" that it ought to have made "between denying the petition (and bearing the criticism that would inevitably elicit) and granting plenary review (and doing the work)" that applying established legal principles to a particular set of facts would require. Justice Alito would have granted the petition and set the case for argument on the merits.

Two per curiam decisions in October 2021 continued the Court's practice of closely scrutinizing applications of the clearly-established law standard for qualified immunity. In Rivas-Villegas v. Cortesluna, 142 S.Ct. 4 (2021), the Court assumed without deciding that circuit authority could clearly establish the law for qualified immunity purposes. It nonetheless found that applicable circuit precedent did not define the use of force in question such that "every reasonable officer" in the position of the petitioner, Officer Rivas-

Vellegas, would have "understood that what he is doing violates that right." Circuit precedent dealt with a claim of excessive force that arose when the arresting officer, responding to a complaint about noise, "dug" his knee into the suspect's back for a prolonged period. By contrast, Rivas-Villegas allegedly injured the back of the plaintiff, Cortesluna, while placing him under an arrest in connection with a domestic violence dispute. The Court saw three essential differences: the domestic violence context was more serious than a noise complaint, Cortesluna had a knife, and the use of force by placing a knee in the suspect's back was of much shorter duration than in the prior case.

Similarly, in City of Tahlequah, Oklahoma v. Bond, 142 S.Ct. 9 (2021), the Court overturned the Tenth Circuit's conclusion that the use of deadly force to stop a suspect from swinging a hammer at the responding officers violated clearly established law. Officers responded to a call from the suspect's ex-wife, indicating that the suspect was intoxicated, was in her garage, and was unwilling to leave. Officers entered the garage and advanced on the suspect, who grabbed and brandished a hammer. The Tenth Circuit found that use of deadly force, even if objectively reasonable, may violate the Fourth Amendment if the officers' reckless or deliberate conduct created the situation requiring deadly force. Without addressing the theory of Fourth Amendment liability for reckless failure to de-escalate, the Court found that none of the Tenth Circuit precedents provided the necessary clear law. The cases on which the Tenth Circuit relied arose from aggressive police actions directed at a person threatening suicide, a factual setting that the Court viewed as "dramatically different" from the situation in the garage.

Schwartz, *Qualified Immunity's Boldest Lie*, 88 U.Chi.L.Rev. 605 (2021), argues that the Supreme Court's emphasis on factual similarity to decided cases systematically misunderstands what police officers can reasonably be expected to know. In an empirical study of the training and educational materials provided to California law enforcement officials, she found that although "police departments regularly inform their officers about watershed decisions" such as those establishing general prohibitions against the use of excessive force, "officers are not regularly or reliably informed about court decisions interpreting those decisions in different factual scenarios." As an alternative approach, consider the suggestion of Professor Jeffries, Seventh Edition p. 1047 n.10, that it would be preferable to ask whether a defendant's actions were "clearly unconstitutional" in light of general legal principles. See generally Baude, *Is Qualified Immunity Unlawful?*, 106 Calif.L.Rev. 45, 82 (2018) (reporting that the Supreme Court has found a violation of clearly established law in just two of thirty qualified immunity cases since 1982); Blum, *Section 1983 Litigation: The Maze, the Mud, and the Madness,* 23 Wm. & Mary Bill Rts.J. 913 (2015) (surveying and critiquing the mounting obstacles confronting plaintiffs who seek to overcome qualified immunity defenses.

Notwithstanding the Supreme Court's efforts to enhance qualified immunity's protective force and to facilitate dismissals of insubstantial claims prior to trial and discovery, Schwartz, *How Qualified Immunity Fails*, 127 Yale L.J. 2 (2017), maintains that district courts rarely terminate

Section 1983 cases on motions to dismiss. After reviewing 1,183 suits against state and local law enforcement defendants in five federal district courts over a two-year period, Professor Schwartz found that "defendants raised qualified immunity in motions to dismiss in [only] 13.9% of the cases in which they could raise the defense"; that these motions to dismiss were granted in whole or in part on qualified immunity grounds only 13.6% of the time; and that, overall, just 0.6% of the cases in her sample were dismissed on qualified immunity grounds at the motion to dismiss stage and just 2.6% on summary judgment. Professor Schwartz speculates that qualified immunity disposes of so few police misconduct cases on motions to dismiss because it frequently takes fact-finding to determine whether clearly established law applies.

In a subsequent article, *Qualified Immunity's Selection Effects*, 114 Nw.U.L.Rev. 1101 (2020), Professor Schwartz concludes, "[b]ased on a study of almost 1,200 federal court dockets, and surveys and interviews of plaintiffs' attorneys * * * that qualified immunity doctrine * * * likely dampens attorneys' willingness to bring" section 1983 actions. But she further finds that the deterrent effect applies to both meritorious and non-meritorious claims and "does not effectively weed out insubstantial cases at the prefiling stage." In yet another article, Schwartz maintains that because most officials are indemnified by their employers when sued for constitutional violations, qualified immunity is unnecessary to avoid overdeterrence of public-spirited action. Schwartz, *After Qualified Immunity*, 120 Colum.L.Rev. 309 (2020). Her bottom line: "If we take the Supreme Court at its word—that its qualified immunity jurisprudence is motivated by an interest in shielding government officials from the burdens of suit in insubstantial cases, and avoiding overdeterrence of officers and officials—the Court need not fear doing away with qualified immunity."

Apropos of excessive force litigation, Obasogie and Zaret, *Plainly Incompetent: How Qualified Immunity Became an Exculpatory Doctrine of Police Excessive Force*, 170 U.Pa.L. Rev. 407 (2022), reports that qualified immunity evolved from a limited protection of executive privilege into a theory that disproportionately blocks excessive force lawsuits against police officers. After an extensive review of caselaw from the period, the authors call for further exploration of what they describe as the middle history of qualified immunity, which they date to the early 2000s, when the doctrine migrated to excessive force litigation.

For a range of (mostly critical) comments on qualified immunity and the policy justifications most frequently advanced to support it, see Symposium, *Federal Courts, Practice & Procedure: The Future of Qualified Immunity*, 93 Notre Dame L.Rev. 1793 (2018). Prominent criticisms, as summarized in Schwartz, *The Case Against Qualified Immunity*, *id.* at 1797, include the following: (1) qualified immunity has no basis in the common law background to the enactment of § 1983; (2) qualified immunity is unnecessary to protect officials from liability or fear of liability because they are mostly indemnified by their employers anyway; (3) qualified immunity fails to lead to early dismissal of frivolous lawsuits with the frequency anticipated by the Supreme Court, perhaps in part because plaintiffs can plead around it; (4)

qualified immunity "hollows out" constitutional rights; and (5) there is little evidence that qualified immunity encourages courts to expand rights that they would hesitate to expand if the consequence were an immediate imposition of liability. Additional contributions to the Symposium include Blum, *Qualified Immunity: Time to Change the Message* (citing rampant confusion in § 1983 immunity decisions and calling for the establishment of respondeat superior liability, which would " 'fix' the doctrine of qualified immunity by making it largely irrelevant"); Bray, *Foreword: The Future of Qualified Immunity* (highlighting leading questions about the justifiability of qualified immunity doctrine); Chen, *The Intractability of Qualified Immunity* (characterizing qualified immunity doctrine as racked by "tensions," including "the conceptual challenge of distinguishing pure questions of law from mixed questions of law and fact" and identifying "the appropriate level of generality at which 'clearly established constitutional rights' are articulated"); Michelman, *The Branch Best Qualified to Abolish Immunity* (maintaining that qualified immunity is a mistaken and unworkable doctrine that should not be sustained on stare decisis grounds); Nielson & Walker, *A Qualified Defense of Qualified Immunity* (countering assertions that qualified immunity is unlawful because not contemplated by § 1983 and that qualified immunity fails to advance its policy objectives); Preis, *Qualified Immunity and Fault* (arguing that qualified immunity "does not reliably differentiate between * * * faulty and faultless" defendants); Reinert, *Qualified Immunity at Trial* (concluding that although "qualified immunity rarely is the subject of jury deliberations," it can often be "outcome determinative" when judges do charge juries with qualified immunity issues); Shapiro & Hogle, *The Horror Chamber: Unqualified Impunity in Prison* (tracing how qualified immunity interacts with other doctrines to create nearly insuperable barriers to suits by prisoners); and Smith, *Formalism, Ferguson, and the Future of Qualified Immunity* (arguing that qualified immunity is ripe for reconsideration because it is out of step with both the Court's interpretive approach in other relevant areas of the law and "post-Ferguson" demands for "greater accountability for violations of rights"). *A Symposium on Qualified Immunity in Courts and in Practice: Where We Go From Here*, 112 J.Crim.L. & Criminology (2022), includes articles from a number of contributors. Other notable contributions appear in *Symposium on Qualified Immunity*, 17 Duke J.Const.L. & Pub.Pol'y (2022).

Page 1051. Add a new footnote 12a at the end of the carryover paragraph:

[12a] Dawson, *Qualified Immunity for Officers' Reasonable Reliance on Lawyers' Advice*, 110 Nw.U.L.Rev. 525 (2016), reports that the circuits are divided on how, if at all, reliance on lawyers' advice matters to the qualified immunity inquiry. He argues that qualified immunity should depend on the reasonableness of a defendant's trusting in a lawyer's opinion under particular circumstances, not an "extraordinary circumstances" test. How often would those two tests be likely to yield different results?

Page 1053. Add at the end of Paragraph (8)(b):

A study that looked at all court of appeals cases that cited Pearson v. Callahan, Seventh Edition p. 1052, in the years 2009–12 found that the court exercised its discretion to reach the merits only roughly 45% of the time.

Nielson & Walker, *The New Qualified Immunity*, 89 S.Cal.L.Rev. 1 (2015). The courts of appeals ruled for the defendants based on the absence of any clearly established right without reaching the merits in regard to 27% of qualified immunity claims and rejected qualified immunity defenses in 28%. When courts of appeals exercised their discretion to reach the merits, in only 8% of their rulings did they find a constitutional violation.

Page 1055. Add at the end of footnote 17:

See also Wells, *Constitutional Remedies: Reconciling Official Immunity with the Vindication of Rights*, 88 St.John's L.Rev. 713 (2014) (emphasizing plaintiffs' interests in "vindicating" their constitutional rights as a basis for tort remedies independent of compensation and deterrence rationales and arguing that, in light of the interest in vindicating constitutional rights, official immunity should not bar suits for nominal damages).

Page 1055. Add at the end of Paragraph (9):

Reinert, Schwartz & Pfander, *New Federalism and Civil Rights Enforcement*, 116 Nw.U.L.Rev. 737 (2021), suggests that states concerned with police use of excessive force and qualified immunity adopt state laws subjecting state officials to liability for constitutional torts. Based on their survey of state laws, including those adopted in the last few years, the authors find that 24 states have recognized state law analogs to section 1983 (either by statute or by judicial inference). After exploring the implications of an immunity-free liability system, and other changes that would send clearer signals to police officers, the authors offer a model statute on which state and local governments might base law reform efforts.

CHAPTER X

JUDICIAL FEDERALISM: LIMITATIONS ON DISTRICT COURT JURISDICTION OR ITS EXERCISE

---

2. STATUTORY LIMITATIONS ON FEDERAL COURT JURISDICTION

B. OTHER STATUTORY RESTRICTIONS ON FEDERAL COURT JURISDICTION

NOTE ON THREE-JUDGE DISTRICT COURTS, THE JOHNSON ACT OF 1934, AND THE TAX INJUNCTION ACT OF 1937

Page 1090. Add at the end of footnote 5:

Solimine, *The Fall and Rise of Specialized Constitutional Courts,* 17 U.Pa.J.Const.L. 115 (2014), identifies instances in which post-1976 Congresses have included provisions in substantive statutes prescribing exclusive review of constitutional challenges by three-judge district courts, often in the D.C. Circuit, and typically with a right of direct appeal to the Supreme Court. Professor Solimine criticizes such statutes on the grounds that they deny the Supreme Court the benefit of "percolation" of issues through a variety of courts, expedite constitutional review and therefore promote decision on an underdeveloped record. He also contends that by vesting the D.C. Circuit with exclusive jurisdiction over significant questions, these statutes contribute to a politicized process of nomination and confirmation to judgeships in that circuit.

Some suggest that three-judge courts might usefully convene to consider applications for nationwide injunction. Gardner, *District Court En Bancs,* 90 Ford.L.Rev. 1541 (2022) (collecting sources). Gardner also identifies a distinct procedural device, the district court en banc, which she distinguishes from mandatory three-judge courts and from appellate panel en bancs. District court en bancs operate informally "not to reconsider decisions but to decide an issue or a case collectively in the first instance." One would expect broad compliance with the decision by district judges who approve of the result but a group of district court judges cannot necessarily bind the judges in the district as to questions of law, except through the promulgation of district court rules of practice.

Questions sometimes arise as to whether a three-judge court must accord vertical stare decisis effect to the decisions of the circuit in which it sits or only to those of the Supreme Court. After sketching the issues, Morley, *Vertical Stare Decisis and Three-Judge District Courts,* 108 Geo.L.J. 699 (2020), argues that the precedents of the hierarchically superior circuit court bind three-judge district courts, even though direct appellate review of those courts takes place in the Supreme Court. We might predict, though, that the Supreme Court, on appeal, would rarely insist on three-judge court compliance with circuit court authority that the Court does not regard as correct.

Page 1091. Add at the end of the first paragraph of Paragraph C(1):

(The Tax Injunction Act is modeled in part upon the Anti-Injunction Act specific to the federal Tax Code, 26 U.S.C. § 7421(a), which provides that "no suit for the purpose of restraining the assessment or collection of any tax shall be maintained in any court by any person," thereby precluding certain challenges to federal tax collection practices. See Hibbs v. Winn, 542 U.S. 88, 100 (2004) (using federal tax law as a guide to defining the terms of the Tax Injunction Act).[5a])

[5a] For an overview of the history of the federal Tax Code's Anti-Injunction Act and an argument that it should be construed narrowly to permit pre-enforcement review of Treasury regulations and IRS guidance documents, consult Hickman & Kerska, *Restoring the Lost Anti-Injunction Act*, 103 Va.L.Rev. 1683 (2017). For a skeptical take on their argument, see Hemel, *The Living Anti-Injunction Act*, 104 Va.L.Rev. Online 74 (2018).

Page 1091. Add a new Paragraph (1)(a):

(a) The Reach of the Prohibition. In Direct Marketing Association v. Brohl, 575 U.S. 1 (2015), the Supreme Court addressed whether injunctive relief sought in a federal court action challenging the constitutionality of a state sales and use tax notice and reporting scheme could be said to "enjoin, suspend or restrain the assessment, levy or collection of any tax under State law" within the scope of the Tax Injunction Act. In an attempt to capture sales and use taxes that would otherwise be lost to e-commerce transactions,[7a] Colorado required out-of-state retailers, under threat of financial penalties: (1) to inform in-state consumers of their obligations to pay state sales and use taxes; (2) to send annual reports to all Colorado customers who purchased more than $500 worth of products from a retailer in the prior year informing the customers of their obligation to pay the relevant taxes; and (3) to send year-end statements to the Colorado Department of Revenue listing the retailers' Colorado customers along with their known addresses and total amount of purchases in the prior year.

The Supreme Court unanimously concluded that nothing in the Tax Injunction Act precludes a district court from enjoining the enforcement of notice and reporting requirements by state tax officials. The Court reasoned that enforcement of the notice and reporting requirements could not be deemed an act of "assessment, levy or collection" within the meaning of the Act. Drawing upon analogies to the federal Tax Code's Anti-Injunction Act,[7b] Justice Thomas posited that the notice and reporting requirements merely constituted "information gathering" that preceded any formal steps of "assessment" and "collection" of taxes by the state. In the Court's view, the Tax Injunction Act should be read narrowly to draw a clear jurisdictional line that asks "whether the relief [sought in the federal court action] to some

[7a] Quill Corp. v. North Dakota, 504 U.S. 298 (1992), reaffirmed an earlier decision holding that the dormant Commerce Clause prohibits states from requiring a retailer lacking a physical presence within a state to collect sales and use taxes. The Supreme Court overruled Quill Corp. in South Dakota v. Wayfair, Inc., 138 S.Ct. 2080 (2018).

[7b] Justice Thomas's opinion for the Court noted that the Tax Injunction Act was modeled on the Anti-Injunction Act in the federal Tax Code, 26 U.S.C. § 7421(a), and "words used in both Acts are generally used in the same way, and we discern the meaning of the terms in the AIA by reference to the broader Tax Code."

degree stops 'assessment, levy or collection,' not whether it merely inhibits them."[7c]

The Supreme Court arguably expanded upon Direct Marketing in CIC Servs., LLC v. IRS, 141 S.Ct. 1582 (2021). In the latter case, governed by the federal Tax Code's Anti-Injunction Act, a material advisor to taxpayers brought suit seeking to block enforcement of a notice issued by the IRS on the basis that the notice failed to comply with the requirements of the Administrative Procedure Act. The notice in question established certain reporting obligations and, unlike the obligations in *Direct Marketing*, provided for a statutory tax penalty in the event of noncompliance. Writing for a unanimous Court, Justice Kagan explained that the added element of a tax penalty did not alter the calculus for purposes of the Tax Code's Anti-Injunction Act.[7d] Emphasizing that the relief sought by the plaintiff did not attempt to stop the collection of a tax, but instead pertained solely to the reporting rules associated with the IRS notice, the Court held the suit could proceed. Justice Kagan offered three reasons as justification: first, the notice imposed affirmative reporting obligations that triggered "costs separate and apart from the statutory tax penalty"; second, the reporting requirements and tax penalty stand "several steps removed from each other"; and third, a violation of the notice's requirements "is punishable not only by a tax, but by separate criminal penalties." Demanding that a party break the law and risk exposure to criminal penalties, she observed, would not equate with "the Anti-Injunction Act's familiar pay-now-sue-later procedure." Crucial to the Court's holding was the fact that the notice in question did not directly levy a tax, but instead imposed a reporting requirement akin to that at issue in Direct Marketing. However powerful the justifications for both decisions, they seem certain to encourage an expanded array of pre-enforcement challenges to new state and federal tax laws and regulations in order to avoid the reach of the Tax Injunction Act and the Tax Code's Anti-Injunction Act.

[7c] The Court declined to address whether principles of comity counseled in favor of dismissal of the case.

[7d] The Court drew heavily upon Direct Marketing in its analysis by again highlighting the presumption that the words employed in the Tax Injunction Act and the Tax Code's Anti-Injunction Act "are 'generally used in the same way' " (quoting Direct Marketing, 575 U.S. at 8).

———

3. JUDICIALLY DEVELOPED LIMITATIONS ON FEDERAL COURT JURISDICTION: DOCTRINES OF EQUITY, COMITY, AND FEDERALISM

A. EXHAUSTION OF STATE NONJUDICIAL REMEDIES

NOTE ON EXHAUSTION OF STATE NONJUDICIAL REMEDIES

Page 1099. Add at the end of Paragraph (5)(b):

More recently, in Ross v. Blake, 578 U.S. 632 (2016), the Court rejected the rule adopted by some circuits that the exhaustion requirement of the Prison Litigation Reform Act (PLRA) is not absolute and need not be satisfied in cases involving "special circumstances." The case arose when a prisoner brought suit under 42 U.S.C. § 1983 against two corrections officers claiming that they had used excessive force while transferring him from his cell to a segregation unit. The district court dismissed claims against one defendant when he raised the affirmative defense of failure to exhaust. The Fourth Circuit reversed, concluding that it was reasonable for the prisoner to believe that he had exhausted all administrative remedies before filing his federal action, even though he had not done so.

Writing for the Court, Justice Kagan first rejected the Fourth Circuit's "freewheeling approach to exhaustion as inconsistent with the PLRA." Statutory exhaustion provisions are different from judge-made exhaustion requirements, Justice Kagan noted, with the former "foreclosing judicial discretion." This is because "Congress sets the rules—and courts have a role in creating exceptions only if Congress wants them to."[5a] The Court emphasized, however, that the PLRA's exhaustion requirement "hinges" on administrative remedies being " 'available' ", 42 U.S.C. § 1997e(a), a term that should not be understood to encompass administrative procedures that are a mere "dead end"; a scheme that is "so opaque that it becomes, practically speaking, incapable of use"; or a situation in which "prison administrators thwart inmates from taking advantage of a grievance process through machination, misrepresentation, or intimidation."[5b] Under the Court's understanding of congressionally-mandated exhaustion, is there any room left for application of judge-made abstention doctrines in such circumstances?[5c] As a separate matter, is it possible that the Court's framework for assessing availability of administrative procedures often will collapse with the Fourth Circuit's "special circumstances" exception to the PLRA's exhaustion requirement?

[5a] Justice Kagan added that the PLRA's exhaustion requirement contrasted "markedly" from its much " 'weak[er]' " predecessor provision that made exhaustion largely a matter " 'left to the discretion of the district court' " (quoting Woodford v. Ngo, 548 U.S. 81, 84, 85 (2006)).

[5b] More recently, Justice Sotomayor, joined by Justice Ginsburg, suggested that the extraordinary circumstances presented by the COVID-19 pandemic could implicate "the PLRA's textual exception" and therefore "open the courthouse doors where they would otherwise stay closed." Valentine v. Collier, 140 S.Ct. 1598 (2020) (statement of Sotomayor, J.) (observing that "if a plaintiff has established that the prison grievance procedures at issue are utterly incapable of responding to a rapidly spreading pandemic like COVID-19, the procedures may be 'unavailable' to meet the plaintiff's purposes, much in the way they would be if prison officials ignored the grievances entirely"). Months later, Justice Sotomayor, now joined by Justice Kagan, argued in a case involving the same prison that the Court should enforce the PLRA's textual exception and uphold a district court order directing prison reforms in light of the ongoing COVID-19 pandemic. Justice Sotomayor argued that petitioners had shown that the prison's "lengthy" grievance process "offered no realistic prospect of relief" in light of "the speed at which the contagion spread." In her view, it followed under Ross that petitioners should not be required to exhaust administrative remedies before seeking relief in federal court. Valentine v. Collier, 141 S.Ct. 57 (2020) (Sotomayor, J., dissenting from the denial of application to vacate stay).

[5c] Justice Breyer wrote separately to reiterate his earlier view that although he agreed that the PLRA does not permit " 'freewheeling' exceptions" of the kind adopted by the Fourth Circuit, the statute should be read to encompass "administrative law's 'well-established exceptions to exhaustion.' " Woodford v. Ngo, 548 U.S. 81, 103 (2006) (opinion of Breyer, J.).

Page 1099. Add a new paragraph after the first paragraph of Paragraph (5)(c):

A closely divided Court partially overruled Williamson County in Knick v. Township of Scott, Pennsylvania, 139 S.Ct. 2162 (2019), concluding that Williamson County had "effectively established an exhaustion requirement for § 1983 takings claims" by requiring litigants seeking just compensation to pursue available state proceedings in the first instance. Deeming Williamson County poorly reasoned, in tension with the Court's "longstanding position that a property owner has a constitutional claim to compensation at the time the government deprives him of his property", and at odds with Patsy and related decisions, the majority found the arguments favoring respecting *stare decisis* wanting. Instead, consistent with Patsy, the Court held that litigants should have the possibility of pursuing § 1983 takings claims in the first instance in a federal forum. Writing for four dissenters, Justice Kagan complained that the Court's decision "betrays judicial federalism" insofar as it will have the effect of "send[ing] a flood of complex state-law issues to federal courts", thereby rendering "federal courts a principal player in local and state land-use disputes." See also p. 47, *supra*.

B. ABSTENTION: PULLMAN AND RELATED DOCTRINES

NOTE ON ABSTENTION IN CASES INVOLVING A FEDERAL QUESTION

Page 1104. Add a new footnote 1a at the end of Paragraph (1)(a):

[1a] Sutton, 51 Imperfect Solutions: States and the Making of American Constitutional Law (2018), urges federal courts to consider these two paths as well as certification when confronted with cases involving a critical question of state constitutional law. In Judge Sutton's view, federal courts should eschew "intruding on sensitive and complicated issues of state law without giving the state courts a chance to review, and perhaps resolve, the matter first." Further, he suggests that where a federal court maintains jurisdiction over a case involving arguably parallel state and federal claims, it should resolve the state claim first and even consider pointing out "the relevance of state constitutional guarantees to certain disputes" to foster greater development of state constitutional law. Doing so, he writes, marries well with Chief Justice Burger's admonition to state courts in one of his year-end reports that they "first . . . resolv[e] issues arising under their constitutions and statutes [before] passing on matters concerning federal law." Do you agree with this analogy? Does it cohere with the policy underlying Pullman abstention? Why should a federal court resolve a (possibly more difficult) state claim before addressing a federal claim that it may be more qualified to decide and that may moot the state claim?

Page 1105. Insert the following at the end of the penultimate paragraph of Paragraph (1)(d):

For a detailed explication of the context in which the Pullman case arose and the proceedings in the case, see Robel, *Riding the Color Line: The Story of Railroad Commission of* Texas v. Pullman Co., in Federal Courts Stories (Jackson & Resnik eds. 2010), at 163. Among other problems with Pullman abstention, Robel highlights the delays inherent in the procedures, noting that Pullman abstention frustrated efforts by the NAACP to enforce the mandate of Brown v. Board of Education, 347 U.S. 483 (1954). See also Harrison v. NAACP, 360 U.S. 167 (1959) (abstaining from deciding civil rights challenges to a host of Virginia statutes). As Professor Robel notes, only one month after handing down the decision in Pullman, the Supreme Court resisted calls to abstain from determining whether the Interstate Commerce Act mandated equal accommodations for passengers regardless of race, holding that the Act required equal accommodations. See Mitchell v. United States, 313 U.S. 80 (1941).

Page 1108. Add at the end of footnote 11:

See also Gardner, *Abstention at the Border*, 105 U.Va.L.Rev. 63 (2019) (contending that in the international context, federal judges today should generally decline to invoke forum non conveniens or abstention based on notions of comity).

Page 1109. Add a new footnote 11a at the end of Paragraph (3)(e):

[11a] Woolhandler, *Between the Acts: Federal Court Abstention in the 1940s and '50s*, 59 N.Y.L.Sch.L.Rev. 211 (2014–15), argues that abstention became the norm in challenges to state legislation in the 1940s and 1950s but declined in the 1960s as the Supreme Court's deferential stance of the immediate post-Lochner era gave way to less deferential substantive doctrines expanding judicial protection of civil rights.

Page 1112. Add a new footnote 14a at the end of the last paragraph of Paragraph (6):

[14a] For additional discussion, see Sutton, note 1a, *supra*, at 80.

NOTE ON PROCEDURAL ASPECTS OF PULLMAN ABSTENTION

Page 1116. Add at the end of footnote 8:

The time to answer certified questions has lengthened, according to a recent study of practice in three circuit courts. See Cantone & Giffin, *Certified Questions of State Law: An Empirical Examination of Use in Three U.S. Courts of Appeal*, 53 U.Tol.L.Rev. 1 (2021).

Page 1118. Add at the end of Paragraph (5)(c):

Cantone & Giffin compiled a dataset of over 200 certification events in the Third, Sixth, Ninth Circuits from 2010 to 2018, finding a fair amount of variation across circuits in the rate and timing of certification. *Certified Questions of State Law: An Empirical Examination of Use in Three U.S. Courts of Appeal*, 53 U.Tol.L.Rev. 1 (2021). The data suggest that it often takes some time, roughly two years on appeal, before a federal circuit court certifies a question of state law. Once the certification occurs, however, circuit courts typically terminate a case within roughly one year. The authors (researchers for the Federal Judicial Center) conclude that the circuit courts do an effective job in identifying, often on their own motion, what matters would benefit from certification.

Page 1119. Add to the end of Paragraph (5)(d):

After the Fifth Circuit upheld an officer's right to sue under state law for injuries inflicted during a protest in front of a police station, the Court directed the Fifth Circuit on remand to certify questions of state law to Louisiana Supreme Court. See McKesson v. Doe, 141 S.Ct. 48 (2020) (per curiam). Because the officer sought damages from the protest's organizer, rather than from the unknown individual who threw the rock that caused the injury, the Court viewed the matter as presenting First Amendment questions that the clarification of Louisiana state law might render moot.

NOTE ON BURFORD AND THIBODAUX ABSTENTION

Page 1123. Add at the end of footnote 4:

See also Weinberger, *Frankfurter, Abstention Doctrine, and the Development of Modern Federalism*, 87 U.Chi.L.Rev. 1737 (2020) (same).

C. EQUITABLE RESTRAINT

NOTE ON YOUNGER V. HARRIS AND THE DOCTRINE OF EQUITABLE RESTRAINT

Page 1139. Insert the following in place of the first two sentences of Paragraph (2)(b):

(b) Whatever may have been the case in other eras, perhaps by 1971 there was less reason to think state courts generally untrustworthy in cases involving claimed federal rights.[8] During this period, moreover, federal habeas corpus review was both available and robust, see, *e.g.*, Brown v. Allen, Seventh Edition p. 1275, and Supreme Court review of state court criminal decisions was available, see, *e.g.*, Friedman, *A Revisionist Theory of Abstention*, 88 Mich.L.Rev. 530, 561–63 (1989).

[8] But cf. Bright, Can Judicial Independence Be Attained in the South? Overcoming History, Elections, and Misperceptions About the Role of the Judiciary, 14 Ga.St.U.L.Rev. 817 (1998) (arguing that southern state courts, in particular, have continued to reflect legacies of racism and have remained subject to political pressures, including those stemming from judicial elections).

Page 1141. Add a new footnote 11a at the end of Paragraph (6):

[11a] Along similar lines, Smith, *Abstention in the Time of Ferguson*, 131 Harv.L.Rev. 2283 (2018), argues that Younger abstention is inappropriate in cases challenging systemic or structural flaws in local or state criminal justice systems, such as suits challenging policies governing fines, fees, collection practices, and bail. Expressing sympathy for Smith's approach, Traum, *Distributed Federalism: The Transformation of* Younger, 106 Cornell L.Rev. 1759 (2021), considers the ebb and flow of Younger abstention over time. Emphasizing the narrowing of Younger in Sprint Communications, Traum defends what she describes as a pivot away from the early doctrine's all-or-nothing conception of federalism. Drawing on the model of Gerstein v. Pugh, which found Younger inapplicable to a suit challenging pre-trial detention without a probable cause hearing, Traum argues for greater federal engagement with state criminal justice practice and procedure. By distributing federalism concerns along the key points of federal adjudication (pleading, merits, remedies), Traum sees post-pivot doctrine as inviting a more productive collaboration between federal and state actors. Granted that federal courts have taken the narrowing signal in Sprint seriously, does anything turn on whether the post-pivot cases represent a doctrinal change or a more faithful application of the doctrine's limited goal? Many post-pivot cases, like Gerstein, do not raise constitutional issues that the state courts would ordinarily resolve as defenses to a pending state court enforcement proceeding.

NOTE ON STEFFEL V. THOMPSON AND ANTICIPATORY RELIEF

Page 1153. Add a new footnote 1a at the end of Paragraph (1):

[1a] Seinfeld, *At the Frontier of the Younger Doctrine: Reflections on Google v. Hood*, 101 Va.L.Rev. Online 14 (2015), notes that the lower courts are divided over when enforcement proceedings should be deemed pending for purposes of Younger. As Professor Seinfeld notes, some courts view issuance of a subpoena as having initiated state proceedings while other courts view such steps as merely "preliminary" to a subsequent proceeding. See, e.g., Guillemard-Ginorio v. Contreras-Gómez, 585 F.3d 508 (1st Cir. 2009). He argues that the larger principles behind Younger, Steffel, and cases elaborating upon the reach of Younger discussed later in this Note (Huffman v. Pursue, 420 U.S. 592 (1975), Middlesex County Ethics Comm. v. Garden State Bar Ass'n, 457 U.S. 423 (1982), and Ohio Civil Rights Comm'n v. Dayton Christian Schools, Inc., 477 U.S. 619 (1986)), stand for the larger proposition that "a proceeding is not 'ongoing' for Younger purposes until such time as it has been turned over to an impartial state official or, at least, an impartial state actor is able to exercise meaningful oversight authority" of the case. Under this test, Professor Seinfeld concludes, issuance of an administrative subpoena alone does not warrant Younger abstention.

D. PARALLEL PROCEEDINGS

NOTE ON FEDERAL COURT DEFERENCE TO PARALLEL STATE COURT PROCEEDINGS

Page 1181. Add a new footnote 5 at the end of Paragraph (4)(b):

[5] For a survey of how lower courts have applied Colorado River that documents notable inconsistencies, see Note, Colorado River *Abstention: A Practical Reassessment*, 106 Va.L.Rev. 199 (2020).

E. MATTERS OF DOMESTIC RELATIONS AND PROBATE

NOTE ON FEDERAL JURISDICTION IN MATTERS OF DOMESTIC RELATIONS

Page 1189. Add at the end of Paragraph (4):

Pfander & Damrau, *A Non-Contentious Account of Article III's Domestic Relations Exception*, 92 Notre Dame L.Rev. 117 (2016), argues that the domestic relations exception is best grounded in Article III's distinction between "cases" and "controversies." Building on earlier work of one of the authors, see Pfander & Birk, pp. 8–9, *supra*, the authors argue that the term "cases" encompasses "both disputes over federal law between adverse parties and a range of ex parte or non-contentious federal matters", while the term "controversy" extends to "only disputes between the opposing parties identified in Article III." Accordingly, the authors contend that the jurisdictional grant over "controversies" does not permit federal courts to entertain uncontested administrative or ex parte proceedings predicated upon state law, an omission that they argue explains and justifies narrow versions of both the domestic relations and probate exceptions to federal jurisdiction. (For discussion of application of the theory to the probate exception, see below.) Applying their framework, the authors conclude that Article III would permit federal question jurisdiction over non-contentious federal law cases in the domestic realm and that diversity jurisdiction could be extended to contested domestic relations matters involving diverse parties, including surrogacy agreements and divorce proceedings, while also encompassing ancillary matters, such as alimony and child custody. See generally Pfander, Cases Without Controversies, *supra* at p. 9 (situating the domestic relations exceptions in Article III's distinction between cases and controversies and explaining the power of federal courts, in cases, to issue both constitutive and adjudicative judicial decrees).

Page 1189. Add at the end of Paragraph (6)(b):

This view draws support from the fact that in recent Terms, the Court has decided a number of federal question cases implicating marriage and child custody matters. See, *e.g.*, Obergefell v. Hodges, 576 U.S. 644 (2015) (holding that the Fourteenth Amendment requires states to recognize same-sex marriages); V.L. v. E.L., 577 U.S. 404 (2016) (per curiam) (summarily reversing one state's refusal to give full faith and credit to an adoption decree awarded in another state); Pavan v. Smith, 582 U.S. 563 (2017) (holding that state law must recognize same-sex spouse of biological mother as second parent on birth certificate where it would otherwise by default recognize opposite-sex spouse on birth certificate); Monasky v. Taglieri, 140 S.Ct. 719 (2020) (detailing the appropriate inquiry governing habitual residence determinations for purposes of child custody disputes falling under the Hague Convention on the Civil Aspects of International Child Abduction, as implemented in the United States by the International Child Abduction Remedies Act); see also Troxel v. Granville, 530 U.S. 57 (2000) (holding that state court order granting visitation rights to paternal grandparents impermissibly infringed upon mother's due process rights to make decisions concerning the raising of her children); Michael H. v. Gerald D., 491 U.S. 110 (1989) (assessing due process rights of biological father and child in custody dispute with another man to whom the mother was married at time of child's birth).

NOTE ON FEDERAL JURISDICTION IN MATTERS OF PROBATE AND ADMINISTRATION

Page 1190. Add at the end of Paragraph (1):

Pfander & Downey, *In Search of the Probate Exception,* 67 Vand.L.Rev. 1533 (2014), offer a complex explanation, including both statutory and constitutional elements, of the historical origins and scope of the probate exception. Building on earlier work, they argue that Article III "extends judicial power only to 'controversies' or 'disputes' between adversaries on state law matters" and would therefore bar Congress from conferring federal jurisdiction over much of the ex parte work involved in probate proceedings conducted under state law. Despite highlighting that limitation, Pfander & Downey understand the historical record to suggest that Article III does not foreclose federal jurisdiction over "cases" under federal law (as distinguished from "controversies" under state law) that encompass ex parte proceedings. (Here, their examples include applications for naturalization and for warrants.) The authors conclude that Congress "could assign probate administration to the federal courts in connection with otherwise constitutionally proper federal legislation that regulated, say, the commercial implications of estates with ties to more than one state". They similarly contend that because nothing in Article III excludes adversary proceedings between diverse parties that involve probate-related matters under state law, Congress could authorize federal court diversity jurisdiction over such matters. Pfander, Cases Without Controversies, *supra* p. 9, extends this account of the probate exception.

CHAPTER XI

FEDERAL HABEAS CORPUS

---

1. INTRODUCTION

INTRODUCTORY NOTE ON THE FUNCTION OF THE WRIT

Page 1194. Add at the end of footnote 4:

Litman, *The Myth of the Great Writ*, 100 Tex.L.Rev. 219 (2021), analogizes aspects of the writ's function during the Nineteenth Century to Halliday's account of the writ as "an instrument for seizing and building power and control, not solely for constraining it." Going further, Professor Litman argues that when studying the writ's historical role in the American legal system, one must avoid oversimplifying it as a "great writ of liberty" and also confront the ways that courts and other actors have wielded the writ "[l]ike other elements of the American legal system . . . , to discriminate on the bases of race and citizenship and to legitimate government power" over historically subordinated groups. See *id.* (exploring case studies in immigration, Native American affairs, and the law of slavery and freedom).

Page 1194. Substitute the following for footnote 15:

The Supreme Court has not resolved whether a person in custody can challenge conditions of confinement in a habeas petition. See Preiser v. Rodriguez, 411 U.S. 475, 499, 500 (1973) (positing that generally the "proper remedy for a state prisoner who is making a constitutional challenge to the conditions of his prison life, but not to the fact or length of his custody" is an action under 42 U.S.C. § 1983, while leaving open "the appropriate limits of habeas corpus as an alternative remedy to a proper action under § 1983"); see also Ziglar v. Abbasi, 582 U.S. 120, 144–45 (2017) (noting that the Court has "left open the question whether [prisoners] might be able to challenge their confinement conditions via a petition for a writ of habeas corpus"). The lower courts are divided on the question. See, e.g., Aamer v. Obama, 742 F.3d 1023 (D.C.Cir.2014) (noting that D.C. Circuit precedent "establishes that one in custody may challenge the conditions of his confinement in a petition for habeas corpus", while recognizing the lower court split). The matter took on new importance in the context of the COVID-19 pandemic during which time some petitioners challenged prison and immigration detention conditions via habeas. See, e.g. Hope v. Warden, 972 F.3d 310, 325 (3d Cir.2020) (holding that petitioners' challenge to the constitutionality of their conditions of confinement during the pandemic was cognizable in habeas where they sought the remedy of outright release). For further discussion of the intersection of habeas and § 1983 actions, see Seventh Edition Chapter XII, Section 2. Most recently, in Nance v. Ward, 142 S.Ct. 2214 (2022), the Court observed that "the classic prisoner § 1983 suit is one challenging prison conditions—say, overcrowding or inadequate medical care . . . because [such suits] attack not the validity of a conviction or sentence, but only a way of implementing the sentence." *Id.* (holding that a claim arguing that the state's prescribed method of execution is unconstitutional and should be replaced by another method not presently authorized by state law should be advanced as a § 1983 suit rather than in habeas). For additional discussion, see p. 224, *infra*.

---

2. HABEAS CORPUS AND EXECUTIVE DETENTION

NOTE ON THE SUSPENSION CLAUSE OF THE CONSTITUTION

Page 1201. Add a new footnote 1a at the end of the first paragraph of Section A:

[1a] Tyler, Habeas Corpus in Wartime: From the Tower of London to Guantanamo Bay (2017), surveys the Convention and ratification debates and concludes that "a wealth of evidence from this period demonstrates that in the Suspension Clause, the Founding generation sought to constitutionalize the protections associated with the seventh section of the English Habeas Corpus Act and import the English suspension model, while also severely limiting the circumstances when the suspension power could be invoked." For additional discussion, see pp. 169–170, *infra*.

Page 1202. Add a new footnote 4a at the end of the first paragraph of Paragraph (2):

[4a] See also Meltzer, Seventh Edition p. 1237 at 1 (observing that Boumediene "for the first time, clearly held . . . that the Constitution's Suspension Clause . . . affirmatively guarantees access to the courts to seek the writ of habeas corpus (or an adequate substitute) in order to test the legality of executive detention"). Subsequently, in Department of Homeland Security v. Thuraissigiam, 140 S.Ct. 1959 (2020), the Court appeared to walk back this holding. See *id.* at 1969 n.12 (stating that "[t]he original meaning of the Suspension Clause is the subject of controversy" and that it would not "revisit the question" "whether the Clause independently guarantees the availability of the writ or simply restricts the temporary withholding of its operation"). For criticism of this inconsistency, see Tyler, *Thuraissigiam and the Future of the Suspension Clause*, Lawfare (July 2, 2020); Kovarsky, *Habeas Privilege Origination and* INS v. Thuraissigiam, 121 Colum.L.Rev. Forum 23 (2021). For additional discussion of Thuraissigiam, see pp. 171–174, *infra*.

NOTE ON HAMDI V. RUMSFELD AND THE SCOPE OF HABEAS INQUIRY OVER PETITIONS FILED BY ALLEGED ENEMY COMBATANTS

Page 1220. Add a new footnote * at the end of the first sentence of Paragraph (1):

[*] More recently, Justice Thomas opined that "[t]he Founders * * * enshrined" the English suspension model "in the Suspension Clause, which they understood to protect a substantive right"—specifically, "freedom from discretionary detention" at the hands of the executive. Department of Homeland Security v. Thuraissigiam, 140 S.Ct. 1959 (2020) (Thomas, J., concurring). Suspension, Justice Thomas added, "likely meant a statute granting the executive the power to detain without bail or trial based on mere suspicion of a crime or dangerousness," referencing, among other examples, Revolutionary War suspensions adopted in the states to authorize detention without charges of persons supporting the crown. Do these statements suggest that Justice Thomas's position has evolved since Hamdi? For additional discussion of Thuraissigiam, see pp. 73–74, *supra*, and pp. 171–172; 172–173, 174, *infra*.

Page 1221. Add a new footnote 1a at the end of the first paragraph of Paragraph (2):

[1a] In subsequent work, Bradley and Goldsmith detail the expansion of the reach of the AUMF to encompass military operations against the Islamic State and argue that one of the legacies of the Obama Administration is its interpretation of the AUMF to "support presidential discretion and flexibility." Bradley & Goldsmith, *Obama's AUMF Legacy*, 110 Am.J.Int'l L. 628 (2016).

Page 1221. Substitute the following for the last sentence of Paragraph (2):

Defending the plurality's approach in Hamdi, Fallon and Meltzer argue that "a common law approach to habeas corpus issues has been not only historically dominant," but also that "[m]uch of the most important jurisdictional and substantive doctrine [in the habeas context] has been and remains judge-made." Fallon & Meltzer, Seventh Edition p. 1221 at 2044.[1b] Tyler, *A "Second Magna Carta": The English Habeas Corpus Act and the Statutory Origins of the Habeas Privilege*, 91 Notre Dame L.Rev. 1949 (2016) (from a Symposium honoring Daniel Meltzer), suggests a more complicated picture. She posits that the English Habeas Corpus Act of 1679 "was enormously significant in the development of English law's habeas jurisprudence." Going further, she observes that "extensive evidence of the Act's influence across the Atlantic dating from well before, during, and after the Revolutionary War demonstrates that much of early American habeas law was premised upon efforts to incorporate the Act's key protections rather than developed through judicial innovation."

In separate work, Tyler details the role that the English Habeas Corpus Act played in the Revolutionary War legal framework, noting that "determinations regarding the reach and application of the English Habeas Corpus Act of 1679 were of tremendous consequence" during this important period in American history. Tyler, *Habeas Corpus and the American Revolution*, 103 Calif.L.Rev. 635 (2015). As she notes, when asked for guidance as to the legal status of American prisoners brought to English soil for detention during the war, Lord Mansfield advised the North Administration that "in England, where the Habeas Corpus Act was unquestionably in force, it promised a timely criminal trial to those who could and did claim the protection of domestic law—a category of persons long understood to encompass traitors." It was against this backdrop that the Administration requested a suspension from Parliament "to legalize the detention in England of American rebels—considered traitors by the Crown—in the absence of criminal charges." By its terms, the Revolutionary War suspension applied to American colonists captured outside the geographic reach of the Habeas Corpus Act who were then brought within the realm, where the Act would have otherwise been in full force and theirs to claim as British subjects. As Tyler also explains, it was not until independence became a foregone conclusion that Parliament allowed the suspension legislation to lapse and declared Americans remaining in custody to be prisoners of war subject to exchange under the laws of war. Taking the story forward, Tyler, p. 168, *supra*, surveys the Convention and ratification debates and concludes that the Founding generation sought to

---

[1b] For a detailed historical account of how English and British courts employed the common law writ in the period leading up to United States independence, see Halliday, Seventh Edition p. 1193. For elaboration of the arguments favoring a common law model in this context, see Fallon, *On Viewing the Courts as Junior Partners of Congress in Statutory Interpretation Cases: An Essay Celebrating the Scholarship of Daniel J. Meltzer*, 91 Notre Dame L.Rev. 1743 (2016) (from a Symposium honoring Daniel Meltzer). See also Vladeck, *Constitutional Remedies in Federalism's Forgotten Shadow*, 107 Calif.L.Rev. 1043 (2019); Freedman, Making Habeas Work: A Legal History (2018).

constitutionalize the English suspension model and with it the protections long associated with the English Habeas Corpus Act. Moving beyond the Founding period, Tyler posits that this understanding of the constraints that the Clause imposed on executive detention largely controlled through Reconstruction, and it was only during World War II, with the forced detention of Japanese Americans in so-called "Relocation Centers" under Executive Order 9066 and resulting military regulations, that this model broke down. See Tyler, p. 168, *supra*, at 222–43 (detailing how senior government officials initially opposed detention proposals during this period on Suspension Clause grounds). See also Ex parte Endo, 323 U.S. 283 (1944) (declining to address the Suspension Clause issues raised by the detention of Japanese Americans during World War II and instead granting a habeas petition brought by a detained citizen on narrower grounds).[1c]

Assessing this same history, White, *Looking Backward and Forward at the Suspension Clause*, 117 Mich.L.Rev. 1313 (2019), focuses on the Civil War as a turning point in the story of the privilege, observing that President Lincoln effectively defended "the outbreak of war [as] justifying suspension of the privilege, and as a result the privilege really did not exist in wartime." This, White suggests, established a new model for the operation of the privilege in wartime pursuant to which one now witnesses "limited executive 'suspensions,'" as occurred during World War II under Executive Order 9066. This shift, in turn, established the foundation for a case like Hamdi, with the result that together, each of these "strategic decisions of the Executive, and their legitimation by the Court, suggest that, at least since World War II, the Suspension Clause has not so much been 'forgotten' as deliberately bypassed."

Assuming that the English model provided the foundation of the Suspension Clause in the United States Constitution, what bearing, if any, should this history have on questions such as those raised in Hamdi?[1d] And if Professor White's conclusion about the function of the privilege in the wake of the Civil War is accurate, what bearing, if any, should that have on the interpretation of the Suspension Clause today?[1e]

[1c] In subsequent work, Tyler explores the contrasting positions of Prime Minister Churchill and President Roosevelt with respect to the domestic citizen internment programs implemented in Great Britain and the United States during the war, highlighting that Churchill pointed to the role of habeas corpus in the English legal tradition as teaching that the British program was unconstitutional and should be ended. Tyler, *Courts and the Executive in Wartime: A Comparative Study of the American and British Approaches to the Internment of Citizens during World War II and Their Lessons for Today*, 107 Calif.L.Rev. 789 (2019). For a different view contending that the habeas privilege should be understood as " 'only' a procedural remedy and * * * not the source of distinct substantive anti-detention rules," see Kovarsky, *Citizenship, National Security Detention, and the Habeas Remedy*, 107 Calif.L.Rev. 867 (2019).

[1d] Meyler, *Originalism and a Forgotten Conflict over Martial Law*, 113 Nw.U.L.Rev. 1335 (2019), explores the intersection of habeas corpus with martial law in the century leading up to ratification, explaining that in the colonies during this period, "the legal framework of England represented not simply a static backdrop for the development of the Constitution but a contested and dynamic space in which military commanders' imperial justifications vied with the arguments of colonial subjects based on English law. . . ." Thus, she concludes, martial law "furnished part of the context out of which the Suspension Clause emerged" and is therefore relevant to understanding the operation of the Clause as an original matter.

[1e] Pfander, *Constructive Constitutional History and Habeas Corpus Today*, 107 Calif.L.Rev. 1005 (2019), poses a similar question this way: "With habeas sidelined, how should we restore the rule of law in light of Lincoln's action?" He responds by proposing that the law

permit persons subject to detention to bring suits for damages against responsible officers. Doing so, Pfander argues, "would preserve the Constitution and the rule of law, while signaling to future presidents that actions taken in the name of military necessity must ultimately face a test of legality."

Page 1222. Add at the beginning of footnote 2:

Potential support for the relevance of the distinction between a citizen and alien to the application of the Suspension Clause may be found in Department of Homeland Security v. Thuraissigiam, 140 S.Ct. 1959 (2020). In Thuraissigiam, after holding that the Suspension Clause does not apply to an asylum seeker who was apprehended shortly after crossing the border challenging his removal following expedited administrative proceedings, the Court distinguished the situation of a citizen who is detained for deportation, clarifying that "today's opinion would not prevent the citizen from petitioning for release." For additional discussion of Thuraissigiam, see pp. 73–74, *supra*, and pp. 171–172; 172–173, 174, *infra*.

Page 1222. Add at the end of Paragraph (3)(a):

When Padilla sought review in the Supreme Court a second time, the government indicted him on various criminal charges and transferred him to the control of civilian authorities. The Court then declined to take up his case anew. Padilla v. Hanft, 547 U.S. 1062 (2006).

———

NOTE ON THE SCOPE OF REVIEW IN IMMIGRATION CASES

Page 1242. Add at the end of Paragraph (2):

The difficulty in drawing a clear distinction between questions of law and fact arose anew in Department of Homeland Security v. Thuraissigiam, 140 S.Ct. 1959 (2020). Petitioner argued (1) that in removal proceedings he had satisfied the "credible fear of persecution" test such that he should be afforded a fuller opportunity to apply for asylum in this country; and (2) that he had been denied a full and fair opportunity to demonstrate that he satisfied the relevant standard in the administrative proceedings. Concurring in the Court's judgment that petitioner was not constitutionally entitled to judicial review of his claims under the Suspension Clause or the Due Process Clause, Justice Breyer, joined by Justice Ginsburg, characterized petitioner's primary claims as "at their core, challenges to factual findings." As for petitioner's additional claims challenging the asylum officer's application of the relevant legal standard, Justice Breyer observed that "[a]t the heart of [what are] purportedly legal contentions * * * lies a disagreement with immigration officials' findings" relating to the underlying facts. Accordingly, he viewed the latter "claims as factual in nature, notwithstanding respondent's contrary characterization," concluding that the Suspension Clause does not require that a "habeas court make indeterminate and highly record-intensive judgments on matters of degree." Justices Sotomayor, joined by Justice Kagan, dissented and disagreed. Deeming petitioner's claims as raising both mixed questions of law and fact and legal challenges to "procedural defects" in the administrative procedures Congress prescribed, the dissent argued that the Constitution required judicial review. Sidestepping the debate, the majority in Thuraissigiam said that it had no occasion to address whatever distinctions existed between petitioner's claims, which the government had labeled as raising "at best a mixed question of law," and those advanced in St. Cyr. The Court instead relied upon the distinction that St. Cyr was already within the United States when he sought review of his claims. For additional discussion of Thuraissigiam, see pp. 73–74, *supra*, and pp. 171–172; 172–173, 174, *infra*.

―――――――

NOTE ON EXHAUSTION OF NON-HABEAS REMEDIES

Page 1245. Add at the end of footnote 5:

Cf. In re Al-Nashiri, 791 F.3d 71 (D.C.Cir.2015) (declining to review, on petition for writ of mandamus, separation of powers challenge to the composition of the Court of Military Commission Review while proceedings before military commission were ongoing and noting that petitioner's arguments could be raised and fully aired on appeal from final judgment); In re Khadr, 823 F.3d 92 (D.C.Cir.2016) (same).

―――――――

NOTE ON BOUMEDIENE AND THE TERRITORIAL REACH OF HABEAS CORPUS

Page 1259. Add a new footnote * at the end of the penultimate paragraph of Paragraph (1):

* For an argument that Anglo-American habeas jurisprudence includes important statutory foundations separate and apart from common law developments, see Tyler, p. 169, *supra* (detailing the significance of the English Habeas Corpus Act of 1679).

Page 1259. Add a new footnote ** at the end of Paragraph (1):

** Tyler, p. 168, *supra*, posits that "Hamdi and Boumediene should be understood as posing distinct questions". In her view, Hamdi was incorrectly decided insofar as it stands at odds with the animating purpose behind the Suspension Clause—namely, to preclude the government from detaining someone deemed to owe allegiance outside the criminal process in the absence of a valid suspension. In Boumediene, by contrast, no Justice questioned the government's authority to detain enemy combatants outside the criminal process as part of the war on terrorism. Boumediene, accordingly, solely implicated the question "what procedural rights attach in habeas proceedings." Tyler then questions "whether there is room for both cases under the umbrella of Suspension Clause jurisprudence", while also asking whether "the Suspension Clause and due process elements of the war on terrorism decisions should be rendered conceptually distinct." *Cf.* Tyler, p. 169, *supra* (underscoring the importance of geography as well as the bond of allegiance with respect to the reach and application of the English Habeas Corpus Act during the American Revolutionary War).

Page 1259. Add at the end of Paragraph (1):

In Department of Homeland Security v. Thuraissigiam, 140 S.Ct. 1959 (2020), the Court held that the Suspension Clause did not apply to a petitioner seeking asylum in this country who was captured 25 yards inside the border and then ordered removed via expedited administrative proceedings. Writing for the Court, Justice Alito framed the Court's analysis as asking whether petitioner's claims would have come within the reach of the Suspension Clause as it was understood in 1789. (The Court framed its inquiry this way after quoting the petitioner's brief to say that " 'there is no reason' to consider whether the Clause extends any further" (p. 1969 (quoting Brief for Respondent 26, n. 12)).) Finding no support for the proposition that "the writ of habeas corpus was understood at the time of the adoption of the Constitution to permit a petitioner to claim the right to enter or remain in a country or to obtain administrative review potentially leading to that result", the Court held that the Suspension Clause did not apply (p. 1969 (observing that at the Founding, "[t]he writ simply provided a means of contesting the lawfulness of restraint and securing release")). For the Thuraissigiam majority, that was the end of the matter.*** Compare the Court's approach in Boumediene, which moved beyond a historical record that it viewed as providing no clear analogy to explore functional considerations in determining the application of the Suspension Clause in the case.

*** It was irrelevant, moreover, that during the Founding period and for decades thereafter, federal policy provided an " 'open door to the immigrant' " (citation omitted), rendering it such that a challenge to a limitation on review of immigration determinations would never have arisen during that period. Concurring in the judgment in Thuraissigiam but reserving judgment on future cases that might present different considerations, Justices Breyer and Ginsburg relied upon Boumediene for the proposition that habeas corpus "is an 'adaptable remedy,' and the 'precise application and scope' of the review it guarantees may change 'depending upon the circumstances' " (p. 1989 (quoting Boumediene v. Bush, 553 U.S. 723, 779 (2008))).

Page 1260. Add a new footnote 1a at the end of Paragraph (2)(b):

[1a] See also Kent, *Piracy and Due Process*, 39 Mich.J.Int'l L. 385 (2018) (exploring the political and legal treatment of piracy in the period leading up to and immediately following ratification and concluding that the history cuts against any historically inflected arguments supporting the concept of global due process).

Page 1261. Add at the end of Paragraph (2)(c):

The Supreme Court's most recent intervention in this debate came in Agency for International Development v. Alliance for Open Society International, Inc., 140 S.Ct. 2082 (2020), in which it rejected the proposition that foreign affiliates of American organizations could bring a First Amendment challenge to conditions that Congress attached to funding grants to combat HIV/AIDS abroad. Writing for the Court, Justice Kavanaugh (joined by Chief Justice Roberts and Justices Thomas, Alito, and Gorsuch), posited that "it is long settled as a matter of American constitutional law that foreign citizens outside U. S. territory do not possess rights under the U. S. Constitution" (citations omitted).[1b] He distinguished the situation of foreign citizens inside the United States, who "may enjoy certain constitutional rights", such as "the right to due process in a criminal trial." Finally, Justice Kavanaugh set apart those cases in which "under some circumstances, foreign citizens in the U. S. Territories—or in 'a territory' under the 'indefinite' and 'complete and total control' and 'within the constant jurisdiction' of the United States—may possess certain constitutional rights" (pp. 2086–87 (quoting Boumediene, 553 U.S. at 755–71)). In dissent, Justice Breyer, joined by Justices Ginsburg and Sotomayor, opined that the plaintiffs should not be understood as foreign organizations but as instead affiliates of their American counterparts. Regardless, he rejected the Court's assessment of prior caselaw on matters of extraterritoriality, writing that it "does not reflect the current state of the law." "At most, one might say that [foreign citizens abroad] are unlikely to

[1b] In reaching this conclusion, the majority emphasized that "[i]f the rule were otherwise, actions by American military, intelligence, and law enforcement personnel against foreign organizations or foreign citizens in foreign countries would be constrained by the foreign citizens' purported rights under the U. S. Constitution. That has never been the law" (pp. 2086–87 (citing Verdugo-Urquidez, 494 U.S. at 273–74; Eisentrager, 339 U.S. at 784)).

enjoy very often extraterritorial protection under the Constitution. Or one might say that the matter is undecided. But this Court has studiously avoided establishing an absolute rule that forecloses that protection in all circumstances" (p. 2099). The dissent further cited Boumediene's rejection of a "formalistic" approach and its holding that "'questions of extraterritoriality turn on objective factors and practical concerns' present in a given case" (p. 2100). Arguing that questions of territoriality were not presented or briefed in the case, the dissent would have left open such matters in light of the many complications that they may raise (pp. 2100–01 (listing examples of potential future cases presenting different circumstances)).

Page 1261. Add a new Paragraph (2)(f):

(f)   In applying the Suspension Clause, how should a court determine whether a petitioner is inside the United States? In Department of Homeland Security v. Thuraissigiam, 140 S.Ct. 1959 (2020), the Court concluded that an alien seeking asylum in the United States should be treated differently than one who is "already in the country [and] held in custody pending deportation." Unlike the alien in the latter scenario, one seeking entry stands on a different footing for purposes of the application of both the Suspension Clause and due process principles. This conclusion followed from Congress's "plenary authority to decide which aliens to admit" (citation omitted).[3] It was therefore of no relevance to the inquiry that petitioner had actually crossed the border and been apprehended some 25 yards inside the United States. The decision reveals that the border remains an important factor in constitutional analysis and that the Court defers extensively to Congress in the immigration context. As several Justices observed in Thuraissigiam, the decision could have important ramifications for those who enter the United States without legal authorization who are apprehended years later and put into removal proceedings. See *id.* (Breyer, J., concurring in the judgment); *id.* (Sotomayor, J., dissenting). For additional discussion of Thuraissigiam, see pp. 73–74, 171–172; 172–173, *supra.*

[3]   The Thuraissigiam Court distinguished Boumediene as involving individuals who "had been 'apprehended on the battlefield in Afghanistan' and elsewhere, not while crossing the border" (p. 1981 (quoting Boumediene, 553 U.S., at 734)), and observing that "[t]hey sought only to be released from Guantanamo, not to enter this country."

Page 1261. Add a new Paragraph (3):

(3) The Application of the Due Process Clause to Aliens Held Abroad. In Al-Hela v. Trump, 972 F.3d 120 (D.C.Cir.2020), a D.C. Circuit panel rejected claims brought by a Guantanamo Bay detainee that his detention violated both his substantive and procedural due process rights. In the panel's view, "the Due Process Clause may not be invoked by aliens without property or presence in the sovereign territory of the United States." The D.C. Circuit vacated the panel opinion and reviewed the case en banc. The en banc majority declined to "decide whether due process protections apply to Guantanamo detainees, because", it held, "even assuming the Due Process Clause applie[d]" to al-Hela, his hearing in the district court afforded him procedural due process. Al-Hela v. Biden, 66 F.4th 217, 222

(D.C.Cir.2023) (en banc). Speaking specifically to the relationship between the Suspension Clause and due process, the en banc court concluded that "the procedures employed by the District Court in its effort to satisfy the Suspension Clause also provided whatever process would be required to satisfy [the] context-dependent Due Process Clause framework" of Mathews v. Eldridge, 424 U.S. 319 (1976). See 66 F.4th at 231 (relying as well on Hamdi v. Rumsfeld, Seventh Edition p. 1206). The court similarly concluded that even if the Due Process Clause applies as a substantive matter to Guantanamo Bay detainees (a matter that it did not decide), al-Hela's claims that his detention violated substantive due process also failed.

In the wake of al-Hela, it is still unclear exactly what the relationship is between the Suspension Clause and due process. Further unsettled is whether there remain any claims under the Due Process Clause that Guantanamo Bay detainees may advance challenging the fact or length of their detention and/or how they came to be classified as enemy combatants. (One could imagine claims challenging continuing detention being predicated upon arguments that the underlying hostilities justifying detention no longer exist, a contention al-Hela did not advance in his case, see 66 F.4th at 243, or claims that continuing detention once an individual has been cleared for transfer run afoul of constitutional concerns similar to those flagged by the Court in the immigration context in Zadvydas v. Davis, 533 U.S. 678 (2001), see Seventh Edition p. 338 n.5.) Also unresolved is the question whether detainees may bring due process claims challenging the procedures or rulings of the military commissions operating at Guantanamo.

---

3. COLLATERAL ATTACK ON CRIMINAL CONVICTIONS

A. COLLATERAL ATTACK ON STATE CONVICTIONS

INTRODUCTORY NOTE ON THE OPERATION OF FEDERAL HABEAS CORPUS JURISDICTION FOR STATE PRISONERS

Page 1272. Add a new footnote 24a at the end of the carryover sentence:

[24a] One recent study found that between 2013 and 2017, federal habeas courts granted relief for claims relating to the guilt phase at a significantly higher rate in capital murder cases than non-capital murder cases. See Note, *Is Death Different to Federal Judges?*, 72 Stan.L.Rev. 1655 (2020).

Page 1272. Substitute for the third sentence in the first full paragraph the following:

To date, only one state, Arizona, has qualified for the procedural benefits available to states in federal capital habeas corpus cases. Arizona did so under new procedures that empower the Attorney General to certify qualifying states.[26] No other state has qualified, perhaps because most find the benefits not worth the cost of supplying counsel in state post-conviction proceedings.

[26] Section 507 of the USA PATRIOT Improvement and Reauthorization Act of 2005, Pub.L.No. 109–177, 120 Stat. 192, 250 (2006), amended AEDPA by shifting from the federal courts to the Attorney General the authority initially to certify that states have established mechanisms for providing counsel in state post-conviction proceedings and by specifying that no additional requirements for certification shall be imposed beyond those set forth in the statute—namely, "whether the State has established a mechanism for the appointment, compensation, and payment of reasonable litigation expenses of competent counsel in State postconviction proceedings brought by indigent prisoners who have been sentenced to death" and "whether the State provides standards of competency for the appointment" (§ 2265(a)(1)). In 2013, the Attorney General issued a final rule implementing the certification procedure. See 78 Fed. Reg. 58,160 (Sept. 23, 2013) (to be codified at 28 C.F.R. pt. 26).

The Attorney General thereafter certified Arizona in 2020, see 85 Fed. Reg. 20,705, and declared his notice effective retroactively to May 19, 1998. The certification was under review in the D.C. Circuit, see Office of the Federal Public Defender et al. v. Barr, No. 20–1144 (D.C.Cir.), but in response to a motion by the Department of Justice, that court remanded the matter back to the Department for further consideration, see Order dated Mar. 26, 2021. Previously, in Spears v. Stewart, 283 F.3d 992 (9th Cir.2002), a Ninth Circuit panel held that Arizona's system could qualify, but refused to enforce the provisions of §§ 2261–2264 in that case because Arizona had not complied with its own rules requiring timely appointment of counsel.

INTRODUCTORY NOTE ON THE HISTORICAL DEVELOPMENT OF FEDERAL RELITIGATION IN CRIMINAL CASES

Page 1274. Add at the end of Paragraph (4):

Professor Vázquez notes that during the nineteenth century, those convicted in state courts enjoyed direct appeal as of right to the Supreme Court of any federal question decided against them. Surveying the cases between the 1916 introduction of discretionary review of state court criminal cases by the Supreme Court and the Brown decision in 1953 that follows on Seventh Edition p. 1275, Vázquez concludes that during this period the Justices debated whether review of such questions remained the exclusive province of the Supreme Court on direct appeal or whether lower federal courts could examine them in habeas proceedings. Thus, Vázquez argues, disagreement centered not on whether a federal court would review such questions generally, but instead over which federal forum should do so. See Vázquez, *Habeas as Forum Allocation: A New Synthesis*, 71 U. Miami L.Rev. 645 (2017).[8a]

[8a] Vázquez's conclusion therefore contrasts with that reached by Professor Bator in his survey of the same period. See Bator, Seventh Edition p. 1283.

NOTE ON THE RULE OF BROWN V. ALLEN AND ON HABEAS CORPUS POLICY

Page 1281. Add at the end of the first paragraph of footnote 3:

See also Vázquez, *supra* (arguing that Supreme Court members favored shifting review of state criminal cases from direct appeals to federal habeas proceedings during the period leading up to Brown).

Page 1284. Add a new footnote 7a at the end of Section C, Paragraph (1)(b):

[7a] Two recent contributions to this debates include Huq, *Habeas and the Roberts Court*, 81 U.Chi.L.Rev. 519 (2014) (criticizing King and Hoffman's broader proposals to scale back collateral federal habeas corpus review and questioning the plausibility of the fiscal tradeoffs they propose); and Wiseman, *What is Federal Habeas Worth?*, 67 Fla.L.Rev. 1157 (2015) (estimating expenditures associated with non-capital habeas review in the federal courts to constitute "a tiny fraction" of criminal justice spending).

Page 1284. Add a new paragraph (C)(2):

(2) Recent Criticism. In Edwards v. Vannoy, 141 S.Ct. 1547 (2021), Justice Gorsuch, joined by Justice Thomas, criticized Brown v. Allen in a concurring opinion. In his view, "Brown not only upended centuries of settled precedent and invited practical problems; it produced anomalies as well." Both before and after the expansion of federal habeas jurisdiction during Reconstruction, Justice Gorsuch argued, the Court consistently declined to award relief to state prisoners "unless the state court had acted without jurisdiction." In his view, Brown not only disregarded that historical practice, it also denigrated the role of state courts, which are obligated to follow federal law under the Supremacy Clause, and provided for unnecessary additional layers of review of criminal convictions. Relying heavily on Justice Jackson's dissent in Brown, Justice Gorsuch contended that in the intervening period, "habeas became little more than an ordinary appeal with an extraordinary Latin name" and "[t]he haystack just grew too large." With respect to the anomalies created by Brown's approach, Justice Gorsuch pointed to the Court's decision in Burns v. Wilson, 346 U.S. 137 (1953) (plurality opinion), which, on his description, rejected Brown's "fix-any-error approach for final judgments issued by military courts," resulting in the oddity that "federal courts wound up with more power to reopen the judgments of a different sovereign's courts than the administrative proceedings of the federal government itself."

Justice Gorsuch continued his criticism of Brown v. Allen while writing for the Court in Brown v. Davenport, 142 S.Ct. 1510 (2022). Once again invoking Justice Jackson's dissent in Brown v. Allen, Justice Gorsuch criticized that decision for disregarding "[t]he traditional distinction between jurisdictional defects and mere errors in adjudication" such that "[f]ull-blown constitutional error correction became the order of the day." As in Vannoy, Justice Gorsuch asserted that in the period leading up to Brown v. Allen, federal habeas courts granted relief only to state prisoners whose convictions arose out of proceedings in which state courts did not have proper jurisdiction.

Writing for three dissenters in Davenport, Justice Kagan complained that Justice Gorsuch's "law-chambers history" was not relevant to the issues before the Court in Davenport. Justice Kagan nonetheless challenged Justice Gorsuch's assertion that Brown v. Allen broke new ground. To that end, she emphasized the breadth of the grant of habeas jurisdiction in the 1789 Judiciary Act and the 1867 expansion of that act, the latter of which by its terms broadly permitted federal courts "to grant writs of habeas corpus in all cases where any person may be restrained of his or her liberty" in violation of the federal Constitution (citing Act of Feb. 5, 1867, 14 Stat. 385). She then catalogued a number of the Court's decisions and contemporary treatises pre-dating Brown, all of which, in her view, demonstrate that Brown "built on decades and decades of history." See *id.* (Kagan, J., dissenting) (citing, among others, Ex parte Lange, 85 U.S. (18 Wall.) 163 (1874) (granting habeas relief to a convicted prisoner under the Double Jeopardy Clause); Ex parte Wilson, 114 U.S. 417 (1885) (granting habeas relief where petitioner had not been indicted by a grand jury); Callan v. Wilson, 127 U.S. 540 (1888) (granting habeas relief where petitioner had been denied jury trial); Moore v. Dempsey, 261 U.S. 86 (1923) (granting relief in habeas proceedings where petitioners were denied due process in their state-court trial); Johnson v. Zerbst, 304 U.S. 458 (1938) (holding that a petitioner may win relief in collateral habeas proceedings for denial of effective assistance of counsel at trial)).

One of the cases relied upon by Justice Kagan in her Davenport dissent, Moore v. Dempsey, 261 U.S. 86 (1923), involved the prosecution of several African American men for an alleged interracial murder in Arkansas. In response to what had been mob domination of the trial, the Court held in an opinion by Justice Holmes that if "the whole [state-court] proceeding is a mask [and] counsel, jury and judge were swept to the fatal end by an irresistible wave of public passion, and . . . the State Courts failed to correct the wrong," then a federal habeas court is empowered to set aside the state convictions of the prisoners who were denied due process of law. See also Seventh Edition p. 1274 (discussing Frank v. Mangum, 237 U.S. 309 (1915), and Moore v. Dempsey). Is it fair to say that Moore v. Dempsey, which predated Brown v. Allen by decades, sweeps beyond the narrow jurisdictional model of habeas that Justice Gorsuch presents in his Davenport opinion?

More generally, do the context in which Congress adopted the 1867 Act and its expansive terms also matter to this debate? In the lead up to the adoption of the 1867 Act, for example, a resolution by the House of Representatives explained that expanded habeas legislation was needed "to enforce the liberty of all persons under the operation of the constitutional amendment abolishing slavery." Cong. Globe, 39th Cong., 1st Sess. 87 (1865). Congress was also concerned at the time with the protection of federal officials from recalcitrant state governments. For more on the 1867 Act, see Wiecek, *The Great Writ and Reconstruction: The Habeas Corpus Act of 1867*, 36 J.So.Hist. 530 (1970). For additional discussion of Davenport, see p. 185, *infra*.

Recent scholarship has explored habeas jurisprudence in the decades preceding Brown v. Allen, see, *e.g.*, Vázquez, p. 176, *supra* (describing Brown as the culmination of a decades-long expansion of federal habeas review of state convictions), with some noting that terminology employed by habeas courts in the past may not equate with modern understandings, see, *e.g.*, Siegel, *Habeas, History, and Hermeneutics*, 64 Ariz.L.Rev. 505 (2022); see also *id.* at 510 (observing that "[a]s amended by AEDPA, the federal habeas statute plainly assumes and confirms the availability of habeas relief in cases beyond" those Justice Gorsuch outlines in his Vannoy concurring opinion).

Page 1287. Substitute the following for the second sentence of footnote 13:

This position was later rejected in Dickerson v. United States, 530 U.S. 428 (2000), 7–2, although it was revived at least in part in Vega v. Tekoh, 142 S.Ct. 2095 (2022), where a Court majority, 6–3, again labeled the Miranda warnings as "prophylactic." Going further, the Tekoh Court held that "a violation of *Miranda* does not necessarily constitute a violation of the Constitution, and therefore such a violation does not constitute 'the deprivation of [a] right . . . secured by the Constitution' " under 42 U.S.C. § 1983. In its decision, the Tekoh Court discussed Withrow without calling the decision into question. See *id.*

———

NOTE ON THE SUSPENSION CLAUSE AND POSTCONVICTION REVIEW

Page 1292. Add a new Paragraph (3)(c):

In Jones v. Hendrix, 143 S.Ct. 1857 (2023), the Supreme Court rejected a Suspension Clause challenge to statutory limits on the filing of successive motions by federal prisoners under 28 U.S.C. § 2255, where the prisoner raised a claim of legal innocence predicated upon intervening Supreme Court authority narrowing the scope of a federal criminal statute. Writing for the Court, Justice Thomas held the Suspension Clause inapplicable because "[a]t the Founding, a sentence after conviction 'by a court of competent jurisdiction' was ' "in *itself* sufficient cause" ' for a prisoner's continued detention (quoting Brown v. Davenport, 142 S.Ct. 1510, 1520–21 (2022) (quoting in turn Ex parte Watkins, 38 U.S. (3 Pet.) 193, 202 (1830))). For this proposition, the Jones Court relied heavily on Chief Justice Marshall's opinion in Ex parte Watkins, which observed that a habeas court has no power to "look beyond the judgment" of a criminal proceeding to "re-examine the charges on which it was rendered"—even where the "court ha[d] misconstrued the law, and ha[d] pronounced an offence to be punishable criminally, which [was] not so." Watkins, 38 U.S. (3 Pet.) at 202, 209. Thus, the Jones Court posited, traditionally there was no power to look beyond a conviction rendered after trial in a court of general criminal jurisdiction. Going further, the Court observed that "[t]he principles of *Watkins* guided this Court's understanding of the habeas write throughout the 19th century and well into the 20th."

———

NOTE ON RETROACTIVITY AND NEW LAW IN HABEAS CORPUS

Page 1298. Add at the end of Paragraph (4)(b):

After over three decades of never finding a claim to fit within Teague's second exception, a divided Supreme Court eliminated the category altogether in Edwards v. Vannoy, 141 S.Ct. 1547 (2021). In the petition for certiorari, Edwards presented the question whether Teague's second exception encompasses a claim brought in habeas seeking to benefit from the Court's recent holding that the Sixth Amendment's requirement of a unanimous jury applies to the states under the Fourteenth Amendment. See Ramos v. Louisiana, 140 S.Ct. 1390 (2020) (overruling Apodaca v. Oregon, 406 U.S. 404 (1972)). Writing for six justices, Justice Kavanaugh began by observing that "applying Ramos retroactively would potentially overturn decades of convictions obtained in reliance on Apodaca." Turning to the Teague inquiry, he classified the Ramos rule as procedural because it "affects 'only the manner of determining the defendant's culpability'" (quoting Schriro v. Summerlin, 542 U.S. 348, 353 (2004)). Because, moreover, "[t]he starkest example of a decision announcing a new rule is a decision that overrules an earlier case", Justice Kavanaugh explained, it was clear that Ramos established a new rule of constitutional law that but for Teague's exceptions would not apply retroactively.

Justice Kavanaugh next analyzed whether Teague's second exception for watershed rules of criminal procedure encompassed Ramos. But the exception, he stressed, has "[i]n practice * * * been theoretical, not real." On this score, Justice Kavanaugh observed that with the exception of the right to counsel recognized in Gideon v. Wainwright, 372 U.S. 335 (1963), "[t]he Court has never identified any other pre-Teague or post-Teague rule as watershed. None." After identifying a number of important decisions that the Court has declined to bring within the watershed exception, Justice Kavanaugh saw no reason to hold differently with respect to the rule of Ramos. This conclusion, he explained, also begged a larger question: "If landmark and historic criminal procedure decisions—including Mapp, Miranda, Duncan, Crawford, Batson, and now Ramos—do not apply retroactively on federal collateral review, how can any additional new rules of criminal procedure apply retroactively on federal collateral review? At this point, some 32 years after Teague, we think the only candid answer is that none can". Justice Kavanaugh observed that "[c]ontinuing to articulate a theoretical exception that never actually applies in practice offers false hope to defendants, distorts the law, misleads judges, and wastes the resources of defense counsel, prosecutors, and courts." Finally, he argued that an exception that never applies in practice could not be said to have generated reliance interests. It followed, on the Court's view, that there existed no reason to retain Teague's second exception.[6a]

[6a] Justice Thomas, joined by Justice Gorsuch, concurred, opining that the Court need go no further than apply 28 U.S.C. § 2254(d) to resolve the case and deny relief. In other words, he argued that AEDPA superseded Teague, including its exceptions. For additional discussion, see *infra* p. 156. Justice Gorsuch, joined by Justice Thomas, also concurred and wrote separately. Although in his view, "Teague did much to return the writ to its original station" by "insisting that final judgments cannot be reopened as a 'general rule,'" its prohibition on retroactive application of so-called "new" rules does not make sense with respect to new Supreme Court holdings, like Ramos, that purport to "realign th[e] Court's decisions with the original meaning" of the Constitution. Regardless, he argued, it should be irrelevant whether "Members of this Court happen to think the rules they announce are 'new' in some sense or insufficiently 'fundamental' in another." Instead, Teague's default proposition should govern in all cases: specifically, habeas corpus should "not authorize federal courts to reopen a judgment issued by a court of competent jurisdiction once it has become final." It followed, Justice Gorsuch posited, that Edwards' elimination of the second Teague exception "advances the progress" toward

Writing for herself and Justices Breyer and Sotomayor, Justice Kagan dissented. Labeling the Ramos decision "historic," she observed that "[i]f you were scanning a thesaurus for a single word to describe the decision, you would stop when you came to 'watershed.' " Justice Kagan also believed that the precedents on which the majority relied to reject classifying the Ramos rule as "watershed" were not comparable.[6b] Ramos, she noted, emphasized the importance of jury unanimity, declaring it "an 'essential element[ ]' of the jury trial right," and therefore " 'fundamental to the American scheme of justice' " (quoting Ramos, 140 S.Ct. at 1396–97). Going further, the dissent reiterated that Ramos did away with nonunanimous juries because the practice was adopted " 'to dilute the influence [on juries] of racial, ethnic, and religious minorities,'—and particularly, 'to ensure that African-American juror service would be meaningless' " (quoting Ramos, 140 S.Ct. at 1394). Against this backdrop, Justice Kagan observed: "If a rule so understood isn't a watershed one, then nothing is."

Observing that no party had asked the Court to eliminate Teague's second exception, Justice Kagan pointed out that the majority author had written in Ramos that under the Court's doctrine of *stare decisis*, it " 'typically does not overrule a precedent unless a party requests overruling' " (quoting Ramos, 140 S.Ct. at 1419, n.4 (Kavanaugh, J., concurring in part)). Justice Kagan concluded by asserting that "[a] decision like [Ramos] comes with a promise, or at any rate should. If the right to a unanimous jury is so fundamental—if a verdict rendered by a divided jury is 'no verdict at all'— then Thedrick Edwards should not spend his life behind bars over two jurors' opposition."

Does Edwards mark a major retreat from Teague? Does the decision have much practical significance? In the wake of Teague, the Court had never found a single one of its decisions to establish a watershed rule of criminal procedure. In some respects, therefore, the majority's decision is not remarkable. Or might this conclusion beg the question whether the Court should have identified more watershed rules? Should Teague, in any case, apply a new rule retroactively when announced in a case that purports to align criminal procedure doctrine with the Constitution's original meaning?

To be sure, the majority's approach respects state reliance interests by avoiding the need for retrials, sometimes years after the fact when witnesses' memories have faded and evidence may be lost. See Bator, Seventh Edition p. 1283; Friendly, Seventh Edition p. 1284, at 149–50. The majority's position also could encourage the Court to recognize more procedural rights on behalf of criminal defendants if doing so will prove less disruptive. See Seventh Edition, Paragraph (2), p. 1293. (exploring the Warren Court's approach to

---

"retir[ing] a test that was unknown in law until 1989 and whose contours remain unknowable decades later." Although Justice Gorsuch was writing about Teague's second exception in his Edwards opinion, his views might be read to suggest that he questions the legitimacy of Teague's first exception as well.

[6b] Justice Kagan also rejected the majority's assertion that the Court had never applied a procedural rule retroactively before Teague, citing Brown v. Louisiana, 447 U.S. 323 (1980), which, she explained, retroactively applied the rule of Burch v. Louisiana, 441 U.S. 130 (1979) (holding that a six-person jury verdict must be unanimous). The majority disputed her reading of Brown's application of Burch to collateral cases.

retroactivity). At the same time, Edwards once again raises fundamental questions about why a prisoner whose conviction became final one day before Ramos should be treated differently from a prisoner whose conviction became final one day after Ramos. See also Seventh Edition Note (C)(2), p. 1299.

Page 1299. Add at the end of footnote 6:

Notwithstanding the Supreme Court's failure to recognize any watershed procedural rules within the meaning of Teague's second exception since Teague, a number of state court decisions have done so. See Fox & Stein, *Constitutional Retroactivity in Criminal Procedure*, 91 Wash.L.Rev. 463 (2016) (listing examples).

Page 1299. Substitute the following for the last sentence of Paragraph (4)(c):

The Court extended this reasoning in Montgomery v. Louisiana, 577 U.S. 190 (2016), holding that its decision in Miller v. Alabama, 567 U.S. 460 (2012), was substantive for Teague purposes. Miller had held that a juvenile convicted of a homicide offense could not be sentenced to life in prison without parole absent consideration of whether the defendant's crimes reflect " 'irreparable corruption' " (pp. 479–80) (quoting Roper v. Simmons, 543 U.S. 551, 573 (2005)). The same Term, the Court extended its decision in Bousley v. United States, 523 U.S. 614 (1998), holding retroactive its decision in Johnson v. United States, 576 U.S. 591 (2015), which struck down as unconstitutionally vague a provision calling for enhanced sentences in cases involving possession of a firearm by a felon. See Welch v. United States, 578 U.S. 120 (2016).[6c] Given these extensions of Teague's first exception, and with Teague's second exception now eliminated, it would be accurate to restate Teague and its exceptions this way: new substantive rules apply retroactively; new procedural rules do not.

[6c] For additional discussion of Montgomery, see pp. 186–204 *infra*. For additional discussion of Welch, see pp. 212–214, *infra*.

Page 1300. Add a new Paragraph (5) to Section C:

(5) **Teague's Foundations.** What is the basis for Teague's mandate? The Constitution or the federal habeas statute? The Court explored this important question in Danforth v. Minnesota, 552 U.S. 264 (2008), and Montgomery v. Louisiana, 577 U.S. 190 (2016), included below as a principal case. See also pp. 82 and 107–108, *supra*; pp. 186–204, *infra*.

Page 1301. Add at the end of Section D:

The Court revisited the questions raised in Danforth v. Minnesota, 552 U.S. 264 (2008), in Montgomery v. Louisiana, 577 U.S. 190 (2016). In Montgomery, the Court held that Teague's first exception establishes a constitutional rule that state courts must apply in collateral proceedings. Writing for the Court, Justice Kennedy concluded that "[i]f a State may not constitutionally insist that a prisoner remain in jail on federal habeas review, it may not constitutionally insist on the same result in its own postconviction proceedings." For further discussion, see pp. 82, and 107–108, *supra*; pp. 186–204, *infra*.

In applying Griffith and Teague, the threshold question of whether a state-court proceeding is direct or collateral is significant. In McKinney v.

Arizona, 140 S.Ct. 702 (2020), a closely divided Court concluded that where a federal habeas court orders a state court to reweigh aggravating and mitigating factors in determining the appropriateness of a death sentence, the subsequent proceeding should be treated as collateral for Teague purposes. Accordingly, Griffith did not apply, and the state court was not required to apply intervening Supreme Court decisions that postdated the conclusion of the petitioner's original direct appeal. Citing the state supreme court's labeling of the reweighing proceeding as occurring on "collateral review," the Court found "no good reason" to second guess that classification. Dissenting for four Justices, Justice Ginsburg read the majority opinion "not [to] hold that the classification a state supreme court assigns to a proceeding is inevitably dispositive of a retroactivity question." Instead, she understood the test to "look[ ] first to the State's classification of a proceeding, and then ask[ ] whether the character of the proceeding warrants the classification." Applying that test, Justice Ginsburg viewed the reweighing proceeding as a reinstatement of petitioner's direct appeal: the state supreme court conducted a *de novo* review of McKinney's sentence, used the docket number from his original direct appeal, and labeled McKinney's original appeal as " 'reinstated.' " In her view, McKinney was therefore entitled to the benefit of all relevant Supreme Court decisions that predated the reweighing proceeding (Ginsburg, J., dissenting) ("Whether the Constitution requires the application of law now in force is a question of federal constitutional law, not an issue subject to state governance."). McKinney raises several questions. First, will any new proceedings ordered by a federal habeas court short of a full retrial alter the date of finality for Teague purposes? Second, is there a convincing distinction to be drawn between McKinney's circumstances and those presented in Magwood v. Patterson, 561 U.S. 320 (2010)? In Magwood, the Court held that where a federal habeas court orders a state court to resentence the petitioner, the ensuing proceeding results in a "new" judgment for purposes of AEDPA and a subsequent federal habeas petition is therefore not "second or successive" to any prior petition; instead, the petition should be treated as "challeng[ing] a new judgment for the first time." For additional discussion of Magwood, see p. 212, *infra*.

NOTE ON TERRY WILLIAMS V. TAYLOR AND 28 U.S.C. § 2254(d)(1)

Page 1314. Add a new footnote * at the end of the first paragraph of Paragraph (2):

   * In a recent article, Professor Vázquez contends that the Court's approach in these cases is the product of its erroneous interpretation in *Terry Williams v. Taylor* of the standard set forth in § 2254(d)(1). In support of Justice Stevens's minority position, Vázquez contends that the *Williams* Court "could just as plausibly have read 'unreasonable' to mean 'contrary to' " when parsing AEDPA's text. He further argues that the weight of the legislative history and President Clinton's signing statement both strongly support the conclusion that AEDPA was not intended to alter the prior *de novo* review standard applied by federal courts to questions of federal law in collateral habeas corpus cases. Vázquez, *AEDPA as Forum Allocation: The Textual and Structural Case for Overruling* Williams v. Taylor, 56 Am.Crim.L.Rev. 1 (2019).

Page 1314. Add a new footnote ** at the end of the fifth sentence of the second paragraph of Paragraph (2):

** The Court found § 2254(d)(1) satisfied in McWilliams v. Dunn, 582 U.S. 183 (2017). Reversing the Court of Appeals, the Court held, 5–4, that Alabama's provision of mental health assistance to a capital defendant "fell so dramatically short" of the requirements set forth in Ake v. Oklahoma, 470 U.S. 68 (1985) (holding that where certain threshold criteria are met, states must provide indigent defendants with access to a mental health expert to "assist in evaluation, preparation, and presentation of the defense"), that petitioner had made the requisite showing under § 2254(d)(1).

Page 1314. Add a new footnote *** at the end of the second paragraph of Paragraph (2):

*** The Court's decisions from the 2014 and 2015 Terms continued the trend. During this period, the Court decided eight cases implicating 28 U.S.C. § 2254(d). In all but one, the Court reversed lower court decisions granting relief. Four of those cases came out of the Ninth Circuit, and three came out of the Sixth Circuit. See Kernan v. Hinojosa, 578 U.S. 412 (2016) (per curiam); Woods v. Etherton, 578 U.S. 113 (2016) (per curiam); White v. Wheeler, 577 U.S. 73 (2015) (per curiam); Davis v. Ayala, 576 U.S. 257 (2015); Woods v. Donald, 575 U.S. 312 (2015) (per curiam); Glebe v. Frost, 574 U.S. 21 (2014) (per curiam); Lopez v. Smith, 574 U.S. 1 (2014) (per curiam). In one, the Court concluded by "again advis[ing] the Court of Appeals that the provisions of AEDPA apply with full force even when reviewing a conviction and sentence imposing the death penalty." Wheeler, supra, at 81. More recent Terms have witnessed additional reversals of lower court decisions granting habeas relief as insufficiently deferential under § 2254(d). See, e.g., Mays v. Hines, 141 S.Ct. 1145 (2021) (per curiam) (positing that "[i]f [§ 2254(d)] means anything, it is that a federal court must carefully consider all the reasons and evidence supporting the state court's decision"); Shoop v. Hill, 139 S.Ct. 504 (2019) (per curiam) (vacating award of relief under § 2254(d) where court of appeals relied in part on a Supreme Court decision rendered after the date on which defendant-petitioner's conviction became final); Dunn v. Madison, 138 S.Ct. 9 (2018) (per curiam) (reversing the lower court's granting of habeas relief in a death penalty case for failing to give sufficient deference to state court judgment under § 2254(d)); Sexton v. Beaudreaux, 138 S.Ct. 2555 (2018) (per curiam) (reversing lower court for failing to accord sufficient deference under § 2254(d) to state court's resolution of Strickland claim). Further, several of the Court's recent opinions highlight that state court decisions involving underlying claims that are generally reviewed deferentially are entitled to "double" deference under AEDPA. See, e.g., Etherton, supra (applying deference under § 2254(d)(1) in addition to the "strong" presumption of Strickland v. Washington, 466 U.S. 668 (1984), that counsel provided adequate representation); Wheeler, supra (applying "doubly deferential" review under AEDPA to claim challenging trial judge's decision to excuse a juror for cause); see also Shinn v. Kayer, 141 S.Ct. 517 (2020) (per curiam) (reversing grant of habeas relief on Strickland grounds while reiterating that because " 'the Strickland standard is a general standard, a state court has even more latitude to reasonably determine that a defendant has not satisfied that standard' ") (quoting Knowles v. Mirzayance, 556 U.S. 111, 123 (2009)).

Page 1316. Add at the end of Paragraph (4):

In Wilson v. Sellers, 138 S.Ct. 1188 (2018), the Court revisited the question of how federal habeas courts applying § 2254(d) should interpret summary dispositions by state courts. After a Georgia trial court rejected Wilson's post-conviction challenge to the effectiveness of his counsel during the sentencing phase of his capital trial, the Georgia Supreme Court summarily denied his application for a certificate of probable cause to appeal. Writing for the Court, Justice Breyer concluded that in applying § 2254(d), which requires deferring to state court decisions "on the merits," a federal habeas court should " 'look through' the unexplained decision to the last related state-court decision that does provide a relevant rationale," and "presume that the unexplained decision adopted the same reasoning." The Court also held, however, that this default proposition may be overcome where a party can demonstrate that the summary affirmance "relied or most likely did rely on different grounds than the lower state court's decision, such as alternative grounds for affirmance that were briefed or argued to the state supreme court or obvious in the record it reviewed." This "look through" presumption, the Court posited, is most consistent with earlier habeas jurisprudence as articulated in Ylst v. Nunnemaker, 501 U.S. 797 (1991), Seventh Edition p. 507, which held that a federal habeas court should presume that where the last reasoned state court decision in a case determined that a federal claim had been procedurally defaulted, that reasoning similarly informed any summary affirmances by higher state courts.

Dissenting for three Justices, Justice Gorsuch argued that the presumption adopted by the majority was at odds with the presumption applied in summary dispositions of federal court decisions, which posits that summary affirmances may be construed solely as approving of a lower court's judgment and not its reasoning. See Comptroller v. Wynne, 575 U.S. 542 (2015). The dissent also contended that the majority's presumption "requires [federal habeas courts] to treat the work of state court colleagues with disrespect we would not tolerate for our own." Nonetheless, Justice Gorsuch concluded that regardless of which default rule controls, the majority's invitation to federal habeas courts in appropriate cases to review materials beyond the last reasoned state court decision renders the debate over the proper presumption not especially significant. Is Justice Gorsuch right, or is the majority's default presumption likely to govern in most cases given the amount of labor and potential speculation that could be involved where a federal habeas court looks beyond the last reasoned opinion in reviewing state court judgments? And, *contra* Justice Gorsuch's suggestion, can it be said that the majority's presumption, which enables state courts to clarify where their decisions do not conform with the last reasoned opinion, respects the state courts? *Cf.* Michigan v. Long, Seventh Edition p. 494.

Page 1316. Add a new sentence at the beginning of Paragraph (5):

In Shoop v. Hill, 139 S.Ct. 504 (2019) (per curiam), the Court unanimously held that "clearly established law" for purposes of § 2254(d) does not encompass Supreme Court decisions rendered after the date on which defendant-petitioner's conviction became final. In doing so, the Court vacated a court of appeals decision granting habeas relief that "lean[ed] heavily" on such a decision.

Page 1317. Add a new footnote 4a at the end of the final sentence of Paragraph (6):

[4a] In Brown v. Davenport, 142 S.Ct. 1510 (2022), the Court took up how its judge-made harmless error doctrine intersects with AEDPA in habeas proceedings. The Court held, 6–3, that where a state court has reviewed a petitioner's constitutional claim and found the alleged error to be harmless, a federal habeas court reviewing the state court's decision may not grant relief unless it finds both that the error in question was not harmless under the test adopted in Brecht v. Abrahamson, 507 U.S. 619 (1993), *and* that the habeas petitioner satisfies § 2254(d). (For discussion of *Brecht*'s test, which governs harmless error review in habeas proceedings and shifts the burden of showing harmlessness from the government to the petitioner, consult Seventh Edition p. 1286 n.11.)

Page 1319. Add a new Paragraph (10):

(10) The Different Standard Governing Review of State Post-Conviction Proceedings on Appeal. In the 2018 Term, a divided Court remanded for reconsideration a capital case on appeal from state post-conviction proceedings after having previously reversed the federal court of appeals' grant of relief to the same petitioner based on similar claims. See Madison v. Alabama, 139 S.Ct. 718 (2019) ("Madison II"); see also Dunn v. Madison, 138 S.Ct. 9 (2018) (per curiam). Explaining the difference in outcomes with respect to the claims, which turned on the application of Ford v. Wainwright, 477 U.S. 399 (1986), and Panetti v. Quarterman, 551 U.S. 930 (2007), to a capital defendant suffering from dementia, the Court majority emphasized that in Madison II, "[b]ecause the case now comes to us on direct review of the state court's decision (rather than in a habeas proceeding), AEDPA's deferential standard no longer governs." Madison, 139 S.Ct. at 726; *id.* at 725 (contrasting the Court's earlier decision as "premised on AEDPA's 'demanding' and 'deferential standard' ") (quoting Madison, 138 S.Ct. at 11).

Perhaps at least in part because the review of state post-conviction proceedings on appeal is not subject to AEDPA's standards of review, recent Terms have witnessed an uptick in the number of cases that the Court has reviewed in this posture, notwithstanding earlier decisions stating that direct review of state post-conviction cases is disfavored. See Ahdout, *Direct Collateral Review,* 121 Colum.L.Rev. 159 (2021) (documenting trend and celebrating this development, arguing that it "restores federal judicial primacy in developing constitutional law" in the criminal justice arena).

Page 1319. After Paragraph (10), add the following principal case and accompanying Notes:

———

INTRODUCTORY NOTE: RETROACTIVITY AND THE OBLIGATIONS OF STATE AND FEDERAL COURTS IN COLLATERAL REVIEW PROCEEDINGS

In Montgomery v. Louisiana, below, the Court explored the question of the retroactive application of new constitutional holdings in state-court post-conviction proceedings. As indicated in the Note following the case, the decision is likely to bear significantly on federal habeas corpus proceedings and the questions raised in Tyler v. Cain, Seventh Edition p. 1318, particularly Justice O'Connor's concurring opinion.

———

Montgomery v. Louisiana

577 U.S. 190, 136 S.Ct. 718, 193 L.Ed.2d 599 (2016).
Certiorari to the Supreme Court of Louisiana.

■JUSTICE KENNEDY delivered the opinion of the Court.

This is another case in a series of decisions involving the sentencing of offenders who were juveniles when their crimes were committed. * * *

I

Petitioner is Henry Montgomery. In 1963, Montgomery killed Charles Hurt, a deputy sheriff in East Baton Rouge, Louisiana. Montgomery was 17 years old at the time of the crime. [After his first conviction and death sentence was reversed on appeal, Montgomery was retried and a jury found him "guilty without capital punishment." Under Louisiana law, Montgomery automatically received a life sentence without possibility of parole. At the time, therefore,] Montgomery had no opportunity to present mitigation evidence to justify a less severe sentence. That evidence might have included Montgomery's young age at the time of the crime; expert testimony regarding his limited capacity for foresight, self-discipline, and judgment; and his potential for rehabilitation. Montgomery, now 69 years old, has spent almost his entire life in prison.

Almost 50 years after Montgomery was first taken into custody, this Court decided Miller v. Alabama, 576 U.S. 460 (2012). Miller held that mandatory life without parole for juvenile homicide offenders violates the Eighth Amendment's prohibition on " 'cruel and unusual punishments.' " Miller required that sentencing courts consider a child's "diminished culpability and heightened capacity for change" before condemning him or her to die in prison. Although Miller did not foreclose a sentencer's ability to impose life without parole on a juvenile, the Court explained that a lifetime in prison is a disproportionate sentence for all but the rarest of children, those whose crimes reflect " 'irreparable corruption.' " (quoting Roper v. Simmons, 543 U.S. 551, 573 (2005)).

After this Court issued its decision in Miller, Montgomery sought collateral review of his mandatory life-without parole sentence. [One form of collateral review available under Louisiana law "allows a prisoner to bring a collateral attack on his or her sentence by filing a motion to correct an illegal sentence." The relevant state statute provides that "[a]n illegal sentence may be corrected at any time by the court that imposed the sentence."]

Louisiana's collateral review courts will * * * consider a motion to correct an illegal sentence based on a decision of this Court holding that the Eighth Amendment to the Federal Constitution prohibits a punishment for a type of crime or a class of offenders. [Here, however, the trial court denied Montgomery's motion for collateral relief on the ground that Miller was not retroactive on collateral review, and the

Louisiana Supreme Court then denied his application for a supervisory writ.]

II

[The Court first addressed the question whether it had jurisdiction to decide the case.]

[The argument against jurisdiction proceeds as follows:] [A] State is under no obligation to give a new rule of constitutional law retroactive effect in its own collateral review proceedings. As those proceedings are created by state law and under the State's plenary control * * * , it is for state courts to define applicable principles of retroactivity. * * *

If, however, the Constitution establishes a rule and requires that the rule have retroactive application, then a state court's refusal to give the rule retroactive effect is reviewable by this Court. *Cf.* Griffith v. Kentucky, 479 U.S. 314, 328 (1987) (holding that on direct review, a new constitutional rule must be applied retroactively "to all cases, state or federal"). States may not disregard a controlling, constitutional command in their own courts. See Martin v. Hunter's Lessee, 1 Wheat. 304, 340–341, 344 (1816). * * *

Justice O'Connor's plurality opinion in Teague v. Lane, 489 U.S. 288 (1989), set forth a framework for retroactivity in cases on federal collateral review. [The argument against jurisdiction rests on the proposition that] Teague was an interpretation of the federal habeas statute, not a constitutional command; and so, the argument proceeds, Teague's retroactivity holding simply has no application in a State's own collateral review proceedings. [But] Teague originated in a federal, not state, habeas proceeding; so it had no particular reason to discuss whether any part of its holding was required by the Constitution in addition to the federal habeas statute. * * *

The Court now holds that when a new substantive rule of constitutional law controls the outcome of a case, the Constitution requires state collateral review courts to give retroactive effect to that rule. Teague's conclusion establishing the retroactivity of new substantive rules is best understood as resting upon constitutional premises. That constitutional command is, like all federal law, binding on state courts. This holding is limited to Teague's first exception for substantive rules; the constitutional status of Teague's exception for watershed rules of procedure need not be addressed here.

* * * Justice Harlan defined substantive constitutional rules as "those that place, as a matter of constitutional interpretation, certain kinds of primary, private individual conduct beyond the power of the criminal law-making authority to proscribe." Mackey v. United States, 401 U.S. 667, 692 (1971) (opinion concurring in judgments in part and dissenting in part). In Penry v. Lynaugh, decided four months after Teague, the Court recognized that "the first exception set forth in Teague should be understood to cover not only rules forbidding criminal

punishment of certain primary conduct but also rules prohibiting a certain category of punishment for a class of defendants because of their status or offense." 492 U.S. 302, 330 (1989). Penry explained that Justice Harlan's first exception spoke "in terms of substantive categorical guarantees accorded by the Constitution, regardless of the procedures followed." *Id.*, at 329. Whether a new rule bars States from proscribing certain conduct or from inflicting a certain punishment, "[i]n both cases, the Constitution itself deprives the State of the power to impose a certain penalty." *Id.*, at 330.

Substantive rules, then, set forth categorical constitutional guarantees that place certain criminal laws and punishments altogether beyond the State's power to impose. It follows that when a State enforces a proscription or penalty barred by the Constitution, the resulting conviction or sentence is, by definition, unlawful. [Here, the Court contrasted procedural rules and observed that "a trial conducted under a procedure found to be unconstitutional in a later case does not, as a general matter, have the automatic consequence of invalidating a defendant's conviction or sentence."]

By holding that new substantive rules are, indeed, retroactive, Teague continued a long tradition of giving retroactive effect to constitutional rights that go beyond procedural guarantees. See Mackey, *supra*, at 692–693 (opinion of Harlan, J.) ("[T]he writ has historically been available for attacking convictions on [substantive] grounds"). Before Brown v. Allen, 344 U.S. 443 (1953), "federal courts would never consider the merits of a constitutional claim if the habeas petitioner had a fair opportunity to raise his arguments in the original proceeding." Desist v. United States, 394 U.S. 244, 261 (1969) (Harlan, J., dissenting). Even in the pre-1953 era of restricted federal habeas, however, an exception was made "when the habeas petitioner attacked the constitutionality of the state statute under which he had been convicted. Since, in this situation, the State had no power to proscribe the conduct for which the petitioner was imprisoned, it could not constitutionally insist that he remain in jail." *Id.*, at 261, n. 2 (Harlan, J., dissenting). * * * It follows, as a general principle, that a court has no authority to leave in place a conviction or sentence that violates a substantive rule, regardless of whether the conviction or sentence became final before the rule was announced.

[The Court next conceded that the precedents "do not directly control the question the Court now answers for the first time," although noting that they nonetheless "have important bearing on the analysis necessary in this case."]

There is no grandfather clause that permits States to enforce punishments the Constitution forbids. To conclude otherwise would undercut the Constitution's substantive guarantees. * * * If a State may not constitutionally insist that a prisoner remain in jail on federal habeas review, it may not constitutionally insist on the same result in its own postconviction proceedings. Under the Supremacy Clause of the Constitution, state collateral review courts have no greater power than federal habeas courts to mandate that a prisoner continue to suffer punishment barred by the Constitution. If a state collateral proceeding is open to a claim controlled by federal law, the state court "has a duty to grant the relief that federal law requires." Yates v. Aiken, 484 U.S. 211, 218 (1988). * * *

As a final point, it must be noted that the retroactive application of substantive rules does not implicate a State's weighty interests in ensuring the finality of convictions and sentences. Teague warned against the intrusiveness of "*continually* forc[ing] the States to marshal resources in order to keep in prison defendants whose trials and appeals conformed to then-existing constitutional standards." 489 U.S., at 310. This concern has no application in the realm of substantive rules, for no resources marshaled by a State could preserve a conviction or sentence that the Constitution deprives the State of power to impose. See Mackey, 401 U.S., at 693 (opinion of Harlan, J.) ("There is little societal interest in permitting the criminal process to rest at a point where it ought properly never to repose"). * * *

III

* * * Miller announced a substantive rule that is retroactive in cases on collateral review.

The "foundation stone" for Miller's analysis was this Court's line of precedent holding certain punishments disproportionate when applied to juveniles. 567 U.S., at 470, n. 4. Those cases include Graham v. Florida, *supra*, which held that the Eighth Amendment bars life without parole for juvenile nonhomicide offenders, and Roper v. Simmons, 543 U.S. 551, which held that the Eighth Amendment prohibits capital punishment for those under the age of 18 at the time of their crimes. [The Court discussed the holdings in Miller, Roper, and Graham, observing that Miller "took as its starting premise the principle established in Roper and Graham that 'children are constitutionally different from adults for purposes of sentencing.' " The Court continued by noting that Miller "made clear that 'appropriate occasions for sentencing juveniles to this harshest possible penalty will be uncommon.' "]

Miller, then, did more than require a sentencer to consider a juvenile offender's youth before imposing life without parole; it established that the penological justifications for life without parole collapse in light of "the distinctive attributes of youth." *Id.*, at 2465. Even if a court considers a child's age before sentencing him or her to a lifetime in prison, that sentence still violates the Eighth Amendment for a child whose crime reflects " 'unfortunate yet transient immaturity.' " *Id.*, at 2469 (quoting Roper, 543 U.S., at 573). * * * [Miller therefore] rendered life without parole an unconstitutional penalty for "a class of defendants because of their status"—that is, juvenile offenders whose crimes reflect the transient immaturity of youth. Penry, 492 U.S., at 330. As a result, Miller announced a substantive rule of constitutional law. Like other substantive rules, Miller is retroactive because it " 'necessarily carr[ies] a significant risk that a defendant' "—here, the vast majority of juvenile offenders—" 'faces a punishment that the law cannot impose upon him.' " Schriro v. Summerlin, 542 U.S. 348, 352 (2004) (quoting Bousley v. United States, 523 U.S. 614, 620 (1998)).

Louisiana nonetheless argues that Miller is procedural because it did not place any punishment beyond the State's power to impose; it instead required sentencing courts to take children's age into account before condemning them to die in prison. * * * Miller, it is true, did not bar a punishment for all juvenile offenders, as the Court did in Roper or Graham. Miller did bar life without parole, however, for all but the rarest of juvenile offenders, those whose crimes reflect permanent incorrigibility. For that reason, Miller is no less substantive than are Roper and Graham. * * *

To be sure, Miller's holding has a procedural component. * * * There are instances in which a substantive change in the law must be attended by a procedure that enables a prisoner to show that he falls within the category of persons whom the law may no longer punish. * * * The procedure Miller prescribes is no different. * * *

[The Court next defended Miller's decision not to require trial courts to make findings of fact regarding a child's incorrigibility: "When a new substantive rule of constitutional law is established, this Court is careful to limit the scope of any attendant procedural requirement to avoid intruding more than necessary upon the States' sovereign administration of their criminal justice systems."]

* * * Giving Miller retroactive effect, moreover, does not require States to relitigate sentences, let alone convictions, in every case where a juvenile offender received mandatory life without parole. A State may remedy a Miller violation by permitting juvenile homicide offenders to be considered for parole, rather than by resentencing them. See, e.g., Wyo. Stat. Ann. § 6–10–301(c) (2013) (juvenile homicide offenders eligible for parole after 25 years).

Extending parole eligibility to juvenile offenders does not impose an onerous burden on the States, nor does it disturb the finality of state convictions. Those prisoners who have shown an inability to reform will continue to serve life sentences. * * *

* * * In light of what this Court has said in Roper, Graham, and Miller about how children are constitutionally different from adults in their level of culpability, however, prisoners like Montgomery must be given the opportunity to show their crime did not reflect irreparable corruption; and, if it did not, their hope for some years of life outside prison walls must be restored.

■ JUSTICE SCALIA, with whom JUSTICE THOMAS and JUSTICE ALITO join, dissenting.

The Court has no jurisdiction to decide this case, and the decision it arrives at is wrong. I respectfully dissent.

I.   Jurisdiction

* * * [A] majority of this Court, eager to reach the merits of this case, resolves the question of our jurisdiction by deciding that the Constitution *requires* state postconviction courts to adopt Teague's exception for so-called "substantive" new rules and to provide state-law remedies for the violations of those rules to prisoners whose sentences long ago became final. This conscription into federal service of state postconviction courts is nothing short of astonishing.

A

Neither Teague nor its exceptions are constitutionally compelled. Unlike today's majority, the Teague-era Court understood that cases on collateral review are fundamentally different from those pending on direct review because of "considerations of finality in the judicial process." Shea v. Louisiana, 470 U.S. 51, 59–60 (1985). That line of finality demarcating the constitutionally required rule in Griffith from the habeas rule in Teague supplies the answer to the not-so-difficult question whether a state postconviction court must remedy the violation of a new substantive rule: No. A state court need only apply the law as it existed at the time a defendant's conviction and sentence became final. See Griffith, *supra*, at 322. And once final, "a new rule cannot reopen a door already closed." James B. Beam Distilling Co. v. Georgia, 501 U.S. 529, 541 (1991) (opinion of Souter, J.). Any relief a prisoner might receive in a state court after finality is a matter of grace, not constitutional prescription.

B

The majority can marshal no case support for its contrary position. * * *

[T]he Supremacy Clause cannot possibly answer the question before us here. It only elicits another question: What federal law is supreme? Old or new? The majority's champion, Justice Harlan, said the old rules apply for federal habeas review of a state-court conviction: "[T]he habeas court need only apply the constitutional standards that prevailed at the time the original proceedings took place," Desist, 394 U.S., at 263 (dissenting opinion), for a state court cannot "toe the constitutional mark" that does not yet exist, Mackey, 401 U.S., at 687 (opinion of Harlan, J.). Following his analysis, we have clarified time and again—recently in Greene v. Fisher, 565 U.S. 34, 38–40 (2011)—that *federal* habeas courts are to review state-court decisions against the law and factual record that existed at the time the decisions were made. "Section 2254(d)(1) [of the federal habeas statute] refers, in the past tense * * *. This backward-looking language requires an examination of the state-court decision at the time it was made." Cullen v. Pinholster, 563 U.S. 170, 181–182 (2011).

Until today, no federal court was *constitutionally obliged* to grant relief for the past violation of a newly announced substantive rule. Until today, it was Congress's prerogative to do away with Teague's exceptions altogether. Indeed, we had left unresolved the question whether Congress had already done that when it amended a section of the habeas corpus statute to add backward-looking language governing the review of state-court decisions. See Antiterrorism and Effective Death Penalty Act of 1996, § 104, 110 Stat. 1219, codified at 28 U.S.C. § 2254(d)(1); Greene, 565 U.S. at 39, n. A maxim shown to be more relevant to this case, by the analysis that the majority omitted, is this: The Supremacy Clause does not impose upon state courts a constitutional obligation it fails to impose upon federal courts.

C

All that remains to support the majority's conclusion is that all-purpose Latin canon: *ipse dixit*. The majority opines that because a substantive rule eliminates a State's power to proscribe certain conduct or impose a certain punishment, it has "the automatic consequence of invalidating a defendant's conviction or sentence." What provision of the Constitution could conceivably produce such a result? The Due Process Clause? It surely cannot be a denial of due process for a court to pronounce a final judgment which, though fully in accord with federal constitutional law at the time, fails to anticipate a change to be made by this Court half a century into the future. The Equal Protection Clause? Both statutory and (increasingly) constitutional laws change. If it were a denial of equal protection to hold an earlier defendant to a law more stringent than what exists today, it would also be a denial of equal protection to hold a later defendant to a law more stringent than what existed 50 years ago. No principle of equal protection requires the criminal law of all ages to be the same.

The majority grandly asserts that "[t]here is no grandfather clause that permits States to *enforce punishments the Constitution forbids*." (emphasis added). Of course the italicized phrase begs the question. There most certainly is a grandfather clause—one we have called *finality*—which says that the Constitution does not require States to revise punishments that were lawful when they were imposed. Once a conviction has become final, whether new rules or old ones will be applied to revisit the conviction is a matter entirely within the State's control; the Constitution has nothing to say about that choice. * * *

The majority's imposition of Teague's first exception upon the States is all the worse because it does not adhere to that exception as initially conceived by Justice Harlan—an exception for rules that "place, as a matter of constitutional interpretation, certain kinds of primary, private individual *conduct* beyond the power of the criminal lawmaking authority to proscribe." Mackey, 401 U.S., at 692 (emphasis added).

Rather, it endorses the exception as expanded by Penry. * * * [But t]he "evolving standards" test concedes that in 1969 the State had the power to punish Henry Montgomery as it did. Indeed, Montgomery could at that time have been sentenced to death by our yet unevolved society. * * *

II.   The Retroactivity of Miller

* * * Having distorted Teague, the majority simply proceeds to rewrite Miller.

* * * Miller stated, quite clearly * * * : "Our decision does not categorically bar a penalty for a class of offenders or type of crime—as, for example, we did in Roper or Graham. Instead, it mandates only that a sentencer *follow a certain process*—considering an offender's youth and attendant characteristics—before imposing a particular penalty." 567 U.S., at 483 (emphasis added).

* * * Under Miller, bear in mind, the inquiry is whether the inmate was seen to be incorrigible when he was sentenced—not whether he has proven corrigible and so can safely be paroled today. What silliness. (And how impossible in practice, see Brief for National District Attorneys Assn. et al. as Amici Curiae 9–17.) * * *

But have no fear. The majority does not seriously expect state and federal collateral-review tribunals to engage in this silliness, probing the evidence of "incorrigibility" that existed decades ago when defendants were sentenced. What the majority expects (and intends) to happen is set forth in the following not-so-subtle invitation: "A State may remedy a Miller violation by permitting juvenile homicide offenders to be considered for parole, rather than by resentencing them." Of course. This whole exercise, this whole distortion of Miller, is just a devious way of eliminating life without parole for juvenile offenders. The Court might have done that expressly (as we know, the Court can decree *anything*), but that would have been something of an embarrassment. After all, one of the justifications the Court gave for decreeing an end to the death penalty for murders (no matter how many) committed by a juvenile was that life without parole was a severe enough punishment. See Roper, 543 U.S., at 572. How could the majority—in an opinion written by the very author of Roper—now say *that* punishment is *also* unconstitutional? The Court expressly refused to say so in Miller, 567 U.S., at 479. So the Court refuses again today, but merely makes imposition of that severe sanction a practical impossibility. And then, in Godfather fashion, the majority makes state legislatures an offer they can't refuse: Avoid all the utterly impossible nonsense we have prescribed by simply "permitting juvenile homicide offenders to be considered for parole." Mission accomplished.

■ JUSTICE THOMAS, dissenting.

* * * We have jurisdiction under 28 U.S.C. § 1257 only if the Louisiana Supreme Court's decision implicates a federal right. * * *

I

A

No provision of the Constitution supports the Court's holding. The Court invokes only the Supremacy Clause, asserting that the Clause deprives state and federal postconviction courts alike of power to leave an unconstitutional sentence in place. But that leaves the question of what provision of the Constitution supplies that underlying prohibition.

The Supremacy Clause does not do so. That Clause merely supplies a rule of decision: *If* a federal constitutional right exists, that right supersedes any contrary provisions of state law. Accordingly, as we reaffirmed just last Term, the Supremacy Clause is no independent font of substantive rights. Armstrong v. Exceptional Child Center, Inc., 575 U.S. 320, 324–325 (2015).

[Justice Thomas then discussed other possible bases for the Court's decision. Article III, he wrote, "defines the scope of *federal* judicial power. It cannot compel *state* postconviction courts to apply new substantive rules retroactively." Turning to due process, Justice Thomas noted that "[q]uite possibly, ' "[d]ue process of law" was originally used as a shorthand expression for governmental proceedings according to the "law of the land" *as it existed at the time of those proceedings*' " (quoting In re Winship, 397 U.S. 358, 378 (Black, J., dissenting) (emphasis added)).]

[The Equal Protection Clause] prohibits a State from "deny[ing] to any person within its jurisdiction the equal protection of the laws." Amdt. XIV, § 1. But under our precedents "a classification neither involving fundamental rights nor proceeding along suspect lines . . . cannot run afoul of the Equal Protection Clause if there is a rational relationship between the disparity of treatment and some legitimate governmental purpose."

The disparity the Court eliminates today—between prisoners whose cases were on direct review when this Court announced a new substantive constitutional rule, and those whose convictions had already become final—is one we have long considered rational. * * *

B

The Court's new constitutional right also finds no basis in the history of state and federal postconviction proceedings. Throughout our history, postconviction relief for alleged constitutional defects in a conviction or sentence was available as a matter of legislative grace, not constitutional command.

The Constitution mentions habeas relief only in the Suspension Clause, which specifies that "[t]he Privilege of the Writ of *Habeas Corpus* shall not be suspended, unless when in Cases of Rebellion or Invasion the public Safety may require it." Art. I, § 9, cl. 2. But that Clause does not specify the scope of the writ. And the First Congress, in prescribing federal habeas jurisdiction in the 1789 Judiciary Act, understood its scope to reflect "the black-letter principle of the common law that the writ was simply not available at all to one convicted of crime by a court of competent jurisdiction." Bator, *Finality in Criminal Law and Federal Habeas Corpus for State Prisoners*, 76 Harv.L.Rev. 441, 466 (1963). Early cases echoed that understanding. *E.g.*, Ex parte Watkins, 3 Pet. 193, 202 (1830) ("An imprisonment under a judgment cannot be unlawful, unless that judgment be an absolute nullity; and it is not a nullity if the court has general jurisdiction of the subject, although it should be erroneous"). * * *

II

A

Not only does the Court's novel constitutional right lack any constitutional foundation; the reasoning the Court uses to construct this right lacks any logical stopping point. If, as the Court supposes, the Constitution bars courts from insisting that prisoners remain in prison when their convictions or sentences are later deemed unconstitutional, why can courts let stand a judgment that wrongly decided any constitutional question? * * *

B

There is one silver lining to today's ruling: States still have a way to mitigate its impact on their court systems. * * *

Only when state courts have chosen to entertain a federal claim can the Supremacy Clause conceivably command a state court to apply federal law. As we explained last Term, private parties have no "constitutional . . . right to enforce federal laws against the States." Armstrong, 575 U.S., at 325. Instead, the Constitution leaves the initial choice to entertain federal claims up to state courts, which are "tribunals over which the government of the Union has no adequate control, and which may be closed to any claim asserted under a law of the United States." Osborn v. Bank of United States, 9 Wheat. 738, 821 (1824).

States therefore have a modest path to lessen the burdens that today's decision will inflict on their courts. States can stop entertaining claims alleging that this Court's Eighth Amendment decisions invalidated a sentence, and leave federal habeas courts to shoulder the burden of adjudicating such claims in the first instance. Whatever the desirability of that choice, it is one the Constitution allows States to make. * * *

NOTE ON MONTGOMERY V. LOUISIANA AND RETROACTIVITY IN STATE POST-CONVICTION AND FEDERAL COLLATERAL REVIEW

(1) The Montgomery Case and the Constitution. The Montgomery decision raises a number of complicated questions about the intersection of new law, retroactivity, and collateral review of "final" criminal convictions in both the state and federal courts. What is the basis for Montgomery's holding that "Teague's conclusion establishing the retroactivity of new substantive rules is best understood as resting upon constitutional premises" and, accordingly, that Miller must be applied retroactively to cases that would otherwise be considered final?[1] The Supremacy Clause? Due Process? Equal Protection? The Suspension Clause? Might the Eighth Amendment have some bearing on the retroactivity question? How convincing are the arguments of Justices Scalia and Thomas that the Constitution contains no mandate to reopen final convictions? *Cf.* Harper v. Virginia Dept. of Taxation, 509 U.S. 86 (1993), and Reynoldsville Casket Co. v. Hyde, 514 U.S. 749 (1995), discussed at Seventh Edition pp. 758–759. How do (a) the Court's discussion of the role of the Supremacy Clause in Testa v. Katt, 330 U.S. 386 (1947), see Seventh Edition p. 437, and (b) Justice Thomas's dissent in Haywood v. Drown, 556 U.S. 729 (2009), see Seventh Edition p. 444, factor into the equation?

In Griffith v. Kentucky, 479 U.S. 314 (1987), see Seventh Edition pp. 55, 1294, the Court relied on Justice Harlan's view of retroactivity for two propositions: (1) to " 'disregard current law in adjudicating cases' " still on direct review would be " 'quite simply an assertion that our constitutional function is not one of adjudication but in effect of legislation' " (quoting Mackey v. United States, 401 U.S. 667, 679 (1971) (Harlan, J., concurring in part and dissenting in part), see Seventh Edition p. 1294); and (2) "selective application of new rules violates the principle of treating similarly situated defendants the same" (citing Desist v. United States, 394 U.S. 244, 258–59 (1969) (Harlan, J., dissenting in part), see Seventh Edition p. 1294). Does this reasoning apply equally to cases like Montgomery that are no longer pending on direct review? For further consideration of these aspects of Montgomery v. Louisiana, see pp. 82 and 107–108, *supra*.[2]

(2) Substance v. Procedure. Despite having announced in Miller that the decision "does not categorically bar a penalty for a class of offenders or type of crime" but "mandates only that a sentencer follow a certain process", the Montgomery Court classified Miller's holding as substantive for Teague

---

[1] In Danforth v. Minnesota, 552 U.S. 264 (2008), the Court posited that the Teague doctrine was properly understood as "an exercise of th[e] Court's power to interpret the federal habeas statute" (p. 278).

[2] In the wake of Montgomery, the Supreme Court held that its decision in Johnson v. United States, 576 U.S. 591 (2015), is a substantive decision that applies retroactively to federal prisoner cases on collateral review. See Welch v. United States, 578 U.S. 120 (2016). Johnson held that the residual clause of the Armed Career Criminal Act, 18 U.S.C. § 924(e)(2)(B)(ii) (ACCA), which served as a basis for sentencing enhancement in cases involving possession of a firearm by a felon, was unconstitutionally vague. In Welch, with Justice Kennedy once again writing for the majority, the Court held that Johnson had announced a new rule that "changed the substantive reach of the ACCA, altering 'the range of conduct or the class of persons that the [Act] punishes' " (quoting Schriro v. Summerlin, 542 U.S. 348, 353 (2004)). Because "[t]he residual clause is invalid under Johnson," the Court held, "it can no longer mandate or authorize any sentence." The Court continued that "whether a new rule is substantive or procedural" requires a consideration of "the function of the rule," and it rejected the argument that the inquiry depends on whether "the underlying constitutional guarantee [being asserted by the petitioner] is characterized as procedural or substantive." As in Montgomery, Justice Thomas dissented, arguing that the first Teague exception had become unmoored from its origins in the jurisprudence of Justice Harlan. For further discussion of Welch, see pp. 166–168, *infra*.

purposes. Is there a valid distinction to be drawn, as Justice Scalia suggests, between cases involving constitutionally protected conduct and cases involving sentences later deemed to be in violation of the Constitution? Relying on Teague's extension to cases like Penry v. Lynaugh, 492 U.S. 302 (1989), Seventh Edition p. 1298, the Montgomery Court reasoned that such a distinction was unfounded. More generally, does Montgomery reveal the elusiveness of the distinction between substantive and procedural rules?

(3) Justice Thomas's Dissent and Its Implications. Before Montgomery could pursue federal habeas relief, he had to exhaust all available state remedies. Justice Thomas argues that states can simply eliminate post-conviction proceedings to avoid implementing the Court's decision in Miller.[3] Can his position be reconciled with the majority's apparent holding that the Constitution forbids a state from continuing to insist that a prisoner whose claim falls under Teague's first exception remain in jail? *Cf.* Case v. Nebraska, 381 U.S. 336 (1965), Seventh Edition p. 1290 n. 15; Martinez v. Ryan, 566 U.S. 1 (2012), Seventh Edition p. 1339; Haywood v. Drown, 556 U.S. 729 (2009), Seventh Edition p. 444. If Justice Thomas is right, is Congress under an *obligation* to provide for collateral habeas review of Miller claims in federal court?

Professors Vázquez and Vladeck argue that post-Montgomery, state courts must provide post-conviction relief for petitioners seeking the benefit of new rules of substantive constitutional law where all avenues of direct review are foreclosed. See Vázquez & Vladeck, *The Constitutional Right to Collateral Post-Conviction Review*, 103 Va.L.Rev. 905 (2017). The authors argue that imposing such an obligation upon federal habeas courts would upend longstanding assumptions underlying Article III, including the Madisonian Compromise and the widely held view that "federal habeas corpus [is] constitutionally gratuitous as a means of postconviction review." Fallon & Meltzer, Seventh Edition p. 1293 n. 2, at 1813. Nor do Vázquez and Vladeck read the Court's line of cases following from Testa v. Katt, 330 U.S. 386 (1947), see Seventh Edition p. 437, as foreclosing the conclusion that state courts must be open in such cases. In their view, any limitation on state court jurisdiction to provide collateral relief to prisoners claiming the benefit of a new rule of substantive federal law "would be based, at bottom, on disagreement with the policies underlying the Constitution, as interpreted in Montgomery," and therefore would not constitute a "valid excuse" under Testa as applied in Haywood v. Drown, 556 U.S. 729 (2009), see Seventh Edition p. 444. This conclusion also follows, in the authors' view, under the Court's decision in General Oil Co. v. Crain, 209 U.S. 211 (1908), see Seventh Edition p. 759, which held that a state court's determination regarding its jurisdiction to award a potentially constitutionally-required remedy is not an adequate and independent state ground precluding Supreme Court review of the decision. In support of their conclusion, the authors read Haywood to limit the range of "neutral" rules or "valid excuses" that will justify closing

---

[3] In a different case the same Term, Justice Alito posited that "[s]tates are under no obligation to permit collateral attacks on convictions that have become final, and if they allow such attacks, they are free to limit the circumstances in which claims may be relitigated." Foster v. Chatman, 578 U.S. 488, 520 (2016) (Alito, J., concurring in the judgment).

state courts to federal claims. They also reject the proposition that closing state courts entirely to a particular class of claims based on state law necessarily will justify the same jurisdictional limitation with respect to analogous federal claims.[4]

Professors Woolhandler and Collins dispute many of the premises on which Vázquez and Vladeck construct their argument, contending that evidence suggests that "the Framers did not contemplate compulsory state court jurisdiction over affirmative federal claims". Woolhandler & Collins, *State Jurisdictional Independence and Federal Supremacy*, 72 Fla.L.Rev. 73, 77 (2020). Viewing Haywood as inconsistent with this backdrop, the authors separately read Crain as a "modest" decision lending support to the proposition that any obligations upon state courts to afford constitutional remedies "tend to surface when lower federal court jurisdiction is disfavored or unavailable." It follows, on their view, that where federal courts are able to supply such remedies, arguments in favor of compelling state courts to do the same falter. They also worry that imposing such obligations on state courts "could discourage states from providing different answers to the problems of state government illegality."

In response, Vázquez and Vladeck argue that their account is more consistent with the Madisonian Compromise and "[t]he default regime established by the Constitution," which "was one in which enforcement of federal law mainly depended on state courts." Vázquez & Vladeck, Testa, Crain, *and the Constitutional Right to Collateral Relief*, 72 Fla.L.Rev. 10, 13 (2021). The authors likewise contend that "the availability of a *constitutionally* required remedy should not depend on a congressional decision to confer jurisdiction on the lower federal courts". Finally, Vázquez and Vladeck emphasize the fact that the Court decided Ex parte Young, 209 U.S. 123 (1908), see Seventh Edition p. 922, the very same day as Crain. The availability of a Young action, they argue, strongly suggests Crain did not turn on the availability of federal remedies.

What is left of the "valid excuse" doctrine under the interpretation of Testa and Haywood embraced by Vázquez and Vladeck, given that they reject the proposition that state legislatures could eliminate entirely state post-conviction review? Separately, are Vázquez and Vladeck correct with respect to the significance of the fact that the party seeking to prevent enforcement of an allegedly unconstitutional tax in Crain arguably could have brought a Young action in federal court? For further discussion, see Seventh Edition p. 760.

(4) The Intersection of Montgomery, Teague, and AEDPA. Looking ahead, federal courts will have to determine the application of Montgomery and Miller to habeas proceedings in federal court. Consider two habeas petitioners: (a) one who, because of a failure to meet state procedural requirements, has lost the ability to raise, on direct review in state court, the

---

[4] For elaboration on the ramifications of Montgomery for debates over the role of state courts as enforcers of federal rights, see Vladeck, p. 128, *supra* (positing that "Montgomery may represent the beginning of the Supreme Court's habeas jurisprudence coming full circle—and the vindication of Professor Hart's famous conclusion about the centrality of state, rather than federal, courts to the protection of federal constitutional rights").

Eighth Amendment claim later embraced in Miller, and (b) one who raised and thereby preserved the claim throughout direct proceedings before Miller. Would the two petitioners fare differently in federal habeas? Should they? With respect to the latter petitioner whose claim was presumably rejected on the merits by the state courts, does § 2254(d)(1) permit a federal habeas court to grant relief from a mandatory life sentence? Post-Montgomery, courts will have to wrestle with how Teague and Montgomery intersect with both habeas procedural default jurisprudence and § 2254(d)(1)'s "backward-looking language". Cullen v. Pinholster, 563 U.S. 170, 182 (2011). See also Paragraphs (6) and (7), Seventh Edition p. 1317.[5] Consider also the litigant who has already pursued federal habeas relief on a prior occasion and must overcome the limits on successive petitions set forth in § 2244(b)(2). See Note on Successive and Abusive Habeas Petitions, Seventh Edition pp. 1346–1349. For the petitioner who has not previously presented the claim in federal habeas, does Montgomery, when combined with Miller, establish "a new rule of constitutional law, made retroactive to cases on collateral review by the Supreme Court that was previously unavailable" under § 2244(b)(2)(a)? For discussion of these and other questions raised by the intersection of Montgomery with AEDPA and the procedural default doctrine, along with an argument that some court must be available to award relief where a petitioner seeks the benefit of a new rule of substantive constitutional law, see Vázquez & Vladeck, p. 198, *supra*.

(5) Jurisdictional Infirmities and Montgomery. How, if at all, does the rationale of Montgomery v. Louisiana apply when the original court in which the state successfully prosecuted a criminal defendant lacked jurisdiction? In McGirt v. Oklahoma, 140 S.Ct. 2452 (2020), the Supreme Court held that because a large swathe of Oklahoma constitutes land within the boundaries of Native American reservations, or "Indian country," as a matter of federal law, state courts lack jurisdiction to try crimes committed by Native Americans within that territory. Instead, only federal or tribal courts possess jurisdiction over such matters. Will petitions for habeas relief predicated upon McGirt fall within the first Teague exception?

(6) Retreat from Montgomery? In Jones v. Mississippi, 141 S.Ct. 1307 (2021), the Supreme Court revisited Montgomery. Petitioner Jones had been convicted and sentenced to life without possibility of parole based on a homicide that he committed at the age of 15. On appeal from state post-conviction proceedings, he argued that post-Miller and Montgomery, "a sentencer who imposes a life-without-parole sentence must *also* make a separate factual finding that the defendant is permanently incorrigible, or at least provide an on-the-record sentencing explanation with an implicit finding that the defendant is permanently incorrigible." The Court, 6–3, held

---

[5]   Justice Thomas, joined by Justice Gorsuch, concurred in Edwards v. Vannoy, 141 S.Ct. 1547 (2021), discussed *supra* at 166–168, to express the view that where § 2254(d) applies, there is no reason to do the Teague analysis. If a state court "reasonably relied" on then-existing federal law in "rejecting a claim", the Court's inquiry "beg[ins] and end[s] there—with § 2254(d)(1)'s plain text" providing that "relief 'shall not be granted' " (Thomas, J., concurring) (quoting 28 U.S.C. § 2254(d)(1)). Justice Thomas added that "Congress' decision to create retroactivity exceptions to the statute of limitations and to the bar on second-or-successive petitions but not for § 2254(d) is strong evidence that Teague" does not apply in cases governed by § 2254(d).

that Miller and Montgomery did not require such a finding, whether made explicitly or implicitly. Writing for the majority, Justice Kavanaugh relied heavily on language taken directly from Miller and Montgomery. Miller, he noted, had "mandated 'only that a sentence follow a certain process— considering an offender's youth and attendant characteristics—before imposing' a life-without-parole sentence" (quoting Miller, 567 U.S. at 483). Montgomery, in turn, stated plainly that " 'a finding of fact regarding a child's incorrigibility * * * is not required' " (quoting Montgomery, 577 U.S. at 211). The Court likewise emphasized that Miller "repeatedly described youth as a sentencing factor akin to a mitigating circumstance," such as those required in the death penalty context, which have traditionally not been deemed to "require the sentencer to make any particular factual finding regarding * * * mitigating circumstances." Further, Justice Kavanaugh asserted that "Miller cited Roper and Graham for a simple proposition: Youth matters in sentencing", and nothing more. It followed, on the majority's view, that all Miller requires is that a sentencer "consider youth as a mitigating factor when deciding whether to impose a life-without-parole sentence". Nothing in Montgomery, Justice Kavanaugh continued, added anything "to Miller's requirements."

Justice Kavanaugh next addressed the fact that Montgomery classified the rule in Miller as substantive for retroactivity purposes. In a footnote, he quoted precedent post-dating Montgomery for the proposition that a rule is procedural for Teague purposes "if it regulates ' "only the manner of determining the defendant's culpability" ' " (quoting Welch v. United States, 578 U.S. 120, 129 (2016) (quoting Schriro v. Summerlin, 542 U.S. 348, 353 (2004))). Although nowhere expressly saying that Montgomery erred in classifying the Miller rule as substantive, the majority left little doubt as to its views on the matter, stating: "[T]o the extent that Montgomery's application of the Teague standard is in tension with the Court's retroactivity precedents * * *, those * * * precedents—and not Montgomery—must guide the determination of whether rules other than Miller are substantive." All the same, Justice Kavanaugh concluded by asserting that "[t]oday's decision does not overrule Miller or Montgomery."[6]

Justice Thomas concurred in the judgment. In his view, the Miller rule was procedural and not watershed for purposes of Teague. It followed in his view that Miller should not have been applied retroactively and Montgomery was wrong to conclude otherwise. But, he recognized, Montgomery labeled the Miller rule as substantive and that "[s]ubstantive rules include those that " ' "prohibit[t] a certain category of punishment for a class of defendants because of their status or offence" ' " (quoting Beard v. Banks, 542 U.S. 406, 416 (2004)). This aspect of Montgomery, he wrote, "creates problems for the majority in this case." Justice Thomas then observed that although Montgomery was not entirely consistent as to its reasoning, it did say that " 'Miller drew a line between children whose crimes reflect transient immaturity and those rare children whose crimes reflect irreparable

---

6   The Court observed that "[b]y now, most offenders who could seek collateral review as a result of Montgomery have done so and, if eligible, have received new discretionary sentences under Miller."

corruption.' " Analogizing this "categorical exemption for certain offenders" to insanity or intellectual disability defenses, Justice Thomas argued that under Montgomery, "the 'legality' of Jones' sentence turns on whether his crime in fact 'reflect[s] permanent incorrigibility' " (quoting Montgomery, 577 U.S. at 205). In Justice Thomas's view, following such a course here would mean granting relief to Jones. But, he argued, the Court instead "should just acknowledge that Montgomery had no basis in law or the Constitution." Justice Thomas concluded that the Court had overruled Montgomery "in substance but not in name."

Justice Sotomayor, joined by Justices Breyer and Kagan, dissented, contending that the Court had "gut[ted]" Miller and Montgomery. Agreeing in some respects with Justice Thomas, she read Montgomery to establish that "[o]nly those rare few [whose crimes reflect irreparable corruption] are constitutionally eligible for LWOP under Miller." As such, she wrote, "before imposing a sentence of LWOP, a sentence must actually 'make that judgment,' and make it correctly" (quoting Miller, 567 U.S. at 480). Justice Sotomayor also highlighted that Miller had drawn heavily on Roper and Graham, both of which had prohibited the application of certain sentences to classes of juvenile offenders, suggesting that Miller intended to accomplish the very same end. She continued, "[f]or Montgomery to make any sense * * *, Miller must have done more than mandate a certain procedure."[7] Finally, taking aim at the majority's statement that Montgomery is no longer sound precedent for purposes of determining whether a rule is procedural or substantive for retroactivity purposes, she observed: "How low this Court's respect for *stare decisis* has sunk."

Aren't Justices Thomas and Sotomayor correct that the majority's readings of Miller and Montgomery are next to impossible to reconcile with Montgomery's classification of the rule in Miller as substantive for Teague purposes? This being said, Jones suggests that had the Montgomery Court been clear that it was reading Miller to require a specific finding relating to incorrigibility (or had Miller itself been clear on the point), that would have made all the difference with respect to the retroactivity analysis and required granting Jones the relief he sought.

Only a few weeks after handing down Jones, in Edwards v. Vannoy, 141 S.Ct. 1547 (2021), the Court, 6–3, eliminated Teague's second exception on the basis that it is "theoretical" and "not real." In so doing, the majority appeared to leave intact Teague's first exception, observing in a footnote that "a new *substantive* rule—for example, a rule that particular conduct cannot be criminalized—usually applies retroactively on federal collateral review." Justice Gorsuch, joined by Justice Thomas, concurred separately and appeared to question the legitimacy of both Teague exceptions. For additional discussion, see pp. 179–182. Edwards therefore heightens the

---

[7]   In the dissent's view, if the majority's reading of Montgomery was correct (namely, that it only required discretionary consideration of youth generally but was still a substantive rule for Teague purposes), it followed that a host of earlier cases involving death penalty sentencing procedures (e.g., those requiring consideration of certain mitigating factors) should also be classified as substantive for Teague purposes.

importance of the distinction between procedural and substantive rules of decision for retroactivity purposes.

(7) The Role, if Any, of 28 U.S.C. § 2241. In Felker v. Turpin, 518 U.S. 651 (1996), the Court noted that a potential bypass of AEDPA's limitations on successive petitions may be found in the Court's original writ. Several courts of appeals, moreover, have suggested that § 2241, the modern descendant of the original provision for habeas jurisdiction, § 14 of the 1789 Judiciary Act, may serve as a proper vehicle for relief in certain federal cases where AEDPA otherwise appears to preclude relief. See Seventh Edition pp. 1362–1363. Against this backdrop, if AEDPA is read to preclude relief for a petitioner seeking the retroactive benefit of Miller or another substantive decision falling under Teague's first exception, there is an argument to be made that § 2241's broad language would give a court a proper basis for awarding relief notwithstanding AEDPA's limitations. See 28 U.S.C. § 2241 (providing that a writ of habeas corpus "may be granted" where a petitioner "is in custody in violation of the Constitution or laws or treaties of the United States"). The Court's recent decision in Jones v. Hendrix, 143 S.Ct. 1857 (2023), however, walked back some from Felker, holding that *federal* prisoners with claims predicated upon legal innocence could not turn to § 2241 to bypass the limitations on successive petitions set forth in 28 U.S.C. § 2255. For additional discussion of Jones, see pp. 215–219, *infra*.

(8) Reopening Judgments Under Federal Rule of Civil Procedure 60(b). Federal Rule of Civil Procedure 60(b) permits a district court to reopen "a final judgment, order, or proceeding" for various reasons, including the discovery of new evidence that was previously unavailable and "any other reason that justifies relief." The Supreme Court has interpreted the rule to permit reopening a judgment on the basis of "extraordinary circumstances," although noting that "[s]uch circumstances will rarely occur in the habeas context." Gonzalez v. Crosby, 545 U.S. 524 (2005). In Buck v. Davis, 580 U.S. 100 (2017), with Chief Justice Roberts writing for the majority, the Court held 6–2 that extraordinary circumstances justified reopening a 2006 judgment denying relief to a state prisoner in what was then his first federal habeas petition. In moving to reopen the judgment, petitioner sought the benefit of the Court's decisions in Martinez v. Ryan, 566 U.S. 1 (2012), see Seventh Edition p. 1339, and Trevino v. Thaler, 569 U.S. 413 (2013), see Seventh Edition p. 1341, to excuse his failure to raise in state post-conviction proceedings a claim of ineffective assistance of counsel in his capital sentencing proceedings. The underlying claim related to the decision of petitioner's own counsel to introduce an expert report and related testimony that characterized petitioner's race as a factor increasing his likelihood of future violence. After criticizing the court of appeals for misunderstanding the standard for granting a certificate of appealability,[8] the Court concluded that counsel's performance at his sentencing "fell outside the bounds of

---

[8] Specifically, the Court criticized the court of appeals for conflating the merits of petitioner's arguments with the decision whether to grant a certificate of appealability, an inquiry that asks " 'only if the District Court's decision was debatable' " (quoting Miller-El v. Cockrell, 537 U.S. 322, 327 (2003)). See Seventh Edition p. 1269. The Court left open the question whether an appeal of the denial of a motion under Rule 60(b) requires a certificate of appealability.

competent representation" and thereby prejudiced the petitioner. Turning to the Rule 60(b) inquiry, the Court posited that "extraordinary circumstances" may justify reopening a judgment where there is a " 'risk of injustice to the parties' " or a " 'risk of undermining the public's confidence in the judicial process' " in leaving a judgment intact (quoting Liljeberg v. Health Services Acquisition Corp., 486 U.S. 847, 863–64 (1988)). Finding these factors present in the case, the Court held that the district court had abused its discretion in denying the Rule 60(b) motion. This conclusion followed, in the Court's view, from the fact that the State had confessed error in other cases in which it had relied upon the same expert and the fact that "Buck may have been sentenced to death in part because of his race." Finally, the Court held that the State had waived any Teague arguments relating to petitioner's reliance on Martinez and Trevino for relief. In so doing, the Court declined to speak to the retroactive application of the decisions. Buck v. Davis potentially opens a new avenue of relief for habeas petitioners seeking to rely on new law after the conclusion of federal habeas proceedings. Note, however, that Buck involved (1) the introduction of deeply objectionable and highly prejudicial expert testimony; (2) a confession of error by the State in related cases; and (3) waiver by the State of any Teague arguments relating to the new law on which petitioner sought to rely.

The Supreme Court again took up a prisoner's attempt to reopen his federal habeas proceedings under Rule 60(b) in Tharpe v. Sellers, 138 S.Ct. 545 (2018) (per curiam). After a district court denied a Rule 60(b) motion and the court of appeals denied a COA, the Supreme Court reversed. The case involved evidence suggesting that race may have played a role in a juror's vote to convict and sentence the petitioner to death. As in Buck, the Court stressed "the unusual facts" of the case. Ultimately, however, the Court remanded, acknowledging that the petitioner still "faces a high bar in showing that jurists of reason could disagree" with the district court's conclusion that under § 2254(e)(1) it should defer to the state court's rejection of the import of the relevant evidence. Similarly, the Court observed that "[i]t may be that, at the end of the day [petitioner] should not receive a COA." Deeming the Court's treatment of the case nothing more than "ceremonial handwringing," a dissent for three Justices written by Justice Thomas would have affirmed the district court's denial of relief. Although Tharpe supports the conclusion that the Court's approval of using Rule 60(b) to reopen habeas proceedings potentially opens a significant new avenue for challenging convictions in successive proceedings, Tharpe's disposition suggests that such an avenue will only be available in extraordinary circumstances. For additional discussion, see pp. 210–212, *infra*.

———————

NOTE ON RELITIGATING THE FACTS IN HABEAS CORPUS PROCEEDINGS

Page 1320. Add a new footnote 1a after Paragraph (2)(a):

[1a] In Brumfield v. Cain, 576 U.S. 305 (2015), the Court rejected a state court's factual findings under 28 U.S.C. § 2254(d)(2) as unreasonable. In the wake of Atkins v. Virginia, 536 U.S. 304 (2002), which held that application of the death penalty to persons with intellectual

disabilities violates the Eighth Amendment, Brumfield sought a hearing in state court to prove his intellectual disability. Surveying the evidence presented during Brumfield's capital sentencing procedure, the state court denied his request. Although recognizing that AEDPA requires that state-court findings be given "substantial deference", a five-Justice majority concluded that the state court's denial of a hearing was unreasonable when held up against the evidence in the record. The majority emphasized that under the state's implementing standard for Atkins, Brumfield need only raise a reasonable doubt as to whether he had an intellectual disability in order to secure a full hearing on the question. In dissent, Justice Thomas argued first that the majority had recharacterized a question involving "the application of law to fact" as a "determination of the facts themselves" in contradiction of the Court's § 2254(d)(1) jurisprudence and second that even if § 2254(d)(2) proved the correct standard of review, Brumfield had failed to satisfy it.

Page 1322. Substitute the following for the last sentence of the first paragraph in Paragraph (4):

In affirming, the Ninth Circuit en banc ruled that a habeas court could consider evidence adduced in a federal evidentiary hearing permitted by § 2254(e)(2) when determining under § 2254(d)(1) whether the state court's rejection of a constitutional claim was contrary to, or an unreasonable application of, clearly established federal law.

Page 1322. Substitute the following paragraph for the third paragraph in Paragraph (4):

Justice Sotomayor's dissent on the relationship between § 2254(d)(1) and § 2254(d)(2) stressed that evidentiary hearings are held in only 4 of every 1,000 non-capital cases and 9.5 of every 100 capital cases and that hearings are permitted by § 2254(e)(2) only when the prisoner was diligent or when very restrictive requirements are satisfied. In these limited circumstances, she argued, consideration of new evidence does not upset the balance established by AEDPA. She further contested the majority's linguistic argument by noting that § 2254(d)(2) expressly requires district courts to base their review on the state court record. See 28 U.S.C. § 2254(d)(2) (precluding relief unless the state court adjudication "resulted in a decision that was based on an unreasonable determination of the facts in light of the evidence presented in the State court proceeding"). This direction, she argued, would be unnecessary if the use of the past tense in § 2254(d)(1), which makes no reference to the state court record, required the same result. When § 2254(e)(2) permits a hearing, some courts of appeals had held (incorrectly, she declared) that § 2254(d)(1) simply does not apply; others had followed the approach of the Ninth Circuit, which permits consideration of new evidence adduced in a federal court hearing when assessing the reasonableness of the state-court decision. No court of appeals, however, had followed the majority's approach, which, she said, has the potential to prevent diligent petitioners from introducing evidence in federal habeas proceedings where the state courts are closed to that petitioner.

Page 1323. Add a new footnote 5 at the end of Paragraph (4):

[5] With AEDPA dramatically limiting the opportunities for relief available to habeas petitioners, some scholars have called upon the Supreme Court to take more criminal appeals on direct review. See, e.g., Vázquez, p. 183, *supra*. Some jurists, meanwhile, have lamented that the standards governing most habeas cases are statutory, as opposed to judge-made, with the former far more difficult to adjust as circumstances warrant. See, e.g., Fletcher, *Symposium Introduction*, 107 Calif.L.Rev. 999 (2019). In the absence of expanded direct review by the Court of state criminal convictions, AEDPA's inflexible deferential standards of review give state

courts the last word on most questions of federal constitutional law that arise in state criminal cases.

Page 1323. Add a new Paragraph (5):

(5) The Intersection of AEDPA's Limitations on Evidentiary Hearings and the All Writs Act. In Shoop v. Twyford, 142 S.Ct. 2037 (2022), the Court took up the question whether a district court could invoke the All Writs Act to order a prisoner transported to a medical facility for neurological testing that might lead to the development of new evidence supporting a habeas claim that the prisoner suffers from neurological defects. The All Writs Act authorizes federal courts to "issue all writs necessary or appropriate in aid of their respective jurisdictions and agreeable to the usages and principles of law." 28 U.S.C. § 1651(a). Writing for five justices, Chief Justice Roberts held that the lower court's order improperly "circumvent[ed]" AEDPA's limitations on the admission and relevance of new evidence in collateral habeas proceedings. In the Court's view, "a writ seeking new evidence would not be 'necessary or appropriate in aid of' a federal habeas court's jurisdiction, as all orders issued under the All Writs Act must be, if it enables a prisoner to fish for unusable evidence * * * ." Instead, the Court held, because the petitioner "never argued that he could clear the bar in § 2254(e)(2) for expanding the state court record, or that the bar was somehow inapplicable," the district court should not have ordered the transportation and testing. (The four dissenting justices believed that the Court should not have reached the question.)

––––––––

INTRODUCTORY NOTE ON FEDERAL HABEAS CORPUS AND STATE PROCEDURAL DEFAULT

Page 1326. Add a new footnote 1 at the end of Paragraph (3):

[1]   For additional background on Fay v. Noia and the companion cases that made Noia's claims especially sympathetic, see Yackle, *The Story of Fay v. Noia: Another Case About Another Federalism*, in Federal Courts Stories (Jackson & Resnik eds. 2010), at 191.

––––––––

NOTE ON FEDERAL HABEAS CORPUS AND STATE COURT PROCEDURAL DEFAULT

Page 1336. Add a new footnote 1a at the end of Paragraph (2):

[1a]   Kovarsky, *Delay in the Shadow of Death*, 95 N.Y.U.L.Rev. 1319 (2020), explains why in the capital context habeas petitioners often bring new claims once the state sets an execution date (specifically, due to ripeness issues and lack of representation through much of the earlier process) and why consciously deferring ripe claims is irrational under current procedural default doctrine.

Page 1338. Add at the end of footnote 8:

The Court revisited the question of attorney abandonment in Christeson v. Roper, 574 U.S. 373 (2015) (per curiam), a capital case in which counsel appointed by the district court to represent a habeas petitioner failed to meet with his client and file a petition on his behalf within the one-year AEDPA filing deadline. Reversing the district court's refusal to grant petitioner's motion to substitute new counsel, the Court concluded that substitution served the "interests of justice." Petitioner's only chance to secure habeas review of his underlying claims was to prevail on an argument that appointed counsel's missteps warranted equitable tolling of the one-year filing deadline—an argument that the same appointed counsel unsurprisingly did not make. As Justice Alito noted in his dissent, however, even with new counsel, petitioner still had to satisfy the standard for equitable tolling, no easy task. See Holland v. Florida, 560 U.S. 631, 653 (2010) (holding that equitable tolling of AEDPA's one-year limitations period may be had only upon a showing of diligence and "extraordinary circumstances").

Page 1341. Substitute the following for the final three sentences of Paragraph (5)(b):

In Martinez, the Court stressed that the right is a "bedrock principle" of the criminal justice system. But what about the right to effective assistance of counsel in a criminal defendant's first appeal as of right? The Supreme Court took up this question in Davila v. Davis, 582 U.S. 521 (2017), and sided with the majority of circuits in holding that Martinez and Trevino should be limited to their particular circumstances.[12a]

Writing for a five-Justice majority, Justice Thomas stressed that "Martinez did not purport to displace Coleman as the general rule governing procedural default. Rather, it 'qualifie[d] Coleman by recognizing a narrow exception'" applying only to ineffective assistance of trial counsel claims and only where those claims "'must be raised in an initial-review collateral proceeding.'" Because Martinez and Trevino were focused on trial errors and because "[c]laims of ineffective assistance of appellate counsel" fail to "pose the same risk that a trial error—of any kind—will escape review altogether," the Court concluded that the default of claims by allegedly ineffective appellate counsel should not be excused. In support of this conclusion, the Court posited that "[i]f an unpreserved trial error was so obvious that appellate counsel was constitutionally required to raise it on appeal, then trial counsel likely provided ineffective assistance by failing to object to it in the first instance." In such circumstances, the Court noted, Martinez and Trevino would authorize excusing any default of claims relating to the trial counsels' ineffectiveness. As further support for declining to extend the Martinez line, Justice Thomas cited the likelihood that "[a]dopting petitioner's argument could flood the federal courts with defaulted claims of appellate ineffectiveness" and that such claims in turn "could serve as the gateway to federal review of a host of trial errors."

Writing for four Justices in dissent, Justice Breyer emphasized that prisoners have a constitutional right to effective assistance of counsel "at both trial and during an initial appeal" and that the Court's decisions have labeled the effective assistance of appellate counsel—just like effective assistance of trial counsel—as "critically important." Turning to the majority's claims, Justice Breyer cited several scenarios in which the ineffectiveness of appellate counsel could result in underlying claims never being reviewed by any court. (Among other things, Justice Breyer noted that this would be true under the majority's reasoning with respect to Brady claims that only became apparent after trial.) He also challenged the

---

[12a] See, e.g., Dansby v. Hobbs, 766 F. 3d 809 (8th Cir.2014) (positing that the "right to appeal is " 'of relatively recent origin' " and "so a claim for equitable relief in that context is less compelling") (citations omitted); but see Ha Van Nguyen v. Curry, 736 F.3d 1287 (9th Cir.2013) ("There is nothing in our jurisprudence to suggest that the Sixth Amendment right to effective counsel is weaker or less important for appellate counsel than for trial counsel.").

majority's assertion that a different holding would open up the floodgates with respect to the filing of new habeas petitions.

Given that the Court has labeled both the effective assistance of trial and appellate counsel as critically important to a fair trial, is there a principled distinction underlying the differing results in Martinez and Davila? After Davila, what, if any, avenues of relief remain for defaulted claims that were not available to a prisoner at the time of trial?[12b]

The Court further curtailed the reach of Martinez and Trevino in Shinn v. Ramirez, 142 S.Ct. 1718 (2022). Writing for a six-Justice majority, Justice Thomas there took up the question whether "the equitable rule announced in Martinez permits a federal court to dispense with § 2254(e)(2)'s narrow limits [on the holding of evidentiary hearings] because a prisoner's state postconviction counsel negligently failed to develop the state-court record." In holding that Martinez does not displace AEDPA's "stringent" limitations set forth in § 2254(e)(2), the Court concluded that even where the underlying claim alleges the ineffectiveness of trial counsel, criminal defendants are bound by the actions taken by counsel in state post-conviction proceedings. Specifically, if post-conviction counsel "failed to develop the factual basis of a claim in State court proceedings"—including an ineffectiveness of trial counsel claim—then a federal court "shall not hold an evidentiary hearing on the claim" unless the prisoner satisfies one of the two limited exceptions set forth in § 2254(e)(2)(A). Relying upon Michael Williams v. Taylor, 529 U.S. 420 (2000), Justice Thomas reiterated that the Court has interpreted "failed to develop" in the relevant provision "to mean that the prisoner must be 'at fault' for the undeveloped record in state court." Fault, in turn, " 'is not established unless there is lack of diligence, or some greater fault, attributable to the prisoner *or the prisoner's counsel*' " (quoting 529 U.S. at 432).

The habeas petitioners in Ramirez had argued that it made little sense to go from holding in Martinez that prisoners will not be held responsible for the failure of state post-conviction counsel to raise a claim of ineffectiveness of trial counsel to then hold the prisoner responsible for the same post-conviction counsel's failure to develop the record in state court supporting such a claim. But, Justice Thomas opined, this argument was foreclosed by Congress's enactment of § 2254(e)(2), which, he wrote, "we have no authority to amend." The Court also emphasized the narrowness of the holding in Martinez along with that decision's prediction that it would not "put a significant strain on state resources" (quoting Martinez, 566 U.S. at 15). Permitting evidentiary hearings in the context of Martinez claims, Justice Thomas predicted, would do just that. Finally, Justice Thomas emphasized the state's interest in the finality of criminal convictions and worried that "broadly available habeas relief" may lead to sandbagging by prisoners who may hold certain claims back in state court, reserving them for federal habeas proceedings.

[12b] To date, those circuits that have reached the question have declined to extend the reasoning of Martinez and Trevino to Brady claims discovered after trial. See, e.g., Hunton v. Sinclair, 732 F.3d 1124 (9th Cir.2013).

Justice Sotomayor, joined by Justices Breyer and Kagan, dissented. In her view, Ramirez "all but overrules" Martinez and Trevino, leaving the state prisoner unable to vindicate the constitutional right to effective trial counsel, what the Court only ten years earlier in Martinez described as " 'a bedrock principle' that constitutes the very 'foundation for our adversary system' of criminal justice" (quoting Martinez, 566 U.S. at 12). Calling the majority opinion in Ramirez "perverse" and "illogical," the dissent disagreed that AEDPA required such an outcome. If, Justice Sotomayor wrote, "Martinez and Trevino establish that petitioners are not at fault for any failure to raise their claims in state court in these circumstances," it is only sensible to interpret AEDPA's § 2254(e)(2)'s "failed to develop" language as "incorporating a threshold requirement that the petitioner be at fault for not developing evidence." Such a conclusion, the dissent contended, is consistent with how the Court first interpreted § 2254(e)(2) in Michael Williams v. Taylor, where it noted that " 'a person is not at fault when his diligent efforts to perform an act are thwarted' by an external force" (quoting Williams, 529 U.S. at 432). In the dissent's view, "Martinez cases are among the rare ones in which attorney error constitutes such an external factor."

Continuing, the dissent labeled the majority as "seriously err[ing] by suggesting that AEDPA categorically prioritizes maximal deference to state-court convictions over vindication of the constitutional protections at the core of our adversarial system." Justice Sotomayor added, "AEDPA does not render state judgments unassailable, [it] strikes a balance between respecting state-court judgments and preserving the necessary and vital role federal courts play in 'guard[ing] against extreme malfunctions in the state criminal justice systems' " (quoting Harrington v. Richter, 562 U.S. 86, 102–03 (2011)). Concluding, she observed that here, "[t]wo men whose trial attorneys did not provide even the bare minimum level of representation required by the Constitution may be executed because forces outside of their control prevented them from vindicating their constitutional right to counsel." This result, in the dissent's view, rendered the protections of the Sixth Amendment "illusory."

In states like Arizona, which require criminal defendants to bring claims of ineffective trial counsel in post-conviction proceedings in which they enjoy no Sixth Amendment right to counsel, Ramirez holds that federal habeas courts are bound by the existing state record developed by post-conviction counsel, whether they advanced a claim of ineffective trial counsel or not. (It is only those rare situations falling within the exceptions to § 2254(e)(2) in which a hearing may be held in federal habeas proceedings.) Very often ineffective assistance claims turn on matters that trial counsel did not investigate with respect to the guilt and/or sentencing phase at trial and therefore failed to uncover and enter into the trial record. In such cases, the ability to introduce new evidence in federal habeas is often essential for petitioners effectively to advance their Strickland claims. If that is correct, what is left of Martinez and Trevino after Ramirez?[12c] More generally, for someone who receives constitutionally deficient trial representation and then inadequate representation in subsequent state post-conviction proceedings, what is left of their underlying Sixth Amendment right to counsel under Ramirez's framework?

[12c] And if evidentiary matters are now controlled by § 2254(e)(2) regardless of whether an underlying claim qualifies for equitable exceptions to procedural default doctrine, what, if anything, is left of the Court's decision in McQuiggin v. Perkins, 569 U.S. 383 (2013)? See Seventh Edition p. 1267 n.4 (noting that the decision applied equitable tolling to permit an untimely habeas claim of actual innocence based on new evidence).

Page 1344. Add at the end of footnote 17:

A divided Court extended the reasoning of Flores-Ortega in Garza v. Idaho, 139 S.Ct. 738 (2019), to hold that where an attorney fails to notice an appeal, despite express instructions from a defendant to do so, prejudice to the defendant under the Strickland standard is presumed " 'with no further showing from the defendant of the merits of his underlying claims,' " even where the defendant has signed an appeal waiver as part of a plea agreement (quoting Flores-Ortega, 528 U.S., at 484).

Page 1346. Add a new footnote 19a at the end of Paragraph (2):

[19a] In Johnson v. Lee, 578 U.S. 605 (2016) (per curiam), the Supreme Court reiterated that a state's " 'procedural bar may count as an adequate and independent ground for denying a federal habeas petition even if the state court had discretion to reach the merits despite the default' " (quoting Walker v. Martin 562 U.S. 307, 311 (2011)). See also Beard v. Kindler, 558 U.S. 53 (2009), discussed at Seventh Edition pp. 541–542. For further discussion, see p. 90, *supra*.

———

NOTE ON SUCCESSIVE AND ABUSIVE HABEAS PETITIONS

Page 1349. Add a new Paragraph (4)(a):

(a) Reopening Judgments Under Federal Rules of Civil Procedure 59(e) and 60(b). Federal Rule of Civil Procedure 59(e) permits a litigant to file a "motion to alter or amend a judgment * * * no later than 28 days after the entry of the judgment." In Banister v. Davis, 140 S.Ct. 1698 (2020), the Supreme Court held that a Rule 59(e) motion does not qualify as a second or successive petition for purposes of 28 U.S.C. § 2244(b). Writing for a seven-Justice majority, Justice Kagan stressed the limited nature of Rule 59(e) motions. First, such motions must be filed within 28 days of entry of judgment, without possibility of extension, Fed. Rule Civ. Proc. 6(b)(2) (prohibiting extensions to Rule 59(e)'s deadline). Second, the Court has recognized that the Rule allows a district court " 'to rectify its own mistakes in the period immediately following' " its decision and that federal courts generally have invoked the rule "only" to "reconsider[ ] matters properly encompassed in a decision on the merits" (quoting White v. New Hampshire Dept. of Employment Security, 455 U.S. 445 (1982)). Thus, in reviewing Rule 59(e) motions, courts do not address new arguments or evidence that the moving party could have raised before the decision issued (citing 11 Wright, Miller & Kane, Federal Practice and Procedure § 2810.1, at 163–64 (3d ed. 2012)). Finally, the timely filing of a Rule 59(e) motion " 'suspends the finality of the original judgment' for purposes of an appeal" (quoting FCC v. League of Women Voters of Cal., 468 U.S. 364, 373, n. 10 (1984)). Putting these factors together, the Court held that Rule 59(e) motions pertain to the same, original underlying judgment with respect to the habeas petitioner's first federal petition.

The Court also relied in part upon "historical habeas doctrine and practice" and AEDPA's purposes, which aim to limit " 'piecemeal litigation' " (quoting Panetti v. Quarterman, 551 U.S. 930 (2007)). Justice Kagan distinguished Gonzalez v. Crosby, 545 U.S. 524 (2005), in which the Court held that a motion filed under Federal Rules of Civil Procedure 60(b)[4a] seeking "relie[f] from a final judgment" that denied habeas relief counts as a second or successive habeas application for purposes of AEDPA in certain contexts. Specifically, Gonzalez held that where a Rule 60(b) motion " 'attacks the federal court's previous resolution of a claim on the merits,' " it shall be deemed second or successive. Holding that Rules 59(e) and 60(b) differ "in just about every way that matters to the inquiry" relating to successive petitions, the Banister Court distinguished Rule 60(b) motions as not governed by any strict time limits with respect to when they may be filed[4b]; for giving rise to a separate appeal than an appeal from the original judgment; and for "attack[ing] an already completed judgment."[4c]

The Court's decision in Gonzalez did not encompass Rule 60(b) motions that attack "some defect in the integrity of the federal habeas proceedings," such as a court's incorrect application of a statute of limitations. Although Gonzalez posited that motions of this kind should only be permitted in "extraordinary circumstances" that "will rarely occur in the habeas context," the Court held, 6–2, in Buck v. Davis, 580 U.S. 100 (2017), that such circumstances existed. In Buck, the petitioner sought to reopen the judgment in his first federal habeas petition eight years after the fact based on the intervening Supreme Court decisions in in Martinez v. Ryan, 566 U.S. 1 (2012), see Seventh Edition p. 1339, and Trevino v. Thaler, 569 U.S. 413 (2013), see Seventh Edition p. 1341. Writing for the majority, Chief Justice Roberts emphasized the extraordinary circumstances of petitioner's claims, which suggested that "Buck may have been sentenced to death in part because of his race."[4d] In so doing, the Court suggested that it is appropriate to reopen a judgment under Rule 60(b) where there is a " 'risk of injustice to the parties' " or a " 'risk of undermining the public's confidence in the judicial process' " in leaving a judgment intact (quoting Liljeberg v. Health Services Acquisition Corp., 486 U.S. 847, 863–64 (1988)). In reaching its holding, the Buck Court did not discuss whether petitioner's Rule 60(b) motion was successive and emphasized that the State had waived any Teague arguments in the case. See also Tharpe v. Sellers, 138 S.Ct. 545 (2018) (per curiam) (reversing and remanding the denial of a Rule 60(b) motion in another habeas case).[4e]

More recently, the Court has been far more rigid in enforcing AEDPA's limitations on the pursuit of second or successive motions in the context of federal prisoner filings. See pp. 215–219, *infra* (discussing Jones v. Hendrix, 143 S.Ct. 1857 (2023)).

[4a] Rule 60(b) provides that a court may grant relief from a final judgment if a party can show (1) mistake, inadvertence, surprise, or excusable neglect; (2) newly discovered evidence that, with reasonable diligence, could not have been discovered in time to move for a new trial under Rule 59(b); (3) fraud * * * misrepresentation, or misconduct by an opposing party; (4) the judgment is void; (5) the judgment has been satisfied, released, or discharged [or] reversed or vacated * * *; or (6) "any other reason that justifies relief."

4b Federal Rules of Civil Procedure 60(c)(1) provides that Rule 60(b) motions should be filed within a "reasonable time."

4c Banister is consistent with the Court's earlier decision in Magwood v. Patterson, 561 U.S. 320 (2010). There, the Court held that if a prisoner secures relief resulting in a material change to the original judgment, such as an order requiring resentencing, the ensuing judgment is deemed "new" and any federal habeas petition that follows is not treated as second or successive.

4d For additional discussion of Buck, see pp. 203–204, *supra*.

4e For additional discussion of Tharpe, see p. 204, *supra*.

NOTE ON PROBLEMS OF CUSTODY AND REMEDY

Page 1355. Add a new footnote 3a at the end of the carryover paragraph:

3a Citing Maleng, the Supreme Court recently reiterated that for purposes of federal collateral habeas review, one is not deemed to be in custody under a state court judgment for purposes of § 2254(a) on the basis that a prior state conviction could serve as a predicate for a subsequent federal conviction. Alaska v. Wright, 141 S.Ct. 1467 (2021) (per curiam).

Page 1355. Add at the end of footnote 7:

In Ziglar v. Abbasi, 582 U.S. 120 (2017), the Supreme Court lent support to the proposition that at least some form of injunctive relief might be available to prisoners challenging conditions of confinement. The case involved a Bivens lawsuit for damages brought against federal officials by individuals detained as part of the investigations into the attacks of September 11, 2001. Writing for a 4–2 majority, Justice Kennedy held that the prisoners could not proceed with their Bivens claims alleging abusive detention conditions in part because other avenues of relief were available to them. "To address" decisions related to the prisoners' conditions of confinement, Justice Kennedy posited, "detainees may seek injunctive relief." The Court left open whether such relief should be specifically available in habeas proceedings, noting that it has never resolved the question. It nonetheless held out "the habeas remedy" as "a faster and more direct route to relief than a suit for money damages" in such cases. In dissent, Justice Breyer contended that "[n]either a prospective injunction nor a writ of habeas corpus . . . will normally provide plaintiffs with redress for harms they have already suffered," and more generally questioned the ability of prisoners denied, as the respondents alleged they were, "access to most forms of communication with the outside world" to pursue habeas proceedings during their detentions. Given the custody requirement for habeas jurisdiction to lie, how effective would a habeas remedy be under the circumstances presented in cases like Abbasi? For additional discussion of Ziglar, see pp. 108–112, 148, and 167 *supra*.

B. COLLATERAL ATTACK ON FEDERAL CONVICTIONS

NOTE ON 28 U.S.C. § 2255 AND ITS RELATIONSHIP TO FEDERAL HABEAS CORPUS

Page 1359. Add at the end of Paragraph (5)(a):

In Welch v. United States, 578 U.S. 120 (2016), the Court relied on Bousley v. United States, Seventh Edition pp. 1358–1359, to hold retroactive the rule of Johnson v. United States, 576 U.S. 591 (2015). Johnson had held that the residual clause of the Armed Career Criminal Act, 18 U.S.C. § 924(e)(2)(B)(ii) (ACCA), which provides for enhanced sentences in cases of possession of a firearm by a felon, was unconstitutionally vague in violation of due process.[4a] After pleading guilty to one count of being a felon in possession of a firearm, Welch received an enhanced sentence under the Act based on three prior violent felony convictions. Throughout the proceedings that followed, Welch contended that one of his prior convictions fell outside the reach of the ACCA, rendering him ineligible for a sentence enhancement. After losing the argument before the district court in a motion under 28 U.S.C. § 2255, Welch applied to the Court of Appeals for a certificate of appealability, which it denied. Shortly thereafter, the Supreme Court decided Johnson. Welch then sought certiorari review before the Court of the merits of his claim as well as the question whether Johnson announced a substantive rule that should be given retroactive effect to cases on collateral review.

Reaching only the second question raised by Welch's petition, Justice Kennedy concluded that Johnson had announced a new rule for purposes of Teague. He then turned to the question whether Johnson's rule "falls within one of the two categories that have retroactive effect under Teague." Relying on Schriro v. Summerlin, 542 U.S. 348, 353 (2004), and Montgomery v. Louisiana, 577 U.S. 190 (2016), pp. 187–196, supra, he concluded that it did. The Court had long indicated that a substantive rule under Teague " 'includes decisions that narrow the scope of a criminal statute by interpreting its terms' " (quoting Schriro, 542 U.S. at 353). Because of Johnson, the ACCA's residual clause "can no longer mandate or authorize any sentence" for those who might otherwise fall under that provision. It followed, in the Court's view, that the decision in Johnson was substantive in nature.

The Court explained that its Teague jurisprudence determines "whether a new rule is substantive or procedural by considering the function of the rule." The Teague analysis, Justice Kennedy wrote, does not depend on whether "the underlying constitutional guarantee [being asserted by the petitioner] is characterized as procedural or substantive." Finally, citing Bousley, Justice Kennedy deemed it irrelevant to the Teague analysis that Congress retained power "to enact a new version of the residual clause that imposes the same punishment on the same persons for the same conduct, provided the new statute is precise enough to satisfy due process."

Justice Thomas dissented on two grounds. First, he argued that the lower courts never had before them the question whether Johnson (which had not yet been decided) applied retroactively, a fact that precluded the Court's review of the claim. On this view, the Court of Appeals correctly

---

[4a] The ACCA imposes a sentence enhancement of five years or more where a felon is found to possess a firearm and after three or more convictions for a "serious drug offense" or a "violent felony," the latter of which is defined in two ways. First, the "elements clause" defines a violent felony as involving any crime that "has as an element the use, attempted, use, or threatened use of a physical force against the person of another". Second, the "residual clause" provides that the crimes of burglary, arson, and extortion, and crimes involving the "use of explosives" qualify as violent felony, as well as crimes involving "conduct that presents a serious potential risk of physical injury to another." 18 U.S.C. § 924(e)(2)(B). Johnson held that the "serious potential risk" residual language gave insufficient guidance as to the scope of its application. For further discussion of Johnson, see pp. 38–39, supra.

denied a certificate of appealability.[4b] Second, Justice Thomas complained that the majority had "erode[d] any meaningful limits on what a 'substantive' rule is" under Teague. Because "the Government remains as free to enhance sentences for federal crimes based on the commission of previous violent felonies after Johnson as it was before", Justice Thomas argued, Johnson's rule should not be deemed substantive under the Court's precedents. Bousley "applied only to new rules reinterpreting the text of federal criminal statutes in a way that narrows their reach." Johnson, by contrast, "announced only that there is no way in which to narrow the reach of the residual clause without running afoul of the Due Process Clause." Reading Johnson as substantive, on this view, will mean that "if any decision has the effect of invalidating substantive provisions of a criminal statute," it will be treated as substantive, "no matter what the reason for the statute's invalidation."

In closing, Justice Thomas argued that the Court's Teague jurisprudence, while "profess[ing] to venerate Justice Harlan's theory of retroactivity", has moved well beyond the limited category of substantive claims Justice Harlan viewed as entitled to retroactive application. In support, Justice Thomas pointed to the Court's extension of Teague's first exception to rules prohibiting certain punishments in cases like Penry v. Lynaugh, 492 U.S. 302 (1989), Seventh Edition p. 1298; to federal prisoners challenging the reach of federal criminal statutes, as in Bousley; and to state post-conviction proceedings, as the Court did over his dissent in Montgomery v. Louisiana, 577 U.S. 190 (2016), pp. 187–196, *supra*. "With the Court's unprincipled expansion of Teague," Justice Thomas complained, "every end is instead a new beginning."

Does Justice Thomas successfully distinguish Bousley? Regardless, is he correct that the Court has moved far beyond Justice Harlan's definition of substantive rules warranting retroactive application? See Mackey v. United States, 401 U.S. 667, 692 (1971) (Harlan, J., concurring in part and dissenting in part) (referring to rules that render "certain kinds of primary, private individual conduct beyond the power of the criminal law-making authority to proscribe"); see also Seventh Edition p. 1294 (Paragraph (3)). For discussion of some of the complications likely to arise as prisoners seek the benefit of Johnson and Welch, see Paragraph (8), at Seventh Edition pp. 1362–1363.

Page 1361. Substitute the following for footnote 9:

[9] Section 2255(h) requires that in order to proceed, any "second or successive motion must be certified as provided in section 2244 by a panel of the appropriate court of appeals" to be predicated upon "newly discovered evidence that, if proven and viewed in the light of the evidence as a whole, would be sufficient to establish by clear and convincing evidence that no

---

[4b] The majority reversed the Court of Appeals' denial of a certificate of appealability on the basis that "reasonable jurists at least could debate whether Welch is entitled to relief" under Johnson. Justice Thomas's dissent labeled the Court's conclusion "preposterous" given that Welch had sought the benefit of Johnson for the first time in an untimely motion for reconsideration of the Court of Appeals' prior denial of his application for a certificate. In Justice Thomas's view, the Court of Appeals could not be criticized for "denying Welch the opportunity to 'appeal' a claim that he failed to raise," which was based on "a decision that did not yet exist." Justice Thomas argued that the majority's standard means that a lower court can avoid being reversed in such circumstances only with "judicial clairvoyance" and "by inventing arguments on the movant's behalf."

reasonable factfinder would have found the movant guilty of the offense" or "a new rule of constitutional law, made retroactive to cases on collateral review by the Supreme Court, that was previously unavailable." Thus, by its terms, § 2255 permits a successive petition based on newly discovered evidence of innocence without § 2244(b)(2)(B)(i)'s further requirement that "the factual predicate for the claim could not have been discovered previously through the exercise of due diligence."

With respect to second or successive motions that involve claims previously presented, courts have interpreted § 2255 to incorporate the restrictions on successive petitions found in 2244(b)(1) & (2), despite the fact that those provisions are expressly limited to claims "presented in a second or successive habeas corpus application under section 2254." See, e.g., In re Baptiste, 828 F.3d 1337 (11th Cir.2016) (per curiam) (holding that § 2255 incorporates § 2241(b)(1)'s requirement that claims presented in a prior motion be dismissed); White v. United States, 371 F.3d 900 (7th Cir.2004) (same). Along similar lines, many circuits have concluded that denials of certification under § 2255(h) to proceed with a second or successive petition may not be appealed, incorporating the standard of § 2244(b)(3)(E), which is not expressly limited to petitions filed under § 2254. See, e.g., In re Graham, 714 F.3d 1181 (10th Cir.2013) (per curiam); Lykus v. Corsini, 565 F.3d 1 (1st Cir.2009) (en banc) (per curiam).

Page 1362. Replace the first sentence of the third paragraph of Paragraph (8) as follows:

Many, but not all, circuits have stated that petitioners who were convicted for conduct that has been rendered non-criminal by a subsequent authoritative decision, and who are barred from resorting to § 2255, may resort to § 2241 in some circumstances.

Page 1363. Add a new footnote 12 at the end of Paragraph (8):

[12] Some circuits have extended this reasoning to encompass petitions brought pursuant to § 2241 for relief based on new decisions that would have rendered the petitioner ineligible for sentencing enhancements that were imposed at sentencing. See, *e.g.*, United States v. Wheeler, 886 F.3d 415 (4th Cir.2018); Hill v. Masters, 836 F.3d 591 (6th Cir.2016). But see McCarthan v. Director of Goodwill Industries-Suncoast, Inc., 851 F.3d 1076 (11th Cir.2017) (en banc) (holding that "a change in caselaw does not make a motion to vacate a prisoner's sentence 'inadequate or ineffective to test the legality of his detention' " under § 2255(e)).

Page 1363. Add at the end of Paragraph (8):

In Jones v. Hendrix, 143 S.Ct. 1857 (2023), the Supreme Court finally addressed the intersection of § 2255(e), the so-called "saving clause", and § 2241. Jones had been convicted of unlawful possession of a firearm by a felon in violation of 18 U.S.C. § 922(g). Well after Jones filed his first § 2255 motion (which was unsuccessful), the Supreme Court decided Rehaif v. United States, 139 S.Ct. 2191 (2019), holding that a defendant's knowledge of the status that disqualifies him from owning a firearm is an element of § 922(g). Thereafter, Jones sought to file a habeas petition under § 2241, arguing that he should benefit from the holding in Rehaif and that the limitations on successive § 2255 motions set forth in § 2255(h) rendered § 2255 "inadequate or ineffective to test the legality of his detention" per the terms of the saving clause, § 2255(e).

Writing for the Court, Justice Thomas disagreed. Instead, he concluded, the saving clause "does not permit a prisoner asserting an intervening change in statutory interpretation to circumvent AEDPA's restrictions on second or successive § 2255 motions by filing a § 2241 petition." In the Court's view, the saving clause had long been understood to cover solely "unusual circumstances" such as where "it is impossible or impracticable for a prisoner to seek relief from a sentencing court," offering the example of a court that Congress has subsequently dissolved.[13] The "straightforward negative inference" of the two conditions set forth in § 2255(h) permitting successive petitions, the Court added, is that "a second or successive collateral attack on a federal sentence is not authorized unless one of" the conditions in § 2255(h) is satisfied. Relevant to the Court's reasoning was the fact that Congress expressly limited relief under § 2255(h) to application of "new rules of constitutional law" and not "*nonconstitutional* law." "Any other reading" of the relevant provisions, Justice Thomas concluded, "would make AEDPA curiously self-defeating. It would mean that, by expressly excluding second or successive § 2255 motions based on nonconstitutional legal developments, Congress accomplished nothing in terms of actually limiting such claims."

The Court saw no constitutional concerns raised by its reading of the statute. There was no problem under the Suspension Clause, Justice Thomas asserted, because "[a]t the Founding, a sentence after conviction 'by a court of competent jurisdiction' was ' "in *itself* sufficient cause" ' for a prisoner's continued detention (quoting Brown v. Davenport, 142 S.Ct. 1510, 1520–21 (2022) (quoting in turn Ex parte Watkins, 38 U.S. (3 Pet.) 193, 202 (1830))). As for due process, Justice Thomas opined that it "does not guarantee a direct appeal" (citing McKane v. Durston, 153 U.S. 684, 687 (1894)), much less "the opportunity to have legal issues redetermined in successive collateral attacks on a final sentence." Nor did the Eighth Amendment raise any concerns. Quoting the Amendment's text to impose limitations solely upon "the kinds of punishments governments may 'inflic[t]' ", Justice Thomas wrote that it does not offer a "freestanding entitlement to a second or successive round of postconviction review."

In adhering to a narrow view of the saving clause, the Court distinguished its previous holding that a party could overcome AEDPA's statute of limitations based upon a colorable claim of "actual innocence" in McQuiggin v. Perkins, 569 U.S. 383 (2013). Justice Thomas reasoned that there is a significant difference between invoking equitable considerations to set aside the statute of limitations and doing the same to displace restrictions on second or successive motions; in so doing, he rejected a clear statement rule calling for clearer evidence that Congress intended to foreclose such a "workaround." He added:

"Statutes of limitations merely govern the *timeframe* for bringing a claim. AEDPA's second-or-successive restrictions, by contrast, 'constitute a modified res judicata rule,' Felker v. Turpin, 518 U. S. 651, 664 (1996), and thus embody Congress' judgment regarding the central policy question of postconviction remedies—the appropriate balance between finality and error correction. Insisting on a heightened standard of clarity in this context would effectively mean adopting a presumption against finality as a substantive value. We decline to do so."

---

[13] The Court added that the saving clause does not displace § 2241 in situations where a prisoner attacks their *detention*, as opposed to *sentence*, such as where "a prisoner * * * argue[s] that he is being detained in a place or manner not authorized by the sentence, that he has unlawfully been denied parole or good-time credits, or that an administrative sanction affecting the conditions of his detention is illegal."

Justices Sotomayor and Kagan penned a joint dissent in which they decried the "disturbing results" of the Court's holding—namely, that "[a] prisoner who is actually innocent" will be "forever barred" from challenging his sentence because he previously did so before intervening caselaw "confirm[ed] his innocence." They argued that the saving clause should instead be read consistent with the Court's pre-AEDPA decisions holding that "federal prisoners can collaterally attack their convictions in successive petitions if they can make a colorable showing that they are innocent under an intervening decision of statutory construction" (citing Davis v. United States, 417 U. S. 333, 344–47 (1974), and McCleskey v. Zant, 499 U. S. 467, 493–95 (1991)).

Justice Jackson also dissented. In her view, the Court's opinion misread both § 2255(e) and § 2255(h) and undervalued the constitutional concerns at stake. The former should be read "to 'save' any claim that was available prior to § 2255(h)'s enactment where Congress has not expressed a clear intent to foreclose it," which, like the other dissenters, she observed included claims of legal innocence. Justice Jackson also pointed to aspects of AEDPA's legislative history suggesting that Congress did not intend to preclude legal innocence claims brought in successive petitions. She further observed that Congress modeled § 2255(h) on AEDPA's provision governing successive petitions brought by state prisoners, § 2244(b). But state prisoners, she wrote, do not generally raise federal *statutory* claims. Thus, she noted, "it is plausible (and perhaps even likely) that Congress did not appreciate fully that the modeled-after language establishing a successive-petition bar did not capture the full scope of available claims for federal prisoners." Arguing that a clear statement rule should apply that assumes Congress legislates in this area aware of the longstanding existence of habeas court equitable powers, Justice Jackson labeled the Court's interpretation "stingy" (citing Ex parte Yerger, 75 U.S. (8 Wall.) 85, 95, 102 (1869), see Seventh Edition p. 307 n. *; INS v. St. Cyr, 533 U.S. 289, 298 (2001), Seventh Edition p. 336; Demore v. Kim, 538 U.S. 510, 517 (2003), Seventh Edition p. 337 n. 3; and Manning, Seventh Edition p. 656, at 121–22). Accordingly, she argued, "the signal from Congress that justifies reading a statute as foreclosing access to venerated post-conviction review processes—*cannot be derived from negative inferences drawn from statutory text.*"

Justice Jackson also argued in favor of application of the canon of constitutional avoidance. With respect to the Eighth Amendment, she wrote, "[t]here is a nonfrivolous argument that the Constitution's protection against 'cruel and unusual punishment' prohibits the incarceration of innocent individuals." Although she cautioned that "[t]his is not to say that the Eighth Amendment creates a 'freestanding entitlement to a second or successive round of postconviction review'" (quoting the majority opinion), she distinguished Jones as seeking "a single meaningful opportunity to have a federal court consider his claim of legal innocence." Justice Jackson also argued that legal innocence claims implicate the Suspension Clause because they call into question the validity of the jurisdiction of the convicting court. Finally, she observed that the majority had, in her view, misinterpreted the intent of Congress in adopting its cramped reading of § 2255 and thereby "create[d] an opening for Congress to step in and fix this problem."

Jones v. Hendrix marks yet another Supreme Court decision in recent Terms scaling back opportunities for post-conviction review while elevating the principle of finality. Cf. Friendly, Seventh Edition p. 1284. It is, in this respect, in considerable tension with decisions from only a few Terms prior, such as Banister v. Davis, 140 S.Ct. 1698 (2020), see *supra* p. 210–211; Buck v. Davis, 137 S.Ct. 769 (2017), see p. 203–204, *supra*; and Tharpe v. Sellers, 138 S.Ct. 545 (2018) (per curiam), see p. 204, *supra*, all of which permitted workarounds to AEDPA's preclusion of second or successive habeas petitions in extraordinary situations. (Specifically, those cases permitted habeas petitioners to attempt to alter or amend or reopen judgments in federal habeas proceedings after-the-fact based on Federal Rules of Civil Procedure 59(e) and 60(b).) The Court also walked back from its suggestion in Felker v. Turpin, 518 U.S. 651 (1996), that a potential bypass of AEDPA's limitations on successive petitions for state prisoners may be found in the Court's original writ.

Jones is also in considerable tension with the Court's earlier decision in McQuiggin v. Perkins. Is Justice Thomas's distinction between Jones and that case convincing? Why should equitable tolling apply to permit an actual innocence claim to go forward in the face of a clear legislative statute of limitations precluding the claim but analogous equitable considerations not dictate that a legal innocence claim may be heard despite a statutory limitation on successive petitions? Is the relevant difference one between claims of actual versus legal innocence? If so, should the Court draw such a distinction? And is it helpful or harmful to the petitioner's case that his claim of legal innocence parallels a claim Congress expressly permitted to go forward in a successive petition in § 2255(h)(2) (permitting successive § 2255 motion based on "new rule of constitutional law")? Justice Thomas thought the express reference to new rules of constitutional law implied the exclusion of claims based on new *statutory* holdings, but could one argue that it does suggest that Congress was concerned as a general matter with permitting legal innocence claims to get around the bar on successive petitions?

It is also noteworthy that the majority in Jones was unfazed by any constitutional concerns implicated by its interpretation of § 2255. In this respect, the Court's refusal to apply the canon of constitutional avoidance in Jones stands in considerable tension with the Court's approach just seven years earlier in Montgomery v. Louisiana, 577 U.S. 190 (2016), see pp. 187–196, *supra*. Recall there the Court held the Constitution requires that a state post-conviction court be open to grant relief to a state prisoner detained under a now-outdated understanding of constitutionally permissible punishments. See p. 190, *supra* (citing Mackey v. United States, 401 U.S. 667, 693 (1971) (opinion of Harlan, J.) ("There is little societal interest in permitting the criminal process to rest at a point where it ought properly never to repose")). In both Jones and Montgomery, the Court faced the argument that limitations on post-conviction availability precluded the relevant courts from awarding relief to the petitioner. In one (Montgomery), the Court held the Constitution required it. In another (Jones), the Court upheld the limitation and held there were no constitutional concerns implicated. What is the critical distinction between Montgomery and Jones? Is it that Montgomery's underlying claim sounded in the Eighth Amendment as opposed to the proper interpretation of a federal statute? And should that distinction matter? Or does Jones signal further erosion of Montgomery more generally?

In the end, Justice Jackson is surely correct that the result of the Court's decisions in Rehaif and Jones is to create a claim for release that is retroactively available to only a "sliver of eligible prisoners"—in Justice Jackson's telling, "those who have not had the temerity to file a prior motion". Justice Jackson calls this point of repose "palpably absurd" and argues that Congress could not have desired such a result. In so doing, does she assign too little significance to the considerable changes and new hurdles imposed by AEDPA to both the § 2254 and § 2255 schemes? Or is she correct that Congress likely did not realize when it modeled § 2255(h) off of § 2244(b) that federal prisoners will have additional legal innocence claims beyond those sounding in the Constitution? In all events, she calls upon Congress to step in and address the result in Jones. How likely is Congress to do so?

CHAPTER XII

ADVANCED PROBLEMS IN JUDICIAL FEDERALISM

---

1. PROBLEMS OF RES JUDICATA

INTRODUCTORY NOTE

Pages 1365–66. Replace the text of Paragraph (1) with the following:

(1) Claim Preclusion. Under the doctrine of claim preclusion, once a court has entered a valid final judgment, a subsequent action on the same claim by any party to that judgment, or by one in "privity" with a party, is normally precluded. The underlying intuition rests at least in part on waiver: the precluded party could and should have raised the matter in the earlier litigation and has now waived the opportunity to do so. Today, most courts embrace the Restatement 2d view that a claim should be defined in terms of the transaction or transactions that were the subject of the dispute, not in terms of the particular theory of recovery that was advanced. The applicability of claim preclusion does not ordinarily depend on whether the claim in question was actually litigated in a prior proceeding. Rather, the question is whether it could and should have been litigated.

A range of exceptions to the rule of claim preclusion covers such matters as the existence of "consent" to the splitting of a claim and instances in which the prior judgment rested on such preliminary grounds as lack of jurisdiction or improper venue. The exceptions for lack of jurisdiction or venue help to illustrate that the theory of claim preclusion is based on waiver. But if the claim could not have been heard in the prior proceeding—because the court there lacked jurisdiction or venue, or, to take another example, because the claim had not yet accrued—then claim preclusion does not apply, as the litigant can hardly be taxed for having failed to raise a claim that could not have been resolved in that proceeding.

Page 1367. Add a new Paragraph (7):

(7) Preclusion of Defenses. It is unclear whether claim preclusion bars a defendant from raising a defense that might have been, but was not, raised in prior litigation. The Supreme Court touched on this issue in Lucky Brand Dungarees, Inc. v. Marcel Fashions Group, Inc., 140 S.Ct. 1589 (2020). It explained that "defense preclusion" is not "a standalone category of res judicata, unmoored from the two guideposts of issue preclusion and claim preclusion." Rather, any preclusion of a defense "must, at a minimum, satisfy the strictures of issue preclusion or claim preclusion." That principle was enough for the unanimous Court to reject the plaintiff's argument that the defendant was precluded from asserting a defense to an alleged trademark violation it did not raise in prior litigation between the parties, since the two lawsuits "were grounded on different conduct, involving different marks, occurring at different times", and thus "did not share a 'common nucleus of operative facts'" (citing Restatement 2d § 24 cmt. b, at 199).

In a footnote, the Court raised the possibility that claim preclusion may never apply to defenses, since "'[v]arious considerations, other than actual merits, may govern' whether to bring a defense, 'such as the smallness of the amount or the value of the property in controversy, the difficulty of obtaining the necessary evidence, the expense of the litigation, and [a party's] own situation'" (alterations in original) (quoting Cromwell v. County of Sac, 94 U.S. 351, 356 (1877)). It declined to reach the issue, however, since the plaintiff had not satisfied the "identity of claims" requirement.

Should defense preclusion ever be available? On the one hand, it appears to promote efficiency and finality by forcing parties to litigate defenses as early as possible. On the other hand, as the Court suggested, parties often have good reasons for not raising all conceivable defenses, and forcing them to do so on pain of preclusion might unnecessarily expand the earlier lawsuit and raise overall litigation costs. How should the Court sort out these competing policy arguments? What sources of law should it look to?

A. LITIGATION WITH THE FEDERAL GOVERNMENT

NOTE ON RES JUDICATA IN FEDERAL GOVERNMENT LITIGATION AND ON THE PROBLEM OF ACQUIESCENCE

Page 1374. Add at the end of Paragraph (1):

Another question is whether the growing spate of federal district court injunctions that bar the federal government from enforcing federal statutes or regulations against nonparties in other districts and circuits is consistent with Mendoza. In recent years courts have been particularly aggressive in enjoining the government "nationwide" from enforcing immigration laws in contexts ranging from the Trump administration's sanctuary city policy, see, e.g., City of Chicago v. Barr, 961 F.3d 882 (7th Cir.2020), and executive order limiting entry into the United States, see Hawaii v. Trump, 878 F.3d 662 (9th Cir.2017) (third executive order), reversed, Trump v. Hawaii, 138 S.Ct. 2392 (2018), to the Obama administration's program to establish lawful presence for aliens for various federal-law purposes, see Texas v. United States, 86 F.Supp. 3d 591 (S.D.Tex.), aff'd, 809 F.3d 134 (5th Cir.2015), aff'd by an equally divided Court, 579 U.S. 547 (2016) (mem.), to the Biden administration's efforts to pause the removal of aliens already subject to a final order of removal, see Texas v. United States, 524 F.Supp.3d 598 (S.D.Tex. 2021). But the nationwide injunction trend is not limited to immigration. See Bray, *Multiple Chancellors: Reforming the National Injunction*, 131 Harv.L.Rev. 417, 428–45, 457–61 (2017) (documenting rise and prevalent use of nationwide injunctions in numerous contexts).

By preventing the government from litigating the enjoined issue in other courts against other parties, a nationwide injunction operates like nonmutual offensive collateral estoppel against the government. It flips Mendoza's policy priorities by elevating efficiency concerns and by frustrating the percolation of legal issues before different courts and in different factual contexts that Mendoza found vital to optimal Supreme Court decision-making and the proper development of federal law. It also has an adverse asymmetrical impact on the government, which is frequently involved in lawsuits against different parties involving the same issues, and which has powerful incentives to appeal every adverse nationwide injunction or risk foreclosing further review of the issue everywhere. In an opinion concurring in the Supreme Court's grant of a stay of a nationwide injunction, Justice Gorsuch, joined by Justice Thomas, mentioned most of these factors as reasons to oppose nationwide injunctions, but he did not invoke Mendoza. See Dep't of Homeland Security v. New York, 140 S.Ct. 599 (2020).

Does it follow from these considerations that Mendoza rules out nationwide injunctions? The proper policy balance in the context of developing a federal common law of preclusion against the government is an analytically separate issue from the proper balance of the equities for purposes of assessing the scope of injunctive relief against the government in a particular context. Which set of concerns should have priority, and how should the concerns be integrated? For arguments that Mendoza is an impediment to nationwide injunctions, see Morley, *Disaggregating Nationwide Injunctions*, 71 Ala.L.Rev. 1, 31 (2019) (stressing that "[n]ationwide defendant-oriented injunctions are flatly inconsistent with Mendoza"); Bray, *supra*, at 469–81 (invoking Mendoza's policy rationale among other considerations to argue that injunctions should protect the plaintiff but not non-parties); Berger, *Nationwide Injunctions Against the Federal Government: A Structural Approach*, 92 N.Y.U.L.Rev. 1068, 1090 (2017) (invoking Mendoza's policy rationale among other considerations to argue that injunctions against the federal government should be geographically limited by circuit); Cass, *Nationwide Injunctions' Governance Problems: Forum-Shopping, Politicizing Courts, and Eroding Constitutional Structure*, 27 Geo. Mason L.Rev. 29, 71 (2019) (invoking Mendoza to argue against nationwide injunctions that "intrude into the political-policy domain, either directly or by facilitating one administration's or party's ability to freeze policy determinations going forward"); *cf.* Trammell, *Demystifying Nationwide Injunctions*, 98 Tex.L.Rev. 67, 97–101 (2019) (arguing that Mendoza's policy considerations should guide judges in crafting nationwide injunctions). For arguments that downplay Mendoza's relevance, see Sohoni, *The Lost History of the "Universal" Injunction*, 133 Harv.L.Rev. 920, 994–95 n.487 (2020) (suggesting that Mendoza is relevant but not dispositive); Clopton, *National Injunctions and Preclusion*, 118 Mich.L.Rev. 1, 20–44 (2019) (maintaining that Mendoza is not a strong argument against nationwide injunctions, but proposing that it be overruled in any event); Frost, *In Defense of Nationwide Injunctions*, 93 N.Y.U.L.Rev. 1065, 1112–13 (2018) (arguing that Mendoza can be squared with nationwide injunctions). For a recent symposium on national injunctions that addresses many of the issues in this Note, see Symposium, *National Injunctions: What Does the Future Hold?*, 91 U.Colo.L.Rev. 779–1034 (2020).

————

2. OTHER ASPECTS OF CONCURRENT OR SUCCESSIVE JURISDICTION

NOTE ON THE PREISER-HECK DOCTRINE

Page 1400. Add a new footnote 2a at the end of the second paragraph:

[2a] A question that followed in the wake of Skinner is when the procedural due process claim accrued for purposes of calculating the statute of limitations under § 1983. In Reed v. Goertz, 143 S.Ct. 955 (2023), the Court held that when a prisoner pursues state post-conviction DNA testing through the state courts, the clock on a § 1983 procedural due process claim begins to run when the state litigation ends. For more discussion of Reed, see p. 139, *supra*.

Page 1404. Replace the text of Paragraph (3)(c) with the following:

In Nelson v. Campbell, 541 U.S. 637 (2004), and Hill v. McDonough, 547 U.S. 573 (2006), the Court considered § 1983 actions challenging the constitutionality of a particular method of execution. In both cases, a habeas petition would probably have been barred by 28 U.S.C. § 2244(b) as an improper successive petition. Likewise, in both cases it was not clear that a successful challenge would prevent the use of alternative methods of execution under existing state law and therefore it could be argued that the lawsuits did not challenge the relevant underlying sentences.

More recently, the Court went further in Nance v. Ward, 142 S.Ct. 2214 (2022). Writing for five justices, Justice Kagan reaffirmed that § 1983 remains the proper vehicle for challenging the method of execution even if the alternative method of execution sought is not currently available under state law. Even though securing the relief sought might require a change in state legislation, the Court concluded that "Nance's requested relief still places his execution in Georgia's control." It also observed that "One of the 'main aims' of § 1983 is to 'override'—and thus compel change of—state laws when necessary to vindicate federal constitutional rights" (quoting Monroe v. Pape, 365 U.S. 167, 173 (1961)). Justice Barrett dissented. She wrote that the Court was circumventing "the more rigorous, federalism-protective requirements of habeas . . . with a theory at odds with the very federalism interests they are designed to protect." By contrast, she argued, "I would take state law as we find it in determining whether a suit sounds in habeas or § 1983." For additional discussion, see *supra* p. 167.

If habeas corpus is generally thought to be more protective of federalism than § 1983, can the Court use principles of federalism in resolving conflicts between them? Doesn't it have to first resolve the conflict in order to know which federalism principles apply?

CHAPTER XIII

THE DIVERSITY JURISDICTION OF THE FEDERAL DISTRICT COURTS

1. INTRODUCTION

NOTE ON THE HISTORICAL BACKGROUND AND CONTEMPORARY UTILITY OF THE DIVERSITY JURISDICTION

Page 1416. Add at the end of footnote 1:

For an argument that emphasizes the Framers' experience judging prize case appeals during the Revolutionary War, see Mask & MacMahon, *The Revolutionary War Prize Cases and the Origins of Diversity Jurisdiction*, 63 Buff.L.Rev. 477 (2015).

Page 1419. Add at the end of footnote 9:

Freer, *The Political Reality of Diversity Jurisdiction*, 94 S.Cal.L.Rev. 1083 (2021) (arguing that diversity jurisdiction is now justified both by concerns about region-based bias and by the need for efficient resolution of complex litigation). See also Dodson, *Beyond Bias in Diversity Jurisdiction*, 69 Duke L.J. 267 (2019) (arguing that bias against out-of-state litigants no longer justifies diversity jurisdiction but "[p]romoting aggregation [of litigation] across state lines" may do so).

2. ELEMENTS OF DIVERSITY JURISDICTION

NOTE ON COMPLETE VERSUS MINIMAL DIVERSITY AND ON ALIGNMENT OF PARTIES

Page 1428. Replace footnote 8 with the following:

[8] The Supreme Court clarified the scope of Section 1453(b) in Home Depot U.S.A., Inc. v. Jackson, 139 S.Ct. 1743 (2019). The issue in Home Depot was whether a third-party counterclaim defendant—that is, a new party brought into the suit by the original defendant's counterclaim against the original plaintiff—can remove a suit that otherwise qualifies for original federal jurisdiction. In an opinion by Justice Thomas, the Court ruled that a third-party counterclaim defendant cannot remove because it is not a "defendant" under the relevant removal statutes. The Court first addressed removal under 28 U.S.C. § 1441(a), which permits a "defendant" to remove a "civil action * * * of which the district courts" have "original jurisdiction". It reasoned that since the original complaint alone determines whether a federal court has original jurisdiction over a civil action, the defendant who can remove is the one named in the original complaint, not a party named in a counterclaim. The Court then turned to Section 1453(b), which presented "a closer question" primarily because its broader language permits removal by "any defendant" to a "class action". It concluded that removal was not available under this Section either. The Court explained that the clauses in Section 1453(b) that use the term "any defendant" concern CAFA's relaxed removal requirements—namely, its elimination of both the requirement that all defendants in a diversity case must consent to removal, see 28 U.S.C. § 1446(b)(2)(A), and the bar on removal if any defendant is a citizen of the state where

the action is brought, see 28 U.S.C. § 1441(b)(2). But nothing in Section 1453(b) alters Section 1441(a)'s limitation on what type of party can remove. Section 1453(b) thus does not expand who is a "defendant" under the removal statutes, but rather clarifies what restrictions apply to eligible parties seeking removal for certain class actions. The Court noted that this conclusion was reinforced by the fact that Sections 1453(b) and 1441(a) both rely on the procedures for removal in 28 U.S.C. § 1446, which employs the term "defendant" and thus suggests that that term should have the same meaning in both Sections. In dissent, Justice Alito disagreed sharply with the Court's statutory analysis of both removal provisions, and argued that the Court created an unjustified "loophole" in Section 1453(b) to Congress's clear aim of making class action removal easier. For a useful discussion of the issues in Home Depot, see Tidmarsh, *Finding Room For State Class Actions in a Post-CAFA World: The Case of the Counterclaim Class Action*, 35 W.St.U.L.Rev. 193 (2007).

Page 1429. Add at the end of the first paragraph of footnote 10:

Wolff, *Choice of Law and Jurisdictional Policy in the Federal Courts*, 165 U.Pa.L.Rev. 1847 (2017) (arguing that Klaxon is no barrier to federal courts developing federal choice-of-law rules in CAFA cases to resolve state-law conflicts).

NOTE ON THE TREATMENT OF CORPORATIONS, UNINCORPORATED ENTITIES, AND LITIGATION CLASSES IN THE DETERMINATION OF DIVERSITY

Page 1435. Eliminate the last sentence of Paragraph (1) and replace Paragraph (2) with the following:

(2) **Partnerships, Business Trusts, and Other Unincorporated Entities.** In Americold Realty Trust v. ConAgra Foods, Inc., 577 U.S. 378 (2016), the Court reaffirmed Bouligny and ruled broadly that "[w]hile humans and corporations can assert their own citizenship, other entities take the citizenship of their members." The question in Americold was whether the citizenship for diversity purposes of a Maryland "real estate investment trust" should be determined by the citizenship of the trust or of its members. The Court described Letson's identification of corporate citizenship with the state of incorporation as a "limited exception", ratified by Congress in 28 U.S.C. § 1332(c), to Deveaux's general rule that "only a human could be a citizen for jurisdictional purposes." The Court thus affirmed that the citizenship of all "artificial entities other than corporations, such as joint-stock companies or limited partnerships", is determined by the citizenship of all of its members. The Court further explained that the appropriate "membership" of unincorporated entities is determined by state law, and that under the law of Maryland, which created the investment trust, the relevant members were its shareholders. The Court distinguished Navarro Sav. Ass'n v. Lee, 446 U.S. 458 (1980), which some lower courts had interpreted to hold that a trust possesses the citizenship of its trustees alone rather than the shareholder beneficiaries. It clarified that Navarro held only that when trustees file suit in their name (as opposed to the trust's name), their jurisdictional citizenship is the state to which they belong. But when the trust itself is a litigant, its citizenship is determined by its members in accordance with state law.